RESTORING AMERICA

One County at a Time

Joel McDurmon

AMERICAN VISION PRESS
POWDER SPRINGS, GEORGIA

Restoring America One County at a Time
by Joel McDurmon

Published by:
American Vision, Inc.
PO Box 611
Braselton, Georgia 30517
www.AmericanVision.org

Printed in the United States of America.

Cover design by Joseph Darnell

ISBN: 978-1-936577-20-0

To

Gary and Sharon North
for all the help,
and in hope
for your grandchildren

Upon the whole, we are too apt to charge those misfortunes to the want of energy in our government, which we have brought upon ourselves by dissipation and extravagance. . . . No government under heaven could have preserved a people from ruin, or kept their commerce from declining, when they were exhausting their valuable resources in paying for superfluities, and running themselves in debt to foreigners, and to each other for articles of folly and dissipation:— While this is the case, we may contend about forms of government, but no establishment will enrich a people, who wantonly spend beyond their income.

—*Candidus* (1787)

But supposing our future rulers to be wicked enough to attempt to invade the rights of conscience; I may be asked how will they be able to effect so horrible a design? I will tell you my friends—The *unlimited power of taxation* will give them the command of all the treasures of the continent; a *standing army* will be wholly at their devotion, . . . These powers, if they should ever fall into bad hands, may be abused to the worst of purposes.

—*An Old Whig* (1787)

Preface

This book was conceived one day as I neared completion on *God versus Socialism: A Biblical Critique of the New Social Gospel*. On that day, Gary North and Gary DeMar were standing in my office discussing the work. One of them noted, "Well, you've written the *critique*; next you need to write the book that gives a *positive* plan of *what to do*." North's constant refrain came to mind once again: "You can't beat something with nothing." If I had a nickel…

It's by far the most prominent question we get in emails and at conferences. After hearing about biblical worldview, biblical law, godly governments, and Christian liberty; and after hearing our critiques of liberalism, secularism, humanism, and radical end-times madness, the number one question is always: "What do we do now?" This book represents the fruit of my efforts to answer that question.

Before you get into the meat of the book, let me explain its nature and structure. This will help you to make the best use of it either as an individual, a teacher or leader, or as a group.

First, this is a *practical* project. It focuses on things that *can be done* and *done now*. In most of these areas, there are things we can do immediately to have an impact. Many people are already doing them with considerable success. In other areas, the practical steps depend on larger social changes before they can be implemented, so we plan and work in the interim to be in a position to accomplish these long-term goals when the time comes. But the more we concentrate on the things we must do—and which we *can do now*—to restore a free society, the more we will open up possibilities for more substantial change. We have to rebuild the foundations first in order to have something lasting on which to build the rest of society. Consequently, I've made an attempt to prioritize the topics of this course according to their practicality for the average individual *now*.

Second, this project focuses on *localism*, not Nationalism or national politics, or even so much states' rights (although states' rights will play an important role). Patriots primarily love their homeland, their roots, not their Nation-State (that was a later perversion of patriotism). Historically, the county was the fundamental unit of government—people rarely had contact with or obligation to any government official beyond that. This should become an ideal once again, and it can. Focusing on localism—"County Rights"—we can take very practical and meaningful steps toward saving this country from all forms of tyranny. If we don't have the vision, and the integrity, and the willingness to sacrifice to take back freedom in our homes, neighborhoods, towns, and counties in areas of life where we can *now*, then the dream of taking back America at large is a delusion. So, here we'll have an emphasis on restoring America *county by county—your* county, *one county at a time*. And the overall goal is to inspire individuals and cell groups in each of America's 3,143 counties to advance and eventually *implement* the vision we will discuss.

Third, this project is only for people *serious* about freedom. There are very real sacrifices that you will have to make in your personal lifestyle, especially in the areas of personal finances, time management, self-improvement, and family education. It is simply going to take a commitment of time and money and discipline toward a better future. I will frankly, honestly, openly address the issue of sacrifices; we will talk about the stumbling blocks and psychological hurdles we'll have to get over in order to restore America to the freedom it once had. As part of this, we will address how we have grown accustomed to living off government "benefits" at all levels of government, and what it will mean to live in a world where you personally refuse to accept those benefits (while they still exist right in front of your face, ripe for the taking), and eventually a world where those benefits no longer exist as a function of State coercion. If you want to escape the trap of tyranny, you will have to acquire the mentality of the wise mouse who said, "To heck with the cheese, let's get out of this trap." (You will encounter the the phrase "Don't take the cheese." several times throughout this book.) So this is for serious lovers of freedom only—those willing to change their lifestyle, to sacrifice, in order to recover individual and social integrity.

Finally, this is a *long-term* project. I am planning and working in order to make a better life for my children, but even more importantly, for my grandchildren and their children. You will not take back America overnight no matter how you go about it, and anyone—especially a politician—who promises you that you can is lying to get your vote. But, you also will never restore America without implementing *lasting* changes, and this requires a multi-generational vision. Involved in this mentality is one of the sacrifices I just mentioned—that is, we are probably not going to reap all the benefits of a free society in our lifetimes. But if we don't work toward that goal doing the things we *can* do now, then our future generations will have to start from scratch in an even more degraded society. So, we'll focus on commitment to steady, slow, yet meaningful progress toward a much larger, long-term vision of a free society.

This is the nature of our project: 1) practical efforts, 2) locally focused, 3) requiring personal sacrifice, 4) to accomplish a long-term vision.

We can summarize these with the following ideas: 1) Get things done 2) County-by-County. 3) Don't take the cheese. 4) Plan for your grandkids.

These are not only aspects of a truly free society, they are all biblical Christian concepts, and we'll discuss that some in each of the topics we cover as well.

As for the structure of this book: it covers ten topics, each a major aspect of our social lives. I give a summary of these in the Introduction. I then cover each of these topics in a separate chapter, each in three major sections: First, how America was once free; Second, how that freedom was lost; and Third, steps to get freedom back. In this third section lies the key: practical steps to answer that question of what we can do.

This work is much more than an action manual, however. It presents the type of iconoclastic history lessons, biblical studies, moral challenges, unpopular truths, and reformational remedies a restored Christian republic will require. This is a training series meant to be incorporated throughout your larger education and worldview.

A full video version of the ten topics is available on DVD and also *free* online at our website (*American Vision.org*), and on our YouTube channel (*americanvisiontv*). I highly recommend these for home schools and general personal education. Visit out web store (*American Vision.com*) to learn more.

JOEL MCDURMON
Powder Springs, Georgia
October 2012

Contents

Preface vii

Introduction. 1

   1: Education 9

   2: Welfare 41

   3: County Rights 71

   4: States' Rights 111

   5: Taxation 153

   6: Money 183

   7: Markets 211

   8: Courts 245

   9: Defense 285

   10: The Executive 349

Epilogue 391

Appendix:

   Repeal the Seventeenth Amendment 395

Introduction

It is hard to miss the plethora of books, websites, radio shows, and even political campaigns chiming on the tune of "Restore America" with every possible permutation of the idea: take back, comeback, turn around, hope for, uniting, and the list goes on. When generalities run low, you read about restoring America's *fill-in-the-blank*: faith, freedom, prosperity, goodness, greatness, economy, markets, military, conscience, promise, justice, neighborhoods, future... you get the picture.

While many grand ideas surface in nearly all of these publications, most of them with few exceptions fall short of presenting the hardest of the hard truths, and virtually none of them provide real, viable, practical steps that average Americans can actually take to restore any of the virtues mentioned, let alone our fundamental foundations of liberty. If this is ever going to change, someone must set forth the issues, ideas, history, hurdles, and blueprints of the way forward.

Among that plethora of "Restoring America" resources, one book at least recognizes a large part of the real problem: the neglect of localism. The very few resources that do provide practical steps aim at *national-level* political solutions—a refrain we have heard, rehearsed, and sung for decades while observing no progress—only gridlock at best, and more often than not, steady decline. This one writer noticed the problem:

> There's another important step: don't waste your energies by campaigning for a presidential candidate. Instead, focus your energy where it can count—focus on the local

level. Taking America back begins by taking back your
city councils, your county boards, your zoning boards,
your sheriff's departments—all the local government
bodies. Then use those agencies and governing bodies to
resist Washington's power grab, to say no to federal intrusion, to fight Big Government's mandates.[1]

Yet even when this author—who provides many great
suggestions (e.g., home schooling)—arrives at a "twelve step
action program," he provides very little of real practical substance. (Indeed, three of that author's twelve steps are self-
promotions for books and websites.)

Another recent book presents interviews with a couple
dozen leaders from the Christian right, asking what in the world
went wrong between 1980 and now, during which intervening
decades Christians essentially have been used by conservative
politicians while making very little if any political progress. *We
won't get fooled again* is the catch phrase. And yet, after inter-
viewing so many prominent Christian leaders, the authors can
offer little more than generalities—"principles before process,"
"issues not personalities"—beyond the simple step, "Pray."

It seems that even the boldest of Christian leaders today can
rarely advance us beyond the lessons we were taught in Sunday
school. Because of this, a hug gap exists between actual biblical
teachings, western history, and the vague, motionless cries for
faith and freedom that abound today.

We hear a lot about "Christian America" these days, about
how "America was founded as a Christian Nation," and about
how we need to get back to the Christian freedoms of our
founding fathers. There is no doubt we need to recover Christian—indeed, *biblical*—freedom in this country. Unfortunately,
the historical truth is not quite as clear as many would have
us to believe, or indeed as we ourselves would so strongly like
to believe. It simply requires greater qualification. (Accepting

---

[1] Joseph Farah, *Taking America Back: A Radical Plan to Revive Freedom, Mo-
rality, and Justice* (Nashville, TN: WND Books, 2005), 208.

this truth is one of those psychological hurdles mentioned in the Preface.) In order to find the *true* Christian foundations of this country, we need to look back before those who are often mistakenly called "founders" to discover the clear biblical ideas that existed in society and government *before* their era—principles which were lost, neglected, marginalized, or even suppressed during the later "founding" era. Much of what we have come to associate with "Christian America" was actually the product of a late nineteenth-century progressive, imperialism which was Christian in name only and rarely if ever could cite the Bible to confirm its political and social policies. Aside from some Christian rhetoric—which was more political than biblical—there has remained a gap between Sunday school lessons and any comprehensive application of biblical ideals to society from the Pilgrim and Puritan era until today.[2]

That huge gap needs filling. Even if you may disagree with the lessons provided, disagree with the emphases, analyses, or the action steps called for, yet even still, an honest attempt to address the erosion of Christianity and liberty in this nation must take a long, hard look at how freedom was lost *specifically*, and how it can be *actually* regained. The suggestions offered for *Restoring America One County at a Time* are intended to begin to fill this need.

A Hard-Core, Ten-Step Training Course

It will not do to content ourselves with lip service to patriotism, faith, and freedom. We must have real, substantial plans and real, practical action items. These must be *clear* and they must be *broad*, addressing every area of life in which freedom must be restored. Keeping in mind the four principles outlined in the Preface above, we need practical, local, selfless, and visionary plans to restore America if we are ever to make real progress toward the type of freedom we once had. There are at

---

[2] There are exceptions to this, of course, which we will examine.

least ten areas in which concerned American Christians *can and must act*, locally, practically, seriously, *now*:

1. *Education*: Education is one area in which you can still exercise almost complete control. We're not just talking about educating yourself, we're talking about your children too. Education in a free society can only be *private*, never government-run at any level. Whether you choose to employ a private school or to teach your children at home, government-operated, tax-funded schools cannot be an option if we are to have a free society. Regaining liberty here requires no change in existing laws—only one's lifestyle. Many people could implement these changes tomorrow, if not over a few months. It's only a test of desire—Do you *really* want a free society? There are economic and psychological hurdles here, and we will address those. For now, we must understand that government schools are at the heart of the problem of government-dominated society. We can change this personally *now*, and we should. All that is stopping us is the perceived benefit of free schooling and daily childcare. This is the cheese in the trap. Don't take the cheese. Do we *really* want a free society, or do we depend on tax-funded benefits like the liberals and socialists we criticize? This is priority number one. If we are serious about freedom, we have to start with education. *If we can't accomplish change in this one area, then forget the rest.* Nothing about truly restoring America will be easier or more readily obtainable than taking free control over your family's education. There's nothing stopping us here.

2. *The Welfare State*: Social Security is a problem, but it doesn't have to be a trap. This means we need to learn about options for securing our own financial futures, privately, while we opt out of Social Security over time. The issue here is that welfare of all forms should be a privately funded and insured affair, not supported through taxation. Family and charity can replace the Welfare State. Again, we must refuse the benefit. Don't take the cheese. Of course, this will certainly mean per-

sonal sacrifices. Again, we will outline the personal impediments in the chapter, speak frankly about how to overcome them, and determine what the costs will be.

3. *Localism*: The real practical solution to big-government intrusion in our lives is not so much states' rights, but *county* rights. This involves returning government and community to a more grass-roots level where it ought to be. *Support your local sheriff* is a good way to remember this. We will emphasize a truly local vision—confronting local waste and corruption, and focus on smaller, practical things we can impact now. In this process, we will expose the areas where the sovereignty of local communities is compromised by receiving Federal and state funds for perceived benefits. We will emphasize learning about, monitoring, and interacting with local authorities, and we will emphasize local applications of "Don't take the cheese."

4. *State Sovereignty:* This chapter includes a history of the Nationalist takeover of America which began immediately after the Constitution's ratification. We will discuss the agenda of big banks, the military-industrial complex, and national taxation, as well as the politicians who engineered the plan and why. From this we will be in a position to recommend ways of living that minimize our personal involvement in this tyranny, and discuss the roles of nullification and interposition which are becoming more popular today. While we emphasize County Rights primarily, States' Rights are important also as a buffer, and as part of a truly federal system of government.

5. *Taxes*: Taxation must be returned exclusively to the local level—in keeping with the way this country was founded and designed to be run. We'll cover the Income Tax amendment and the drastic change in American society it represents. We will discuss the nature and scope of taxation in a truly federal society; we will see why the power to tax is the power to destroy; and we will discuss the role of taxation—if any—in a truly free local society.

6. *Money* (Breaking the Federal Reserve System): We will

review the question, "What has government done with our money?" We will discuss money and currency in American history, particularly the several instances of failed paper currency. We will discuss the role of government coercion in banking and debt: counterfeiting laws, war, welfare, restrictions on states, etc., and why these laws exist. We will discuss who profited (and still does) from these arrangements, and what happened to real wealth in each case. We will discuss alternative currencies, banking, the benefits and sacrifices of freedom in money, and also how to protect your personal wealth from a devalued paper/digital currency. Gold is wealth, why is it not money? What's the government got against gold? Find out why one American statesman once complained that debtors were chasing down their creditors and *"paying them without mercy"*!

7. *Free Markets*: The sanctity of private property, the enforcement of contracts, and the right *not* to engage in contracts. We will discuss the role government coercion and money manipulation has played in business and the economy: inflation, legal tender laws, the business cycle, government corporatism (essentially fascism here in America), etc.

8. *Courts*: We'll see how the Constitution centralized power over the various local courts in this land, and how this was immediately exploited to favor big-government agendas. We'll trace subsequent expansions of government based on that early precedent. The remedy to recover freedom is the decentralization of courts, local and separate jurisdictions, and even private courts (perhaps especially), all with only local law enforcement. We'll see one check and balance against the Court in the Constitution most people don't even know exists, and yet it's been used to protect mainly big-government interests so far—even recently. The key to the abortion issue, family protections, and much more lies in the issue of decentralizing the judiciary. Believe it or not, there are actually practical steps you can take here as well.

9. *Defense*: One of the most important areas—and perhaps that in which Christians are most deceived—is in regard to our military. We must support and demand a decentralized defense system instead of the national standing army and empire we've allowed, and even promoted, for over a century. We'll take a close look at biblical rules for the military and war. *Patriotism* does not mean *Militarism*. *Patriotism* does not mean *Empire*. Being patriotic and conservative does not mean always supporting everything the military does. Anti-war is not Anti-American. We will discuss how the military was originally decentralized and strictly defense-oriented, and how it was transformed incrementally to become a powerful centralized force designed to serve the varied interests of the central government, eventually being used in prolonged international conflicts. We will show how and why this was done in American history, and who profited from it at the expense of millions of lives and trillions of dollars. We will propose practical steps that you can take *now* to gain the moral high ground at least, in the process of returning from offensive corporate-state militarism to true armed patriotism.

10. *The Executive*: We take a look at treaties, Executive Orders, and emergency powers. How do they work? What safeguards do we have against them if necessary? Why are we vulnerable to international organizations because of them? How have they already been abused? And how can we best work to protect ourselves from them?

These are the ten basic topics; some of them may sound large and intimidating, and that's because some of them are. But keep in mind, we're going to focus on accomplishing a long-term vision by small practical changes—through personal sacrifice and local service. None of this will change overnight, but if we don't lay the necessary foundations for freedom, it will never change (and in fact, it will get worse). So if you're serious about freedom, please invest the time to read these lessons, watch the video versions online, and teach them to your children. Then pass them on to your friends, family, pastors, and while you're at it, pass it on to your in-laws, ex's, and enemies too. We all need Christ, faith, family, and freedom.

Unless we invest the time and sweat to get these things back, we have no one to blame for society's erosion but ourselves. And of course, all the books in the world won't help you restore America—even if the authors decide to wake up and finally tell you how to do it. So, by all means, read this book. Then go out and get things done.

1. Education

The first and foremost area we can and must restore now is education. If you want to restore America, you have to start by restoring freedom in education first. So let's talk about the idea of education in a free society.

Education in a Free America

Education in a free society means *exclusively* "private" education. We are never free as long as we are subjected to compulsory government education shored up by threats, penalties, fines, and taxes—to any degree or at any level. This is, of course, not to deny the prime importance, and even necessity, of education, but in education, as in all areas of life, the primary issue is *sovereignty*: who has legitimate control, legitimate command? To the extent that civil government has control, it will force us to comply with its standards and dictates, and, to that extent, we are not free individuals. We're not free as long as someone else tells us what to do and forces us to do it how they want us to do it, and then forces us to pay for it. Apart from God alone, no person or agency has that level of authority—and the person or institution that usurps that position assumes the role of God in that area of life. This applies to our individual liberties, freedom of expression, freedom of speech, etc., but it also applies to education as much as anything else.

In view of our responsibility for our own education as well as for that of our children, we must ask: to whom are we ultimately responsible? To God, or to man? Who is sovereign?

Who has the right to tell you who, what, when, where, how, etc., to educate? Who has that right? What man has the right to compel you to attend any given school, and what man has the right to compel you to pay for someone else's attendance at school? I submit to you that no man or group of men has that absolute right, and yet that is the accepted norm for society today. In a free society, this would not be the case.

In regard to the issue of sovereignty in education, two important issues need to be addressed at the outset. First, we must expose *the impossibility of neutrality*, and second, we must consider *the purpose of education*.

Ideological neutrality is a myth. No middle ground actually exists concerning education or any other isue because there is no place in between faithfulness to God and submission to a man-dictated, man-driven, man-enforced system that denies God, excludes God, and replaces God. Either our society is faithful to God, or it is not. And just as there is no middle ground between faithfulness to God and subjection to man, there is also none between freedom and coercion in education. Either we are free, responsible individuals and families before God, or we are coerced and cajoled by other forces.

The points here are simple: 1) you must choose between faithfulness and unfaithfulness in education, and 2) no one has the right to force another to choose (or to fund) one way or the other.

Secondly, the issue of sovereignty immediately raises the issue of *purpose*. What is education, after all? Is education necessary? Why and for what reasons do we educate? And who decides what those reasons are? Who gets to impose their reasons for education, ideas of education, and meanings of education on society, if anyone should impose them at all?

What is education? The bare minimal meaning of the word "education" comes from its Latin derivation: *e+ducatus* from *e+ducere—e* meaning "out of," *ducere* meaning "to lead." sO, the most basic import of the word *education* is "to lead out."

This seems simple enough, but it immediately raises questions. Who, exactly, is leading? And leading "out" of what, exactly? And into what? Ostensibly, education leads one out of ignorance and into knowledge, but who defines what ignorance is? Conversely, what is the wisdom or knowledge or truth into which the student is to be led? Who determines this? I submit to you that whoever is in control of education determines these purposes and definitions, even if they do not pronounce them explicitly or submit them to public scrutiny.

This pertains not only to the basic existence and structure of education in society—whether we will have purely private institutions versus compulsory civil-government institutions and penalties—but to the impossibility of neutrality and the necessity of an overarching purpose that dictates every other issue of education. Whoever has control decides what is taught (and what is *not* taught), when it is taught, how it is taught, what you can or cannot criticize, with whom you will or will not associate, how discipline is administered, and a thousand other very important issues. Whoever controls education determines all of these issues for you and your child, and therefore, for your entire legacy. In a free society, *all* of these decisions would be left to the individual and the family and never made an issue of coercion from the State. You should be accountable to God and no one else for these decisions.

What does education look like in a truly free society under God?

1. Parents exercise personal responsibility for, and authority over, their own children.

2. Federal, state, and local governments have no jurisdiction in this area, and no ability (legal or otherwise) to coerce free individuals and families in any way.

3. Parents pay for their own children's education.

4. No one is forced to fund the education of other people's children in any way (directly or indirectly).

5. No one demands that anyone else fund their child's education (indeed, a free citizen would not even allow or accept funding derived from coercive means—taxation or otherwise).

The issues of sovereignty, non-neutrality, and purpose all mean that *you have to make the choice for liberty*—it will not happen for you. If you leave the decision for someone else, then you have abdicated your individual responsibility. If you accept that civil government can coerce you or others to pay for other people, then you have abdicated the principle of liberty. So, the question of control and command of education forces us before God to choose who shall lead and how.

Not only do we have to stop thinking of this thing called "education" as primarily an institution of the State, but we must discontinue thinking of education as an institution at all. There is no reason (certainly no biblical reason) why civil government should have education as one of its functions, or even have regulatory oversight over education. In a free society, the primary focus of leadership in education should always and only be the family, and the church—and anyone whom the family freely decides to hire. This is the ideal of freedom both in the Bible and in the Christian founding of this land, through the founding years of American history up until the 1830s and really even beyond. Let's look at these two realities—the biblical and historical.

The biblical Christian case is simple and brief. In both the Old and New Testaments, education was the responsibility primarily of the family, and secondarily of the church:

> Hear, O Israel: The Lord our God, the Lord is one. You shall love the Lord your God with all your heart and with all your soul and with all your might. And these words that I command you today shall be on your heart.

> You shall teach them diligently to your children, and shall talk of them when you sit in your house, and when you walk by the way, and when you lie down, and when you rise. You shall bind them as a sign on your hand, and they shall be as frontlets between your eyes. You shall write them on the doorposts of your house and on your gates. (Deut. 6:4–7)

In this passage, God makes it clear that education is to be carried out in the home, is to be pursued constantly using every opportunity and resource, and is to reflect the content of God's teachings. In the New Testament, the same educational principle appears in Paul's reiteration of the fifth commandment:

> Children, obey your parents in the Lord, for this is right. Honor your father and mother (this is the first commandment with a promise), that it may go well with you and that you may live long in the land. Fathers, do not provoke your children to anger, but bring them up in the discipline and instruction of the Lord. (Eph. 6:1–4)

So whatever else we may derive from Scripture, the two most basic places that address education of children apply it directly to the family, and in such a way that God's Word and godliness compose the central, sacred purpose. In no place in Scripture is it even intimated that civil government should have a hand in this process.

At least until the 1830s, American culture generally reflected these biblical ideals of freedom and individual responsibility. This should not surprise us. The American colonies were founded and settled almost completely by Bible-believing Christians who established towns and communities on Christian principles and were generally averse to any government-established churches or institutions.

This is confirmed by perhaps the most widely accepted source on the history of American education, Lawrence Cremin. Cremin was a liberal and a progressive, so he had no particular fondness for America's Christian history, and yet, while writing his definitive four-volume history, he was faced with and was compelled to transmit these clear facts:

1. The Bible was "the single most important cultural influence in the lives of Anglo-Americans."[1] It thus formed the core of American literary and moral education.

2. The household or family was "the principal unit of social organization," and "the most important agency of popular education." "The family undertook the training of children 'in some honest calling, labor or employment.'"

3. In cases where the family was unable to advance education any further in a calling or trade, businesses or apprenticeships would provide a "direct example" and "immediate participation" in a trade through which a young person could learn a trade, find employment, and contribute to society.

4. Entrance into apprenticeship programs was free and easy. Unlike in Europe or Britain at the time, there was high demand for skilled laborers, an absence of guilds that monopolized and controlled labor, no informers, no legal obstacles, no Statute of Artificers, no fees, and no property restrictions.[2]

5. Additionally, there were private night schools for working adults to improve their English and vocational skills.

Another great scholar of American history, Samuel Eliot Morison, notes the main exception to private education in the American colonies: Boston. But its handful of public schools

---

[1] Lawrence A. Cremin, *American Education: The Colonial Experience, 1607–1783* (New York: Harper Torchbooks, 1970), 40

[2] Cremin, 133–135.

admitted children only after they had learned to read. Where did they learn to read? Morison answers:

> Boston offers a curious problem. The grammar (Boston Latin) school was the only public school down to 1684, when a writing school was established; and it is probable that only children who already read were admitted to that . . . they must have learned to read somehow, since there is no evidence of unusual illiteracy in the town.[3]

One of the famous graduates of that Boston Latin School, by the way, was Benjamin Franklin, who had little good to say about it later in life. Morison then reports a rather illuminating statistic:

> [A] Boston bookseller's stock in 1700 includes no less than eleven dozen spellers and sixty-one dozen primers.[4]

In other words, with no need for compulsory attendance laws or any other government regulation of education, people were educating themselves and their children just fine. They took the task so seriously that they had already created a huge demand for textbooks which the free market had already met with a huge supply—a randomly sampled store had a stock of 132 spelling books and 732 primers.

It's clear that during the founding of America from the Pilgrims all the way up until the middle of the nineteenth century, education was a private affair. In fact, as late as 1860, throughout all the states, there were only about 300 public schools. At this time there were over 6,000 private institutions, but the vast majority of educational "institutions" were at home.

Yet, though education was a thoroughly private affair at the time, masses of children did not fall through the cracks. In fact, literacy was extremely high even in rural western areas,

---

[3] Samuel Eliot Morison, *The Intellectual Life of Colonial New England*, 2nd Ed. (Ithaca, NY: Cornell University Press, 1956), 71–72.

[4] Morison, 72.

comparable to educated Britain at the time and close even, one could argue, to the U.S. today.

For example, roughly 48% of rural Britons could read at the time, compared to roughly 70% in rural America. Urban Britain was 74% literate, whereas urban America was nearly 100% (based on signatures on deeds, wills, militia rolls, voting registers).

Far western, rural Connecticut (e.g., the town of Kent) saw nearly 100% literacy; they took private education so seriously that the locals chartered a school even before the church, and the ministers taught at the school—and it was private. In rural South Carolina, like in most places, education was also carried out mainly by local pastors. Literacy there was 80% in general, and even 90% among the German population.

Cremin concludes, "[T]hese rates are extraordinary, and stand as eloquent testimony to the power the tradition of learning had acquired in the minds of provincial Americans," and he notes that this was driven purely by churches and households.[5] And, remember, Cremin had no allegiance to the Christian underpinnings of colonial America, he was merely reporting relevant educational facts. From just these facts and figures, it is safe to say that family and church-led education is the original American way—*and it works.*

As for the issue of sovereignty and leadership in education, this free family-driven American way provides many benefits, also seen in the history of the time.

A free market in education creates a vast array of pedagogical choices. For example, from 1740 to 1776, Philadelphian newspapers included ads for no fewer than 125 distinct private schoolmasters advertising their services. (They were like lawyers in the phonebook today!) Don't like that antagonistic teacher your child is having problems with? Hire another. No problem. (After two or three different tutors, you may

---

[5] Cremin, 543.

learn the problem's not the teacher after all!) This, of course, also means teachers have to compete, and thus the quality of teaching improves as teachers try to become better teachers in order to attract enough students to make a living.

At the time, different churches offered private schools as centers of their own denominational missions. You want a Scottish Presbyterian education? German Reformed? Wesleyan Methodist? No problem. No one was forced to go anywhere that denied his faith or even the distinctives of his denomination.[6]

Freedom in education means freedom in curriculum. This in turn will begin to favor the needs of the real world, individual faith, and economical options. Available jobs spur specialized education for personal advancement; printed news drives a demand for literacy for anyone wishing to know about or participate in current events; and religious education, as I noted, helps drive this as well for those who wish to follow their religious confession or history. All of these phenomena were observable in the early and freer period of American history.

Freedom affects how we fund education. It means we can no longer force others to pay our way, and we will no longer be forced to pay for others. There is no government money involved, and thus there are no government regulations—the strings attached to the "free" benefit. But this means we must also have personal initiative, planning, and individual sacrifice to educate ourselves and our children effectively. But when private money is involved, then a private interest develops concerning who teaches, what is taught, when, where, how, how much, etc., is taught—*and* you have the fundamental inalienable right one hundred percent of the time to demand, direct, change, or alter any or all of those things. It takes time and money, but we've all said it once or twice: "Freedom ain't free."

---

[6] The shell of this tradition is still visible today in some Lutheran circles and Roman Catholic private schools—although in both cases the education is little more than secular education with a weekly prayer service.

Freedom gives education a more long-term, generational prospect. Now you are passing a legacy of not only reading, writing, and arithmetic to your children, but also your own chosen worldview. Now your children, and, Lord willing, *their* children, will inherit a family heritage and religion, perhaps a family business or trade, and a commitment, if you are successful, to local politics and culture. In short, a free society will tend to reinforce itself because children will mirror the models and advance the principles of their very hard-working, self-sacrificing parents.

So we can see that 1) a free society, in order to be called truly free, must accommodate only private education with neither taxation to subsidize education nor civil government coercion to enforce attendance; and 2) such a free view of education was in fact the American way for a very long portion of our history. It is the only view that we can properly call "free." It was once the norm, and it worked very well.

So the question is, "Why did it change?" What brought about the colossal transformation, and even reversal, of the American educational model? Now home schools and private schools are the tiny minority, looked upon with suspicion and, in some cases, ridicule. Tax-funded government schools, on the other hand, are the norm, and the vast majority of Americans believe that the civil government should force some people to pay for other people's education. Not only do they accept this tyranny, they actively fight to keep it that way—calling it right and proper and "American" and even "Christian." How could Christians vehemently argue for a system of coercive taxation that imposes *anything*—much less a secular humanist, pluralist, anti-Christian system of education? There are some who say that changes in society have required changes in education. Is this true? How was our basic educational freedom lost?

How Freedom Was Lost

In the last section, we discussed how free, purely private education was the American way, and it worked. We mentioned how this was the norm up until at least the 1830s and really even beyond. How was this high level of freedom and individual responsibility lost? How did a once completely free system come to be dominated by government mandates and taxation—that is, government confiscation of private property?

Some claim that changes in society necessitated educational reform. For some reason or other, upswings in technology, mechanization, the industrial revolution, etc., changed the face of society so drastically that the only way to bring the masses of common people up to speed was for the civil government to intervene and redistribute wealth to provide public schools. Does this argument have any basis in fact? Only to a very limited extent. The truth involves much more than that.

The four most important social factors that precipitated educational "reform" involved: *First*, a rival religious ideology; *Second*, reactions to mass immigration in the late 1840s and forward; *Third*, the forces of big business; and *Fourth*, the promise of "free" education (in the sense of no personal financial cost) to the masses.

The Rival Religion

Unitarianism, particularly prevalent in New England congregational churches, championed the idea that mankind could be perfected through proper education and training because mankind was essentially divine, good. Unitarians taught that this divinity of man is most pronounced when mankind is considered collectively as a whole; consequently, they believed that the civil State was the highest expression of divinity on earth and the ultimate parent and benefactor of individuals.

Perhaps the most important Unitarian in regard to the American educational transformation was the so-called father

of public schools in America, Horace Mann. Mann, a Congrega-
tionalist minister, argued that human rights derive from Nature;
and this Nature—with a capital *N*—he interpreted, "proves an
absolute right to an education of every human being that comes
into the world." This is the classic "entitlement mentality" which
characterizes leftism, communism, socialism, etc., before and
since, which today is often applied to healthcare, employment,
etc.—here Horace Mann applied it very early to education, by
which he meant *public* education.

He argued two basic propositions about education: *education should be secularized*—geared toward civic virtue and efficiency rather than religious worldview—*and education should
be a function of the civil government, not families.* In fact, he
sought to replace the family with an explicitly paternal state. He
called Society collectively a "godfather for all its children," and
said, "Massachusetts is *parental* in her government."

Unitarian activists, such as Horace Mann, were ready and
willing to employ government force in order to remake society in their own image—in fact, most radical Unitarians considered government force, or any kind of force really, to be the
first and primary agent of change. In the mid-1850s, the radical
revolutionary John Brown committed several acts of violence
and murder in Kansas and in Virginia intending to start a slave
rebellion that he thought would eventually bring about abolition. The underlying belief was in the legitimacy of violence to
impose better social values. Shortly before his death by hang-
ing, Brown himself made this point explicitly. He said he was
"quite certain that the crimes of this guilty land will never be
purged away but with blood," and that this would never be done
without "very much bloodshed." He was a homegrown American terrorist who carried out acts of terrorism on American soil
in the name of social and political renovation.

Brown had studied in Massachusetts to be a Congregation-
alist minister, but quit due to financial and health problems.
While there, he established radical connections that would

later help finance his homicidal intrigue. The least publicized aspect of Brown is this: the six main financiers who funded his terrorism and then idealized it to the New England masses as a righteous social crusade were all Unitarian Congregational ministers. And while not every Unitarian believed in Brown's brand of revolutionary violence, they all believed in using the force of government to bring about whatever social changes they considered desirable.[7]

Mann certainly held this position in regard to public education. He believed education was a right, property should be socialized, and individual preferences were subservient to the will of the collective (as represented by the decisions of the civil government, of course). He wrote:

> The successive generations of men, taken collectively, constitute one great commonwealth.
>
> The property of this commonwealth is pledged for the education of all its youth, up to such a point as will save them from poverty and vice, and perhaps to prepare them for the adequate performance of their social and civil duties.

Note the language of salvation: the common right of education mecessitated a "pledge" (theft) of private property in order to "save" society's youth from "poverty and vice." So here you have not only a messianic State, but also America's first State-imposed war on poverty. (And this first war on poverty boasted no greater or more lasting victories than the similar wars LBJ waged in the '60s.) Notice also that property would be appropriated "up to such a point as will save them [society's youth]." In other words, taxation and theft would con-

---

[7] The force of civil government is really not much different than vigilante revolutionary force when it comes to unbiblical social crusades. It's comparing one version of unwelcome coercion to another, and, in both cases, the terms of compliance are imposed by an enitity that thinks it knows better than the "masses" and believes it has the right and authority to impose its view on them by force.

tinue until the social crusaders felt they had fulfilled their mission—which is to say, indefinitely and without limit. Mann concluded by expressing what can only be called socialism:

> The successful holders of this property are trustees, bound to the faithful execution of their trust by the most sacred obligations; and embezzlement and pillage from children and descendants have not less criminality . . . than the same offenses when perpetrated against contemporaries.

In the public schooling worldview, you do not own your property! You can never be a property *owner*; but only a *trustee* for property that rightly belongs to Society. It is society that determines who will get what and for what purpose, and any resistance to the government's dictates in this area is considered a crime of "embezzlement and pillage" (both crimes committed, by definition, with reference to *other people's* property). Note again the religious language: payments made for State-run education are "the most sacred obligations" which require "faithful execution."

The alleged natural "right" which entitles every human being to an education is so sacred that it transcends the biblical protection of private property. Mann said:

> No one man, nor any one generation of men, has any such title to, or ownership in these ingredients and substantials of all wealth, that his right is invaded when a portion of them is taken for the benefit of posterity.

In other words, we're going to tax you for education, and you'll pay the tax and shut up, because you have no right to complain about it. It's not really your property to begin with, and what we're doing is for you own good and the good of posterity. Make this note: public education, from its inception, was incapable of existing without socialism, and this is still the case. The very nature of the system requires the government to claim ownership over at least a portion of every individual's property.

Proponents for State education worked tirelessly to convince the American populace that compulsory schooling was in the public interest. In 1835, Thaddeus Stevens used this very argument on the floor of Pennsylvania's legislature to defend a public schooling law the state had passed just a year before. To those who objected that it was morally wrong to tax some people to pay for other people's education, he responded, "It is for their own benefit, inasmuch as it perpetuates the government and ensures the due administration of the laws under which they live, and by which their lives and property are protected." In other words, the paternal state knows what is best for you, and what is the best use of your money, and, besides, such measures "perpetuate the government" that knows all this! Who could be against that?

Mann made his views very explicit. Public schooling was the path to social salvation; all ills would be cured by its full implementation:

> The common school is the greatest discovery ever made by man. . . . Other social organizations are curative and remedial; this is a preventative and an antidote; they come to heal diseases and wounds; this to make the physical and moral frame invulnerable to them. Let the common school be expanded to its capabilities, let it be worked with the efficiency with which it is susceptible, and nine-tenths of the crimes in the penal code would become obsolete; the long catalogue of human ills would be abridged; men would walk more safely by day; every pillow would be more inviolable by night; property, life and character held by a stronger tenure; all rational hopes respecting the future brightened.

This is language of healing and of hope. This is the language of religion, and Mann wanted it funded by the State. The scholar who studied the history of the state-takeover of education noted what action step Mann really had in mind here. It was the same thing public schools have said ever since:

"Give us the money and we can do it; our failure thus far is your fault in that we have received insufficient funds." And Mann, like most public school advocates ever since, believed that the school and its parent State had a right—an entitlement—to appropriate those funds from private people.

Overrun by such Unitarian thought, Massachusetts was the first state to create a State Board of Education in 1837. As its first chairman, they appointed Horace Mann. The timing of this secular board's creation is of interest. Up until 1832, the Congregational Church was an established state church—receiving funding from the state to pay ministers, etc. That was abolished in 1832 (Massachusetts was the last state to do so), and the state-funded education program was in place only five years later. And in that same year, 1837, Mann brokered a political deal that immediately doubled the budget for public education. Common schools were already being funded in Massachusetts by local taxes, but this was the first time school funding and standards had been centralized at the state level. The astute observer will note what many public school critics have already pointed out—the established churches were replaced by the public schools as the religious centers of the state. The state now had an officially secularized state church, with double the taxes at the outset and more than double the tyranny.

It is not only the facts and coincidences of history that indicate that secular public schools were the harbingers of a newly established state religion. The very activists who founded and administered the new educational system made this connection manifest in their speeches and writings. And this perception lasted well into the twentieth century and exists still in the minds of many today, Christian or not.

One representative figure who stated the truth explicitly was James Earl Russell, Dean of Columbia Teachers College for thirty years (1897–1927). The task of education, he wrote in 1922, was "making democracy safe for the world," and this meant "teaching the proper appreciation of life-values."

Indeed, "The doctrine that all shall get what they deserve presupposes that the largest possible number shall be taught to want what it is right that they should have." In other words, democracy will be great only as long as the schoolmasters can first train the people what to want and how to vote. Put more succinctly, you can have whatever you want, as long as you want only whatever we see fit to give you! Russell believed that once his ideal democracy was fully in place, the wholesale replacement of the church could become explicit. He believed a "well-trained" future generation would "find it expedient to substitute for the established church of the old regime a state-supported and state-controlled school system."[8]

Of course, this state-controlled system was the antithesis of the free and private system which had served America well over the two preceding centuries. Russell knew this, yet he saw the change as *progress* nonetheless. Before, teachers had to compete with each other—and this generated greater choice, improved quality, lowered costs, etc. But socialists like Russell demeaned this system under which he believed "the teacher was a chattel sold on the open market."[9] Instead, he touted "the teacher as a civil servant whose foremost duty is the promotion of the welfare of the State."

He did get one thing right when he called this scheme "a new conception in American life." It certainly was: In the original American way, the civil State was an educational nonfactor, and the very idea, let alone practice, of civil coercion as a tool for social change militated against basic American freedoms: of religion, property, business, and family. All of these traditional American liberties had to be overturned and the value system that upheld them had to be replaced in order to impose the grand scheme of State-supported and State-controlled education. Indeed, it was nothing less than a complete secularized replacement of the established church.

---

[8] James Earl Russell, *The Trend in American Education* (New York: American Book Company, 1922), 201–208.

[9] Russell, 215.

At least one religious group, the Roman Catholic Church, saw what was going on, and within just a few years, they began starting their own private schools as an alternative—a haven for traditional religious education. Consequently, the rise of Catholic parochial schools coincided with the rise of secularized Unitarian public schools. But these Catholic schools would not have been able to survive financially had it not been for the second major factor in the story of the public school: mass immigration.

Mass Immigration and "Americanism"

Irish Catholics who fled the Irish potato famine beginning in 1845 made up a large number of the immigrants during this time. In 1825, there were only about 5,000 Irish in Boston. In 1845, the number had multiplied six times to 30,000—constituting about 30% of the population. These immigrants saw State education as a toll for imposing a secularized version of Protestantism, so they started their own schools. Most of the other early immigrant groups, most of whom came from Northern Europe, and were either Lutheran or Dutch Reformed, also started private schools to avoid the secularized indoctrination of the public school system. These denominations still continue these traditions today.

Many Americans, particularly the Unitarian-minded, "civic religion" types, hated Catholicism and saw immigrants as a threat, so they tried to use the force of government to unilaterally enforce their version of American culture. To them, public education was not only a means to perfect mankind and cure society of all ills, it was a means of turning immigrants into good Americans. And over time, the secularized religious motive fell further into the background, and the promotion of *Americanism* became the thrust of public schooling. Of course, the ideal America these establishments promoted was already a long way from the America that had once been free. Throughout this whole process, many orthodox Protestants were hoodwinked by the façade of Christianity in the Unitarian-driven school system, and thus accepted that "their" public schools must certainly be Christian.

Immigration caused cultural and religious tensions, but it also created economic tensions as the labor market was flooded with hundreds of thousands of new workers. Of course, with the industrial revolution gathering steam in the 1830s and forward, the waves of immigrants provided a source of very cheap labor. But factories and large business owners quickly learned what type of temperament and mentality was best suited for the tasks of factory labor—they wanted employess who were accustomed to repetition and schedules, monotony, quiet obedience, single file lines, etc. And these wealthy influences in society quickly learned they could harness public education to produce such workers.

The Public School as a Factory

So the third factor contributing to the loss of liberty in education was the rise of big business, corporations, and particularly the influence of industrialization and factory mechanization. This factor not only contributed directly to a loss of freedom, but, more importantly, it acclimated the populace to a freedomless environment so that they ceased even to notice their chains.

There is some truth (albeit very limited) to the contention that industrialization required changes in society. But here is the important qualification: the phenomenon itself did not *require* politically effected changes in education, but, rather, big business found it *profitable* to leverage big government power—just as the Unitarian ideologues had done—in order to mass produce suitable workers to meet the demand for factory labor. Soon, public schools were mass-producing workers in the same way factories were mass-producing widgets.

The public school environment was perfectly suited for this training. In 1880, one education reformer, Charles Francis Adams Jr., recalled that initial atmosphere of educational mechanization:

> Most of you, indeed, cannot but have been part and parcel of one of those huge, mechanical, educational machines, or mills, as they might more properly be called. They are, I believe, peculiar to our own time and country, and are so organized as to combine as nearly as possible the principal characteristics of the cotton-mill and the railroad with those of the model state's prison. The school committee is the board of directors; while the superintendent — the chief executive officer — sits in his central office with the timetable, which he calls a programme, before him, by which one hour twice a week is allotted to this study, and half an hour three times a week to that, and twenty hours a term to a third; and at such a time one class will be at this point and the other class at that, the whole moving with military precision to a given destination at a specified date. He can at any given moment tell you exactly where any squad, or class as he would term it, is, and what it ought, at least, to be then doing. Mechanical methods could not be carried further. The organization is perfect. The machine works almost with the precision of clock-work. It is, however, companyfront all the time. From one point of view children are regarded as automatons; from another, as india-rubber bags; from a third, as so much raw material. They must move in step and exactly alike; they must receive the same mental nutriment in equal quantities and at fixed times: — assimilation is wholly immaterial, but the motions must be gone through with. Finally, as raw material, they are emptied in at the primaries and marched out at the grammar grades;— and it is well![10]

---

[10] Charles Francis Adams Jr., *The New Departure in the Common Schools of Quincy*, 6th Ed. (Boston: Estes and Lauriat, 1881), 61.

And he should have added that, after graduation, the well-trained automoton funneled directly into the industrialized workforce having been trained for the past several years to pursue a boring, task-oriented life compartmentalized for him by his superiors. He merely exchanged a school bell for a work whistle. Horace Mann had been interested in education as the tool to accomplish the perfection of society. The industrialists couldn't care less about *perfectibility*, they only cared about the *trainability* of man. And that legacy has been with us ever since.

There is, by the way, much truth in Adams' comparison of public schools to not only mills and railroads, but state prisons. The same Unitarian spirit that gave us the institution of public schools also produced, in the same era, the penitentiary, the insane asylum, and the poorhouse. All of these were built on the same theory that *society* was the bed of corruption, so the proper way to train people was to put them in a controlled atmosphere where the allegedly corrupt external influences could not affect them. This very popular theory was applied to the "rehabilitation" of criminals, the insane, the mentally ill, and the poor—and to the education of children. So in the 1820s–30s, America witnessed both the explosion of official institutions for all of these purposes *and* the consequent ballooning of taxation and government controls.

As decades passed, it became clear that the original theory was bogus—that no genuine reform was made in criminals or madmen, and that corporate interests had commandeered the schools—in short, that the whole system was a failure. Yet in spite of all this, educational bureaucrats continued to blame the failure of the system on a deficiency of funds and a need for greater control. One of the few historians of the asylum phenomenon concluded his assessment of its legacy with a statement that applies equally well to all the failed government engines of social reform: "Failure and persistence went hand in hand."[11]

When correctional institutions failed, advocates shifted their emphasis from "cure" to "prevention"—thus, education became all the more important as preventative medicine—more schools, they said, would mean fewer prisons. This was used, then, as an argument for greater government involvement in and support of education.

The Real Cost of "Free" Education

Yet finally, as a sort of capstone upon these three major contributing factors to the ascendancy of State schools, Americans began to abandon home and private education due to the illusion that government schools were *free*. But not everyone who subscribes to public education is equally hoodwinked. Some buy the illusion completely: the school costs them nothing while it educates their children and simultaneously provides free childcare during the day. People who don't own property are the most likely to be deluded in this way, since they never pay a property tax directly. But even property owners may not recognize the true weight of the tax, since it is usually escrowed automatically. Other people who know the true cost of public schools merely live content with the illusion. They know they actually pay taxes to support public education, even if indirectly through increased rents, yet they accept this as a moral obligation or a bearable reality at least. These people, too, upon receiving the benefits, will defend the system that proved profitable to *them* even if *other people* have to pay for it. Even among public officials who know better, the misleading language is simply modified to maintain the ruse: public education is free "at the point of delivery" (which is, of course, an admission that it's *not* free).

---

[11] David Rothman, *The Discovery of the Asylum: Social Order and Disorder in the New Republic* (Boston and Toronto: Little, Brown and Co., 1971), 240.

The perceived benefit of "free" education powerfully motivates those who are dependent upon the system to fight for its perpetuation. In short, once they are *dependents*, they become *advocates*. Yet the system, used and defended by so many conservatives and Christians, is based on an anti-Christian, socialistic system of values *at its very core*.

So how was liberty lost in the area of education? First, anti-Christian ideologues leveraged State power to impose a State-funded, State-controlled utopia. They established a whole new secular state "church" in the name of getting rid of state churches. Second, mass Catholic immigration prompted misguided Protestants to use government power to oppose Catholicism and turn Europeans into Americans. Third, the educational mass-production possibilities of public schools served the financial and practical interests of corporate industrialists who needed dutiful, reliable, interchangeable workers for their factories. Fourth, the majority of Americans believed the myth that public education is indeed free, and we have now grown vastly dependent on its "benefits."

These things, all combined together, created a very powerful culture that entirely eliminated *fiscal freedom* in education (we're all forced to pay for public schools even if we don't use them), and almost totally destroyed educational freedom altogether. Over the past few decades, many Christians and others have begun to realize the need to reclaim our freedom in education; many are already practicing it as much as they can; and the tools and resources to make it viable, effective, and easy are so vast and accessible today that no lover of liberty has any good excuse for not pursuing a complete emancipation from public education.

As I have already said repeatedly, this is the one area you can change drastically toward the cause of freedom right now. Nothing toward that cause will be easier, more effective, and more life-transforming for all involved, than restoring freedom for yourself and family in the area of education.

How to Get It Back

When we talk about restoring freedom, we have to be careful not to be too romantic about the past. It is one thing to survey how things used to be free, and we can certainly apply the lessons we learn there to modern times; it is another thing, however, to think that the goal is to literally turn the clock back to 1776. We can't return to that world in many regards: socially, technologically, culturally, geographically, demographically, or economically. But we can certainly restore many of the ideals and principles of that time. After all, the highest morals and ethics of Christianity do not change; the ideals of life, liberty, and property do not to change. Rather, it is our commitment to ideals that changes society.

So how do we restore the ideal of individual and economic freedom in education? Obviously, you're not going to change the whole system overnight, but you can commit to do what you can, and then begin to model for and persuade others. The first step can be stated simply, and, for many, can be performed tomorrow if they are willing: don't accept the apparent benefit that comes with government control. Don't want the trap? Don't take the cheese. Put bluntly: *Pull your children out of public school.*

You may not consider this the top priority; you may think that education can be left alone for the time being while we fix the really big problems over in Washington. But this mentality has been in play for well over a century, and it's a myth—it's totally backwards. If you can't rein in the socialism in your own *county*... if you can't even discontinue your *family's* complicity in it, for that matter, you don't have a chance at changing anything greater. And even if you did accomplish some "big" change in Washington, it wouldn't matter socially, because you would still be allowing tyranny at the only level where it actually matters: the local level.

Why do I say this is the one area you can take control of now—the first point at which you must start? In later chapters, we're going to cover things like the role of the Supreme Court, the Federal Reserve, the Constitution—*you can't change these things*. You don't have any control over what currency you use, unless of course you live in a very tightly controlled community that relies purely on barter (*nota bene*: not even the Amish do this). You have absolutely no power to change those things at this point, and very little in the way of alternatives. For all practical purposes, you're stuck with tyranny in these areas (although, not to be completely pessimistic, there are some things you can do which we will discuss). Regarding Federal policies, the best you can do in most cases is cast your vote—one vote among a hundred million—about like standing up a sandcastle against a tsunami. In the area of education, however, you can take nearly complete control right here, right now. No election required, no legislation required, no vote required, no amendment to the Constitution required; you don't have to hire a lawyer, call your Congressman—nothing. There are no substantial legal, social, or economic barriers preventing you from being free in this area. It is purely, one hundred percent, a lifestyle decision.

If we don't reassert liberty here first, we won't really do it anywhere else. Because if we're not willing to make changes when and where we *can*, then we certainly won't do it where we're impeded at every turn. If we're not willing to make the sacrifices in lifestyle necessary in order to take personal responsibility *here*, where it's perfectly legal and feasible, then pretending anything beyond that is an absolute parade of showmanship. We readily devote tons of time and effort, and maybe even money, to ambitions that can promise only marginal improvements at best; we'll spend countless hours and expend measureless energy campaigning, rallying, attending speeches, waving flags and signs, passing out buttons and bumperstickers, watching the news every night to see what politician on what side said what. We'll post clips of news reports and interviews on YouTube and Facebook, adding positive commentary ("We need more guys like this."; "I wish this guy was president!"), or, conversely, advancing one of our indisputable criticisms. Nevertheless, all our efforts avail very little, yet we press on (what was that about failure and persistence?) instead of concentrating our time and energy on exercising freedom in the one arena that promises instantaneous success and long-term improvement.

It speaks volumes as to why we're in the shape we're in: we've taken the benefit. We take the easy way out—the path of least resistance. And our attempts to regain freedom reflect this very complacency: it's easy to mount a bumpersticker, to attend a rally, to get in a group and shout at the marble façade of a building that houses corrupt politicians. It's easy to click on an internet link, and to share it on Facebook. It's easy. We do what's easy.

But home school a child? Pay for private school? We've got a thousand reasons why we wouldn't, shouldn't, couldn't do such a thing, but in all but a small minority of cases, those thousand reasons are all excuses.

We have to *work hard* for liberty. All human government begins with self-government. The moment you believe it's legitimate to coerce someone else "legally" to benefit yourself, you have sown the seeds of destruction for both Christianity and liberty. And it just so happens that the easy way out means just that: the destruction of both Christianity and liberty. We have to reassert individual responsibility where we can. And you *can*. If ever there were an area of life in which people today need to hear the mantra "Yes we can," it's in the area of reasserting individual liberty in education.

Educational Choices: A Few Scenarios

So what does this mean on a personal level? It will depend on your personal family situation, and it will depend on what alternative to government schools you choose. I personally favor home schooling for a variety of reasons; but you may decide private schooling is better for you and your children.

The purpose in either decision is to reassert individual control, which means individual liberty, and to begin ending the civil government domination of education and, in fact, *all* educational coercion. Let's consider a few case examples:

In an ideal traditional family scenario, the husband works and the wife stays at home. If their children are currently in government schools, the only changes that would need to be made are very minor, especially if the decision is to switch to a private school. Here the only changes are logistical: deciding what school, enrolling, and attending; and the greatest burden would be paying tuition, which would mean revising the budget. A home schooling scenario is relatively easy as well, however, and cheaper: the stay-at-home mother (or, in some cases, father) simply needs encouragement and a few resources to start home schooling. The encouragement can be found in many churches, support groups, co-ops, and other organizations devoted to home education. These same people and institutions can direct you to a million curriculum and teaching resources; American Vision sells a few as well. There is no reason for traditional families to keep their children in public schools. For Christians, it could be argued persuasively that it would be sinful to do so.

But the majority of families today are clearly not traditional. Most pseudo-traditional families today have two parents working, and the children, if not at public school, are often in day care. In these cases, the decision whether to switch to private school or home school will mean a more extensive look at the budget. Private school will require tuition, and home schooling will necessitate either a private nanny/tutor, or, more commonly, one of the parents staying home. But in order to stay home, one of the parents would have to forfeit a full-time salary at least and, more than likely, would need to quit work altogether. This is the most common excuse I hear in regard to home schooling. People always say that their family needs the whole of both incomes in order to pay the bills.

While I suspect that may sometimes be the case, I am skeptical that it has been true as frequently as I've heard it. In most cases, the two-income dependent family has a large suburban home and comfortable lifestyle to match. If families require two incomes in order to maintain this, and this makes government taxation for childcare and education necessary, then don't we need to start evaluating our lifestyle? In this scenario, taxation is not so much subsidizing education as subsidizing their high standard of living, cable TV, etc. And is it really the case that the total of both incomes is *necessary* to pay the necessary living expenses—house payments, utility bills, insurance, etc. In many cases, cutting back here and there, sacrificing a few luxuries, and tightening the budget a little across the board would be sufficient to pay for educational freedom. What is the price of freedom, after all? Is the price of freedom living beyond our means while forcing others to pay for one (at least) of our fundamental responsibilities?

And then there are the actually difficult cases: single parent families. How in the world can we expect a single parent to work and provide for the necessities of life, and at the same time home school? How can we expect a single mom to be able to afford to pay for private schooling? I don't think the latter issue is as difficult as the home school issue. A single mom is really not much different than any other one-income household paying tuition at a private school. And in these cases, many churches which have private schools will give discounts to church members. At any rate, many private school tuitions are not that much more expensive than day care rates.

But the single parent home school dilemma is definitely difficult. Even here, depending on state requirements, nothing says you have to home school during the day. You can find the required number of hours in the afternoon and evening. The author personally knows at least one business-class working mom who has successfully home schooled a child into their teenage years. It can be done.

The only real question here is the same question at the root of all these cases: What sacrifice are you willing to make to restore freedom?

Steps to Restoring Educational Freedom

So here are a few practical steps: First, educate yourself. Educate yourself concerning the processes of beginning and managing your decision (whether home school or private). Really, the easiest to way for a beginner to learn is to Google something like, "How do I get started homse chooling?" and add to this the name of your state (e.g., "Georgia") because every state has slightly different laws. You will be able to choose from an endless list of helpful sites, the top few probably being the most popular organizations in your state. For this example, one is the Georgia Home Educators Association. Study especially the relevant laws for compulsory attendance, reporting, etc., and find out exactly how to initiate your home school legally (if necessary) and what is required of you beyond that. Then see what resources are available for curriculum in all price ranges, read reviews, talk online and in person with people who know, and make an *educated* decision.

Second, write the letters, order the necessary books, and start the process. Here's one tip: don't jump at first into one of those thousand-dollar all-in-one curriculum packs, because if you get half way through and don't like it, or find something better for much less, you will have wasted your money. Most people I know prefer to design their own curriculum piece by piece.

Also, get some books for *yourself*: learn how to become more than just a housewife going through the motions; learn how to become an effective communicator and a good teacher, planner, organizer, and scholar. Improve yourself as much as you do your child.

Educate yourself, make the investment, and then start doing it. Jump in and start. That's more important than trying to get everything perfect beforehand, because then you'll never start. You'll make mistakes, but you'll learn, and the child will learn—and you'll both be better for it. There will always be more to learn down the road, no matter how good you become.

In addition to re-establishing individual and family educational freedom, we should also pursue broader political goals concerning education, beginning at the local level: the ultimate goal should be to abolish all public taxation and funding for schools in general—to get the civil government completely out of the education business. But a medial step could be a law that exempts from property tax anyone who is private schooling or home schooling their children. No one should be taxed to pay for other people's educations, but private and home schoolers don't even use the service themselves. As it currently stands, these people are bearing what is essentially double the tax burden.

Not only would this be economically fair for those who already pay for their own educational needs, but this fairness in itself would become an incentive for more people to pull out of public school, and for more people to become private tutors and teachers. A greater demand would stimulate the creation of more private schools. When more and more property owners realize that they could afford a more than adequate home school curriculum for way less than the price of their property taxes, they would certainly want to move in that direction (not to mention the additional educational benefits of home schooling). And if more people opted for private schooling, not only would options increase in that market, but a range of affordability would develop to accommodate the different tuitions people were willing to pay. And depending on your status and property, when the market reaches an equilibrium not distorted by the State's virtual monopoly on education, you would soon be able to afford yearly tuition for a superior education at one of *many* private schools for equal to or less than the amount of your property tax—and that's considering an average middle-class property owner. This is probably already true for many people.

If the essential government *monopoly* over education were broken, a free market in education—considering today's technology and vast information resources—would produce options that we probably can't even currently imagine. Charitable organizations could start schools that surpassed public schools in capability and efficiency, and serve even the poorest of the poor, and do so in a way superior to the current one-size-fits-all model of government education.

We should also, if we were to consider the political side, look further into revenues. We have just discussed the perfectly reasonable option of personal exemptions, but what about the county and state governments? The sovereignty of a county's administration is compromised to the extent that it accepts funding from the state and Federal government. These funds always come with mandates, regulations, and other strings attached. In order to reassert effective and independent local district control (which is the basis, after all, behind most people claiming, "Our schools are different."), the source of funding must remain always and only local (or by privately funded organizations with all contracts publically disclosed). The truth is that nationwide, most local school districts receive about half of their funding from state governments, about another ten percent from the Feds, and only the remaining 40% from local taxes. Of course, taxpayers actually foot the entire bill, but when more and more centralized levels of government are in control, the revenues get consolidated and then reapportioned in a more equal manner than they were collected. In other words, it's one more deceptive way to redistribute wealth. Local districts should reassert local control, and could do so by refusing to accept centralized handouts. Of course, this would require pressure on the school board from the community, and again, a willingness on the part of all involved to make sacrifices to function within the limitations of their own means. But this should be done, and it should come in addition to local, state, and Federal exemptions for anyone not directly using the system. The bottom line is that no one should in any way, at any level, be forced to fund someone else's education.

The goal is to exercise what freedom we can in the area of education. In doing so, we could create a movement that will make it socially viable to free up education completely. This, I realize, will not be easy, but it is the easiest thing we can do right now in the effort to restore America. It sits there right in front of us waiting to be done. All it takes is a little commitment and a little sacrifice.

What are you willing to sacrifice? What do you consider important: freedom, integrity, honesty? Can these be compromised for the causes of convenience and comfort? Should they be? That's the question at the root of *Restoring America One County at a Time*, and it begins with the issue of education. If we can't take action here, we can forget the rest.

2. Welfare

Having grown up in the twentieth and twenty-first centuries, most of us have a narrow mental window through which to view the subject of human welfare and insurance. It is almost impossible for us to imagine a world in which Social Security, Medicare, and the myriad other State-funded benefits do not exist. This world seems normal because it's the way it's always been for most of us: the State provides social security and social insurances for the aged and the needy. But this is not the way it's always been.

Welfare in a Free America

There are still a few people out there who can remember the time prior to the passage of America's first Social Security Act in 1935. Aside, perhaps, from some memories associated with the Great Depression (which was both an uncommon and temporary event), they can vouch for what I am about to express here: in a free society, private interests (whether individual, family, business, or charitable interests) are solely responsible for providing cradle-to-grave welfare. And, contrary to popular assumption today, these few people can also establish that, in such a society, people do not commonly go hungry in old age, nor go bankrupt and become homeless due to medical expenses, or suffer any of the many nightmare scenarios that are brought up any time welfare privatization is discussed. Those things simply did not happen except in extraordinary circumstances, and they still happen in some circumstances today in spite of vast socialistic measures. In other words, in a free society, private welfare and insurance are sound both in *principle* and *practice.*

The Principle of Welfare in a Free Society

A truly free society will exercise individual liberty and responsibility in all areas of human welfare—health insurance, retirement planning, survivors' benefits, disability, unemployment, and all things of that nature. Free people learn how to provide for themselves and their own families, how to manage their resources, and how to plan for the future. In times of need, they are taken care of by their own private arrangements, their own private funds, insurance benefits, and their own family whatever extent necessarye—and, preferably, they utilize a combination of these helps.

As long as the State is involved in funding or regulating any of these matters, however, we do not have a free society. The State is, by definition, an agency of legal *coercion*—of force. To place a social concern (like welfare) within the jurisdiction of the State is to argue implicitly that God endorses the use of force—even lethal force—in the administration of that concern. In the case of restitution for a crime, legal coercion is mandated by the Scriptures, yet it is nonetheless a negation of (the criminal's) freedom. A criminal who is under civil penal sanctions is to that degree a slave (and the Thirteenth Amendment to the Constitution allows for this explicitly) because the very nature of *being compelled* is by definition *a loss of liberty.* Coercion means servitude. Since this is so, the more we expand the State's power to coerce people, the more we constrict freedom and liberty in society. The very moment we begin to expand the State's functions and institutions *beyond the proper punishment of crime,* that same moment we begin to make slaves out of free men. And thus, the moment we begin to place basic welfare issues beneath the coercive arm of civil government—that is, the moment we legitimize the Welfare State to the slightest degree—we have subverted a free society.

Many people defend the existence and expansion of the Welfare State because they believe it is legitimate to use force to reshape society as they see fit—to make it "virtuous," or "equitable" (or whatever other sweet-sounding word they may employ to make their intentions seem honorable). Many liberals and progressives have long since been very open about this; and many conservatives hold the same belief, although they are less often open about it—if they are even conscious of holding it. The belief that justifies State coercion of law-abiding people must be seen for what it is, however: anti-Christian, unbiblical, and against every reasonable idea of liberty on which this country was founded.

There was certainly no Welfare State when Thomas Jefferson penned those immortal words "that all men are created equal, that they are endowed by their Creator with certain unalienable Rights, that among these are Life, Liberty and the pursuit of Happiness." Nor when Benjamin Franklin published *Poor Richard's Almanack* and started his own printing and news business. The framers of the Constitution did not design one, and there was no subsequent Welfare State in America through virtually all of the nineteenth century (although it did begin to creep in). The Welfare State had no place in the original American way, and some people living today can still remember life before the imposition of that system. They can tell you—it was a family-based society, and human welfare was a family-based and business-based affair. *And it worked.*

The Practice of Welfare in a Free Society

In practice, welfare must be family-based. Primarily, the family meets the most basic welfare needs of society, and the church serves as a secondary welfare ministry. There is the reality of social debt: All people come into this world helpless and with no property—entirely dependent on the love and provision of their parents. This dependence runs longer for humans than any other living being in the natural world—anywhere from 18 to 20 or more years. During nearly this entire period, a child is indebted to his parents' welfare. Parents have a moral obligation to provide this welfare in the form of food, clothing, shelter, and education (as well as many intangibles like discipline, love, etc.). In turn, as children remain indebted for these many years of provision, they can repay their familial debt if their parents need provision and care in their elderly years. In the typical family scenario, there is always at least one bread winner distributing food to several dependents.

The cementing of this family commitment has been, for several thousands of years, the marriage vow. This oath—legally binding—joins a man and a woman into a covenant of, among other things, perpetual welfare for each other and their progeny. We tend to lose sight of the very weighty, material implications of the marital oath; it gets obscured by the romantic feelings, the flowers and kisses, and the cake and the champagne. But listen again to the actual words of those vows. Here's the traditional wording from the Anglican prayer book upon which nearly all American Protestants have based their marriage vows:

> The groom says, "I ,_____, take thee ,_____, to be my lawful wedded Wife, to have and to hold from this day forward, for better for worse, for richer for poorer, in sickness and in health, to love and to cherish, till death us do part, according to God's holy ordinance; and thereto I plight thee my troth."

The bride promises essentially the same thing with minor, though important, differences. Then, as the groom places the ring on the bride's finger, he says the following:

> "With this Ring I thee wed, with my body I thee worship, and with all my worldly goods I thee endow: In the name of the Father, and of the Son, and of the Holy Ghost. Amen."

Notice the extent to which these vows concern a commit-ment of material wealth and provision for material health (in sickness and in health) until death. And toward these ends, the vow includes a pledge of bodily devotion (i.e., the entirety of one's physical capacity and labor) and worldly goods. This is a welfare program, period. And, by the way, it is the original prenuptial agreement—because, until *after* this vow is taken and the marriage is consummated, the covenant is not yet in force. Today, we think of a prenuptial agreement as something a rich partner does to limit the loss of his or her wealth in the event of a divorce (in other words, to limit the scope of the traditional vow on his material wealth). In effect, it is divorce protection. In contrast, the original and fundamental prenup-tial agreement is the traditional marital vow, and it is a bind-ing, legal oath to provide for the partner's welfare and health until death (with exceptions, of course, for adultery or some-times abandonment). And it was legally enforceable.

It is not surprising, then, that the rise of the Welfare State has closely paralleled the decline of the family, and the out-right debasement of marriage through easy, no-fault divorce. In other words, the State-dominated system has helped destroy the nature of the marriage commitment (and in many cases, e.g., the Marxist and other secular traditions, *it was consciously designed to do so*).

So in the original American way, and for most of West-ern—especially Christian—history, the marriage vow was the foundation of social insurance—both for the provision and education of children, and for the care of the elderly.

The same was true of health care: it was primarily carried out by the family. The church did have a large role in the creation of hospitals in the middle ages, but these were not widely put to use by the general population, especially not in the way hos-pitals and doctors are used today. When they were employed, it was a private affair, and often charitably subsidized by a sponsoring church—not the State. Since healthcare was largely decentralized, with families providing for themselves, there has always been—in America at least, until more recent times—a broad base of health care providers in the free market.

Additionally, in the nineteenth century, there was a tremendous development of a wide variety of private insurance companies— for life, fire, travel, shipping, crop, and deposit insurance. Eventually, there was even *reinsurance*—for insurance companies that faced losses in payments. People learned quickly that, by paying a small premium, they could pool their risk and protect themselves against losses. Premiums were kept affordable by constant advances in actuarial tables and, most importantly, by the fact that insurance companies had to compete in the free market—unregulated and unsubsidized by the State.

In the originally free American way, the government was not involved in funding or managing these affairs, nor was it involved in any attending redistribution of wealth. The only legal aspects to the whole system were first, the enforcement of the marriage vow, which itself had been entered into freely. If a party abdicated its responsibility to either spouse or children, the government could enforce sanctions in relation to the legally binding nature of the marital oath—this protected the innocent and the children. Second, the civil government attended to the enforceable aspects of insurance contracts, which had also had been entered into freely.

Benefits of Freedom in Welfare

This ideal of liberty in human welfare has the following beneficial features:

First, individuals retain sovereignty over their own decisions regarding retirement, old age, health, and all forms of insurance. It's *your* decision, not some bureaucrat's. (If, however, you prefer it to be someone else's decision, you are certainly free to contract with someone for such consultation; but, in a free society, you're not allowed to demand or force anyone else to pay for that decision.)

Second, there's a much greater value placed on the family. When that happens, more families stick together. Marital vows function again as the basis of human society. Churches and private-based charities are restored. This also re-establishes the true nature of charity as voluntary care for the helpless, and it decentralizes the determination of who truly deserves aid. This inhibits those who would take advantage of charitable systems, yet, at the same time, it allows for latitude in those decisions from charity to charity.

Third, property is protected. No one can confiscate your property for redistribution, and you can't demand that anyone else's property be confiscated and given to others.

Fourth, the civil government cannot penalize anyone who has not committed a crime, and it cannot impose obligations without your consent. The State would, of course, uphold voluntary vows and contracts in a court of law—these alone would be legally enforceable. You can choose to abstain from a marital vow, insurance contract, or any other binding commitment that may obligate you to pay taxes or fines or penalties or premiums. This means *you* must bear the consequences of *your choices*: If you have chosen to rely entirely on your own personal means, you will fall upon the mercy of charity, if any is available, should you face an emergency beyond your limited resources.

Fifth, the next generation has obligations to the previous primarily in regard to its familial connections. Parents, in turn, must be honored and respected (this is the fifth commandment!). This being so, the government will not be operating an inter-generational ponzi scheme (which is essentially the nature of the Social Security system).

So, as with education in a free America, the original private welfare system preserved individual freedom and responsibility in both principle and practice. Welfare was a matter of individual and family liberty, and it worked.

These principles are not only traditionally American, but they are also biblical. They uphold the centrality and integrity of the family in society, family legacies and trusts, the honoring of parents, and the protection of inheritance. That's social freedom—that's freedom in social security and insurance.

So, how was this freedom lost? How did our society come to be dominated by so-called "cradle-to-grave" programs administered by a paternal state? Why do we have a massive Welfare State where a free society once thrived? As with the discussion of the State takeover of education, the answer illuminates our current predicament by revealing the darkness of its roots.

How Freedom was Lost

In a free society, the legal institution of the family, private insurance arrangements, and private charity provide entirely for human welfare. That's the way it used to be in America, and people didn't starve because of it. So what changed? Why the monumental change from freedom to coercion, free markets to taxation and fines, from families and parents to a paternal State?

We've already mentioned, in our discussion of education, the rise of the secular, Unitarian belief system and, with that, the rise of remedial social institutions—the asylum, prison, alms house, and public school—aimed at conditioning individuals through the corrective influence of an environment designed and controlled by "experts." And with this, grew the "need" for government power to impose those institutions on society. Then, as these institutions failed over and over, their proponents cried for even greater government control and even larger budgets. This shows that there was already a mentality at work among a small, self-dubbed *elite* who believed in using government control to "improve" mankind. This was in America as early as the 1830s, among Horace Mann and others, and it grew from there.

Eventually, the floodgates were completely opened to this type of thinking among civil government officials. One of the most important contributions to this process was the creation, in 1883, of Otto Von Bismarck's socialist Prussia—the first socialist Welfare State in modern history. While Bismarck was not necessarily a hero on American soil, his socialist model was systematized in America a decade later by a sociologist named Lester Frank Ward who revolutionized the field with his work *Dynamic Sociology*. This massive 1200-page work presented a completely new version of social Darwinism— one that demanded a paternal State to accomplish its goals. Ward's basic thesis eventually swept American academia and politics, and, when it came time later to implement his views on a massive scale, the propagandists immediately referenced the once unpopular *Bismarck* to defend their views!

Bismarck's Dubious Legacy

So let us first take a look at what happened in Prussia under his majesty the Chancellor, Otto von Bismarck. By 1883, there were already many socialist and communist movements in Europe. *The Communist Manifesto* of Karl Marx and Friedrich Engels had already been published in the German language in 1848, and there were certainly many cells of socialist and communist thinking at the time. Ironically, Bismarck insisted that his system was a *defense* against the growing demands of socialists and communists. He argued that his system was in fact *not* socialism, but simply welfare, or as he put it, "practical Christianity legally demonstrated."[1]

Many critics of his system pointed out the obvious—Bismarck's measures to impose social insurance and health insurance via State taxation (up to a third of one's income) was no different than the socialism which he claimed to combat. In a speech defending his measures, he first brandished the label "practical Christianity," a label he used from then on and

---

[1] Quoted in Marjorie Shearon, *Wilbur J. Cohen: The Pursuit of Power, A Bureaucratic Biography* (Marjorie Shearon, 1967), 5.

often. A famous early twentieth-century professor of German history at Harvard saw the hypocrisy very clearly. He wrote that Bismarck "was the sworn enemy of the Socialist party— he attempted to destroy it, root and branch; yet through the nationalization of railways and the obligatory insurance of workmen he infused more Socialism into German legislation than any other statesman before him."[2] Eventually, Bismarck himself would refer to his "practical Christianity" as "our State Socialism"—which, of course, everyone already knew.[3]

Everyone also knew that Bismarck's socialism was really no defense against the more revolutionary Socialists and Communists. Instead of haulting the march toward centralization, it put it in motion and accelerated it; and even worse, it turned the very people who opposed it into its dependents. There was no way out after that. Interestingly, William Shirer, perhaps the most famous biographer of Adolf Hitler, recognized that the culmination of Bismarck's policies was Nazi Germany. In his book, *The Rise and Fall of the Third Reich*, he wrote:

> To combat socialism Bismarck put through between 1883 and 1889 a program for social security far beyond anything known in other countries. It included compulsory insurance for workers against old age, sickness, accident and incapacity, and though organized by the State it was financed by employers and employees. It cannot be said that it stopped the rise of the Social Democrats or the trade unions, but it did have a profound influence on the working class in that it gradually made them value security over political freedom and caused them to see in the State, however conservative, a benefactor and a protector. Hitler, as we shall see, took full advantage of this state of mind. In this, as in other matters, he learned much from Bismarck. "I studied

---

[2] Shearon, 4.

[3] Moritz Busch, *Bismarck: Some Secret Pages of His History* (New York: Mac-Millan, 1898), 2:282.

Bismarck's socialist legislation," Hitler remarks in *Mein Kampf*, "in its intention, struggle and success."[4]

Bismarck's system became the model not only for Hitler, but for Welfare States all over the world. Politicians and activists studied its laws and its methods. They studied how it was passed, and the way rhetoric and euphemisms were used to sell it to the public. For example, in this country, the taxes used to fund Social Security have been called "contributions" from day one, by design. It's not a "tax," it's a "contribution." It's not "socialism," it's "practical Christianity." These are word games used to deceive people. But it's common practice. When Bismarckian programs finally got a firm foothold in America in the 1930s, under FDR's so-called "New Deal," it was openly admitted that Bismarck was the model. One biographer and propagandist of FDR's administration wrote:

> Social security is not a new idea. . . . Other nations of the world are far ahead of the United States in battling this important economic problem [financing retirement]. Von Bismarck, the founder of the German Empire, nearly fifty years ago launched a plan for social security. The Iron Chancellor, who could hardly be called the precursor of radicalism, was only putting into effect sentiments that had been uttered by statesmen before him.[5]

Socialism and Social Darwinism

So that was the influence of Bismarck which would not have gained a foothold in America without the seminal work of sociologist Lester Frank Ward. His magnum opus, *Dynamic Sociology*, was published in America in the same year Bis-

---

[4] William L. Shirer, *The Rise and Fall of the Third Reich: A History of Nazi Germany* (New York: Simon and Schuster, 1960), 96.

[5] P. J. O'Brien, *Forward with Roosevelt* (Chicago: The John C. Winston Co., 1936), 84. This open acknowledgment remains even today on a page of the Social Security Administration's own website (http://www.ssa.gov/history/ottob.html).

marck passed his first social insurance measures. Up until Ward, social Darwinists had simply taken Darwin's biological theory of natural selection and applied it to the marketplace and the political sphere. In particular, the idea of "survival of the fittest" was used by men like Herbert Spencer in England and William Graham Sumner in America to argue for laissez-faire economics. Competition should rule the day and there should be no artificial leveling of results. The winners win and the losers lose, period. The fittest survive and the unfittest don't. That's nature and we shouldn't try to change it.

And while that philosophy might resonate in general with most lovers of free markets, it had an unfortunate tone of harshness and uncharitableness that made for bad PR. The field was ripe for some progressive to come along with a system that sounded more like it had everyone's best interest in mind, and not just that of the fittest. This is exactly what Ward did.

Ward posited that, though biological life does evolve just as Darwin taught, *sociological* life need not be so undirected. With the evolution of man and his complex brain, the ability to reflect, reason, and plan has brought about a change in the *nature* of evolution. No more is it to be a blind natural force, for mankind has been endowed by evolution with the ability to plan and direct his own development. Now, instead of ramming and trampling each other, man can build institutions for governing and improving the race, and thereby to advance the species. This is the advent of evolutionary social planning.

This theory suited the reforming elites and progressives just fine—since the 1830s, they had already seen themselves as the reformers and directors of society. Now Ward provided academic justification for their actions. He soon dominated the field of sociology, becoming the first president of the American Sociological Association. His line of thinking began to produce a whole new generation of academic and political leaders who believed in progressive intervention in society via government power.

There was an immediate effect on the administration of Teddy Roosevelt, and an even more dramatic change during for Woodrow Wilson's tenure—especially after the beginning of World War I. From that point on, academics and activists began to pour out of the universities and into bureaucratic positions and think tanks funded by organizations like the Rockefeller Foundation. These formed a tireless behind-the-scenes army writing legislation and scheming to get it passed as soon as possible.

Harry Hopkins, who was a close adviser to FDR and chairman of the Works Progress Administration, exemplified the mentality of a ruling elite cramming legislation through in a time of crisis. He was quoted in a 1934 *New York Times* article:

> You aren't going to get health insurance if you expect people to do it voluntarily. I am convinced that by one bold stroke we could carry the American people along not only for health insurance but also for unemployment insurance. I think it could be done in the next eighteen months.[6]

FDR got his Social Security Act passed in 1935, but unlike Bismarck, FDR implemented only one main piece of social welfare—Social Security. The bureaucrats and activists who drew up the law, however, had much more in mind. In the meantime, however, the Constitutionality of even the Social Security Act was being challenged.

Of note, the original bill included a mandate for lawmakers to begin working on similar measures for health insurance, but this was written out of the bill during committee. Congress expressly removed this authorization for further Congressional studies from the original Social Security Act. But this did not stop the activists. And Congress had made one important oversight: it forgot to remove three little words—"and related matters"—from a pertinent section of the bill. Liberal activist

---

[6] Harry Hopkins, quoted in Shearon, 48.

Isidore Falk would leverage this phrase as statutory authority to conduct continuing researches and publications regarding health insurance and other forms of social control.

In fact, the socialists didn't even wait for the Supreme Court ruling: they already had papers and laws prepared beforehand. Marjorie Shearon, who was an insider aide to the bureaucrats during this time (and who, by the way, later repented of what she had been a part of and defected, writing a book about it) relates that, "With the validation of the Social Security Act, the bureaucratic world within the agency went wild. Expansionist plans, hidden in desk drawers and files up to that time, came out boldly into the open."[7]

Immediately after the Supreme Court validated the Act in 1937, Shearon writes that her boss at the time, who was Isidore Falk himself, turned to her and said:

> "I want you to study and make yourself an expert in compulsory health insurance. Old-age and unemployment insurance are now here to stay. They will be modified and expanded, but health insurance will be the great new advance in social insurance. It's the coming thing and *we* will draft the new laws."[8]

In 1946, Falk published a booklet in the Congressional Record called *Medical Care Insurance*.[9] Shearon describes that this book "must be regarded as the *Mein Kampf* of the nationalization of American Medicine."[10] It contained

> the most comprehensive description of the plans to capture every aspect of health and medical care in this country that has ever been published. It explained the necessity for Federal control of personal health services, the unification of preventative and curative services, medical edu-

---

[7] Shearon, 43.

[8] Isidore Falk, quoted in Shearon, 49.

[9] Senate Committee Print No. 5 of 1946; 79th Cong., 2d Sess.

[10] Shearon, 150.

cation, medical research, hospitals, health centers—everything, all under the control of one agency and, though not stated explicitly, there was the implication that one man would be the Czar of Medicine: Isidore S. Falk.[11]

The goal was a total socialized State. Jane Hoey, Director of the Social Security Board's Bureau of Public Assistance, published a book called *Common Human Needs* in which she stated it plainly: "Social security and public assistance programs are a basic essential for the attainment of the socialized state envisaged by democratic ideology, a way of life which so far has been realized only in slight measure."[12]

From this we learn at least two things: first, the people who wrote and promoted the laws saw them plainly as measures of socialism—a "socialized state"; and second, activists of this kind were not and are not satisfied until they've reached a *fully* socialized state. Until then, they keep working, and the end justifies the subversive, lying, elitist means.

The "Ratchet Effect"

This brings up an important component of leftist ideology and practice: the "ratchet effect." If leftists can't accomplish their full plan all at once, they will fight for as much of it as they can get, knowing that once it's in place, people will get addicted to the benefit, and as much as gets put in place will never be rescinded—thus constituting the starting point for the next piece of legislation. Many of them viewed their work explicitly in these terms. Sydney Webb, who was one of the most active and influential socialists in the Fabian group in England a century or more ago, said it openly: "No nation having once nationalized or municipalized any industry has ever retraced its steps or reversed its action."[13]

---

[11] Shearon, 150.

[12] Quoted in Shearon, 34

[13] Quoted in Shearon, 1.

This is exactly what we find in the socialized takeover of America: socialism by small, creeping increments. The major encroachments, of course, came in 1935 with Social Security and then, in 1965, with the Medicare expansion. But we should also include Bush's expansion of Medicare in 2003, and then Obamacare in 2010. But even these major increments don't tell the whole story. You originally had welfare as part of Indian pacification (in the 1840s), but the slippery slope began in earnest after the Civil War. Union veterans who had been wounded in battle received government benefits; then their wives and children were included in these benefits; then all Union veterans (wounded or not); then all their families; then their extended families... Pretty soon, labor unions began to recognize the effectiveness of collective agitation to keep welfare payments coming during recession. Then WWI hit and Wilson's War State centralized everything and set a precedent for what was to follow in this country. Social activists accomplished this by creeping increments—a little here, a little there—until the trap was closed. We took the cheese, and now we're in the trap... Except, it doesn't have to be a trap. There is still a beginning of a way out.

How to Get it Back

In chapter one, we discussed how we still have the option of almost complete freedom in education, and we should fully exercise that liberty. Combatting the welfare state is similar in that regard. Aside from the taxes extracted from us in order to maintain the government-run scheme, we are still at liberty to save for old age, and to buy different forms of insurance freely. The major exception to that is Medicare—Americans over 65 effectually have little to no private health insurance options and are thereby forced to be dependent on the system. Other than this, with sacrifice and self-discipline, we can take a large portion of our freedom back and plan for a day when the "benefit" does not exist.

We have to end our personal dependence on the Welfare State: Social Security is a problem, but it doesn't have to be a trap. This means we need to plan for our own financial futures, privately, while we also plan to phase out Social Security. All forms of welfare should be privately funded and insured, not supported through taxation. Family, Church, and private charity can replace the Welfare State. And again, we'll have to learn to refuse the proferred benefit. (*Don't take the cheese.*) This means personal sacrifice, but we can do it with effort.

The Evils of Social Security

Before we get into the practical steps, I want to drive home the immoral nature of the Social Security system, and why it has become so much of a problem. First, Social Security *is not* a retirement program, or any kind of savings program at all. It is not the case—and even the Social Security Administration makes this abundantly clear—that we are paying into a discreet personal fund in our name so that we can draw from that fund in the future. That may be how FDR sold it to the masses, but it is legally and practically *not* that.

I want to share with you an exchange that took place recently, between a reporter and a man named David Walker. Walker was the Comptroller General of the U.S. for ten years, overseeing all matters relating to all Federal public funds, and then he went on to head the Peterson Foundation which specializes in bringing public awareness to the looming collapse of the Social Security and Medicare programs. So if anyone understands the system, it's this guy. I want you to listen to how candidly he describes the Social Security system. In light of the fact that it will probably collapse (it's already in the red), the reporter asks a question:

> [Q:] *Is the Social Security program fair to younger workers?*
> . . . The way to look at it, rather than young versus old,

is really income level. The Social Security system is designed to provide a better deal for workers who make less money because the replacement ratio that you receive compared to your earnings is much higher for lower-income workers than it is for higher-income workers.

But the reporter was no dummy, and she pounced on this answer: "So it sounds unfair to both younger workers and higher-income workers."

Then came the outright admission by Walker:

> Social Security is not an investment program. You shouldn't look at it as a rate of return. It's intended to provide a safety net of retirement income. By definition, it's structured so lower-wage workers will get a higher relative benefit. So, by definition, there's an element of transfer payment.
>
> When people look at it as, "Give me the money, I'll invest and do better," it depends on what your income level is. Middle and upper incomes would do better because it would eliminate the subsidy to the lower income. But that's not what the program is. I hear young people saying, "I'm not getting a good deal." That's technically right, but it doesn't reflect the nature of what Social Security is.[14]

So a major government official who oversaw the program, who is now an activist in regard to reforming the program, openly admits that the program is unfair to both younger payers and middle- and upper- income payers. It is, he says, not a retirement or savings program, but rather a *wealth-transfer* program. And of course, a wealth-transfer program is—for the net-losers in that transfer—just the opposite of a savings program. It is in fact a "losings" program, or an un-recouped tax.

---

[14] David Walker interviewed by Kimberly Palmer, "David Walker explains Social Security's Future," June 16, 2009, http://money.usnews.com/money/personal-finance/articles/2009/06/16/david-walker-explains-social-securitys-future (accessed April 21, 2011).

So, instead of thinking of Social Security as some kind of investment program, a fund you're paying into on which you can draw in the future, you need to see it for what it is—a tax now, spend now scheme (tax *you* now, and spend on *others* now scheme). Not a penny of what you pay in now will be put into a fund that will collect interest and be there when you get old and need it—*not a penny*. And this is not only because the system is losing money and will probably be bankrupt when you get to that age, but because the system was never designed that way to begin with. What you pay now goes 100% to pay elderly and other people now; and the promise is then given that when you get to the proper age, the government will then collect from *other* young people to pay *you*. It is not savings, but a tax and spend wealth-transfer program underwritten by government coercion. There is no fund, only a gun—pointed at workers, forcing them to pay for the retired generation.

Social Security is the government's promise to tax young people on behalf of anyone over 65. It is an inter-generational wealth-transfer scheme. And the cost to the older generation for this agreement is that they were once the taxed generation having a portion of their income transferred to the older. In essence, the younger advocate says to the government, "I agree to pay taxes for older people now, if you agree to extract money at gunpoint on my behalf in the future." So, it is wealth-transfer system sustained by the self-interest of the retirees and based on threats of violence.

This understanding is important when we begin to talk about phasing out or ending the system. So many people get nervous and upset, "But I've paid so much into the system. I want my fair share back out!" But, of course, this assumes that the system is a savings plan and not a tax-and-spend transfer. What you have paid all of your life is nothing but a recurring tax—no matter what else they officially name it. What they promise to give you is not actually your money—rather, it is future taxes on your children and grandchildren, and other people's children and grandchildren. Instead of having an actual entitlement to actual assets, you have an alleged entitlement to the government's ability to tax future generations—and that ability is growing weaker and weaker as time goes on for more than one reason. So we have to get into the mindset that we have not been saving for ourselves, but have been robbed on behalf of others. This is not *saved* money, it is *lost* money.

Any attempt to fix this immoral and broken system is inevitably going to involve someone, somewhere suffering a financial loss (and more likely it will be everyone, everywhere). A sacrifice is inevitable. And like all of the financial crises which have threatened government with bankruptcy in the past, the longer we wait to make the necessary sacrifice, the worse and more painful that sacrifice will become. We must prepare for it, and we must prepare *now*. If you want to have a free society, you have to plan to be free of government control in the area of old age and welfare, and this means we have to plan now to replace that system with private options—not just "privatized" options that are still largely controlled by the government, but fully private and voluntary options.

How To End Social Security

A lot of people talk about phasing out or privatizing Social Security, but few actually present any details. As far as I know, only one person has published a serious, comprehensive plan for phasing out Social Security. And while that plan has some great ideas, it has one fatal flaw: Because it seeks to minimize the sacrifices required of the dependent generation, and those young people who have already been paying into the system, it takes *forty years* to complete the plan. And it's just not reasonable to expect people to take progressive cuts in benefits over that long of a period without complaining, and thus, it's even more unreasonable to expect politicians to stay the course on a painful and unpopular program (at least unpopular with most of the beneficiaries) over the course of ten presidential terms and twenty Congressional elections. It'll just never happen. So the process of regaining private control of welfare needs to include quick, substantial, and decisive actions—be they political or private—or it's just not going to happen.

So two ways are available to us: either completely abolish the Social Security system immediately, or do so in steps over a relatively short period of time. Either way will be difficult. Abolishing it immediately would cause widespread hardship for those who are entirely dependent on the system. Phasing it out gradually risks never truly breaking free from it. But I think the gradual option is probably the better of the two practically speaking, as long as it is done definitively and in a short enough span of time.

The primary immediate goal, as in education, should be to allow people to opt out of the system. If they exclude themselves, they would never be allowed to draw benefits, but, most importantly, they would be exempt from any taxes designated for the system. This is the main step toward a free society: the ability to opt out of the system if you want to. But this freedom will require sacrifices, both material and psychological, in the mean time. These pertain specifically to the things we can do personally, *now.*

The first thing you need to do is plan—personally, financially, for yourself—as if you will receive *nothing* from Social Security. Pretend as if it already does not exist—even though it does. This involves financial and mental planning. Planning financially is a no-brainer: you begin to save money at a rate that will allow you to have substantial resources (in fact, adequate resources) set aside for a later time of need (notice I did not say "when you retire"—retirement and elderly need are two different things). You've got to have a large nest egg, and that means saving and investing a substantial percentage of your income now, from as early in your life as possible. You have to create financial independence for yourself for the day that you are no longer able to work, so that you can erase the need for dependence on the government's system. You erase that dependence completely; you replace it with personal independence.

By first making ourselves and our families independent of the need for Social Security, we can begin to delegitimize the program. If we average people prove we can live without it, that means most people in general don't need it. In turn, that means only a small percentage of people truly do need wealth transfers in old age in order to live a modest lifestyle or, in extreme cases, to survive. But once we reach that point, we are talking about an entirely different social circumstance: a few cases of real need can easily be handled by private charity from families, businesses, and churches (as the apostle Paul commanded in 1 Timothy 5). And this means we don't need a government-run program *at all*, and, therefore, we should dismantle it. Through self-discipline, self-sacrifice, self-funding, and private charity, we can delegitimize the system even while it exists; and delegitimizing the system will stimulate the political will to abolish it.

Achieving Personal Financial Independence

But making that first step for ourselves is the hard part—it will require a major sacrifice for most people. We have unconsciously trusted in the Social Security system as *the* means for old age security, and we have not saved money and wealth at a rate anywhere near high enough to sustain us in that time. Most people, resting on the government promise, save very little if any beyond a 401k contribution (which means little more than a few percent usually). And yet, if people actually sat down and calculated—based on life expectancy, standard inflation, and their annual expenses based on their expected lifestyle—how much money they will actually need in old age, they would see a huge disparity between what they will *have* and what they will *need*. Add to this savings set aside for an emergency like temporary unemployment, uninsured auto accident, etc. Ideally, people should be saving at least twenty perecent of their income regularly—and putting it back in a safe investment for future needs. But this would greatly hamper most people's current lifestyles, because people currently spend what they should be saving and even borrow beyond that. In lieu of saving, people buy the largest house possible (with ninety-five or sometimes one hundred percent mortgages), the finest cars available, plus many additional perks like $100/month cable TV plans, and much, much more. And much of the "investment" in these areas is mortgaged and sometimes second-mortgaged—and people are financially *stuck*. Millions of people are now upside-down in their mortgages—they could not sell their house for anywhere near what they bought it for—and thus would have great difficulty transitioning into a lifestyle of thrift and saving. It's a trap—a self-set, self-sprung trap. Becoming financially independent will mean a major lifestyle sacrifice (perhaps seemingly impossible for some), but they must start saving a large percentage of their income if they want to reach the goal of independently financed old-age security.

How can this be done? Well, you have to set your mind on personal sacrifice. This relates to my second piece of practical advice: preparing mentally for sacrifice. Whether we phase out Social Security over time, or the State starts trimming benefits in order to save, or the system goes completely bankrupt overnight on its own (as some predict), nearly all people are going to take a financial hit in some way anyway. Before that time comes, we who wish to decentralize political power and take personal responsibility and restore freedom need to accept the fact that we are going to lose at least some money in that system and because of that system. You're going to get robbed, and the cash is going to be lost forever. Accept it; get over it; move on. But that sacrifice is short-term. The long-term gain we get for that short-term sacrifice is the freedom and independence we say we want. The time to prepare for a better way of living—for both moral and practical reasons— is *now*. Mentally forfeiting and foregoing alleged future benefits will help us train our minds to accept a lifestyle of thrift and sacrifice in general. That mental preparation will get us over the initial hump of beginning to plan for an independent financial future, and will then help sustain us as we carry that new vision out day-by-day into the future. From that mentality, then, we begin voluntarily to trim and pare down our lifestyles to more conservative and viable proportions.

For the person who has simply refused to save up to this point, and whose mortgage and lifestyle have maxed out their income and beyond, there needs to be a tremendous personal accounting, and then cutting back. You need to sit down and take a scalpel to your budget. Do you really need all the appointments, pool and gym memberships, more new clothing and shoes and jewelry, TVs, gadgets, expensive food and shopping, eating out, expensive lattés every morning? The list is nearly infinite for many people. Hundreds if not thousands of dollars are spent every month on unnecessary consumption. And most spending on consumer items is irredeemable— it is wealth gone forever rather than invested. So the capital is lost, and any interest the wealth would have gained had it been invested is also forfeited. Meanwhile, these same people rest assured that they will retire some day (maybe even sooner rather than later) at least partially on Social Security, which is taxation on the younger generation. In other words, they live to the max now, giving no thought for the future, and then live off government coercion in the end. For anyone who accepts this arrangement and refuses to change, I have no sympathy, no desire to help, and frankly, I consider it immoral that anyone else should be taxed to sustain gluttonous, careless people in their old age. It's immoral to tax people for that purpose in general; it's *grossly* immoral when done in these cases.

Why should anyone living a maxed-out, debt-ridden, gluttonous lifestyle be entitled to one red penny of someone else's money for their retirement? I understand that there is a genuine charity case in the poorest of the poor and the truly vulnerable (but we can easily address that problem), but don't tell me it's moral and necessary and right to tax anyone for the benefit of those who have squandered their entire income all their life, never saved a penny, and lived as high a lifestyle as they could along the way. No one owes them anything, and they deserve to reap the benefits of their own immoral decisions. They should live the latter part of their lives in financial distress *as a fitting punishment* for their earlier wastefulness. If you want "social justice," *that's* social justice.

In the meantime, those who have currently entrapped themselves in debt and wasteful living, yet desire to rise out of it, need to commit both mentally and practically to cutting back. The security of their financial future depends on how they choose to perform in that endeavor.

And this really applies to all of us. We all need to make plans, and make cuts, to return to a level of lifestyle that allows us to save money, purchase private insurance, and put ourselves in a position either to demand freedom from the government system, or to live freely when it collapses. In other words, if we're really about freedom, if we're really serious about breaking free from government control, then we will make the sacrifices necessary to do so.

Opting Out of the System

The way forward is to delegitimize the government wealth transfer system by replacing it with a genuine private savings and retirement system. The means to do this is through personal sacrifice, responsibility, thrift, saving, and a public demand for individual freedom. And only when we have exercised the prerequisite discipline, will we have a legitimate political demand to be removed from the system. This has to start with those of us who value freedom. We have to make the sacrifice, expecting nothing in return, until we can form enough of a base to demand exemption from the system—and an option of freedom for all who choose to live free.

There is already precedent for this in certain religious com-munities—notably the Amish and Mennonites. Due to their resistance to the tax back in 1961, they received a legal exemp-tion from the system—both the program and the taxation. And they received exemption because they already had a viable independent system in place, and had a religious conviction against being involved in a coercive government scheme. The legislative exemptions were worded so that they really apply to only their groups. But, this does set a precedent. There is no reason the legal language has to remain so restrictive. There is no reason the exemption should not be extended to anyone with religious convictions against public insurance. This is a very serious thought for a future goal.

A very similar approach should be taken to Medical Insur-ance—for everyone and the elderly. Now this is more diffi-cult than mere savings. Saving money in the face of taxation is one thing, but the effects of Medicare upon the insurance industry for people over 65 makes opting out very difficult. Private plans, if you can find one, could run around $2,000 *per month*, which makes it tough for most people; and even then, those plans won't cover anything that Medicare cov-ers. There are already private Christian sharing programs that are very affordable and very effective in covering healthcare costs—such as Samaritan Ministries—and since they are not insurance programs, they are exempted from government regulation and pressure and were specifically exempted from Obamacare. This is the type of private system that can provide a viable way forward.

Plus, Medicare is provided *only* if people receive Social Security benefits, and opting out by law means one must also forfeit Social Security benefits and pay back all previously received Social Security benefits. A judge upheld this federal statute in September 2011, denying a senior's legal request to opt out without penalty. U. S. Circuit Judge Henderson noted, "[T]he actual question placed before this Court is whether the Social Security Administration can lawfully promulgate a quasi–regulatory provision that penalizes individuals who seek to decline coverage under Medicare, Part A, by requiring them to forfeit their Social Security retirement benefits."[15] The appeal was squashed the following Spring. So there are significant obstacles for anyone over 65 who wants to opt out.

But the main point here is that we must put ourselves in a position of the moral and financial high ground. Make the mental preparations to abandon government dependence, despite the losses. Then, start planning, cutting, downsizing, and saving for your own retirement. Start now with your own life insurance arrangements while you're young and can lock in cheap rates. Only with that in place first will we have a good shot at gaining legal exemptions from the corrupt system of taxation and wealth transfer.

There is yet a more radical option to pursue. We could demand the *immediate* abolition of the system, and if successful in attaining it, we would then fend for our own financial futures as I just described—only, *immediately.* In such a case, the very fact that we find ourselves outside of the system (and without the so-called safety net), might in itself be adequate motivation for making the tough changes in mindset and lifestyle we've talked about. Tough decisions sometimes require tough motivation.

---

[15] *Hall v. Sebellius* (2011); The appeal was squashed by Judge Brett Kavanaugh, who added to Henderson's notes: "We obviously cannot do anything here about the coverage practices of private insurers. And the statute simply provides no mechanism for a person who is 65 or older and has signed up for Social Security to disclaim his or her entitlement to Medicare Part A benefits (or to "disenroll," as plaintiffs put it). . . . One of the consequences of the expanded social safety net fashioned by the Federal Government is that private entities or charities sometimes adjust benefits based on whether a recipient is otherwise entitled to government-provided benefits. We recognize that plaintiffs are frustrated with this particular manifestation of that broader phenomenon. But absent a constitutional or statutory violation, it is not our role to police that allocation of government and private resources." (http://www.cadc.uscourts.gov/internet/opinions.nsf/8A1A2C 8F6BD52E3C85257A0E00502466/$file/11-5076-1376121.pdf).

This option, however, would also result in a large-scale social need for millions of people already dependent on the system; they would have to find another source of income immediately (possibly from families, or churches where applicable). There would probably be considerable furor from large numbers of people demanding the money they've already "paid into the system," even though, as we've already discussed, the system never functioned that way. There would definitely be riots. The better approach, I think, is simply to work toward the freedom to opt out of the system—both its taxes and benefits. That would begin the end of the system.

So how do we get financial freedom back? The best way is two-fold: first, we can immediately begin to plan and save and change our lifestyles in order to meet our own needs for our own old age security. That is, despite the system's continued existence, we can function independently of it, resigning ourselves to the fac that all the taxes we've already paid into it are stolen and lost (which they are). Refuse all future entitlements, and galvanize your minds against the bribery of the promises. This delegitimizes the system, and earns us the moral high ground to demand freedom from the system. Second, we aim politically at making that demand as broad and as public as we can, and we can even seek to erect local and state political protections against Federal intrusion into our payrolls.

Now I would like to make one important point in closing. The freedom of opting out of the system and gaining the moral high ground from which to make that demand—that freedom already exists. We can, legally, morally, rightly, make that political demand to be free *right now* without having made any other preparation. We have the right to be free from that system. I am not saying that possibility won't exist until *after* we prepare ourselves mentally and financially. It exists now, and we can and should announce this from every street corner, and in every election. What I outlined here is a more practical approach to achieve the manifestation of that right in our whole society. By joining our personal efforts with our public demand, we create a very powerful witness in society; and whether we succeed politically or not, we will, in effect, make ourselves financially independent of that Federal system of taxation and redistribution.

And if enough people do that for themselves, we will see two things emerge. First, we will see a growing awareness of the situation. As people who take responsibility for themselves begin to become a more visible portion of society, they more readily influence others, thus creating a real community and a real social ethic. And from this, second, we will see very quickly that these communities emerge in concentrated areas of the country, and they will be widespread in the more conservative areas, which are the vast majority of counties in this nation. And when that happens, we just may begin to see local communities and counties, perhaps even entire states, protect their people, politically and physically, from Federal intrusions.

But the best way to begin this process is to prepare *yourself* for independence financially and psychologically, as if the system already does not exist, while sacrificing what they take in the meantime. Only by that sacrifice and preparation will we have a real shot at restoring a free society in the long run.

3. County Rights

The basic premise of localism—and therefore, the basic premise of what I call "County Rights"—is that civil government power should be as decentralized as possible. *This is the heart of the program.* This chapter covers that principle of localism: the ideal of freedom and how we once had it in America.

Local Government in a Free America

We need to acknowledge that an emphasis on states' rights—though an improvement over centralized nationalism—is not a good enough answer to national tyranny. "States' Rights are for sissies," as a friend of mine says. Give me "County Rights." *That's* decentralized power. But lest my libertarian friends needle me by pointing out that counties can cajole and extort too, I prefer to argue even more generally: civil government power should be as decentralized as possible. If it is possible to have a well-ordered society with little government beyond the family and perhaps voluntary community organization, then we should welcome this.

As we shall see here, localism and decentralized power is the best expression of freedom in government, and it was on this original principle that America was founded. This is the way it used to be in America, and it worked. So I would like to discuss, briefly, localism or "County Rights," in both *principle* and *practice*.

In principle, limited and localized government is an out-growth of specifically Christian thinking; particularly the demands that 1) rulers are not divine, but are themselves subject to a higher law, 2) private property is to be protected and property owners invested with powers against encraochments even from government, 3) social relationships are based on legally binding contracts, and 4) power enables corruption and should therefore be limited, checked, and safeguarded. In short, we have a society based on religious faith, property rights, honoring of contracts, and individual responsibility—all fundamental things derived directly from the Ten Commandments. And, of course, with all of these things is assumed the right to and protection of life.

To understand these things properly, as it pertains to western civilization, and particularly America, we need a little background. What is a "county"? Where did such a name come from? The answer to that question rests in the medieval feudal system of government ("feudalism" is not a bad word, despite what many might say). A "county" was the area of land governed by that member of the land-owning hierarchy of nobility called a "Count." A "count" owned and governed a "county," just as a "duke" did a "duchy." This was the French name for the rank. In England, the equivalent division of land was a "shire"—a name coming from the Latin word *scire,* meaning "to cut" or "to divide" (we get our words "scissors," "shears," "schism" and others from this same word, including our word "share," as in "shareholder"). It was a division of land apportioned to a particular property owner (usually as granted by the King or other higher property owner, but *ownership* was the basic issue). After the Norman invasion of 1066, the English usage of "shire" gradually diminished and was replaced by "county." Later, in the American colonies, there were only six divisions ever called "shires" (in 1634 in Virginia). A few years later, these were renamed "counties" and that name has persisted throughout America ever since. Regardless of the name, however, the point stands that our most basic units of government are derived from the original basic units of property ownership. The basic premise of government is one of private property—that each owner of property is the governor of what he owns. And of course, in a Christian society, owners would govern according to God's Law, not their own.

In such a society, ideally, there would be no need for higher governors. But of course, this is neither possible nor practical yet. We live in a world still marred by sin, and crime exists and needs to be discouraged and punished. But, sin and crime exists in all men, including those in higher ranks. And if sinful men fill positions of power as well (perhaps especially), we should seek to distribute the authority to punish and use force throughout society so that no individual or group ever has either too much power or power over too great an area. If there's going to be a tyrant or corruption in civil government, it's better to have administrative units as small as possible and as separated and independent as possible, so that 1) the tyranny is limited to that area, 2) the tyrant has limited resources with which to work, and thus can't easily spread, 3) people in that limited area can easily escape to better places, and 4) that tyrant will be facing a whole host of surrounding jurisdictions and forces ready to intervene for, at the very least, the sake of peace. When there's another layer of government above the local (which is usually the case), the local units can appeal to the higher powers; disputes between locals can be settled by private arbitration between them, or by appeal to the higher courts if necessary. If the higher powers try to exert tyranny, the local governments must resist, and if necessary band together to resist as a group.

This is exactly what happened in Anglo-American history, during the construction of that famed document the *Magna Carta*. In 1215, during the Feudal Age, the Kings had for several generations gradually moved closer to absolute power. The land barons—the property owners—were fed up. This was the twilight of the old feudal system, and because the King kept grasping at more and more power, absolutism was gaining early strength. It was the representatives of the local land owners who gathered together to oppose King John's extensive attempts to consolidate absolute power and aise their taxes to do so: These protectors of private property drafted the *Magna Carta*, falling back on the old feudal idea of fixed mutual contractual obligations. The land owners would pay a predictable and tolerable tax to which they agreed, and the King was subject to the powers of law upheld by a representative assembly of the barons (as well as protection and proper courts, etc.). The document is often perceived as some advance in political theory because it looks a little like modern representative government being advanced against ancient monarchy, but in reality, it was a *conservative* document. It aimed to secure the ancient rights of property owners, the rule of law, and the upholding of contracts—things that had already been established in Christian England *for centuries.*

As I said, this society is rooted deeply in Christian thinking and biblical law. In the right to life, we see the commandment against murder. In the sanctity of private property, we see the commandments against theft. In the enforcement of contractual obligations, we see the commandment against false witness. We could also explore the centrality of the family which finds support in the fifth and seventh commandments or the guarding of property and inheritance against the jealousies of others, found in the tenth commandment. At least one modern political philosopher noted this derivation:

> The limited state is a creation of Christian thinking, particularly of Augustine. It arose from the fundamental experience of the Incarnation, the appearance of God in human form at a definite place and time of human history. Christian thinking about politics was based on a new discovery about the destiny of man: man lived in order to attain fellowship with God.[1]

---

[1] Gerhart Niemeyer, "Two Socialisms," *Modern Age: The First Twenty-Five Years, a Selection*, ed. George A. Panichas (Indianapolis, IN: Liberty Press, 1988), 587.

In other words, the idea of limited civil government is based in Christian theology: it is a political development based upon the previous theological development of the historic Church councils, particularly Nicaea (A.D. 325) and Chalcedon (A.D. 451). Because only Jesus Christ is the perfect man, and the only God-man, this means He alone has the final word of human jurisdiction. He is prophet, priest, and king. No mere human government, therefore, has the right to wield supreme or final power on earth, whether in family, church, or state. All people and all rulers must bow the knee to King Jesus, obey his commandments, and love one another as equals before God.[2] All of these biblical and theological ideas are visible in and fundamental to the old feudal system, despite its flaws.

This is relevant to United States history because the idea of *federalism* is related directly—both in principle and in name— to feudalism. "Federal" and "feudal" have the same etymological root (*foedus*, Latin for *pact* or *covenant*) and refer to governmental relationships based on contractual agreements, or covenants, between various levels of government. The contract established a bond between the parties—for example, a King and a Colony, or a Colonial Government and its counties— which established obligations for each party, and protected each party in regard to those obligations being performed. If those obligations were not met, then sanctions could be enforced, or the bond could be declared null and void.

It was this very type of covenantal relationship which the American colonists in 1776 argued had been violated in regard to them by their feudal head, King George III. The colonies had each been established with charters which themselves established feudal land grants and recognized the ancient feudal rights of free Englishmen. But things had gradually changed— especially in England—over the decades. In 1688, Parliament overreached its bounds by usurping the absolutism to which

---

[2] See my book *Manifested in the Flesh*, 2006, chapters 8–9.

the King had once aspired. It began a series of attempts to extract taxes from the colonies. King George—whose duty it was to protect the colonies from outside governmental influences—did nothing, and the colonies rightfully regarded this as a failure on his part. They in fact considered him complicit in Parliament's act of aggression and tyranny. The Declaration of Independence was a federal document, announcing that the King had failed to do his part of the contract, and thus it had become necessary "to dissolve the political bands which have connected them with another."

The Declaration—aside from the famous language of "life, liberty, and the pursuit of happiness," which is all we normally recall—goes on to list two long trains of grievances. The first list includes abuses on the part of the King himself, and the second, those in which he has "combined with others"— namely Parliament—"to subject us to a jurisdiction foreign to our constitution, and unacknowledged by our laws; giving his Assent to their Acts of pretended Legislation." The colonists considered Parliament a foreign party to their colonial charters and governments, and thus King George's failure to protect the colonies against Parliament's encroachments and taxes was a breach of the governmental contract on his part. For this failure, and in order to retain the freedoms they expected under the original agreement, the colonists united with the willingness to fight and die if necessary.

Thus, it is instructive to look at the nature of early American government—especially during the time still *before* the Constitution—in order to see what a decentralized, truly free and federal society looks like, especially as derived from the old system of *genuine* federalism. Let's consider the *practice* of limited government:

The Practice of Localism in the Colonies

The fundamental unit of government was the county. The so-called Anti-Federalists during the Constitutional ratification period argued for local sovereignty on the part of their states, as opposed to the nationalists (improperly named "Federalists") who wanted a strong central national government with a powerful military and direct jurisdiction over individuals with the attending powers of taxation (overriding the state and local governments as it became convenient). Men such as Patrick Henry rightly argued that a truly federal system would allow a national government to interact with only the states, not the counties, townships, towns, or people. In a truly federal system, only counties dealt with people, states dealt with their own counties, and the federal government under the Constitution should deal with the states. Anti-Federalists were obviously fighting for states' rights in the particular context of the Constitution, but the principle for which they stood goes much deeper—all the way to the county and smaller. And long prior to the Constitution, American civil government was firmly oriented around county sovereignty.

The Massachusetts General Court in 1635 made an Act that delegated most governmental authority to the local level. It read:

> Whereas particular towns have many things which concern only themselves, it is therefore ordered that the freemen of every town, or the major part of them, shall have only power to dispose of their own lands and woods, with all privileges and appurtenances of the said towns to grant lots and make such orders as may concern the well-ordering of their own towns . . . to levy and distrain, . . . also to choose their own particular officers, as constables, surveyors of highways and the like.[3]

---

[3] Quoted in Thomas Jefferson Wertenbaker, *The Puritan Oligarchy: The Founding of American Civilization* (New York: Grosset and Dunlap, 1947), 44–5. It is important to note that the phrase "the freemen . . . shall have only power" in the language of that era really means to indicate that "only the freemen" shall have the powers described, as the context makes clear.

The historian Thomas Jefferson Wertenbaker explains, "Under this act the town became to the State what the congregation was to the Church. Localism in religion, which had become so vital a feature of Puritanism, was to be matched in New England by localism in government."[4] Note two things: 1) that their form of *civil* government explicitly mirrored their form of *church* government, and therefore, 2) their civil government was radically decentralized. This system descended directly from the old English feudal arrangements. Although the New England Congregationalists delegated even greater powers to the local level than did other groups (New Jersey Presbyterians, for example), the system was generally consistent throughout the colonies.

Remnants of this decentralized system of government lasted at least into the 19th century. Even as late as the 1830s, when the famous French observer Alexis de Tocqueville toured the country, he left with the impression that "every village forms a sort of republic, accustomed to govern itself."[5]

And at the local level, a deciding influence for all forms of local government and culture was—as a *federal* society would have it—a Christian covenant. Some of these covenants were simple; for example, the early Pilgrims used the following as the basis for their society: "We covenant with the Lord and with one another and do bind ourselves in the presence of God to walk together in all His ways, according as He is pleased to reveal Himself unto us in His blessed word of truth."[6] Others were much more detailed. The Northampton covenant read:

> Disclaiming all confidence of, or any worthiness in, ourselves either to be in covenant with God or to partake of the least of His mercies, and also all strength of our own to help covenant with Him . . . by relying upon His tender

---

[4] Wertenbaker, 45.

[5] Alexis de Tocqueville, *Democracy in America* (London: Everyman's Library, 1994), 406.

[6] Quoted in Wertenbaker, 58.

mercy and gracious assistance of the Lord through Jesus Christ, we do promise and covenant in the presence of the Lord, the searcher of all hearts, and before the holy angels and this company, first and chiefly to cleave forever unto God with our whole hearts as our chief, best, yea and only good, and unto Jesus Christ as our only Savior, husband and Lord and only high priest, prophet and king. . . . We promise and engage to observe and maintain . . . all the holy institutions and ordinances which he has appointed for His Church. . . . And as for this particular company and society of saints, we promise . . . that we will cleave unto one another in brotherly love and seek the best spiritual good each of other, by frequent exhortation, seasonable admonition and constant watchfulness according to the rules of the Gospel.[7]

The Benefits of Decentralization

The benefits of such a decentralized society are many. For starters, taxation is specifically and only local. No state or Federal agencies have any direct access to your property or income. Though I don't support a property tax in general,[8] the historical institution of the property tax indicates that the fundamental unit of government in America was at the county level, and it is one aspect of county sovereignty that persists today. The county is the only civil agency that has the authority to tax you directly on your property.

And since this system is entirely local, all the aspects of it are tied to a local vote: the level of taxation, the type of taxation, and the agents of taxation. The tax officials in most counties are elected officials. These can be voted out, impeached, removed, overridden, or defunded. In the very worst scenario,

---

[7] Quoted in Wertenbaker, 58.

[8] He who faces forfeiture or distrainment of his property should he fail to pay a recurring tax on it does not really own the property in question. Thus, property taxes are violation of the biblical protection of private property.

a citizen could move to a new jurisdiction with little effort. Taxation should be a *locally controlled* issue.

Secondly, in a decentralized society, law is generally *local* law: Nationalized healthcare, welfare, taxation, military draft, and any other national measures could not be forced upon a citizen by distant, disaffected, self-interested legislators. There would be no issue if your local county or town votes almost unanimously to display the Ten Commandments in its court, or even to require candidates to take a Christian test oath to hold a public office. The neighboring counties may not approve of it, but that's the beauty of decentralization—you can move two miles and be in a jurisdiction you prefer. Or, if you like your chances, you can stay and work for political change at home. It is easier to achieve change locally than as it is transform national policy. Life is so much better when you can freely choose from three dozen options rather than having a single one-size-fits-all government "solution" crammed down your throat.

Localism means both civil law and criminal law are local law. When criminal law is local, the main law enforcement in society is the county sheriff. The old John Birch Society had a similar vision with its "support your local police" campaign, but it appears to me to take this too far. More on that at another time. When criminal law is local, the legislation itself, as well as the agents of its interpretation and enforcement, are *elected*. This is seen in our county legacy: sheriffs and local judges are elected—as are county commissioners and other local legislators and directors.

Remember the old Robin Hood scenario? Remember Robin Hood's great enemy? He was the *Sheriff* of Nottingham. Our word "sheriff" comes from the Old English "shire"—which we've already discussed—and "reeve," a representative of the king. The "Shire-reeve" was the King's agent who came to the local shire to collect taxes. He was an agent of the central government. But not in America! Here, he is a locally elected official, accountable to his local shire (county), and susceptible to being removed at the next election. And if the local population becomes morally lax and will not vote our a corrupt official, again, it would not be hard to move to a new county, if you saw it necessary, and if it came to that. In short, when the sheriff is the agent of the central government, you have tyranny; but when the sheriff is a local elected representative, you are closer to freedom.

Likewise, civil law was county law mostly—locally determined. I can assure you, for example, gay marriage would not be acceptable in my county. There would be no deliberation about it, and the first judge or official who peeped in favor of it would be voted out in the next election if not impeached on the spot. Let that liberal joker move to one of those indigo blue counties on the west coast—not in my back yard. Instead of having to win a washed-out general election stacked against us by all the forces of politics and media and big money across the whole country, our grass roots would be the ultimate voice in law and leadership. Your society would reflect your values, instead of being weaseled by special interests, spineless politicians, and activist judges.

This is a taste of localism: a world in which government is as small as possible, people are generally free, their societies mirror their own values, government is accountable and generally unable to spread tyranny. It is based on the Christian concepts of protecting life, protecting family, property, and contracts, and holding public officials accountable to the law before God. This is the only way to maintain a free society. And having such an emphatic local focus is the only way we will ever be able to restore freedom in America. The focus on Washington and the Supreme Court will do nothing but rearrange the forces of top-down, centralized tyrannical "solutions." States' rights will not even do it, though it is important. We need localism. We need county rights.

We have also seen that this vision of local government was the original American way. And it worked. The next question,

of course, is, how was it lost? And how was it so far lost that
we've never even heard about how it really used to be until
now? While it would be fun to skip ahead to the "how to get it
back" part, understanding what has come to pass in this country is vital to knowing what exactly to overturn. And we must
learn our history, else we are doomed to repeat it. We will
talk about how America grew from the radically decentralized,
voluntarily settled, free society of 1776 and earlier, to the massive government bureaucracy, empire, and centralized near-
police state that it is today.

How Freedom was Lost

The conservative sociologist Robert A. Nisbet once said that
up until the year he was born, 1913, the only contact the average individual ever had with the Federal government was the
Post Office.[9] The Income Tax Amendment and the Federal
Reserve Act both appeared that same year, and they have since
enslaved the average person to the Federal government, overriding and consuming the roles of state and local governments
in many places along the way. Both of these new develop-
ments greatly overstepped the role of government envisioned
by most of the Framers in 1787, and even further beyond that
of colonial Americans. Was this the turning point?

It was certainly *a* turning point. The erosion of local sovereignty and freedoms has mostly been a long, slow, gradual
process, although punctuated at key times—usually times of
war—by rapid increases in centralized power. Many people
recognize one or more of those rapid government power-
grabs—the Civil War, the Wilson war state and the leftist progressives, FDR's New Deal, LBJ's Great Society, Vietnam, the

---

[9] An autobiographical anecdote oft-referenced by Nisbet's student, Gary
North, for example, in his article "Robert Nisbet: Conservative Sociologist," August 15, 2002, http://www.lewrockwell.com/north/north120.html (accessed Sept.
21, 2012).

Patriot Act, Obamacare, and so on. Some have even pointed out that abuses against the Constitution took place as early as Jefferson's unprecedented, and many would argue unconstitutional, Louisiana Purchase in 1803. But it is just as important, I think, to consider what enabled all these great power grabs to begin with. What has enabled the long, slow, and gradual erosion from the start?

The Instrument of Centralization

I would argue that the first major round—and the most hotly contested round—of the American conflict between proponents of centralized power and proponents of freedom ended in favor of centralization when the U.S. Constitution was installed in 1789. It is the Constitution that has enabled the proponents of centralized power to carry out their various agendas at various subsequent points in U.S. history— whether their encroachments advanced rapidly, or slowly and gradually. If power over state and local sovereignties had not been fused together and vested in one centralized institution, the types of abuses we have since endured would have been at least much more difficult for tyrants to perpetrate, if not almost impossible.

And, ironically, nearly all of the various forms of tyranny we decry today were predicted and denounced by the original critics of the Constitution. Many of the principal fathers of the American Revolution saw today's problems already taking root in their own time. But, due to nostalgic sentimentality and the textbook versions of American history, these most prescient men are the least known, least read, and most often forgotten figures of that time. They are not Washington, Madison, and Hamilton. They are not the authors of the *Federalist Papers*. These were in fact considered agents of tyranny by these critics of nationalism and the Constitution.

I am talking about the so-called *Anti*-Federalists—the authors who argued against ratifying the Federalist Constitution. Few people today bother to read even the much more well-known *Federalist Papers*. The *Papers'* language and concepts are oftten found too lofty and difficult, despite the fact that they were *newspaper editorials* in their time. Consequently, few people even *know about them*. Even fewer people actually *read* them. And even fewer still read the majority position of that day—the Tea Party platform of that day—the *Anti-Federalist Papers*.

Yet these liberty-minded leaders recognized that the centralizing forces at work during their day were the sinews of tyranny. They knew *absolutely* where centralized government power would lead. On this principle, they opposed the Constitution itself, for it ceded too much power to the central government. Let me give you some examples:

One of them, writing under the pseudonym "The Federal Farmer" (possibly Richard Henry Lee), foresaw the direction of centralizing power as a departure from a free society, but also as the long-term agenda of a few ambitious leaders:

> The plan of government now proposed [the Constitution] is evidently calculated totally to change, in time, our condition as a people. Instead of being thirteen republics, under a federal head, it is clearly designed to make us one consolidated government. . . . This consolidation of the states has been the object of several men in this country for sometime past. Whether such a change . . . can be effected without convulsions and civil wars; whether such a change will not totally destroy the liberties of this country—time only can determine.[10]

The number of writings of these more freedom-minded individuals well outnumbered those in favor of a new Constitution. And by most accounts, the number of those actual people who opposed the Constitutional centralization greatly outnumbered those who desired it. But—as is the case with

---

[10] In *The Complete Anti-Federalist*, 7 vol., ed. by Herbert J. Storing (University of Chicago Press, 1981), 2:226.

most decentralized forces compelled into a hasty debate on a national stage—the Anti-Federalists were up against a political machine of ambitious lawyers and financiers who had the motivation, resources, and savvy to accomplish their goals in spite of popular objections. In short, the scenario was one in which the forces of freedom had numbers on their side, but the forces of centralization succeeded due to an organized agenda, good planning, a powerful political machine, and a good deal of ambition and energy.

To avoid rehearsing too many Anti-Federalist quotations (as choice as many of them are), it is most convenient here to use a summary of their concerns provided by one of their writers, "A Plebeian," who, in his words, represented the opinion "among writers, and in public bodies throughout the United States." Among other things, he warned that:

1. [The Constitution] is calculated to, and will effect such a consolidation of the states, as to supplant and overturn the state governments. . . .

2. The representation in the general legislature is too small to secure liberty, or to answer the intention of representation. . . .

3. It gives to the legislature an unlimited power of taxation . . . direct and indirect. . . .

4. It is dangerous, because the judicial power may extend to many cases which ought to be reserved to the decisions of state courts, and because the right of trial by jury is not secured in the judicial courts of the general government, in civil cases. . . .

5. The power of the general legislature to alter and regulate the time, place, and manner of holding elections . . . will place in the hands of the general government, the authority, whenever they shall be disposed, and a favorable opportunity offers, to deprive the body of the people, in effect, of all share of government. . . .

6. The mixture of legislative, judicial, and executive powers in the senate;

7. The little degree of responsibility under which great officers of government will be held;

8. And the liberty granted by the system to establish and maintain a standing army, without any limitation or restriction. . . .[11]

In short, Plebeian foresaw a surrendering of political power, representation, taxation, judicial power, and military power to a centralized state.

Since this list was but a summary of what many Anti-Federalist writers had said in many places, it is easy to find these critiques most eloquently defended by the others. One of the major writers among them wrote under the name "Brutus," and could likely have been the delegate from New York, Robert Yates, who left the Constitutional Convention early in disgust. He decried the seemingly unlimited powers of taxation,

> for they extend to every possible way of raising money, whether by direct or indirect taxation. Under this clause may be imposed a poll-tax, a land-tax, a tax on houses and buildings, on windows and fire places, on cattle and all kinds of personal property:—It extends to duties on all kinds of goods to any amount, to tonnage and poundage on vessels, to duties on written instruments, newspapers, almanacs, and books:—It comprehends an excise on all kinds of liquors, spirits, wines, cider, beer, etc. and indeed takes in duty or excise on every duty or conveniency of life; . . . In short, we can have no conception of any way in which a government can raise money from the people, but what is included in one or other of three general terms. We may say that this clause commits to the legislature every conceivable source of revenue within the United States.[12]

---

[11] "Address by A Plebeian," in *The Complete Anti-Federalist*, 6:137.

[12] *The Complete Anti-Federalist*, 2:390.

So he recognized the eventual likelihood of the 1913 income tax. In fact, he considered it within the scope of the proposed central government's powers. He later described such power to tax in terms of the absolute invasion of private lives:

> This power, exercised without limitation, will introduce itself into every corner of the city, and country will wait upon ladies at their toilett [vanity], . . . their domestic concerns, . . . to the ball, the play, and to the assembly; it will go with them when they visit, and will, on all occasions, sit beside them in their carriages, nor will it desert them even at church; it will enter the house of every gentleman, watch over his cellar, wait upon his cook in the kitchen, follow the servants into the parlor, preside over the table, and note down all he eats or drinks; it will attend him to his bed-chamber, and watch him while he sleeps; it will take cognizance of the professional man in his office, or his study; it will watch the merchant in the counting-house, or in his store; it will follow the mechanic to his shop, and in his work, and will haunt him in his family, and in his bed; it will be the constant companion of the industrious farmer in all his labor, it will be with him in the house, and in the field, observe the toil of his hands, and the sweat of his brow; it will penetrate into the most obscure cottage; and finally, it will light upon the head of every person in the Unites States. To all these different classes of people, and in all these circumstances, in which it will attend them, the language in which it will address them, will be GIVE! GIVE! . . .
>
> I say, such a power must necessarily, from its very nature, swallow up all the power of the state governments.[13]

And he foresaw the massive administrative law and bureaucracy needed to carry this out:

---

[13] *The Complete Anti-Federalist*, 2:396–397.

> Not only are these terms very comprehensive, and extend to a vast number of objects, but the power to lay and collect has great latitude; it will lead to the passing a vast number of laws, which may affect the personal rights of the citizens of the states, expose their property to fines and confiscation, and put their lives in jeopardy: it opens a door to the appointment of a swarm of revenue and excise officers to prey upon the honest and industrious part of the community, eat up their substance, and riot on the spoils of the country.[14]

The language here came directly from Jefferson's in the Declaration of Independence. Brutus was reiterating the exact same charge the colonists had levied against King George: he had "sent hither swarms of Officers to harass our people and eat out their substance." The advocates of the Constitution, then, were installing the same tyranny from which the people had just fought to free themselves.

And even above and beyond this, Brutus criticized the proposed Federal power to make all laws "necessary and proper" to carry out their desires:

> It is truly incomprehensible. A case cannot be conceived of, which is not included in this power. . . . The command of the revenues of a state gives the command of everything in it.—He that has the purse has the sword, and they that have both, have everything; so that the legislature having every source from which money can be drawn under their direction, with a right to make all laws necessary a proper for drawing forth all the resource of the country, would have, in fact, all power.[15]

These things alone amounted to destruction of state power, let alone local:

---

[14] *The Complete Anti-Federalist*, 2:390.
[15] *The Complete Anti-Federalist*, 2:391.

> [T]his power in its operation, would totally destroy all
> the powers of the individual states. . . . [T]his power,
> given to the federal legislature, directly annihilates all
> the powers of the state legislatures.[16]

These fears in regard to the vast powers to tax did not wait until 1913 to materialize. Almost immediately after the Constitution was ratified, Hamilton proposed and helped pass a national tax targeting that group of people with the least representation, the least organization, and possibly the least ability to organize resistance—whiskey makers. And when they did pull together a local force to resist the national tax-collection agents, the Anti-Federalist fear of the newly centralized standing army also materialized as Washington and Hamilton themselves mounted horseback and led 13,000 troops to suppress the so-called Whiskey Rebellion. It was a rebellion indeed, but, more particularly, a tax revolt.

Plebeian's list, representing the opinion of many other Anti-Federalists, includes a warning against the power of the Supreme Court:

> It is dangerous, because the judicial power may extend
> to many cases which ought to be reserved to the deci-
> sions of State courts, and because the right of trial by
> jury is not secured in the judicial courts of the general
> government, in civil cases. . . .[17]

Brutus, likewise, warned clearly, "If . . . the legislature pass any laws, inconsistent in the senses the judges put upon the constitution, they will declare it void; and therefore in this respect their power is superior to that of the legislature."[18] Another, "The Federal Farmer," added: "we are in more danger of sowing the seeds of arbitrary government in this depart-

---

[16] *The Complete Anti-Federalist*, 2:391.

[17] *The Complete Anti-Federalist*, 6:137.

[18] *The Complete Anti-Federalist*, 2:440.

ment than in any other."[19] "Candidus," attributed to Samuel Adams, warned that it would "occasion innumerable controversies; as almost every cause (even those originally between citizens of the same state) may be so contrived as to be carried to this federal court."[20] This means, effectively, the end of state and local sovereignty, because a partisan Court could construe any decision, and then that decision would stand as law for every state.

This fear also materialized shortly after the nationalist proponents pressured the states to adopt the Constitution. Within a mere fifteen years, the nationalist John Marshall framed the system and then decided the very case he framed—*Marbury v. Madison* (1803)—in favor of centralizers against the Jeffersonian view. The decision established the doctrine euphemistically called "judicial review" wherein the Supreme Court essentially legislates through its decisions.

In 1819, Marshall decided perhaps the most damaging antebellum case against state power. In *McCulloch v. Maryland*, he decided that the Federal government could operate branches of the Federal central bank within state jurisdictions, run by unelected board members for their own profit, and the states could neither regulate the bank nor tax its income. Marshall reminded the states that the Federal Congress could pass whatever laws were—in those disputed words—"necessary and proper" in order to carry out their other Constitutional powers; and once passed, states could do nothing to violate these Federal laws.

But what about the Tenth Amendment?! Even the Tenth Amendment, which was included as a means of preserving for the states all powers not delegated in the Constitution, was not enough to stop Marshall from overriding states' rights. He found just enough of a hair to split:

---

[19] *The Complete Anti-Federalist*, 2:316.
[20] *The Complete Anti-Federalist*, 4:129.

Even the 10th amendment, which was framed for the purpose of quieting the excessive jealousies which had been excited, omits the word "expressly," and declares only, that the powers "not delegated to the United States, nor prohibited to the states, are reserved to the states or to the people;" thus leaving the question, whether the particular power which may become the subject of contest, has been delegated to the one government, or prohibited to the other, to depend on a fair construction of the whole instrument.[21]

In other words, by saying "delegated" instead of "expressly delegated," Marshall decided, the Tenth Amendment left him room to determine exactly what powers could and could not be added to the national government. Thus, as Plebeian and those he represented had predicted, the Federal government did "supplant and overturn the state governments."

The power of the Court would be expanded again by *Cohens v. Virginia* (1821), as Marshall interpreted the Constitution to extend Federal jurisdiction to criminal as well as civil cases.

Further abridgement of state powers came in 1824 when Marshall ruled against the state of New York in *Gibbons v. Ogden*. He struck down a shipping monopoly granted to a New York company operating between New York and New Jersey; this he did on grounds that Federal licensing statutes took precedence over state laws, and thus a state could not license monopolies when engaging in interstate commerce—a sphere expressly entrusted to the Federal government by the Constitution.

Of course this had been a design of the nationalists all along, despite their denials to the contrary during ratification. In 1821, a Washington D.C. printer and politician named Joseph Gales printed extracts from Robert Yates' notes upon the Constitutional Convention. Upon receiving a copy, James

---

[21] Marshall, 17 U.S. 316, 406.

Madison wrote a letter to Gales in which he dismissed Yates as partisan and prejudiced. In the letter, however, Madison notably confided one of his true purposes at the Convention, "which was among other things to take from that State the important power over its commerce."[22] Perhaps Madison felt safe in admitting his true designs some thirty-two years after the fact.

States' rights were further destroyed and judicial review more firmly entrenched after the Civil War, during Reconstruction, and particularly by the Fourteenth Amendment. Things have only gotten worse since then. So The Federal Farmer's warning came true. Indeed, time has confirmed his predictions almost exactly: States' rights were hijacked by the nationalists, and it took a civil war eventually to cement their tyranny. And of course, that's just states' rights; but local sovereignty has eroded to a greater degree because of it.

Many people today rightfully see the great encroachments of the Federal government in different points in American history, but too often we stop short of the root cause. It is not enough to complain about the Patriot Act, or FDR, or the Progressive Era. These were all overtures against the principles of liberty, true, but they were merely later variations on a theme played upon the original instrument of centralization—the Constitution. Without the nationalization of legislative, judicial, and executive powers, all of these later abuses could never have been successfully imposed.

While problems can also arise under a decentralized system of government, these cannot compare to the tyrannies latent in the opposite. The Anti-Federalist Candidus warned that we must "distinguish between the evils that arise from extraneous causes and our private imprudencies, and those

---

[22] James Madison to Joseph Gales, August 26, 1821, *The Records of the Federal Convention of 1787*, 3 vol., ed. by Max Farrand (New Haven: Yale University Press, 1911), 3:447.

that arise from our government."[23] Candidus realized that power over vital areas of human action (such as commerce, legislation, and defense) was too easily abused to justify leaving it in the hands of just a few men. Decisions in these areas should rather be left as decentralized as possible.

The Anti-Federalist antipathy toward centralization rested on principles—but it was also practical. They realized that wise and benevolent representatives would not always be available to fill the few seats of power. Instead, power-seeking, greedy, and avaricious men would pursue and secure those seats, and the people would suffer for it. Paying lip-service to the beloved leaders of the day, Candidus foresaw that "though this country is now blessed with a Washington, Franklin, Hancock and Adams," elected leaders shall not always possess such integrity, and "posterity may have reason to rue the day when their political welfare depends on the decision of men who may fill the places of these worthies."[24]

What the opponents of the Constitution predicted is exactly what has happened: The state and local governments were overridden by the powers of a national government. The people are not adequately represented, and self-interested powers—usually big banks, big corporations, or special-interest groups—purchase the few seats of power with money or political promises. These powers then begin to use their new positions of power to ensure and expand the advantages of their interests via more powerful government. The government grows consistently over time at the expense of the people and their freedoms and wealth. This was predicted *before* the Constitution, *because* of the Constitution, and history has proceeded almost exactly as was predicted at that time.

---

[23] *The Complete Anti-Federalist*, 4:128.

[24] *The Complete Anti-Federalist*, 4:128.

The Method of Centralization

Even more important, however, than rehearsing this historical "I told you so," is to understand the methods used to implement and impose greater centralized power on states and counties—even beyond what the Constitution allowed. In other words, in a country where freedom and individual responsibility were perceived to be something worth fighting and dying for ("Liberty or death!"), how in the world did the centralizers succeed? And how have they continued to succeed for over two centuries?

There are many answers to that question because there are countless tactics of tyranny. But let us immediately consider first, that a fairly early change in the electoral system altered the nature of representation and gave undue political power to urban areas, a minority of swing voters, and special interest groups. But second, and more importantly, consider the enormous profusion of Federal bureaucracies that have been using Federal funds to buy off state and local governments with all kinds of grants and handouts in exchange for compliance with their regulations. Like many individual beneficiaries of welfare and socialism who have become dependent on the system, counties and local governments have just as much *taken the cheese*, become dependent on Federal money, and thus become trapped in the system.

Centralizing the Electoral System

So first, concerning the change to the electoral system, this was an assault mainly on the power of local government through the state governments. The issue was the Electoral College— the system which elects the president. In the Constitutional design, the Electoral College exactly mirrors the state's representation in Congress: the number of electors shall be "equal to the whole Number of Senators and Representatives." While the precise manner in which electors are chosen and charged to vote is left to the state Legislatures to decide, the Constitutional arrangement implies that the Electoral College was designed to parallel the representation of the Congressional districts—that each district should cast its vote for the candidate of its choice. This was largely followed until 1832, at which time politicians began to replace local district votes with a popular *state-wide* vote, and began using this as the basis for awarding *all* electoral votes to the candidate who won the state-wide majority.

This was party politics gone wild, and it helped solidify the modern "winner-take-all" two-party system at the expense of genuine local representation. Now, all of the rural districts in any given state may vote for one candidate, but have their votes overridden because of one highly-populated urban center that distorts the popular vote in its favor—even by a few percent. For example, in the 1824 election in New York, the electoral votes were cast as follows: Adams 26, Crawford 5, Clay 4, and Jackson 1. In the following election of 1828, Adams won only 16 electors and Jackson 20. But after the popular vote method was installed in 1832, Jackson was able to receive *all* the electoral votes, whereas the loser, Henry Clay, received zero, even though he had gained 48% of the popular votes throughout the districts.[25] This has continued the same since then. And the significant fact is not about who might have won or lost, it is that a tiny minority of voters even in just one district can swing a vast percentage of the electoral votes in all the other districts combined. Thus we have had the rise of the "swing vote," the power of minority-issues and special-interest groups, and the concentration of campaigning and strategizing in just those closely-divided but influential districts—all playing disproportionately determinative roles in national elections. In this arrangement, for example, Chicago can overpower all of Illinois, New York City speaks for the whole state of New York,

---

[25] See R. J. Rushdoony, *The Nature of the American System* (Fairfax, VA: Thoburn Press, 1978), 12–13.

Charlotte for all of North Carolina, and so on. Even in a state where the rural population outnumbers any big city, a single special-interest issue like farm subsidies can swing the difference in favor of liberals, progressives, statists, or other miscreants. It didn't used to be this way.

Federal Cheese to Local Mice

In addition to tampering with the electoral process, the Federal government has also discovered the financial means to entice local governments into accepting Federal tyranny. This is where the "don't take the cheese" warning really comes into play. Federal agencies and bureaus by the multiple dozens, having multi-billion dollar budgets, use grants and handouts as ways to circumvent state and local governments and thus impose national control and national agendas (and even international agendas) on local communities—even without the authorization or consent of local populations. The basic lure is grants of Federal money, and most local district officials can't resist extra money for their struggling budgets. But, with the grants of money come restrictions, regulations, and sometimes massive legal codes imposed on entire regions of a state. Thus, most states and local governments willingly subject their people to Federal regulations so they can increase their revenue at the direct expense of taxpayers or, more likely, the national debt.

And you can bet the Federal government has figured out how effectively this method can corral and bridle local governments: hold the sugar cubes in one hand while the other hand slips the bit in the horse's mouth. Let me illustrate the nature and extent of this problem by referencing one local agency—the police department—as an example. Local police currently have the option of applying for grants with the following Federal Departments: Agriculture, Commerce, Education, Health and Human Services, Homeland Security, Housing and Urban Development, Justice, Labor, and Transportation. That's nine agencies offering bribes for local government compliance with Federal regulations and demands.

Within each one of the major Federal departments, there exist numerous smaller agencies each with their own programs, budgets, and regulations. For example, the Department of Justice alone breaks down into a few dozen major constituent offices and service bureaus. One of them, for example, the Associate Attorney General, governs several others, one of which is the Office of Justice Programs. This Office itself includes about fifteen smaller offices, one of which is the National Institute of Justice. This Institute itself runs several programs, one of which is the DNA Initiative—a Federally funded body that makes grants to local agencies for the purpose of DNA analysis in criminal investigations (up to $1 billion total of the current Department of Justice budget of $27.7 billion).[26] Part of the quid-pro-quo here is that the results of any local law enforcement DNA tests must be shared with a central national database governed by the FBI. It's the beginning of a national DNA registry.

This is just one agency—one program. Local public school districts receive on average about 8% percent of their funding from the Federal government and about 45% from the state.[27] Nearly all public schools and many private schools accept at least some degree of Federal funding due to the attendance of low-income families. As we've already discussed, public schooling is socialistic to begin with, but the fact that local districts are further compromised because of Federal and state handouts should be alarming even to those conservatives who defend public education. And if they're not alarmed, it really does prove my point about how socialistic the system is. The fact that local schools receive over *half* of their funding from higher governmental agencies indicates that they are stuck in

---

[26] http://www.justice.gov/ag/dnapolicybook_exsum.htm (accessed September 21, 2012)

[27] According to the U.S. Department of Education: http://www2.ed.gov/about/overview/fed/10facts/index.html (accessed September 21, 2012).

those regulations and programs because they are dependent on them for the majority of their budget.

In these cases and many more, local leaders—sometimes unelected—subject local citizens to the regulations and standards of higher government bureaucracies in exchange for money. In essence, they literally sell out local sovereignty. Local control is then a commodity to be sold to the highest bidder, or multiple bidders (or bidders). In these grant-related cases, the ultimate problem is not with the higher bodies, but with the local decision-makers that accept the money.

And ironically, the Federal bodies don't really have any money to give out in the first place. The money they grant is money that was created out of thin air by the Federal Reserve and loaned to the U.S. Treasury, and the legislature doles out portions of this funny money to Federal agencies, and the agencies make the grants to local governments. So the Federal government exchanges funny-money for local control. The Federal government is buying local control *for nothing*; it costs them nothing. And local governments are giving up their powers for immoral, debased money. This goes on in every county in the United States today. It could end tomorrow with a city council or school board vote, or a referendum.

So how was freedom in local government lost? It was lost as early as the Constitution, which set a precedent for a continual series of Federal government power grabs throughout American history. It was lost through manipulation of representation at the Federal level, and most importantly, it is lost every day of every year as state and local governments continue to take Federal money and subject their people to the regulations and administrative laws of distant governments.

We have dug ourselves a huge hole, although, in many ways, we could say the hole was dug for us. Either way, we're in a huge hole. Is there any possible way we could even begin to get out? Some people say no, we should just prepare for collapse. Is there anything we can do to begin to restore sovereignty and control to the local level? Believe it or not, there are ways we can fight to restore freedom again, county by county.

How to Get it Back

America was originally settled with nearly all governmental sovereignty entrusted to local authorities. This was the legacy of Christian culture, and the better part of it. Early Americans did not have to worry about their wealth and freedom being voted away by alleged representatives far removed by hundreds of miles and two or three levels of government. This ideal of freedom has been lost gradually over time at many junctures, and always in the name of "emergency" or "the common good." But, more importantly, these several creeping tyrannies were enabled and empowered by that one initial instance of centralizing power, force, and money at the Federal level—the Constitution of 1787. Nevertheless, whatever the causes are ultimately, it is easy to see that we do not enjoy anywhere near the same level of freedom that our ancestors did. The question now is how to get back that freedom back.

We need to develop a new mindset in order to overcome the numerous obstacles, both internal and external, that block the path to restoring local freedom and local sovereignty. By "local sovereignty," I mean the authority and freedom that local governments should have to govern local affairs without countermanding dictates from higher levels of government. We must return to local control, and release local institutions from off the hook of Federal and state mandates baited with grant money. We must end the Federal and state encroachments on local power and decision-making, licensing, and regulations. By the similar phrase "local freedom," I mean the freedom that individuals should have from similar encroachments and impositions on their individual sovereignty by their own local governments.

Obstacles to Local Sovereignty

First, there are many hurdles in the way of gaining this freedom. The enemies of freedom have always been those who stand to profit from public coercion. These people—either for the sake of some form of prestige or money (or both)—will consistently scheme and legislate to benefit themselves. And these lusts exist at every level of government, but also in the hearts of individuals. So, the remedy for restoring freedom to the local level will mean confronting the many, many ways in which both private individuals and government leaders have become addicted to public funds acquired through taxation. Whether this manifests in publicly-funded construction contracts, public education, exorbitant pensions for public employees, union privileges, grants from higher governmental agencies, or numerous other versions of the same evil, the path to freedom is blocked by these appropriations and redistributions of money. We must derail the long train of abuses that has resulted from the alliance between local plunderers who lust for money and the pompous elites who want to plan our lives and think they have the right and wisdom to do so.

The problem ultimately is as much *personal* as it is political. The local and state levels are microcosms of the more extended plundering that goes on in Washington, D.C., but local governments themselves are a reflection of the lusts and corruption that local *individuals* choose to allow. Local governments often suffer under corrupt officials who doggedly pursue more money—more grants from state and Federal governments. But often local citizens either agree with taking, taxing, and borrowing, or they are oblivious or apathetic to it.

So here's the hard truth: if you agree with the appropriations (even if "only at the local level"), then you're complicit in a corrupt system that stretches from your heart all the way to Washington. Don't talk about freedom and fiscal responsibility when you make multi-million dollar exceptions for yourself, your business, your industry, your union, your police and fire, or your local schools. Obama's not the problem; you're the problem. Until you address this problem in your own heart, you have no moral authority to criticize people for doing essentially the same thing you do (albeit on a larger scale and way over your head).

On the other hand, if you are merely oblivious to the problem or don't care, then you're still culpable and complicit by your complacency—and the liberals and statists just love you just the way you are, for your complacency helps them to implement their schemes with less opposition. It's been said that the only thing necessary for evil to triumph is for good people to do nothing. I agree, although I would add that anyone who sits there and does nothing shouldn't be considered good to begin with. We need to confront both corruption and complacency, which is to say we need to wake up and take responsibility—take action.

Knowing that the problem begins with the individual heart and stretches all the way up to Washington, we'll need to confront all levels of corruption at the same time. But we must concentrate our energy and focus on the areas where we'll have the greatest effect—ourselves and our local governments. We have already addressed the personal lifestyle adjustments that are vitally needed to reclaim freedom in education and welfare. We have emphasized the "don't take the cheese" principle in those areas for individuals. Now it is time to focus on that concept at the level of local government also. We must work to ensure local governments do not accept any grants from higher governmental bodies. This is the first step in returning to anything like true local sovereignty to America—her counties must be free of strings attached to higher agencies.

But since that level of freedom does not yet exist, we must still attend as need be to state and national politics until we achieve the desired local conclusion. We have to be careful that the Feds don't creep in the back door while we're busy with local matters. Even when we achieve our goals locally, we cannot rest until surrounding counties, and then the vast majority of counties in the state, have reached a similar level of local sovereignty. Until a majority of counties exist that are willing to assert their freedom simultaneously against higher governments, the few that arrive at near local autonomy will always be vulnerable because of their tiny minority status. In other words, we'll need a lot of free counties voicing their "nullifications" and independences at the same time, or else the Federal government could simply ignore the issue or squash it with little repercussion. We need massive decentralized (yet legitimate) resistance so that no central authority can easily or effectively answer it. Until we reach a time in which a growing number of America's 3,000-plus counties care more about freedom than Federal aid, we must be vigilant in our work and prayers. For until we achieve widespread local autonomy, we will not be safe from Federal threats of violence, force, defamation, and theft.

Solidifying the Vision of Local Sovereignty

Anyone wishing to start a truly grass-roots, bottom-up movement for restoring local sovereignty is going to face multiple levels of opposition—from the higher levels of government, from the vast mainstream media leftist propaganda machines, from entrenched Statism even in local media such as newspapers, corporate forces that use government force to stop competition, and also from corrupt local officials. We must be prepared to meet all of this with the truth, an unwavering commitment to freedom, the courage to act, and yet calmness, confidence, and kindness.

We also need to affirm and solidify this new vision of decentralized power. This vision must be deep and we must commit to it thoroughly. The vision was actually voiced at a crucial time in this country by the famous economist F. A. Hayek. Nearing the end of World War II, he noted that western civilization was going to need to be rebuilt, and that this task would have to be done amidst an atmosphere in which

Communism thrived as a powerful force, in which the forces and ideas behind National Socialism and fascism were still very strong, and Western academia was (as it still is) strongly socialist if not communist. Hayek argued in his famous book, *The Road to Serfdom*, that any attempts at rebuilding along the lines of any large socialized, nationalized State would be doomed to failure sooner or later. And this was his conclusion:

> We shall not rebuild civilization on the large scale. It is no accident that on the whole there was more beauty and decency to be found in the life of the small peoples, and that among the large ones there was more happiness and content in proportion as they had avoided the deadly blight of centralization. . . Nowhere has democracy ever worked well without a great measure of local self-government. . .Where the scope of the political measures becomes so large that the necessary knowledge is almost exclusively possessed by the bureaucracy, the creative impulses of the private person must flag. I believe that here the experience of the small countries like Holland and Switzerland contains much from which even the most fortunate larger countries like Great Britain can learn. We shall all be the gainers if we can create a world fit for small states to live in.[28]

Of course we know that his advice was pretty much ignored—but the vision still remains. And at this point in American history—when leftists and even many conservatives continue to praise and protect the instruments of socialism even while these instruments simultaneously bankrupt the Treasury and society—this vision of decentralized power still remains the only viable expression of freedom and liberty. And that vision today remains ignored, even ridiculed, although it's been essentially untried for the past 225 years.

---

[28] F. A. Hayek, *The Road to Serfdom* (Chicago: The University of Chicago Press, 1944, 1956), 235–236.

The vision is simple. Local governments have to take back sovereignty in every area they can; local people need to pressure local governments to do so and to refuse monetary handouts from higher governments; and people have to hold their local officials accountable to these goals. Local government must begin to resist the enticements, entrapments, and encroachments of the higher levels.

This will eventually mean 1) local individuals will not have to interact with any but local government officials; 2) representation will be much more genuine, as local officials are elected from a much smaller sample of the population; 3) government will be easier to monitor, and be much more transparent; 4) local officials are much more easily held accountable; and 5) if any of these ideals fails miserably and the locality grows intolerable, it won't be hard to move to another county that upholds your values. These are just a few of the benefits of decentralization.

There are disadvantages as well: 1) individuals can no longer enrich themselves from swollen promises paid for by taxing the population at large or borrowing trillions of dollars, plus interest, from your grandchildren; 2) ideologues, leftists, elites, and other pests can no longer impose their values easily on 300 million people by means of only a few-vote majority in Congress and the President's celebrity ink pens; or worse, by means of a 5-4 Supreme Court decision. But these are the kinds of disadvantages I can live with.

Imagine that: a society in which 300 million people are not subjugated by law to the opinion of a mere five. Mind-blowing, isn't it? And really, since a 5-4 decision determines any case, it really only takes the opinion of *one* person to decide the law for 300 million. There is much more we could say in regard to this vision of freedom and liberty, but these are the basics.

Practical Measures in the Meantime

Finally, there are some practical measures to consider in the meantime. This is where taking action starts. First, learn everything you can about your local government. This will take a little time, and will mean shifting the focus of your political engagements from the national to the local scene. Sadly, most people know everything there is to know about Obama and Pelosi, et al, and yet couldn't even tell you the name of one of their local County Commissioners. This needs to be essentially reversed. Read the headlines for national politics; react if necessary; but focus, focus, focus on learning the local stuff. Learn your commissioners' names, backgrounds, beliefs, values, career history, voting records.

Learn the organization of your local government; learn the schedules of all relevant board and commission meetings. Know when they meet. And show up for important issues.

Learn how to find and obtain all publicly available information: meetings, agendas, budgets, revenues, expenditures, bondholders and financiers, contracts, projects, land use plans, rezoning efforts, constitution and bylaws—everything. You will find that information-gathering in itself will begin to generate questions. Numbers and budgets and legal memos have their own way of whispering. You may unintentionally root out the corruption your local officials thought was well-hidden. You may find that a board member is working to give himself or herself special privileges for their career advancement or profit. Maybe not. But the more information you have, the more transparent and accountable you can force the government to be.

Second, start a blog or website dedicated to making your local government as public and transparent as possible. You can be as detailed or selective as necessary. Just keep it honest and open, and focus on only your local government. Post anything relevant you can find. Ask questions, suggest solutions, uncover any clear connections, disclose every cent that is taxed—how it is assessed and collected, and how it is spent. Document every cent borrowed, who profits from borrowing against future taxation, and who holds the bond. Show how much tax money collected for special purposes actually goes to pay for those purposes. Show how much elected officials and public employees of all sorts are paid, and what their public pension benefits look like. This is all perfectly legal. It lies hidden because no one cares enough to do the work to publicize it. Wordpress and other blog sites are absolutely free and easy to use. It would be great to have at least one such website dedicated to ultimate transparency in each of America's 3,000-plus counties. It would be better to have several in each county. Variety, choice, and competition will make them better and more effective. These would make fabulous projects for students; but really, *anyone* could do this, and *everyone* should.

Then, add video. This can be done on YouTube or some similar site, or better yet, embedded in a website or blog. Record meetings and obtain interviews with officials whenever desired and possible. Some local governments already record their meetings and post them themselves. Find these and repost them to your central site. Edit them down to the important details if necessary. The point is to have a clear and open public record and to make everything about local government as accessible and understandable to as many local people as possible. This should lead to a more widespread involvement in local politics; and this will lead, eventually, to the election of board members, judges, sheriffs, assessors, collectors, etc., who better represent the population, and better represent local values. It will increase accountability, and it will help end corruption and waste. Taxes will decrease in many localities, choices will open up, people will be more free.

You should know that these ideas and these tactics are being upheld and implemented already with success. Some counties are beginning to assert local sovereignty against state and Federal encroachments. For example, the lone town of

Sedgwick, Maine recently declared absolute sovereignty over its local food supply. They were tired of state and Federal regulations on local meat, raw milk, etc., so they declared their right and determination to be free of the tyranny. Their new ordinance says, "Our right to a local food system requires us to assert our inherent right to self-government. We recognize the authority to protect that right as belonging to the town of Sedgwick." They considered state and Federal regulations as "usurpation of our citizens' right," and went on to declare, "It shall be unlawful for any law or regulation adopted by the state or Federal government to interfere with the rights recognized by this Ordinance." This was applied also for "any corporation" that would try to interfere. The town further added that claims to local sovereignty are supported by the Declaration of Independence, the Maine State Constitution, and other Maine statutes. They reserved the right even to secede completely if necessary in the face of a legal contest.

That Sedgwick ordinance, all by itself, is creating quite a stir. It's currently being used as a model to resist Federal regulation in many other municipalities across the country. These will certainly lead to court battles and possibly intimidation from higher governments, but all this indicates that the local sovereignty movement is growing and can be implemented. The fight has only just begun, but it has begun indeed.

This is true in other areas of life as well, as some local counties and even states have declared that they will not honor Obama's health care act, but have declared it null within their jurisdictions. Some states have declared all Federal firearm laws null and void within their boundaries for guns or ammo manufactured there. There are at least a dozen or more areas in which states are currently working to nullify Federal laws within their states. And as this precedent becomes more prevalent at the state level, it makes sense that it will extend to counties. Local sovereignty and county sovereignty will then grow more viable as well.

This is, after all, the foundation of American freedom: the first American declaration of independence was not that of 1776, but was written by a single county a full year before that. Mecklenburg County, North Carolina, formally declared independence from Great Britain on May 31, 1775, saying that "the Authority of the King or Parliament, are annulled and vacated." They proceeded to set up an interim government all by their lonesome, until (as they expected) the rest of the Colonies should catch up. So local sovereignty is an American tradition, and it's back on the rise.

Cases of local freedom—individuals asserting control over corrupt local officials—are occurring as well. In one case I was told, a small town council had very quietly been paying itself an exorbitant pension package. When a few local business owners found out, they were of course outraged. At least one council member was opposed to the pensions, so the businessmen approached him with a plan. They showed up unexpectedly at a council meeting with a video camera running. They got the members to confirm the opulent terms of the package, and then asked for a show of hands on the council of all those who disapproved of it. The lone honest member of the council thrust his hand high, and the rest were caught on video exposed. The businessmen then simply thanked the council and left with the video. The council was so scared that it called a recess and chased the inquirers into the parking lot, trembling, asking what there were going to do with the video! They knew good and well.

In a similar case, a seventeen year-old exposed a self-serving shool board's rush appointment of a big-spending school superintendent. By simply showing up at both the interview process and the board meetings with a digital recorder, this intrepid teenager stopped these corrupt thugs dead in their tracks. They were literally trembling in fear.

Another local contact of mine has been fighting these kind of battles for several years. He's watched his community deteriorate from a combination of Federal Section 8 housing and corrupt local investment trusts, much of which arose only after local public schools gained Title 1 status and started receiving massive Federal aid (e.g., the Federal "free school lunch" program). There is much to sort out here, but the bottom line is that corrupt local fat cats have been using government grants to empower and enrich themselves at the expense of the local culture. And they are protected for several reasons by liberal politicians at the state and national level. My contact said he started attending board meetings to record what was said. Very early on, one of these fat cats approached him with a suspicious and menacing demeanor—essentially threatening to get him fired from his job. The man is now very paranoid. He has seen how deeply the corruption goes in his area and how serious some of the insiders are about *keeping it that way*. And it's all happened gradually over the years while local people neglected to attend to their local politics. There is work to be done here.

Another man wrote to tell me how he had won a seat on his local commission because the local conservatives were raising taxes and spending like crazy. He simply took a strong "Tea Party" stand against spending and corruption, and he was elected—despite overwhelming opposition from the local papers, labor unions, and even the local Chamber of Commerce. The local Chamber opposed him because it was dominated by big business interests that favored big government for their corporate welfare. In other words, the local Chamber itself was corrupted by the forces of wealth redistribution. It had taken the cheese, and was now entrapped. My friend won the election anyway, but still faces an uphill fight against complacent and complicit officials, and, as he put it, "the grip that Federal grants place on local units."

There are some successes out there. But there are currently many challenges. Clearly assessing the severe depth and reality of *local* challenges to county sovereignty will help us to realize how much worse it must be at higher levels of government. The nature of the problem is exactly the same; it's just magnified. So if we can't dismantle this tyranny locally, we have no chance of transforming even our state governments, let alone Washington D.C. But this is what is encouraging about the successes we're seeing: we in fact *can* have an effect locally, and many people *are.* There is a lot of work to do, and a lot of hills left to climb. It will take time. But remember, we are planning for our grandchildren. It is time to start, to get busy, and commence a steady pace of reform. So start with these steps of publicizing and controlling local politics.

It begins when people become aware of our dire national condition. It advances when people get focused, study, and understand the problem. It succeeds when they take action. This is the county rights project. It will work only when you get involved. People can be free only if they will be responsible and courageous.

4. States' Rights

The last chapter dealt with the primary issue of decentral-izing government. The ultimate goal is to decentralize as much as possible, leaving individuals as free as possible and dealing only with local units of government. We also saw how America once enjoyed this ideal scenario, how it was lost, and how we can begin to get it back. Now it's time to talk about the important role of states' rights.

Freedom and States' Rights

Related to the protection of local sovereignty, and vital to under-standing American history, is the old notion of states' rights. By upholding states' rights as an essential link in any truly federal system, we protect an indispensable check on national tyranny and adhere more faithfully to the way America was settled and founded. Though defending states' rights alone is not enough to reverse national tyranny, states, if they are returned to their original role, can provide an umbrella of protection against the central government under which local governments can (and must) begin to work independently of Federal regulation and interference. In fact, states could provide the needed impetus for local communities to develop greater independence. In short, even if not *sufficient*, states' rights may be a *necessary* step along the way. More importantly, recognizing the original power and independence of states helps us understand just how complete Federal tyranny has become.

The American colonies were originally settled as feudal land grants, chartered by the English crown. Government took its complexion from the local sovereignty of fiefdoms, the more specific sovereignty of property-owners within those fiefdoms, and a very clear contractual agreement between levels of government all the way up to the king. It is necessary here to remember that each colony was established as a discreet entity—with separate ownership, a separate charter, separate governments, and separate jurisdictions. The operative descriptor in regard to the colonies—later "states"—was "separate." When the colonies declared independence, they established themselves as sovereign states, not a single nation. This colonial history forms the basis for the old claims about states' rights. They have been largely ignored and maligned, but the argument is both crucial and unimpeachable.

The Original States' Rights Debate

Within three decades of the Constitution's framing—within the generation of those who debated its ratification—virtually all the fears of the Anti-Federalists had come true. Power had been centralized at the national level in regard to the judiciary, the military, taxation, legislation, commerce, and much else. Nevertheless, while political power had been centralized in reality from day one, popular sentiment on the topic remained starkly divided. The majority of common Americans assumed the states' rights view,[1] while the victorious party in the Constitutional battle favored the Nationalistic view which was in place. The Jeffersonian party called "Democratic Republicans" represented the majority, while the Federalist Party controlled the day.

The debate over states' rights ultimately hinged upon the interpretation of the nature of the Declaration of Independence. The Anti-Federalists (and later, Jeffersonians) noted what seemed like common sense: once the colonies "dissolved

---

[1] By "states' rights," I am referring to the doctrine that each state in the Union is a sovereign and indpendent jurisdiction interposed between individuals and the federal government.

the political bands" that connected them to the British Crown, they immediately became thirteen "Free and Independent States." These thirteen countries—for this is how we would understand their status today—recognized their need to band together for strength and thus "united," meaning *confederated*. In this unity, they declared their independence, and in this unity, they vowed to support each other to defend it. The same arrangement of independent sovereignties that drafted the Declaration immediately started writing a constitution, and the resulting document was called the Articles of Confederation. Completed in 1777, the Articles were ratified formally in 1781, securing the confederate organization of the Colonies. It stated clearly in Article II, "Each state retains its sovereignty, freedom, and independence, and every power, jurisdiction, and right, which is not by this Confederation expressly delegated to the United States, in Congress assembled."[2]

The nationalist side of the debate, nevertheless, emphasized the unity at the expense of the plurality. Their response to the Anti-Federalists was that "the colonies declared their independence not individually but unitedly, and that they had never been independent of one another."[3]

The dispute over the individual status of the confederated colonies raged during the Constitutional ratification period. Perhaps the most famous remark comes from Mr. "Liberty-or-Death" himself, Patrick Henry. He complained,

> What right had they to say, *We, the People*? My political curiosity, exclusive of my anxious solicitude for the public welfare, leads me to ask who authorized them to speak the language of, *We, the People*, instead of *We, the*

---

[2] Recall John's Marshall's argument that the word "expressly" was absent from the Tenth Amendment? (See pp. 90–91 above.) Here was the origin of that debate. The Articles clearly contained the term. It was purposefully removed from the Tenth Amendment by the Federalist sympathizers.

[3] Herbert J. Storing, *The Complete Anti-Federalist*, 7 vols. (Chicago: University of Chicago Press, 1981), 1:13.

States? States are the characteristics, and the soul of a confederation. If the States be not agents of this compact, it must be one great consolidated National Government of the people of all the States. . . .

The people gave them no power to use their name. That they exceeded their power is perfectly clear.[4]

This argument threw down the gauntlet on the issue of nationalism. Everyone knew the Constitutional Convention had been resolved by Congress "for the sole and express purpose of revising the Articles of Confederation,"[5] and this meant honoring the sovereignty of the states. But this was the very thing the forces behind the Convention wished to change. They got their way by convincing the states' delegates that what everyone had already agreed upon—the Articles of Confederation—was a *wholly* insufficient instrument to provide for the future needs of the nation, and thus, they argued, the Articles should not be revised, *but completely trashed.*

Thus arose the new argument that the Articles of Confederation "were a defective instrument of a preexisting union"[6] which had departed from the true spirit of national solidarity allegedly expressed in the Declaration. Nationalists argued that the newly proposed Constitution was *restoring* the principles of the Declaration from which the Articles had irremediably deviated. The new position was expressed eloquently by General Charles Cotesworth Pinckney, who urged the Constitution on the South Carolina legislature:

The separate independence and individual sovereignty of the several states were never thought of by the enlightened band of patriots who framed this Declaration; the several states are not even mentioned by name in any part of it,—as if it was intended to impress this maxim

---

[4] Storing, *Complete Anti-Federalist*, 5:211.

[5] See *Journals of the Continental Congress*, 32:74.

[6] Storing, *Complete Anti-Federalist*, 1:13.

on America, that our freedom and independence arose from our union, and that without it we could neither be free nor independent. Let us, then, consider all attempts to weaken this Union, by maintaining that each state is separately and individually independent, as a species of political heresy. . . ."[7]

After this position won the day, the victorious Federalist party (and its historical successors: the National Republicans, the Whigs, and the Republicans) used this argument as a means of suppressing the "political heresy" of states' rights.

The most vehement elocution of this position appeared when National Republican John Quincy Adams gave a two-hour lecture to the New York Historical Society in 1839—*The Jubilee of the Constitution*. Adams wrote,

A convention of delegates from eleven of the thirteen states, with George Washington at their head, sent forth to the people an act to be made their own, speaking in their name and in the first person, thus: "We the people of the United States, in order to form a more perfect union, establish justice, ensure domestic tranquility, provide for the common defence, promote the general welfare, and secure the blessings of liberty, to ourselves and our posterity, do ordain and establish this Constitution for the United States of America." This act was the complement to the Declaration of Independence—founded upon the same principles, carrying them out into practical execution, and forming with it one entire system of national government.[8]

. . . It is not immaterial to remark that the signers of the Declaration, though qualifying themselves as the Representatives of the United States of America, in general Congress assembled, yet issue the Declaration, *in the name and by the authority of the good people of the*

---

[7] Ibid., 1:82n40.

[8] John Quincy Adams, *The Jubilee of the Constitution* (Powder Springs, GA: American Vision Press, 2011), 39.

colonies—and that they declare, *not* each of the separate colonies, but *the United Colonies*, free and independent states. The whole people declared the colonies *in their united condition*, of right, free and independent states. . . .

But there still remained the last and crowning act, which *the People* of the Union alone were competent to perform—the institution of civil government for that compound nation, the United States of America.[9]

Adams carries on for pages extending his argument to the finest details of the situation. And yet, for all its detail and rigor, it is easy to get the feeling that Adams "doth protest too much." It is important to remember that the particular choir Adams was addressing was composed of a *minority* of the population—a controlling, wealthy, entrenched minority—but a minority nonetheless. The Democratic-Republican party had grown so overwhelmingly popular that the Federalist faction was forced into oblivion—its nationalist sentiments only allowed to live on as they reemerged within a faction of the Democratic-Republicans called the National Republicans. This was Adams's party. Regardless of how institutionally victorious the nationalists' cause had been, the sentiments of states' rights still gripped a majority of freedom-loving hearts across America. A very tense situation was brewing in which major popular sentiment wished for states' rights and more local control, while elites such as Adams continued to preach vehemently for Union and thus Federal government domination.

So, while I noted above that "virtually all the fears of the Anti-Federalist opponents of the Constitution had come true," there remained one very important fear which had not yet been fulfilled by Adams's time, but it was brewing—civil war. "The Federal Farmer" (likely Richard Henry Lee) predicted—as did many others—that such would occur should the Constitution be forced through:

---

[9] Adams, *Jubilee*, 42.

The plan of government now proposed [the Constitution] is evidently calculated totally to change, in time, our condition as a people. Instead of being thirteen republics, under a federal head, it is clearly designed to make us one consolidated government. . . . This consolidation of the states has been the object of several men in this country for sometime past. Whether such a change . . . can be effected without convulsions and civil wars; whether such a change will not totally destroy the liberties of this country—time only can determine.[10]

Time did determine it. While nationalists and states' rights advocates had *officially* settled their old debate on paper at the Constitutional Convention, that settlement was not fully manifested until it was written in blood at Gettysburg. At that site, Lincoln gave an eloquent eulogy for states' rights, if only in passing: "Four score and seven years ago our fathers brought forth on this continent a new nation. . . ."

That was at the heart of the debate, and Lincoln exploited his military victory at Gettysburg to claim ideological victory for his side. According to Lincoln, the "fathers" had not confederated several states, no. They had brought forth a single, *one*, "new nation"—or as the Anti-Federalists had so often warned, "one consolidated government."

Of all of the major advances that the Federalist party touted as benefits of the new Constitution, not one was ever carried out successfully without an eventual resort to the force of arms. The Civil War was merely the climax of that precedent.

Despite how things were eventually settled, the nationalists' argument in favor of the primacy of the government of the Union was not nearly as sound as Adams, Lincoln, and company would have us believe—for at least a few reasons.

First, The language of the Declaration of Independence makes it clear that the states, though united for a particular purpose, still viewed themselves as plural independent sovereignties in doing so.

---

[10] Storing, *Complete Anti-Federalist*, 2.8.4.

While the Declaration contained language like "the Right of the People" and "one people"—thus favoring the Federalist perspective—it nevertheless concluded by speaking of the new independence not of a single nation but of the "free and independent States" in the plural:

> *These united Colonies are*, and of Right ought to be Free and Independent *States*, that *they* are Absolved from all Allegiance to the British Crown, and that all political connection between *them* and the State of Great Britain, is and ought to be totally dissolved; and that as Free and Independent *States, they* have full Power to levy War, conclude Peace, contract Alliances, establish Commerce, and to do all other Acts and Things which Independent *States* may of right do.[11]

"These united Colonies *are* [plural] . . . Independent States" is a very odd phrase if, in fact, the goal had been to create a single consolidated government.

The details so often make the difference. In fact, it is of great importance that we notice just how even the capitalization of a single letter changes the whole nature of the discussion. In that final paragraph of the Declaration, the original text begins, "We, therefore, the Representatives of the UNITED STATES OF AMERICA. . . ." The same phrase appears in the very heading of the document, with the word "united" even more disproportionately subdued. Note in both cases that the word "united" is not capitalized; it is, therefore, a mere adjective and not part of a proper name. The phrase is not referring to a single government or entity called "The United States of America," but rather to the coming together of the "States of America." Yet, when Adams tells the story, he argues that the assembly which drafted the Declaration were "qualifying themselves as the Representatives of the United States of

---

[11] See original image at http://www.archives.gov/exhibits/charters/slurp_file.php?fileref=1. Emphasis added.

America." This is inaccurate and misleading. Adams argues: "*not* each of the separate colonies, but *the United Colonies*."[12] While the phrase "United Colonies" is used in passing in one place, Adams completely ignores, and in fact misrepresents, the phrase "united States of America" which forms the heading and heads the closing thought. Thus Adams's nationalist view was derived from only a small part—and a minority part at that—of the Declaration's own words. In other words, he had to disregard those Representatives' clear and very definite conclusion in order to presume the Constitution took care of their allegedly unfinished business. It was a political half-truth—really, *less* than a half-truth.

Second, it is helpful in this regard also to understand the usage of the term "state" in the Declaration. Today Americans generally think of a "state" only as one of those divisions within the nation of the United States. We tend to consider a state simply a secondary unit of government below Federal or national government. A "state" is less than a "nation." But, at the time of the Declaration, this was not so. A "state" was regarded as a free and independent, stand-alone, unit of government subject to no other body. In contrast, a *nation* was considered a lesser people-group, often joined together in local community by a common language. Noah Webster, in his 1828 definition of NATION, said: "It often happens that many nations are subject under one government." STATE, on the other hand, was defined as a "whole body of people united under one government, whatever may be the form of the government."

The Declaration did not declare the colonies a free and independent nation, or even a free and independent state, but "Free and Independent States." And in calling Britain herself a "State" as opposed to a "nation" as we would call it today, the Declaration seems to accord *each* of the American "states" that same status, and thus exalts each to the status of what we

---

[12] Adams, *Jubilee*, 42.

would today regard as a nation. Thus it says that "as Free and Independent States, they have full Power to levy War, conclude Peace, contract Alliances, establish Commerce, and to do all other Acts and Things which Independent States may of right do"—all things that mere constituent parts of a single state may not of themselves rightly do.

Finally, the nationalist argument was an *ad hoc* novelty, a little piece of revisionist history designed to justify the Constitution. It was not heard or explicated by anyone before the Convention or ratification process. The states' rights doctrine, however, was confirmed in the Articles immediately after the Declaration. These were not challenged at the time, and no one objected to them on the grounds that the colonies were *actually* acting as a united whole.

Whatever else can be said in defense of having a single, powerful, centralized national government is irrelevant here. What must be clear is that America was not originally settled that way, the colonies did not declare their independence that way, the original instrument of government written by the same people who wrote the Declaration did not confederate in that way, and thus states' rights seems to be the original American way. Whatever undesirable connections became associated with states' rights at a later date must be set aside from the issue itself for the purposes of this discussion.[13]

Now we have already discussed a lot about how states' rights have been trampled and lost over the years. There is still more to tell about this story, however.

---

[13] Many criticize the states' rights movement because the Dixiecrats used "states' rights" as a platform code phrase for "pro-segregation." But whatever they may have used their state sovereignty to promote, the instrument they used, and the logic that supported it, was often quite sound. For example, I recommend James Jackson Fitzpatrick, *The Sovereign States: Notes of a Citizen of Virginia* (Chicago: Henry Regnery Co., 1957). Overlooking Fitzpatrick's support of segregation, his scholarship in regard to the issues is very good, and his writing is very engaging.

How States' Rights were Lost

We have already covered how decentralization in principle was already forfeited by the Constitutional settlement. It is not my intention to rehash that same material for the loss of states' rights—though much of it is relevant. What we have not covered yet, but very much need to, is just how systematic and premeditated that original takeover was. We are not dealing with patriots and patriotism here; we are dealing with the roots, causes, and progress of tyranny.

It is helpful to remember that while great societies often appear to crumble overnight, the cracks in their foundation began long before they collapsed. For example, when the Israelites demanded a "king like other nations" (1 Sam. 8:5), God said definitively that they had rejected Him (1 Sam. 8:7–8). This began the era of the kings in Israel. And yet this God-rejecting society which was "serving other gods" did not disintegrate immediately. Rather, it decayed over centuries to the point that even its most famous reformer-king, Josiah, could not ultimately avert eventual judgment. This era of the kings ended when the people were defeated and carried away captive into Babylon. But, from beginning to end, this decline and fall took about 434 years (1020 B.C. to 586 B.C.). In other words, the inciting cause of a social decline can be present immediately, but its effects may take centuries to manifest fully.

Thus while it may be illuminating to consider the various periods of centralization in America's history—whether it be the Wilson War State, the Civil War, etc.—this is not necessarily the most effective, or most accurate, approach. It may even be detrimental. For example, the Civil War debate can become hopelessly sidetracked with an endless variety of peripheral issues—slavery not the least of them. And yet the issue of slavery—as important and interesting as it is—does not touch the core issue behind tyranny and centralization in American history. Yet it will consume the entire debate, and then breed several side debates of its own. This is unfruitful. It is better to lay the axe at the root of the tree rather than hack away at a thousand branches which always seem to find a way to grow back anyway. While it may involve some digging, sweat, and dirt, we simply must get to that root.

We cannot plan a proper solution to the problem if we misdiagnose it, or focus exclusively on only part of it. For example, we feel free to condemn Wilson or FDR, Johnson or Obama, Socialism or the Fed, and yet we remain timid or even defiantly opposed to criticizing even parts of the Constitution itself. But if the Constitution was the first great act of centralization in this land—the act which enabled and empowered all subsequent centralization in this country (exactly as predicted by its opponents)—then it will do little good to clear away merely its subsequent tyrannies. If the root remains viable, the brambles will grow back. "Return to the Constitution" sounds nice, but what good does it do to return ourselves to the same slippery summit from which we've already fallen?

As it concerns this project, I am not so much interested in debating the evils on one side or the other of the Civil War (Northern Aggression, Southern Rebellion, or any of its other hundred partisan epithets), Reconstruction, or the Progressive Era (either in its Republican or Democrat permutations), or any other issue peripheral to the root of the problem. For that reason, I will use this section to continue the story of centralization that began in the first generation after the Constitutional settlement, adding upon what I've already written under County Rights. I wish to hammer home just how systematically and drastically nationalists grabbed and centralized power during that time, and how this initial centralization prepared the way for the wars, debts, and tyrannies that would come later. Since I have already told some of the story of the ratification debate, and the series of Supreme Court decisions John Marshall used to gradually centralize power in every area that the Anti-Federalists predicted, I now want to cover a different angle of that same takeover. This should further establish that the nationalist takeover was conscious and premeditated, and that it was the real turning point for the country.

One of the prominent Anti-Federalist writers, "The Federal Farmer" (possibly Richard Henry Lee), pointed out both the extreme degree of the change in government and the premeditated nature of it. Very early in the ratification debate, he wrote,

> The plan of government now proposed [the Constitution] is evidently calculated totally to change, in time, our condition as a people. Instead of being thirteen republics, under a federal head, it is clearly designed to make us one consolidated government. . . . *This consolidation of the states has been the object of several men in this country for sometime past.*[14]

The Federalist Agents of Centralization

We need, therefore, to examine the goals and efforts of the most prominent of these early central planners. While there were, of course, many that deserve attention, we have space here to deal with only some of the most famous—Madison, Hamilton, and Washington. Among these, we will mainly concentrate on Hamilton's agenda.

We have already discussed Marshall a bit. Despite the enormity of his contribution, he was only the judicial contingent of the real energy behind the Federalists. Writing on the centennial of Marshall's death, the leftist Max Lerner noted the direction of the judge's agenda: "Much of Marshall's career may be viewed as a process of reading Hamilton's state papers into the Constitution."[15]

Doubtless, there was not a more efficient, effective, energetic, or evil influence toward centralization than Alexander

---

[14] Storing, *Complete Anti-Federalist*, 2.8.4.

[15] "John Marshall's Long Shadow," *Ideas are Weapons: The History and Use of Ideas,* (Transaction Publishers: New Brunswick, NJ, 1991), 31.

Hamilton. Often praised today by conservatives for the tradition of "strong Hamiltonian Federalism"—derived from his
central role in writing the *Federalist Papers* defending the Constitution—his system was anything but truly federal. He was the
liberal progressive of his day in nearly every political sense considerable (except possibly the idea of social welfare which was
not, at least in the modern sense, really invented yet).

Long before the Constitutional Convention, Hamilton displayed a dangerous penchant for obtaining his goals through
top-down, coercive means. As a young soldier, these instincts
served him well, producing examples of bravery and leadership during the Revolution. But during the so-called Newburgh Conspiracy of 1783, when the restless Revolutionary
Army refused to disband without its long-overdue pay, Hamilton suggested that Washington take charge of the army and
use the threat of force to persuade Congress not only to pay
up, but to pass legislation to install his dream of a more centralized financial system. Washington, as much a statist but
less foolhardy than his former aide-de-camp, read Hamilton's
letter "with pain . . . astonishment and horror." He explained,

> The idea of redress by force, is too chimerical to have had
> a place in the imagination of any serious Mind in this
> Army; but there is no telling what unhappy disturbances
> might result from distress, and distrust of justice. . . . The
> Army . . . is a dangerous instrument to play with.[16]

Hamilton's dangerous disposition developed very early. As
a bastard child who was orphaned at about twelve years of age
when his mother died of fever, he was fortunate to find meaningful employment as a merchant's apprentice. A prodigious
self-taught child, his intellect and energy drove him quickly to
a position of responsibility: he was keeping the books and run-

---

[16] Washington to Hamilton, April 4, 1783, *The Writings of George Washington:
Volume 29, January 1, 1783–June 10, 1783*, ed. John C. Fitzpatrick (Washington,
D.C.: Government Printing Office, 1938), 292, 293.

ning the warehouse at twelve while his masters were out at sea. Despite his early accomplishments and promise, Hamilton was bored. He confronted his boredom with dreams of fame and glory. In a letter to a friend, he revealed how he disdained a life of common business: "I contemn the grov'ling and condition of a Clerk or the like, to which my Fortune &c. condemns me." He said he would willingly risk his life to exalt his "Station." And Hamilton had studied the classics; he knew how to achieve advancement and fame. The primary way—according to prominent Greek and Roman writers—was through warfare. Hamilton was ready to risk his life, he said; and thus he wrote, "I shall Conclude saying I wish there was a war."[17]

For a young man of twelve to be considering personal fame and advancement already, and even conceiving plans of how best to achieve it, is extraordinary, to say the least. But discontentment with a promising business career and a willingness to die for fame belies the mindset of a fool. To dismiss (really hate) the value of a steady wealth-producing life due to a lust for fame is indeed a biblical definition of foolishness—that is, running from the basic laws God gave for life, and seeking that way of life that leads to self-glorification and/or death (Psa. 14; Prov. 1–8).

We must not ignore the powerful role that the lust for fame played in the lives of America's framers. It was overwhelming; it was all-consuming for many of them. The historian Douglas Adair, widely respected by colleagues from various perspectives and parties, first alerted American historians to the importance of this concept. It reigned true for most of the famous founders, including Hamilton. Hamilton recognized that "love of fame . . . is the ruling passion of the noblest minds."[18] Later in his life, he would reiterate this in a letter to

---

[17] Quoted in Forrest McDonald, *Alexander Hamilton: A Biography* (New York: W. W. Norton and Co., 1979), 9.

[18] Douglass Adair, "Fame and the Founding Fathers," *Fame and the Founding Fathers: Essays by Douglass Adair*, ed. by Trevor Colbourn (Indianapolis: Liberty

his uncle, suggesting that the "love of fame" was a common "spring of action" for seeking public office.[19] After reviewing how this love of fame infused the lives of Hamilton, Washington and others, Adair concludes,

> The love of fame, and the belief that creating a viable republican state would win them fame, is part of the explanation of the élan, the tremendous energy, the dedicated and brilliantly effective political maneuvers by which a small minority of American . . . nationalists kidnapped the movement to reform the Articles, wrote what they conceived to be a more perfect union, and then managed to get it ratified by the reluctant representatives of an apathetic populace.[20]

An American Caesar

In Hamilton's case, the love of fame seems to have had some attachment to the icon of empire himself—Julius Caesar. In his parlor, Thomas Jefferson had portraits of Bacon, Locke, and Newton, whom he considered the three greatest men the world had ever produced. As a guest in Jefferson's house, Alexander Hamilton rebuffed him: "The greatest man that ever lived was Julius Caesar."[21] Jefferson would conclude of Hamilton that while "honest as a man," he was nevertheless, "as a politician, believing in the necessity of either force or corruption to govern men."[22]

Fund, 1974), 10.

[19] Quoted in McDonald, *Hamilton*, 85; Hamilton to William Hamilton, May 2, 1797, *Papers of Alexander Hamilton*: Volume 21, April 1797–July 1798, ed. Harold C. Syrett (New York: Columbia University Press, 1974), 78.

[20] Adair, *Fame and the Founding Fathers*, 34.

[21] Ibid., 18.

[22] Jefferson to Benjamin Rush, Jan. 17, 1811, *The Works of Thomas Jefferson: Volume 11*, ed. Paul Leicester Ford (New York: The Knickerbocker Press, 1902), 168. The recent hagiographer of Hamilton has called this story "absurd." His evidence however is a combination of strained assumptions and exaggerated circumstantial references. See Ron Chernow, *Alexander Hamilton* (New York: Penguin, 2004), 398. I have rebutted Chernow's (and others') view in my article, "The Resur-

An interesting thread emerges long before Hamilton's visit to Jefferson. As champion of Constitutional centralization, Hamilton was the most vigorous nationalist to undertake its defense in print. But before he and Madison collaborated as "Publius" on the *Federalist Papers*, a curious pair of response letters appeared in a New York newspaper. Here's the story.

The other two delegates from New York left the Convention early in disgust at what they perceived as a coup. They returned to New York City and informed the strongly states' rights (at the time) governor, George Clinton, what was afoot. Merely ten days after the close of the Convention, the proposed Constitution was published in the *New York Journal* for all to read. In that same September 27, 1787 edition, an open letter to the citizens of New York bore a critique and solemn warning about the proposal. The letter was signed with the pseudonym "Cato." The author was (most assume) Governor George Clinton.

The name "Cato" was taken from Cato the Younger (d. 46 B.C.), the ancient Roman statesman known for his commitment to freedom and honesty. After Caesar crossed the Rubicon and usurped power from the Senate, Cato committed suicide. He would rather die than suffer the tyranny of Caesar's military dictatorship. Governor Clinton now saw a group of similarly ambitious would-be Caesars usurping power from the states. He warned the people:

> Deliberate, therefore, on this new national government with coolness; analyze it with criticism; and reflect on it with candor: if you find that the influence of a powerful few, or the exercise of a standing army, will always be directed and exerted for your welfare alone, and not to the aggrandizement of themselves ... adopt it—if it will not, reject it with indignation—better to be where you are, for the present, than insecure forever afterwards. . . .[23]

---

rection of a Demigod, and the Defense of Tyranny," Sept. 1, 2011, http://american-vision.org/5099/the-resurrection-of-a-demigod-and-the-defense-of-tyranny/#. UGIM9Y2PW8k (accessed Sept. 25, 2012).

[23] Storing, *Complete Anti-Federalist*, 2:105–106.

Within a week, the letter received a response in the news-paper. And what pseudonym would the ambitious defender use to oppose Cato? Unbelievably, it was "Caesar." And just like the Caesar who crossed the Rubicon with military force, this young would-be Caesar brandished the threat of military takeover should the people not submit to the proposed gov-ernment willingly. Referring to George Washington as "the American Fabius," he urged Clinton to ease the former gen-eral's journey to the presidency of a new nation:

> I would also advise him to give his vote . . . to the Ameri-can Fabius; it will be more healthy for this country, and this state, that he should be induced to accept of the pres-idency of the new government, than that he should be solicited again to accept of the command of an army.[24]

Scholars for some time considered Hamilton the author of the "Caesar" letters, though this has since been severely questioned.[25] Whoever the author was, he (or she) was cer-tainly of the same Hamiltonian nationalizing spirit, and was very likely of personal association with, or at least known to, Hamilton. This shows that the nationalist New York clique in which Hamilton circulated was willing to appeal immediately to military force in order to get their agenda passed.

---

[24] Paul Leicester Ford, ed., *Essays on the Constitution of the United States, Pub-lished during its Discussion by the People, 1787–1788* (Brooklyn, NY: Historical Printing Club, 1892), 285. Fabius Maximus was the Roman general who won his wars gradually through guerilla tactics. Instead of meeting superior forces head-on, he broke into small bands and executed numerous small sorties, slowly wearing down the enemy's forces and will to fight. George Washington had used similar tactics against the British during the American War for Independence.

[25] While the consensus for some time was that Hamilton was "Caesar"—based on primary-source evidence found by Paul Leicester Ford—a couple scholars have since undermined this position with counterevidence strong enough to leave the question unresolved. (See Jacob E. Cooke, "Alexander Hamilton's Authorship of the 'Caesar' Letters," *The William and Mary Quarterly*, Third Series 17/1 (Jan., 1960): 78–85.) The worst part of this debate is that Ford's primary source evidence was apparently destroyed in a library fire, and is thus not able to be re-entered into the discussion. This allows would-be Hamilton apologists the leverage of further doubt.

So here we have the same Hamilton, who in 1783 urged Washington to leverage military power, aligned with the same "end-justifies-the-means" tactic once again. Clinton (although certainly no saint himself) warned the people that "in case you do not acquiesce, he should be solicited to command an army to impose it on you." In his second letter as Cato, he went on to remind them of the freedom they had just fought for:

> Is not your indignation roused at this imperious style?— For what did you open the veins of your citizens and expend their treasure?—For what did you throw off the yoke of Britain and call yourselves independent?—Was it from a disposition fond of change, or to procure new masters?—if those were your motives, you have your reward before you—go,—retire into silent obscurity, and kiss the rod that scourges you—bury the prospects you had in store, that you and your posterity would participate in the blessings of freedom . . . let the rich and insolent alone be your rulers—perhaps you are designed by providence as an emphatic evidence of the mutability of human affairs, to have the shew of happiness only, that your misery may seem the sharper, and if so, you must submit. But, if you had nobler views, and you are not designed by heaven as an example—are you now to be derided and insulted?—Is the power of thinking, on the only subject important to you, to be taken away? And if perchance you should happen to dissent from Caesar, are you to have Caesar's principles crammed down your throats with an army?—God forbid! . . .[26]

This indeed was a case of Caesar versus Cato, and the governor intended to make it clear to all people that a small group of tyrants intended to grab power over them. He wrote:

> The Convention too, when in session, shut their doors to the observations of the community, and their members were under an obligation of secrecy . . .

[26] Storing, *Complete Anti-Federalist*, 2:107.

For the sole and express purpose [of revising the
Articles of Confederation] a Convention of delegates
is formed in Philadelphia:—what have they done?
Have they revised the confederation, and has Congress
agreed to their report?—neither is the fact.—This Convention have exceeded the authority given to them, and
have transmitted to Congress a new political fabric, essentially and fundamentally distinct from it, in which
the different states do not retain separately their sovereignty and independency, united by a confederated
league—but one entire sovereignty—a consolidation of
them into one government. . . .

The Convention had taken on themselves a power
which neither they nor the states had a right to delegate
to them. . . . it originated in an assumption of power . . .
founded on usurpation. . . .

And yet you are unhesitatingly to acquiesce, and if
you do not, the American Fabius, if we may believe Caesar, is to command an army to impose it.[27]

Caesar's final letter against Cato would reveal his ani-
mosity not only to freedom, but to religion: he wished to see
America as a glorious secular empire destined to steal power
from and begin the decline of Christian nations:

When this glorious work is accomplished, what may
America not hope to arrive at? I will venture to proph-
esy that the day on which the Union under the new
government shall be ratified by the American States,
that that day will begin an era which will be recorded
and observed by future ages, as a day which the Americans had marked by their wisdom in circumscribing the
power and ascertaining the decline of the ancient nations in Christendom.[28]

---

[27] Storing, *Complete Anti-Federalist*, 2:108–109.

[28] Ford, *Essays*, 291.

Surely Hamilton realized that "Caesar" did not have the upper hand in this particular rhetorical battle. He was playing the role of the tyrant, Caesar, against the just lover of freedom, Cato. He was threatening a military dictatorship, or at best a civil war, and he openly opposed Christian civilization at this time. He seemed to play the part of a tyrant well, but the people were not yet ready to accept him in this garb. So Hamilton resolved to change tactics: he presented himself instead as the champion of federalism and liberty, joining with Madison to write the more popular *Federalist Papers.*

A Christian Statesman?

The public denigration of "the ancient nations in Christendom" struck directly (if unwittingly) at the true Christian heritage of America. As we saw in the last chapter, the Christian feudal system (what was good of it), particularly the emphasis on contracts and property ownership, formed the basis of America's settlement. It formed the basis, particularly, of the decentralized nature of colonial government. The nationalist swipe at that heritage—indeed the prophecy of its decline and fall—was an admission of the unbounded tyranny latent in the nationalist philosophy.

Hamilton's relationship with religion is certainly of interest. Adair and Harvey have recognized four different periods of his life in which his attitude toward religion shifted quite distinctly: his youth, his fabulous rise to fame, his partisan activist period, and his decline and fall.[29] Without explaining each part in depth, here are the main points.

During his youth, Hamilton was taken in by a devout Presbyterian family. During these years, he prayed regularly, attended worship services, and received a religious education, though he never joined a church. It seems that during these

---

[29] See Douglass Adair and Martin Harvey, "Was Alexander Hamilton a Christian Statesmen?" *The William and Mary Quarterly*, Third Series 12/2 (Apr. 1955): 308–329.

years he may have been simply going through motions, for, in the second period of his life, he ceases almost entirely from making references to his faith.

It is the second and third periods which concern us most here, for it was during this time that Hamilton exercised his most permanent influence. And it is here that his agenda and worldview are most explicit. During this second period—which covered his military exploits and advance to national stardom, from 1777 to 1792—Hamilton appears religiously indifferent, even hostile. He refers to religion in his writings only twice in these fifteen years, and both times in crude jest. In the first, he said that a certain "Dr. Mendy" fit his mould for a perfect army chaplain except that the parson did "not whore or drink"—suggesting that he expected hypocrisy among Christian ministers.[30] In the second reference, taken from a letter to a friend, Hamilton outlines his qualifications for a good wife. Among having "a good shape" and a large fortune, she must both "believe in God and hate a saint." Aside from these references, we have nothing else regarding religion from Hamilton's own pen during the period.[31]

Hamilton's third period spanned the French Revolution and his political battles with Jefferson. At this point, Hamilton suddenly waxes religious again. His main references to religion during this period make it clear he was using religious rhetoric only for political advantage. Indeed, he speaks explicitly of religion as an "engine" of politics, and explained this at length in letter to William L. Smith (April 10, 1797):

---

[30] Not ironically, the later editor of Hamilton's writings, Henry Cabot Lodge, scrubbed "whore or" from his edition of the letters (the only one available to the public). The lack of irony comes from the fact that Lodge published Hamilton's letters in 1904 as a partisan of the old imperial Progressive Republicans—for whom Hamilton was a hero. Lodge consciously sanitized Hamilton to make him more acceptable to "Christian America."

[31] A couple of anecdotes from Hamilton's contemporaries are also unflattering.

> A politician will consider this [religion] as an impor-
> tant means of influencing opinion, and will think it a
> valuable resource in a contest with France to set the re-
> ligious ideas of his countrymen in active competition
> with the atheistical tenets of their enemies. This is an
> advantage which we shall be very unskilled if we do not
> use to the utmost.[32]

With this plan in place, Hamilton mounted his attack against the Jeffersonians by presenting them as American admirers of the French Revolution, engaged in "a conspiracy to establish atheism on the ruins of Christianity."[33] Yet, as we just noted, it was Hamilton himself who sought to overthrow the ancient heritage of Christianity in society. So nothing of Hamilton in this period evinces a truly Christian worldview; his use of Christianity was hypocritically leveraged for politi- cal gain. Even the secular historians note, "this period in his life hardly deserves to be praised as an era of Christian thought and practice."[34] This is an understatement.

It appears that Hamilton does eventually get true religion, but only after his dramatic fall from fame and popularity in his final four years of life. There are numerous testimonies to his change of heart and perspective in his humbled state. He focused on family, nature, and gardening, and prayed with his sons. He allegedly disagreed with dueling, and yet accepted the code of honor to which he apparently felt bound. Never- theless, he allegedly wrote that he would waste his shot and let Burr kill him. On his deathbed, he pleaded for the sacrament and eventually received it when the parson accepted his faith as genuine. Thus, it appears Hamilton died a Christian.

---

[32] Quoted in Adair and Harvey, "Hamilton a Christian Statesman?", 316n10. Just for the record, while Lodge included an excerpt of this letter in his collection, he suppressed this part of it. Progressive Republican "Christian America" endured.

[33] Ibid.

[34] Ibid., 316.

But all of this came only after his great fall from public grace and influence, and little-too-late to affect his politics in a biblical way. Adair and Harvey observe,

> Hamilton, who in the years of his early success had al-most forgotten God, who in the years of his greatest power had tried to manipulate God just as he manipu-lated the public debt to increase that power, began sin-cerely seeking God in this time of failure and suffering.[35]

This more private religious period is not often referenced as the image of Hamilton's faith. It is rather his period of manipulating God that factors most heavily in this image:

> Ironically, it is his insistence during these years, in tirade after tirade, that "democracy" and "Christianity" were incompatible, that Jefferson, "the atheist," was God's en-emy, that has left a simple-minded American posterity with the false impression that Hamilton throughout his life was a devout Christian in both thought and practice.[36]

Indeed, we have seen that this was not the case. During his most influential years, he was at his most irreligious. And during this time, he had perhaps the largest hand in pushing through massive assumptions of power, beginning with the Constitution, and extending throughout many acts of legis-lation, taxation, military action against Americans, central banking, judicial cases, and many other acts of tyranny. It is tempting to say that it was not by chance that his years of tyr-anny and sacrilege were concurrent.

Washington's New Deal

While little discussed in today's textbooks, Washington and Hamilton held a virtually identical view of government—Washington was just less outspoken and more gentlemanly

---

[35] Ibid., 317.
[36] Ibid., 316.

about it. Some historians have considered Washington a mere front for Hamilton's agenda—the public executive face to Marshall's later back-room judicial maneuvers. But Washington's regular endorsements of "strong and energetic" government rival the best of Hamilton's in substance.[37]

Washington had brought the young Hamilton under his wing as his personal aide-de-camp. It was here that Hamilton reapplied his administrative abilities (first discovered as a bookkeeper in those warehouses when he was twelve), and he realized he could actually have more control from behind the throne, so to speak, than from the spotlight. As noted by prominent historian Forrest McDonald (hardly a sympathizer with the Anti-Federalists or states' rights): "Much as [Hamilton] yearned to prove his worth on the battlefield, he was forced to realize that he could contribute far more as an administrator—for he was a man who could run things."[38] And this was just the beginning.

After the Constitution was ratified, Hamilton was already prepared with legislative papers and proposals. Despite a lethargic start (it took almost a month before enough members showed up to reach a quorum), on April 1, 1789, the first session of the first Congress opened. In a week, Madison was proposing new taxes on imports. Thus began the history of the Federal government: let the taxing begin! The first actual statute enacted by Congress was the establishment of oaths for the members. The second was the Tariff of July 4, 1789. It was Hamilton's plan, even though he was not yet even a member of the President's cabinet. Nevertheless, the "Hamilton Tariff" went through, taxing imports, thus strengthening American manufacturing and weakening southern farmers by increasing the prices of the manufactured goods they needed.

---

[37] See Richard B. Morris, "Washington and Hamilton: A Great Collaboration," *Proceedings of the American Philosophical Society* 102/2 (Apr. 30, 1958), 107–116.

[38] Forrest McDonald, *Alexander Hamilton: A Biography* (New York: W. W. Norton and Co., 1979), 15.

This was a grievance that remained for decades, and became a major cause of the Civil War.

In this way, Hamilton was already exercising significant control in Congress before his promotion to any office. Of course, it had always been his plan. McDonald relates, "Hamilton contemplated an American adaptation of the British scheme of things—with Washington as George II and himself as Robert Walpole. But, like Washington, he had to await the event."[39] Hamilton retained this self-important and monarchical view of things for the duration, referring in 1792 to "my administration," and to himself in the third person as "The Minister" in 1795.[40]

On September 11, 1789, Washington made the fateful appointment. It was confirmed the same day. Hamilton would be Secretary of the Treasury. But this is only part of that story. Washington had informed Hamilton he would get the job months before—only a few days after his inauguration.[41] This gave Hamilton important time to influence Congress so as to outfit the position of Secretary of the Treasury with all the powers he desired. And this he did. McDonald elaborates:

> His hesitancy to make a final commitment, despite his preparations and his dreams, derived from a determination that the conditions of his appointment must be compatible with the success of his grand plan. From his point of view three conditions were vital. One he took for granted: that he would have the support of his friend and erstwhile collaborator James Madison, the ablest and most powerful man in the House of Representatives. The second, of which he was less confident, was that the treasury must be under the control of a single person with ample powers—unlike, for example, the impotent three-

---

[39] Ibid., 126.

[40] Ibid., 392n18.

[41] See McDonald, *Hamilton*, 128; Nathan Schachner, "Alexander Hamilton Viewed by His Friends: The Narratives of Robert Troup and Hercules Mulligan," *The William and Mary Quarterly*, Third Series 4/2 (Apr. 1947), 220.

man Treasury Board that had attempted to administer the Confederation's meager finances in 1784. The third, most important, and least certain condition was that the office must have some measure of independence from the executive and permit direct dealings with Congress.[42]

It would be the new creation by a centralized Congress of a position of power far beyond anything conceived in the Constitution, but nevertheless allowed under the guise of "all things necessary and proper." Hamilton positioned his bureaucracy of finance somewhere between the executive branch (to which it properly belonged), and the legislative branch. Since it had direct influence on legislation and direct oversight of the Congressional purse, Hamilton would be able to exercise some control loosed from Washington's leash.

This was just the type of Constitutional creativity Hamilton had always envisioned. Indeed, he would later refer to the Constitution as a "frail and worthless fabric" propped up by his own powers,[43] it was his own ingenuity and prowess which he trusted to force his agenda ahead. Thus,

> it was almost a matter of indifference to him how the national government was organized: what was important was to organize one and to endow it with as much power in relation to the powers of the states as possible. . . .
>
> [For,] if a strong national government could be established on almost any plan at all, and if he could become minister of finance, he could personally activate the government to "provide for the happiness of our country."[44]

By September 11, the position of minister of finance-was created according to Hamilton's specifications, and two days later, he was at work. He was soon immersed in financial arrangements with Holland and France, and sometimes

---

[42] McDonald, *Hamilton*, 128.

[43] In a letter to Goveurnor Morris, Feb. 27, 1802.

[44] McDonald, *Hamilton*, 96.

with no oversight from or knowledge of others. But the great gift came when Congress recessed for the fall: it requested a report from Hamilton on how to improve public credit. Hamilton presented the report when Congress returned in January, and it put in play one of Hamilton's long-term goals: Federal assumption of state debts.

The measure was essentially socialistic in that it would place an unequal burden on wealthier states to discharge these debts. Indeed, for some states that had already paid off large amounts of their debts, saddling with the arrears of their neighbors was criminal. But the poorer and the delinquent states were quite cheerful at the prospect; and it is no irony that this very scenario had been part of the Federalists' Constitutional ad campaign to those states. For just one example, Federalist William R. Davie tipped his socialist hand during the ratification debates in North Carolina, arguing,

> The whole proportion, of this state of the public debts . . . must be raised from the people by direct and immediate taxation. But the fact is, sir, it cannot be raised, because it cannot be paid; and *without sharing in the general impost, we shall never discharge our quota of the federal debt.*[45]

Hamilton's plan was strongly opposed by Madison and Jefferson. Nevertheless, in what must be the greatest political sellout of all time—in which is seen the shallowness, vanity, self-interest, and giddy exchange of principle for convenience—Hamilton was able to gain their vote in exchange for moving the U.S. Capitol to the Potomac River. Thus, in exchange for a guaranteed local influx of prestige and wealth from the capitol city, these men allowed the Federalist faction to centralize power over national finance. This was a classic example of "taking the cheese," and Hamilton was springing the trap.

---

[45] Jonathan Elliot, ed., *The Debates in the Several State Conventions on the Adoption of the Federal Constitution*, 5 vols. (Philadelphia: J. B. Lippincott Company, 1907), 4:238–239.

After this, came a systematic stream of reports and state papers from Hamilton to Congress. An increase in the Tariffs came in April, 1790. In December, Hamilton provided a second report on public credit, this time calling for a national bank—a proto-Federal Reserve. He finally won consent for it and it arrived in February, 1791. Hamilton had argued for the *necessity* of a national bank as early as April 30, 1781, in a letter to Robert Morris,[46] so he had to have been waiting, planning, and striving for this moment for a decade. In March of 1791, followed his call for a direct tax on liquors, which passed. This precipitated the tax-revolt known as the Whiskey Rebellion which Hamilton and Washington personally helped squash at the head of their newly centralized 13,000-man army. But before they could do this, they had to pass two Militia Acts of 1792, in order to empower the behemoth to conscript every able bodied male from 18 to 45, and then call them up at the President's when.[47] When not threatening otherwise innocent farmers from horseback, Hamilton and Washington furthered their collusion for protectionism and corporate welfare. The effort would result in Hamilton's Report on the Subject of Manufactures calling for regulation of trade via *more tariffs*, and direct subsidies to favored industries, corporations, and projects.[48]

Hamilton and Washington had this idea of corporate welfare in mind for some time. During that very first Congress, Washington addressed a joint session on January 8, 1790. His vision for America was—by comparison to the old decentralized Puritan ideals—a New Deal and War State wrapped into

---

[46] Hamilton to R. Morris, April 30, 1781, *PAH*, Syrett, ed., 2:620.

[47] By comparison, when Shays' Rebellion erupted over a truly corrupt taxation scheme, the governor was unable to muster more than a few hundred to fight for his corrupt cause. This, because the Constitution was not yet around and the national government could not yet commandeer the other state militias; and, the state militia was only voluntary; thus, as in a biblical system, when a potential soldier perceives a cause to be corrupt, he can refuse to fight. Not so much under Hamilton and Washington.

[48] See Stanley Elkins and Eric McKitrick, *The Age of Federalism* (New York: Oxford University Press, 1993), 258.

one. He urged the need "To be prepared for war," as "one of the most effectual means of preserving peace." Toward this end, he encouraged the Congress to "promote such manufactories as tend to render them independent on others for essential, particularly for military, supplies." This call was answered by Hamilton's Report on the subject. Note that it was a call not only to provide a government-funded stimulus plan for manufacturing, but especially to provide for it in regard to military supplies. Thus, Washington created the original military-industrial complex—*in peacetime.*

Not often recognized as a big-government big spender, Washington called for greater Federal control and spending on nearly everything you can imagine in that first-ever State of the Union address: manufacturing, military supplies, defense (particularly the "comfortable support of officers and soldiers"), Indian suppression, agriculture, commerce, transportation, post offices, science, and education, including a national university. And perhaps just in case the actual funds weren't there, he expressed strong "support for public credit." All this, he added, was for "the welfare of our country." It was the nation's first cutting of it's teeth on Welfare-Warfare Statism, and those teeth just happened to be, by legend, wooden. In reality, they were rotten.

Now don't get me wrong! My intention is not just to hammer on Washington. I mean, I love the fact that he went to church sometimes, and I love the pictures of him kneeling openly in prayer at Valley Forge—even though it's probably a piece of historical fiction. I just have to point out how much the centralized, subsidized, nationalized *everything* contradicts the basic freedoms espoused in the Declaration of Independence, and, well, the Bible. For, however sincerely he may have championed his faith, he did not extend it into all areas of life. As a result, he ended up with a form of tyranny. And the precedents of subsidy and regulation that he and Hamilton set, while different in *degree,* differ not at all in *principle* from the socialistic schemes we have today—and just the same, in the name of "welfare"!

It should not surprise us, then, when we see Marshall leg-islating Hamilton's state papers from the bench, that the view we get is one of gradual national tyranny over state and local freedoms. It was designed to impinge upon us from every branch of the national government until all of American life was ruled by a Hamilton-propped "worthless fabric."

In the light of Washington's New Deal, it should not surprise us to see that control especially extended over business, com-merce, and finance. Indeed, power over both the purse and the means of filling it were perhaps the most central aims of many of the Federalists. The Judiciary was the security blanket for these. Thus, more limitation on state powers came in 1824 when Mar-shall ruled against the State of New York in *Gibbons v. Ogden*. He struck down a shipping monopoly granted to a New York company operating between New York and New Jersey; this he did on grounds that Federal licensing statutes took precedence over state laws, and thus a state could not license monopolies for companies engaging in interstate commerce—an area expressly enumerated for the Federal government in the Constitution.

Of course this had been a design of the nationalists all along, as we've already witnessed. As Madison wrote to in 1821 to Joseph Gales, one of his true purposes at the Conven-tion: "was among other things to take from that State [New York] the important power over its commerce."[49]

Madison was thus quite open about his anti-state agenda. He later broke dramatically with Hamilton and helped author the Virginia Resolution of 1798—advocating the doctrine of interposition of states against intrusive Federal laws. But this, helpful as it may be conceptually, was too-little-too-late on Madison's part, especially when you consider the ambition with which he himself had earlier destroyed states' rights dur-ing the Constitutional settlement.

---

[49] James Madison to Joseph Gales, August 26, 1821, *The Records of the Federal Convention of 1787*, 3 vol., ed. by Max Farrand (New Haven: Yale University Press, 1911), 3:447.

While his writings contain many nuances, qualifications, and explanations—all ingenious—Madison gives us a simple enough explanation of the new government. It was designed as a means to bypass state laws and act directly on individuals within the states: "Hence was embraced the alternative of a Government which instead of operating, on the states, should operate without their intervention on the individuals composing them."[50]

Conclusion

What these men—indeed this Triumvirate of Washington, Hamilton, and Madison—accomplished was a "revolution in government" conceived of early by some men, including Hamilton, and designed for the express cause of assuming every power of the states (with few exceptions) by means of centralizing power in a type of *coup*. In an early letter to James Duane, Hamilton expressed his regret that "an excess of the spirit of liberty" left the states with too much freedom, and this must be remedied either by taking direct control of Congress and assuming authority over the states (which Hamilton believed Congress already had anyway), or by calling a Convention for the purpose of circumventing them.[51]

So, we have seen quite a bit now—probably more than you ever wanted to see—of how the original freedom of states' rights was lost. Couple this with the lessons of lost localism covered in the last chapter and the picture is pretty gruesome. But this is not where it has to end. We can recover a vision of decentralized government, even at the state level—one which is devoid of all the nineteenth century baggage of slavery, etc. We can recover the vision, and we can think of some practical steps toward restoring state freedom today.

---

[50] Madison to Jefferson, October 24, 1787.

[51] Hamilton to Duane, September 3, 1780, *PAH*, Syrett, ed., 2:401.

4.3 How to Get Freedom Back

If we are to discuss how to restore freedom in regard to states' rights, we have to make some acknowledgments and qualifications up front. Nevertheless, there is work we can do and which needs to be done.

Remember that this project focuses mainly on things average individuals can do to restore freedom in this country. We have already addressed those areas where we can have the most impact by far. These are education, welfare, and local government. Taking back control in these areas to the maximum extent possible must be the main priority. And much of what needs to take place in these three areas will keep the average family busy for years to come. If we can't accomplish anything here, we shouldn't expect to make any headway where the treading will be more difficult. Concentrating on issues above and beyond these—in both scope and governmental power—will only detract from the primary tasks for most people. As we shall quickly see, most of the steps that need to be taken in regard to states' rights will have to come at the level of state representatives, state assemblies, and above. There is simply no key we can turn, hand we can shake, organization we can join, or person we can vote in (should we be so lucky as to have such a "perfect" candidate), that will magically transform the nation into a states' rights paradise (should such a thing exist) overnight. With that said, however, there are still things average people can do toward restoring freedom in states' rights.

First, self-education is always in order. Just as with local government, most people don't even know the names of their state legislators. Learn who they are and everything about them. Learn their beliefs, platforms, and everything about their voting history. Learn about your state governmental system in all of its branches, departments, procedures. Why not learn some of its history while you're at it. (Do your state and local historical societies have museums? Check them out.)[52] You'll probably discover some interesting connections and notice a few wealthy families stretching from way back all the way to the seats of power today. Special interests tend to be homebrewed and inbred. At any rate, knowledge of your representatives, how the system works, various local and state laws, and what issues are on the floor or in queue are all part of this learning process.

Second, individuals should start websites monitoring state officials just as we described for local governments. These sites should be dedicated exclusively to state matters, and not mixed with either local or national political campaigns, etc.—except inasmuch as local or national political matters directly relate to state sovereignty, etc. The goal here is ultimate transparency. This is the ultimate form of education: revealing to people things they would not normally know or understand. It is also a great service to your fellow citizens. Most people have no clue about such things; they don't even think beyond the normal media and wouldn't know where and how to find important information even if they did consider it. You can provide an invaluable service with a state politics clearinghouse website. Since so few people will take the initiative on something like this, it could be the greatest contribution you can make to the cause of liberty, especially if you have the skills (not a whole lot required!) and time available to do it, and are looking for a way to contribute. It is almost imperative that you begin now.

Part of your own educational process will include learning the vast array of issues where states' rights can restore freedom. One of the best places to observe some of these, currently, is in the work being done by the Tenth Amendment Center (TAC). Now, this acknowledgement is not an unequiv-

---

[52] In my experience, state and local history (as well as state and local government) are not well-emphasized in public school curricula. Most students will graduate with little or no knowledge in these areas—to an even worse degree than in other areas. This means that such education is your responsibility.

ocal endorsement of that organization, but the work they are doing is in fact admirable in both scope and detail. They have drawn up model legislation for a host of issues which states can apply in their own jurisdictions. Consider just a few of the areas in which they are currently working:

- Nullification of Federal Health Care
- State control of state National Guards
- Freedom from Federal firearm regulations
- Protection of intrastate commerce
- Protection of local food and food commerce
- Protection from national ID (REAL ID, etc.)
- Protection from TSA offenses, etc.
- Nullification of unconstitutional legal tender laws
- Nullification of "Cap and Trade" and other EPA regulations
- State regulation of Federal tax collection and revenue
- "Sheriffs First" laws against unwarranted Federal policing activities
- Industrial hemp freedom acts

This is an impressive list, but the potential list is even longer. A move to *practically* nullify *Roe v. Wade* could be effected at the state level, and indeed has already been attempted at least once (it failed by an 11% margin, almost certainly due to a refusal to allow *any* exceptions at all, such as mother's life in danger, etc.). At any rate, it will be helpful to find your local chapter of TAC, and ask how you can help get the word out in your community.

TAC also works for issues that are controversial to some Christians—such as state control over marijuana laws. In defense, the issue here is not about personal stances on marijuana—medicinal or otherwise—but rather on *jurisdiction*. How does the U.S. Constitution apply to this issue? Many would argue it does not, and that acquiescing on this one Constitutional issue legitimizes Federal usurpations in all other areas not explicitly enumerated in the Constitution as well. After all, if we submit to the idea that the Constitutional interstate commerce clause applies to the regulation of marijuana *inside* the state, then that can be used as a precedent when the Feds move to regulate other commerce within the state. But whatever your position on this particular issue (and certainly we must account for our emotions in regard to "drug abuse"), it should not take away from the whole range of other issues TAC is addressing in favor of the Tenth Amendment and states' rights. It is vital that we not throw out the baby with the bathwater (if there's any bathwater to throw out at all). We will return to nullification momentarily.

Also, having learned about your state reps, you may discover that they themselves have little knowledge or ambition in regard to states' rights. And they will likely know nothing about the *potential* that state power offers for reclaiming freedom in the many areas just discussed. You could aid your fellow citizens by informing your state reps of these things, providing them with information to pursue these avenues. This is still part of the educational process, and it is something an average person can do toward advocating states' rights *well within the Constitutional bounds of the Tenth Amendment.*

From this point, then, we move from, "What can *I* do *now*," to "the way things ought to be." Beyond the immediate practical steps, in other words, there are larger goals—but these are *definite*, if lofty, goals for which to aim. Educating your reps is one thing, actually getting them to develop, introduce, and promote states' rights issues in Assembly is quite another. And it is here that individual efforts will be limited. But this should not stop us from discussing them.

Nullification and Interposition

The doctrine of "Nullification" was expressed by Thomas Jefferson in the Kentucky Resolutions of 1798. These resolutions were a reaction against John Adams' atrocious Alien and Sedition Acts which enhanced Federal deportation powers at the President's whim, and made criticism of the administration a criminal act. Jefferson and many others deemed these Acts unconstitutional and argued that when the Federal government passes unconstitutional acts, the states have a right to declare them null and void within their own jurisdictions. Jefferson wrote, "whensoever the general government assumes undelegated powers, its acts are unauthoritative, void, and of no force."[53] For this state power, the Resolutions appealed explicitly to the Tenth Amendment. Nullification, therefore, is a state's declaration that a Federal law exceeds Constitutional powers, and is thereby considered null and void within that state.

At the same time, Madison penned the Virginia Resolution (singular), which posited a similar notion now called "Interposition." The Virginia version exposited the same view of states' rights, although Madison did refer to it as not only a state's right but its "duty." In times of Federal tyranny, states are "in duty bound, to interpose, for arresting the progress of the evil." Some view this as going beyond mere nullification to active resistance. This does not seem to me to be a *necessary* implication of "arresting the progress of evil." A subsequent review by the Virginia legislature asserted that a state declaration could have no legal force upon the Federal government, but was only an expression of opinion, but even this leaves open the possibility that a state may decide in some way actively to resist—either alone, or in concert with other states.

At any rate, the idea of states resisting tyranny from legal lords above comes directly from the history of the Reformation theological social theory. Calvin (and Luther as well, although to

---

[53] Kentucky Resolution 1.

a lesser and less systematic extent) and his disciples developed the idea of the intervening "lesser magistrate" who resists impositions of tyranny from above.[54] It is a biblical and historically Christian concept in which a representative civil ruler acts on behalf of his constituents to uphold civil liberty against the evil of tyranny—this is the civil magistrate's job, after all (Rom. 13).

This is what, historically, the American Declaration of Independence was—an interposition of the colonies in concert against King George III. In this sense, we can speak of "interposition" in a more general way without having to accept all of the technical terminology that comes along with Madison's Resolution. We can also speak generally of nullification in the same way. We can even celebrate Jefferson's fabulous rhetoric in this regard without adopting every jot and tittle of the Kentucky Resolves. Therefore, "let no more be heard of confidence in man, but bind him down from mischief by the chains of the constitution," by which "man" Jefferson meant our civil rulers, and by which Constitutional "chains" he meant the Tenth Amendment.

Ending Abortion

So, what are some of those lofty goals at which state officials could aim? Aside from TAC's long and important list, perhaps the most important and powerful issue for Christians that can be addressed by state power is the abomination protected under *Roe v. Wade*. This was the subject of an informative lecture by Constitutional Lawyer Herb Titus, given at American Vision's annual conference in 2009: "Restoring the Sanctity of Human Life State by State." Without giving an exhaustive account of the arguments, suffice it to say that the Supreme Court decision contains holes that can be exploited, and, more importantly,

---

[54] See Douglas F. Kelley, *The Emergence of Liberty in the Modern World: The Influence of Calvin on Five Governments from the 16th Through the 18th Centuries* (Phillipsburg, NJ: P&R, 1992); and David W. Hall, *Calvin in the Public Square: Liberal Democracies, Rights, and Civil Liberties* (Phillipsburg, NJ: P&R, 2009).

rests on factual assumptions that are today disproven by more advanced knowledge. Therefore, a state could set a precedent with a well-designed, thoughtfully constructed statute which would effectively displace the ruling of *Roe v. Wade—even if the law itself remains on the books!*

Most Christians don't realize that the legal decision of *Roe v. Wade* had nothing to do with determining when life begins. This aspect of the situation was explicitly *not decided* in the case. As the writer of the opinion, Justice Blackmun, states:

> We need not resolve the difficult question of when life begins. When those trained in the respective disciplines of medicine, philosophy, and theology are unable to arrive at any consensus, the judiciary, at this point in the development of man's knowledge, is not in a position to speculate as to the answer.[55]

He went on to discuss different theories, but all this was superfluous to the overall decision. What this allowed the court to do, however, was subsequently forbid the states—on the the sole basis of the same inconclusive facts, by the way—from imposing any single view of the beginning of life upon citizens.

The decision was made based on that ingenious piece of Lincoln's legacy: the 14th Amendment, period. To whom do the Constitutional protections of life and privacy apply? The State of Texas (Wade) argued that a fetus is a "person" within the language of the 14th Amendment. The Supreme Court acknowledged, "If this suggestion of personhood is established, the appellant's case, of course, collapses, for the fetus' right to life would then be guaranteed specifically by the Amendment." The problem was, that Texas's application of that Amendment to the unborn was a novelty—there was nothing explicit in the Constitution saying this. There was absolutely no legal precedent for interpreting it that way,

---

[55] *Roe v. Wade*, 410 U.S. 113, 159 (1973); online at http://caselaw.lp.findlaw.com/cgi-bin/getcase.pl?court=us&vol=410&invol=113 (accessed Sept. 25, 2012).

and there was no historical precedent from the time of the Amendment for such an understanding. As such, the Court ruled this application of "person" to be unconstitutional. For the 14th Amendment itself clearly defines exactly who exactly are "citizens" and thus whose rights are protected: "All persons *born* or naturalized in the United States. . . ." There you have it: the Constitution protects only those who are *born*, not the unborn.[56] This, coupled with the other observations, led the Court to conclude, "the word 'person,' as used in the Fourteenth Amendment, does not include the unborn." Yet since the mother was in fact "born," she was protected: and thus the mother's right to life and privacy is all that was deemed to be left standing.[57] Thus, the famous decision hinged upon a technical argument over a definition, and the application of wording completely unheard-of and unforeseen by the people who wrote the Amendment.

Yet, as I said, the ruling is not airtight—not insurmountable. Even beyond what we have said already, yet another powerful approach is available to states. While the word "person" does not apply to the unborn according to the U.S. Constitution, there is nothing to prevent states from adopting Amendments to their State Constitutions which provide greater protection of life than the U.S. Constitution does. And the beauty of this approach is that the Supreme Court consistently defers to the State Constitution or State Court rulings in order to determine the definitions of state laws. Thus, in short, a state could define "person" to include the unborn, and for any laws passed in regard to that definition, the Supreme Court would abide by the state's

---

[56] A good argument could be made the other way, I think, but the language of the Amendment is in fact terribly unhelpful. On the surface of it, the idea that the Constitution protects the rights of only the "born" in the word "person" is like arguing that the Declaration's phrase "all men are created equal" and have the natural rights of "life, liberty, etc." only technically applies to *men* and not *women*. After all, it *says* "men."

[57] Although the Court did go on to allow for some state regulation in regard to the mother's health, etc.

definition for that case because it afforded a higher protection of life that the U.S. Constitution. Since the State of Texas did not have this in place at the time, its appeal to the 14[th]Amendment was judged by Federal precedents and the definitions derived from the U.S. Constitution alone, and thus, it lost.

If a state amended its Constitution, decided a case, or even perhaps passed a statute that properly expanded the protections of life to unborn persons, then any future Supreme Court challenge would have to deal with the state definition as a higher protection and sustain it. For this reason, there are currently groups advocating "Personhood Initiatives" and working for "Personhood Amendments." These are at both the state and national levels.

Christians in the right-to-life world simply have to learn that a decentralized solution is best and most likely to succeed. The strategy of a "once-for-all" reversal of *Roe* has been ineffective for almost forty years now. This is not to say it's an impossibility. But had the already spent time and money been focused on local solutions instead, we might very likely see life more properly protected in a vast array of states today, with the forces of infanticide pushed to the blue fringes of the nation. Those who will accept only a single, national solution to abortion are saying that, if they cannot outlaw abortion *everywhere*, then they don't want it outlawed *anywhere*. The corollary to this is even more startling: if they cannot *outlaw* abortion *everywhere*, then they'd prefer it to be *legal everywhere*. So the power and potential of a decentralized, states' rights approach should be evident to everyone. Indeed, it should immediately become *imperative* to everyone who cares about the right to life.

State officials who are interested in advancing these measures can seek them out and get involved. Individuals who wish to do what they can—"county rights" style—could get involved with their local and state-wide groups, ask for direction, volunteer their time, and inform any and all of their state representatives, Senators, and other officials of these causes.

Here, this applies directly to right-to-life issues, but it really applies to any of the Tenth Amendment issues already mentioned. Contact the offices of your local and state officials. Ask around. Search the web for groups or local committees involved in whatever states' rights issues you feel most strongly about. Find out what's already being done, and if you find the work worth joining, then get to it. At the very least, you should find worthy causes or groups and support them with donations. If you don't think you have any time to spare, or nothing else to contribute (which is almost certainly false), then give money. The causes of life and liberty can employ your $25/mo. better than a movie channel or dinner at Applebee's this week. But volunteering your skills and time is even better yet.

5. Taxation

We have now laid out the fundamental shape of decentralized government as it ought to be. The county should be fundamental, and people should have to deal with no government official other than their county officials, with perhaps limited exceptions for state elections, etc. This is nowhere more true than with that most hated of all ancient evils—taxation.

Taxation in a Freer America

What we have been demonstrating—based on biblical and historically Christian ideas, as well as their implementation in much of Western history—is the power that true federalism has for restoring and protecting freedom. In theory, in a truly federal system, the National government should govern only states, state governments should govern only counties, and county governments alone should govern individuals (and where there are smaller units below counties, such as townships, towns, cities, etc., then the principle of federalism should extend that much further).

In regard to taxation, true federalism means the National government should have *no power* to tax individuals. The only agency—if any—that should have any authority to tax individuals is the smallest, most local, nearest jurisdiction to that individual. No jurisdiction above that should be able to touch the individual directly unless through that individual's consent. Instead, if higher governments desire to raise revenue through taxation, they should be forced to deal with only the next level of government below them. In other words, the Feds could tax only states, states could tax only counties, and only counties could tax citizens (or municipalities where applicable).

None of this, however, is to justify taxation in general. Ideally, there would be none, and public services would be much more like private services, if not in fact private services. Police and fire services are essentially insurance services for the protection of property, and could be paid for in a very similar way—privately. Public water and sewer services are often already paid in this way, so are some ambulance and EMT services (at least in part); there is no reason police and fire could not be similarly provided for. Even the court system could be improved through greater proliferation and even dominance of private courts. There is very little reason that most currently public services should require taxation in order to exist and function effectively.[1]

But if taxes must exist, they should be as decentralized as possible. Only the most local municipality should have power to tax the individual. Counties must protect their people from the reach of state taxes. They should act in concert, represented at the state level *as counties*, to create a government and tax barrier between individuals and the state. Then, if the state absolutely needs revenue, it must work with the counties in concert in order to arrive at an acceptable level. Thus, county representatives will be negotiating how much of their budgets they shall agree to pro-vide to the state for its services. To the degree that local citizens have control in their counties and are adequately represented in the state assembly, you can be sure that they will not want much of their county's budget to be handed over to the state—nothing beyond necessity. This will strictly limit state power.

The same delicate negotiating balance should also exist between the national government and the states represented in concert (this is one reason the 17th Amendment should be

---

[1] See Gary DeMar, "Financing the Responsibilities of the State," Chapter 16 of *God and Government: A Biblical, Historical, and Constitutional Perspective* (Powder Springs, GA: American Vision, Inc., 2011), 307–329.

repealed).[2] States, being squeezed by the local interests and bargaining power of their counties, will naturally (and rightly) wish to guard their limited revenue from Federal encroachment. This will create pressure against the taxing desires of the national government, and will thus keep its powers limited to that degree—preferably funding only the bare necessities of government, whatever those may be.

Constitutionally speaking, the states have an added bargaining chip. The Feds are allowed—and the states forbidden—to collect duties on exports and imports. Thus the National government already has a unique and exclusive source of revenue, and should not need much if any taxation upon member states. States can point to this as one more reason to deny further Federal taxation.

Taxation in the Bible

What type of tax is best? There is no biblical law regarding any taxation for civil government. This leads me to believe there should be none. Nevertheless, we are given the ecclesiastical precedents of the tithes as a model for which *type* of taxation is best, in the event that a sinful society demands one. There were only two types specified by law: a tithe on increase of produce, and a small flat head tax. The particular flat tax specified in Exodus 30:11–16, however, was explicitly *priestly* in nature, and was paid exclusively by males over 20 years old who were numbered in the army. It was specifically called "ransom money" to protect the lives of God's holy soldiers. It was specifically for atonement. It was collected only when an army was raised for battle. It was not intended to function as a general stream of revenue, and it should thus not be looked to as a good model for civil taxation.[3]

---

[2] See "Appendix: Repeal the Seventeenth Amendment" in this volume, page 391.

[3] Gary North, *Tools of Dominion: The Case Laws of Exodus* (Tyler, TX: Institute for Christian Economics, 1997), 903–912.

The other type seems more suited for the purpose of general revenue: this was the general tithe on an increase of produce. The tithe was ten percent and was payable after harvest at a central location during the appropriate semi-annual festival. It could be paid in produce itself or in monetary form, depending on the taxpayer's preference (Lev. 27:30–33; Deut. 14:22–29). In a modern monetary economy, we would simply call this an income tax. In Deuteronomy, the ten percent was God's requirement for the ecclesiastical institution—not the civil State. The funds were to be used for feasting and making merry, as well as taking care of the widows and fatherless, and the priests and Levites.

Thus, welfare was an ecclesiastical function as well. The Bible gives no such ten-percent stipulation for the civil government. It in fact gives *no percentage at all* for civil government. Yet when Samuel warns the Israelites against the adoption of a king "like other nations" (1 Sam. 8), he spells out the tyranny that would follow. Among the list of confiscations and enslavements to come, Samuel warns that such a king will "take the tenth of your grain and of your vineyards . . . the tenth of your flocks, and you shall be his slaves" (1 Sam. 8:15–17). In other words, when the civil government assumed the right to a ten percent income tax, this evidenced an absolute, unimaginable tyranny equivalent to outright slavery. For when the civil ruler assumes the right to extract as much as God Himself demands, then the civil government is exalting itself above God—saying essentially that its work is more important than the work of God Himself. Thus, while there is no explicit number in Scripture for civil taxes, Samuel certainly indicates that a ten percent income tax has *already* far exceeded the maximum for a free society. At this point, don't call it taxation—call it slavery to the State.

Hardly any Western nation on earth today has a total tax burden below thirty percent (a couple are slightly below, several are over forty percent).[4] This means that nearly every Western nation today needs to slash its tax burden by at least sixty-six percent just in order to return to Samuel's standard of *tyrannical slavery.*

One problem with allowing an income tax, however, is the need for accurately reporting income. This is not an issue with the ecclesiastical tithe, for God allowed no legal enforcement of the tithe. Thus the Church must depend on the free giving and honesty of her members.[5] The State, however, will use legal coercion to extract its duties. Thus, if taxation is based on a percentage of income, it will require reporting of income to make sure it is getting its demanded percentage accurately. To eliminate this requirement, several measures could be taken— all of them undesirable to someone. First, the State could rely on honesty and non-reporting like the Church does. In this case, revenues would certainly *plummet,* just as the Church receives nowhere near the ten percent it is due. Voluntary disclosure would have similar results. Fraud would be rampant. The civil government could require an accurate income statement as qualification to vote. This would disenfranchise many people, especially those who are generally honest and upstanding, but place a high value on personal privacy. (It's also unconstitutional at this point.) There seems to be no good way around this problem, if an income tax is desired.

A property tax is not only problematic, but is not permitted in Scripture, and should in fact be considered unbiblical. Only God has absolute ownership of property; He delegated this to individuals, and gave us a commandment against property theft in all forms.[6] God did not give the civil State any claim of ownership on an individuals' land. It has none, and for it to claim such

---

[4] Also, these are revenues *as a percentage of GPD.* Results for individuals can range from around ten percent total to well over fifty in the U.S.

[5] Proof of paying tithes ought to be considered, however, as a qualification to vote in church elections, especially for financial decisions.

[6] Exod. 20:15; Lev. 19:11, 13; Deut. 19:14; 27:17; Prov. 22:28; 23:10.

a right is to defy God. And what is a property tax except a claim of partial ownership in the land? It is a system of feudal tenure in which the State claims a percentage of the value of your property, yearly, in exchange for the privilege of living on land in its particular jurisdiction. While this type of tax has deep historical roots, it is also deeply unbiblical. And though this tax has historically been collected and spent at the county level—thus demonstrating how the County historically was the fundamental unit of governmental authority in this country—it is nevertheless an unbiblical *form* of taxation and should be replaced with a better form in every place in which it is practiced.

A sales tax seems to be the least intrusive form of taxation on the surface of it. It is enacted not on ownership or income, but only on exchange. Thus it is extracted piecemeal. This means there is never a large tax surprise at the end of the year. As a tax only on voluntary purchases, it gives people an incentive to save as much of their money as possible if they wish to avoid taxation. One problem, however, is that to the extent we have to buy a certain amount of basic necessities, a sales tax places a greater necessary burden on the lower classes than the upper. Of course, it is assumes that wealthier people will indeed spend more and thus pay more in sales tax, but they are certainly not obligated to by necessity. If it is a valid consideration that there is a basic set of human needs most people must purchase *of necessity*, then a sales tax does indeed hit the poor harder. For this reason, many states and municipalities do not assess sales tax on basic food stuffs and some other groceries. Secondly, while the sales tax seems fairly unobtrusive from the shopper's perspective, it requires the business to keep records of all sales and submit accurate reports along with a collective sales tax payment. This additional bookkeeping and reporting creates the same problems for businesses that an income tax creates for individuals. It is also additional and unnecessary expense added to the cost of doing business.

There seems to be no good form of taxation compatible with preserving the inviolability of person, income, or property. Taxation seems to be an inherent compromise of life, liberty, property, and the pursuit of happiness. I believe this is why the Bible prescribes no method for civil taxation: because taxation for the support of civil government is inherently at odds with the type of freedom God desires us to have. The very idea of empowering the coercive arm of society to fund itself by means of its own coercive arm seems at best a recipe for corruption, if not enslavement. If it is fundamental folly to put the power of the purse and the power of the sword in the same hands, then our means of funding the administration of justice in society needs to be radically rethought.

Taxation will always require some degree of servitude. To the extent that it does—and it will vary from time to time and place to place—it means we are not free people, not a free society. To the extent that we must tolerate taxation as Christians—as our inspired writers have told us to (Rom. 13:7; 1 Pet. 2:13–17)—we admit that sin has a grip on society, both among the people and the officials. We must strive to reach a society in which the protections of person and property are ensured through voluntary means. I believe the silence of the Bible on the method and form of civil taxation was deliberate because no method could be prescribed in accordance with God's design for society—even in a sinful world—which would not itself involve some amount of sin.

What principles, then, can we glean from Scripture in order best to rein in taxation? *First*, it should be based on a fixed percentage. The tithe was ten percent for everyone. A graduated percentage is unbiblical and thus unjust—the rich should not pay a greater percentage than the poor, as they are forced to do now. *Second*, the fixed percentage should be nowhere near as much as ten percent total. Ten percent should be an indicator to us all that we are squarely in the grip of tyranny. Social repentance and a return to individual responsibility are in order. *Third*, the only biblical model for a method of taxation is on *income*. Other forms of taxation either have no biblical precedent at all, or run directly against biblical principles of property.

The Right Form of Taxation

Based on these criteria and what has already been established: if we are to suffer the evil of taxation for civil government, it should take only the following form: 1) local governments and local governments alone should tax individuals, 2) only on net income, 3) well under a total of ten percent, and 4) only for the bare necessities required to administer justice. The same principles should apply at each level in the federal system: the taxes collected by counties should be viewed as income, and taxed well under ten percent by states. The totality of revenue collected this way from all counties by the state should be considered the state's income. The Federal government should tax the income of the states for its services, but only well under ten percent.

This system would mean: 1) no individual would ever suffer greater taxation than what occurred at their local county level, and 2) at least ninety percent of your tax dollars would stay in your local community (only a maximum of nine percent would stay at the state level, and one percent to the national level).

For example, the average household income in the U.S. is about $45,000 annually. In today's mad system of taxation, a couple filing jointly will pay roughly 13% in Federal income tax (25% if not married), and (in my state of Georgia) 6% in state income tax. They will also pay their half of Social Security and Medicare (the employer pays the other half), 6.2% for social security and 1.45% for Medicare. (If the earner is self-employed, he or she is liable to *both* halves, and thus 12.4% and 2.9% respectively.) When the order of taxes and all the brackets are considered, the total tax burden here is at least 22.13%.

This does not include the sales taxes we pay, taxes on imported items, increased prices due to government regulations, the hidden tax of inflation, so-called "sin taxes" on tobacco and alcohol, and sundry luxury taxes. Plus, an average American pays roughly 1% to 2% of assessed property value in property taxes. With average home prices around $175,000 in the U.S., just a low 1% property tax rate would mean an additional bill of $1,750. That's an additional 3.88% of yearly income. Including this conservative property tax number raises our former total to 26.01%—a loss of $11,700 in income annually for the *average* couple.

Consider, in contrast, my proposed "biblical" federal model. Let's assume an almost worse-case of 9%—almost to the 10% tyranny threshold— at each level of government. In such a case, the same household would surrender 9% of its earnings to the local government—that's $4,050. He would pay nothing else in taxes. The state would then extract 9% from the county level—$364.50 in this case. The Feds, extracting 9% of state revenue, would get only $32.81 of this one person's contribution.

In the current scenario, people are taxed directly by every level of government for purposes that often conflict with their values, and in a manner about which they have no say. In a free society, people are accountable to only one agency, only at the local level where they can be most accurately represented, and their money is spent mostly in that particular public square. *And even in the worst-case scenario, it costs them far less than half of what they pay under the current scheme.*

Taxes in Colonial America

Decentralization and low taxes are not only good theory, they're more originally American, too. It's closer to the way America used to be. In colonial days, before the Constitution, there was no taxation from a central National government. When the central government (Britain) attempted to impose centralized taxation, it set in motion a series of tax revolts that culminated in the Declaration of Independence—a document which condemned King George III and Parliament, among many other grievances, "For imposing Taxes on us without our Consent."

This is a very general truth, however. This is not to say that the colonies were a tax haven, although taxes were generally lower than anywhere else throughout the British Empire at the time. Nevertheless, there were very many taxes of various types, and they were implemented variously in every colony throughout the period from colonization to the Declaration. There were poll taxes, land taxes, "collective mass of property" taxes, all-livestock taxes, specific taxes on horses and cattle, taxes on stocks, taxes on cash investments, house taxes, slave taxes, and carriage taxes.[7] Only one colony, North Carolina, implemented as few as three of these ten types of taxation during this time; most employed between four and six. So the colonies were not shy about implementing taxes.

Taxes, though various in type, were generally very low. For example, Virginia instituted a poll tax as early as 1619. The yearly tax was one pound of tobacco per male person over sixteen years old. This was about one day's wages for a common laborer.[8] (Compare this to the full 26% described above for *today*, which means the government gets over *three months* worth of the average family's wages.) In the midst of a financial strain, Virginia took on debt. In a few years, the tax was 10 pounds of tobacco. By 1644, it was as high as 18 pounds per male head.[9] Even at this extreme point, the 18-pound tax represented less that 7% of yearly income for a common laborer— the lower classes. It would thus have been much less for a professional of any sort. For a schoolmaster in 1651 making £30 per year, 18 pounds of tobacco would have equaled only 4.5% tax on his income.[10]

---

[7] Robert M. Kozub, "Antecedents to the Income Tax in Colonial America," *The Accounting Historians Journal* 10/2 (Fall 1983): 101.

[8] Based on stats in William B. Weeden, *Economic and Social History of New England, 1620–1789*, 2 vol. (New York: Hillary House Publishers, 1963), 880.

[9] Kozub, "Antecendents," 103.

[10] Weeden, *Economic and Social History*, 881.

Again, this is only one of various taxes to which different people at different times were liable. But these rarely over-lapped, and when they did, they still did not amount to a great collective burden. Overall, the burden to which any person at any given time was subject was very low, especially by today's standards. It was also low in comparison to the tax burdens of the rest of the British Empire at the time. This is why George III chose the American colonies as the place to raise taxes to begin with.

And again, when Britain tried to impose a tax from the central government in addition to these colonial (state) taxes, the colonists resisted and ultimately revolted. The Boston Tea Party was thrown as a result of Britain's "Townshend Acts" of 1767 and the Tea Act of 1773 which had levied a tax on several imports, including tea, and created a government-enforced monopoly on tea. The tax on tea was uncomfortable but not exorbitant by today's standards—8.33% (3 pence per pound when tea was selling at 3 shillings (36 pence) per pound). Con-sider that this was a tax on a single product which was used mostly by the upper and upper-middle classes. This was not a universal sales or import tax. Today, several *states* allow sales taxes on *most* goods at rates higher than the single-product 8.33% for which our ancestors rebelled and shed their blood. Meanwhile, the total per capita tax burden in the colonies was significantly less—only two to four percent—of what was being levied in Britain.[11] And the colonists said, "We would rather die."

Of course, consider the wisdom of the British bureau-crats—imposing taxes on the most outspoken and able peo-ple in the colonies. The Stamp Act of 1765 levied taxes on all printed materials, thereby enraging every minister, lawyer, publisher, and politician in the hemisphere. Then the Townsh-end Acts taxed their tea—a commodity indulged in mostly by

---

[11] Ben Baack, "The Economics of the American Revolutionary War," February 5, 2010, EH.net (accessed Sept. 22, 2011).

the wives of the aforesaid classes. Now you've got disgruntled lawyers with the added aggravation of their annoyed wives nagging them! Then to add insult of intelligence to the original insult, the British imposed a monopoly on the tea with the Tea Act. So the British succeeded in enraging the classes of people most self-interested and most able to rouse the masses against the British: the preachers, the lawyers, and their wives! That would be about as smart as levying a tax on lobbyists, liquor, and prostitution in modern-day Washington, D.C. You would see an immediate tax revolt from the vast majority before you could say "Washington Monument"!

Well, enough has been said so far to demonstrate the point: a biblical view of taxation is greatly decentralized, based on only a fixed percentage, and assessed exclusively on an increase in income. Even this is not fully in line with God's ideal of only voluntary services, and thus, taxation can only be described as a very questionable, necessary evil. And taxation to pay for civil government should always be well less than ten percent of net income annually. And it should only go to local governments. Higher levels must wrangle and negotiate with the more fundamental, local units for their services. Beyond this is to prescribe tyranny. In other words, we live in a tyranny now.

I say it's time for another tea party. Throw off the taxes. Assert fundamental rights and local sovereignty.

How Freedom was Lost

There is that old and reliable indicator of when a politician is lying: his mouth is open. There is, however, an exception to this rule: when he's talking about raising taxes. Then you can trust his announcements.

For this reason, it is no surprise that the word "tariff" derives from an old Arabic root meaning "announcement." It was assumed that any government "announcement" was going to cost you something. Eventually, the word referred to officially-published lists of customs duties throughout the shipping world. So traditionally, a tariff is a tax on imports or exports. In the U.S., tariffs can be levied Constitutionally only on imports.

"Tax" is more general. It comes from the Latin word *tax-are* which means "to handle," in the sense of "examine personally for the purpose of assessment"—a euphemism for "invade one's privacy." *Taxare* is likely a form of the Latin *tangere* which means "to touch," as in "touch what ain't yours." Thus, the taxman first invades someone's privacy, then takes his property. The taxman's "touch" should be considered equivalent to a TSA "enhanced patdown." The latter has his hand firmly on your inseam, the other firmly in your pocket. One takes your dignity, the other your substance. It's government as usual.

The "hand in your pocket" image should be the official logo of the IRS and the SSA, although, granted, the eagle they both use now is even better: the eagle first *spies* its prey, then *grasps* it, then *flies off with it*, and then *consumes it*.

As I said already, taxation in this land used to be extremely low—low even by the standards of the time, microscopic compared to today. Yet, while taxes were very minimal, there never was a time when we actually were "free" in regard to taxation. So, this section is not quite exactly "How freedom was lost." Nevertheless, it is close enough—as they say—for government work (what's good for the goose...).

Before we begin in earnest, let me say that the history of taxation in this country (in virtually any country) is almost inseparable from that country's history of war. The taxes and tariffs that helped spark the American Revolution, for example, were George III's attempt to pay off his war debts from the previous French and Indian War debacle. And since we're talking about sovereign debt, the story is also inseparable from central banking. We have separate chapters for both finance and war later in this book. For now, know that the whole picture of taxation—though gruesome in itself—is without context unless we factor in both wars and central banking.

It is obviously no revelation that our historically-low levels of taxation—"not quite freedom"—were lost, but it will surprise many readers just how quickly and systematically they were lost. For example, as I said before, the revolutionary sentiments were raised in response to the Townshend Acts of 1767. These were a second attempt, after the failed Stamp Act, to raise revenues in the American colonies. The duties imposed were resisted and ultimately repealed on everything except tea, leading to the Tea Act of 1773 and then the Boston Tea Party. So, for the principle of self-government, no doubt, but for the specific case of an 8.33% import tax on tea, American colonists were willing to fight and die if necessary. The irony here is that the Tea Act *lifted* tariffs paid by the British East India Company. These were far higher than what the colonists paid, and thus the Tea Act actually dropped the price of tea significantly for the colonies overall. But they still hated the tax. "No taxation without representation!" "Liberty or death!"

Taxation and the Constitution

The Continental Congress struggled trying to get the states to raise revenues to pay off the debts of their War for Independence—again, war debts. After several failed attempts, the delegates were convened in Philadelphia, and the deed we have referred to so much already was done—the Constitution was written. I have already discussed how the opponents of that move created a public outcry over the centralization of powers—and one of the most crucial of those decried powers was taxation. Recalling those previously rehearsed comments and warnings, my short answer to the question of how freedom in taxation was lost is simple: the Constitution.

Let's just do a quick comparison. Americans were willing to shed their blood to fight off Britain over a very moderate tax on *one* item. Even the Townshend Acts had placed duties on just a few items—imported paper, paint, lead, glass. In other words, George III tried to impose *very limited* taxes to pay off war debts—*and Americans revolted.*

After the Constitution, however, Congress (led by Hamilton's designs) immediately raised tariffs on their countrymen—again in order to pay off war debts—but this would be beyond anything the people could have imagined under Britain. Here's the list (pardon the length!) of items taxed from five to ten percent (more in some cases) under the first Hamilton Tariff of 1789. There were duties

- On all distilled spirits of Jamaica proof, imported from any kingdom or country whatsoever, per gallon, ten cents.
- On all other distilled spirits, per gallon, eight cents.
- On molasses, per gallon, two and a half cents.
- On Madeira wine, per gallon, eighteen cents.
- On all other wines, per gallon, ten cents.
- On every gallon of beer, ale or porter in casks, five cents.
- On all cider, beer, ale or porter in bottles, per dozen, twenty cents.
- On malt, per bushel, ten cents.
- On brown sugars, per pound, one cent.
- On loaf sugars, per pound, three cents.
- On all other sugars, per pound, one and a half cents.
- On coffee, per pound, two and a half cents.
- On cocoa, per pound, one cent.
- On all candles of tallow, per pound, two cents.
- On all candles of wax or spermaceti, per pound, six cents.
- On cheese, per pound, four cents.
- On soap, per pound, two cents.
- On boots, per pair, fifty cents.
- On all shoes, slippers or galoshes made of leather, per pair, seven cents.
- On all shoes or slippers made of silk or stuff, per pair, ten cents.
- On cables, for every one hundred and twelve pounds,

seventy-five cents.

- On tarred cordage, for every one hundred and twelve pounds, seventy-five cents.
- On untarred ditto, and yarn, for every one hundred and twelve pounds, ninety cents.
- On twine or packthread, for every one hundred and twelve pounds, two hundred cents.
- On all steel unwrought, for every one hundred and twelve pounds, fifty-six cents.
- On all nails and spikes, per pound, one cent.
- On salt, per bushel, six cents.
- On manufactured tobacco, per pound, six cents.
- On snuff, per pound, ten cents.
- On indigo, per pound, sixteen cents.
- On wool and cotton cards, per dozen, fifty cents.
- On coal, per bushel, two cents.
- On pickled fish, per barrel, seventy-five cents.
- On dried fish, per quintal, fifty cents.
- On teas imported from India or China. On all teas imported from China or India, in ships built in the United States, and belonging to a citizen or citizens thereof, or in ships or vessels built in foreign countries, and on the sixteenth day of May last wholly the property of a citizen or citizens of the United States, and so continuing until the time of importation, as follows:
  - On bohea tea, per pound, six cents.
  - On all souchong, or other black teas, per pound, ten cents.
  - On all hyson teas, per pound, twenty cents.
  - On all other green teas, per pound, twelve cents.
- On teas imported from Europe. On all teas imported from Europe in ships or vessels built in the United States, and belonging wholly to a citizen or citizens thereof, or in ships or vessels built in foreign countries, and on the sixteenth day of May last wholly the property of a citizen or citizens of the United States, and so continuing until the time of importation, as follows:
  - On bohea tea, per pound, eight cents.

- On all souchong, and other black teas, per pound, thirteen cents.
- On all hyson teas, per pound, twenty-six cents.
- On all other green teas, per pound, sixteen cents.
- On all teas imported, in any other manner than as above mentioned, as follows:—
- On bohea tea, per pound, fifteen cents.
- On all souchong, or other black teas, per pound, twenty-two cents.
- On all hyson teas, per pound, forty-five cents.
- On all other green teas, per pound, twenty-seven cents.
- On all other goods imported from India or China, 12 1/2 per centum ad valorem. On all goods, wares and merchandises, other than teas, imported from China or India, in ships not built in the United States, and not wholly the property of a citizen or citizens thereof, nor in vessels built in foreign countries, and on the sixteenth day of May last wholly the property of a citizen or citizens of the United States, and so continuing until the time of importation, twelve and a half per centum ad valorem.
- On other enumerated articles, 10 per centum ad valorem.
- On all looking-glasses, window, and other glass (except black quart bottles),
- On all China, stone, and earthen ware,
- On gunpowder,
- On all paints ground in oil,
- On shoe and knee buckles,
- On gold and silver lace, and
- On gold and silver leaf,
- On other enumerated articles, 7 1/2 per centum ad valorem.
- On all blank books,
- On all writing, printing or wrapping paper, paper-hangings and pasteboard,
- On all cabinet wares,

- On all buttons,
- On all saddles,
- On all gloves of leather,
- On all hats of beaver, fur, wool, or mixture of either,
- On all millinery ready made,
- On all castings of iron, and upon slit and rolled iron,
- On all leather tanned or tawed, and all manufacture of leather, except such as shall be otherwise rated,
- On canes, walking sticks, and whips,
- On clothing ready made,
- On all brushes,
- On gold, silver, and plated ware, and on jewelry and paste work,
- On anchors, and on all wrought, tin, and pewter ware,
- On playing cards, per pack, ten cents.
- On every coach, chariot, or other four wheel carriage, and on every chaise, solo, or other two wheel carriage, or parts thereof,
- On all other goods, except certain articles, 5 per centum on the value at the time and place of importation.
- On all other goods, wares and merchandise, five per centum on the value thereof at the time and place of importation. . . . [there is more!]

Now that's quite an oppressive list. George III's tyranny was mild in comparison to Congress's and Hamilton's. But this was just a beginning. Within a year, they increased the rates in some cases by a factor of two or even three. Then they did it again in 1792.

Tariffs ultimately became the grounds for a divisive conflict between northern manufacturing and southern agriculture—and the political battle led to the Civil War.

At the same time, Congress began levying excise taxes— taxes on specific domestic items. The first of these came with the "Whiskey Act" of 1791—a tax on all domestically distilled spirits. This led to rural producers revolting in the so-called Whiskey Rebellion—a tax revolt not much different than the

Tea Party and other tax revolts against Britain before the revolution. But this time, instead of having their Continental government behind them, and the option of calling militias from other states to *choose* whether or not to fight and on what side, the rebels watched their government conscript an army of 13,000 men to be used against them. Washington and Hamilton—reliving the old glory days on the battlefield—personally led the charge on horseback.

So the American government almost immediately became a tyranny measurably many times worse than Britain herself would have ever considered. Taxation *with* representation did not look as great up close as it had at a distance.

And *then*, things got really bad. How was the freedom lost, you ask? It was lost with those Hamilton Tariffs of 1789, 1790, and 1792. It was lost with the Whiskey Tax of 1791. It was lost with the excise taxes raised to offset the loss in tariff revenue during the War of 1812. It was lost with the Tariffs of 1816 (raised to pay off the debts of the War of 1812). It was lost with the protectionist Tariff of 1824, and its sister Act in 1828—the "Abomination"—which raised the rates. It was lost with the Morrill Tariff in 1861. This established the highest rates in U.S. history, and set a precedent that reigned until Woodrow Wilson.

It was lost with the first income tax in 1861, and again in 1862. The Confederacy did the same thing in 1863. Income tax was a bipartisan (Northern and Southern) abuse. This lasted for ten years. After a landmark Supreme Court case in 1895, blanket income taxes were considered unconstitutional. Congress sulked. Wait! No problem! Just pass an *Amendment* to the Constitution!

It was lost then again in 1913 with the Sixteenth Amendment and the Revenue Act of 1913. This measure was championed by progressives of both the Democrat and Republican stripe. Since that time, the income tax brackets have been monkeyed with a few dozen times: the lowest tax bracket has not dipped below 10% since 1933. The most exorbitant has reached as high as 92%, though is currently at 35% due to the "Bush tax cuts."

It was lost during and immediately after the Civil War in a series of excise taxes on, again, liquor. This led to the whole legacy of ridge-runners, moonshiners, and their enemies, the revenuers. This led also to the creation of two agencies involved, respectively, with alcohol and the taxation of it— the ATF and the IRS. It was lost as Federal excise taxes today persist on alcohol, tobacco, firearms, tanning, fuel sources, gas *mileage*, coal, phone line usage, trucking, vaccines, water transportation, fishing gear, harbor maintenance, airline tickets, jet fuel, and tires.

It was lost when FDR invented "Social Security." It was lost as Social Security taxes have been raised *20 times* since 1933 to keep propping up the failed socialistic system (beginning at 1%, and reaching to 6.2% today). It was lost when LBJ piggy-backed Medicare onto Social Security in 1965. The result meant *another* payroll tax on top of Social Security. It was lost as Medicare taxes have been raised *eight times* since 1965— beginning at the promised 0.35%, and ending at 1.45% today, an increase of 414%.

And this is considering only *Federal taxes*. Local and especially state governments impose their own versions of these same taxes in conjunction with the Feds. In "total tax burden" per nation considered as a "percentage of GDP," the U.S. comes in high among western nations with just under a 30% total tax burden. But this is misleading in only regarding *income taxes*. This does not consider Social Security and Medicare, as well as state, Federal, and local taxes of every stripe. Including these would send the American percentage much, much higher (to say nothing of the total in other countries).

How was the freedom lost? It was lost for many reasons in many phases. We trusted the Federal government. We have trusted all levels of government to treat us well. They have instead raped us financially. From 1789 until today, we have watched as Washington has gradually taken our money and spent it on frivolities and money pits.

Need we say more? We had something close to freedom in taxation—as much as it could be called freedom. It was lost. And, it was lost decisively in the areas of income, and public choice in schooling, hospitals, and much more. There is no doubt taxes are not only too high, they are out of control. The question is, of course, how do we get it back?

How to Slash Taxes

We have now seen how taxes used to be very low in this nation. We have seen—enough anyway—how that has changed over time. In an earlier section we talked about the "ratchet effect" in the size and power of government. The people cede gradual increments here and there until one day the chains of government are tightened to the point we can't breathe. This is nowhere more evident in American history than in the area of taxation. The question is, can we loosen the screws? Better yet, who's got the bolt cutters?

First let's discuss what needs to be done. Then we will discuss what practical things we can do to help advance the cause of liberty in taxation. What needs to be done? Let me explain the real problem first. If you can grasp this problem, you can get very close to the heart of the loss of freedom in America.

Taxation is the wicked step-sister of spending. They are quite a tandem, let me tell you. Politicians love to promise low taxes, but they rarely talk seriously about cutting spending. Without cuts in spending, there has to be either further taxation or increased debt. There is no other way to get around this. What needs to be done is a drastic cut in unnecessary public spending (most of it), and simultaneously a drastic cut in taxation to match.

While most attention is focused on the national debt, defi-
cits, "debt ceilings," and the specter of spending cuts—and
all for good reason, as these are all important issues—local
spending and waste gets much less emphasis, even by those
people who follow politics closely. But billions of dollars are
wasted unnecessarily all over other nation in local governments, and most of this could be cut and taxes lowered. Local
spending must be attacked and subdued. And if we can't organize to stop the waste locally, if we can't impose some fiscal
discipline and even sacrifice locally, you can forget it at the
state or national levels where the booty is greater by a factor of
a thousand and the entrenched forces greater as well. Indeed,
the local graft often provides the training ground for those
who rise to positions of state and Federal power later.

Cutting Local Taxes

I just checked my local county commission's minutes from
the latest bi-weekly meeting. This was a random check. There
was nothing special about this meeting; it was rather low-
key. And yet, in this one meeting, the commission stamped
$219,000 in new contracts and $59,000 extra for two existing
contracts. Now, in terms of county budgets, a few hundred
thousand is not much. But consider that 1) the board meets
some twenty-five times or more per year, 2) that these are
arguably not *necessary* public expenses, 3) that there are other
projects going on (also arguably unnecessary) which have a
price tag of tens of millions, 4) that we are still living with the
effects of a great recession and on the precipice of a new one,
5) that the money has to come from taxation in some way, 6)
that much of the tax money goes to contractors from outside
the county, and 7) that the decisions to blow away millions of
dollars on behalf of thousands of people are generally made
by just a few people (this is inadequate representation). In
other words, while average people are feeling a great financial
squeeze and many have lost jobs and homes, local govern-

ment officials are spending almost fanatically, without blinking, and with little to no input from the public in regard to the budget. And this is just one example. *This is going on in every county and municipality in the nation.*

In many cases, money is borrowed upon the collateral of *future* taxation. In other words, a government wants to spend more than it currently has. It goes to the bank and says, "Loan us money." The bank looks at the government's budget and sees income already maxed out with no surpluses on hand. It replies, "How will you pay back the loan?" This is hypothetical, of course; the bank already knows how the government will pay it back. "We will raise a new tax," is the reply. The bank looks at the legal situation: it sees that the government has the authority to tax, and it has the force (guns) to collect the taxes. Looks like a pretty safe investment for the bank (which stands to draw interest in the bond, by the way).

Thus, the government borrows money it does not have on the promise of future taxation. In other words, on the decision of just a few people, an entire municipality or county is indebted by millions, with the politician's promise to the bank that the government will extract more money from the people in the future to pay the loan with interest. In other words, I repeat myself, the commissioners say, "These people will pick up my tab." This is implicitly saying that *the people work for the government (and the banks), not the government for the people.* The people are essentially slaves of their government.

The only thing standing in the way of such a maneuver is—in some cases—a vote from the people. Normally, people are opposed to increased debts and higher taxes, and such a deal would never fly. But the government and other interested parties (school boards, teachers unions, etc.) have tricks up their sleeves to get their funds. First, they attempt secrecy and a low profile to keep voter turnout very low. They only publish the proposal to the minimum extent required by law, and hold the vote in a special election. With most average people busy with their lives and disinterested or complacent, very few people even hear about the vote, fewer understand the issue, and even fewer actually vote.

And voter turnout can lead to terribly deceptive conclusions. To illustrate, in my little semi-rural county, the school board has indebted the public to the tune of $146 million over the space of the past decade or so (this tyrannical debt is *mild* compared to many other places). Tax revenues have not covered what was projected (surprise!), so a vote was required to extend a tax increase for a few more years. This would cover, allegedly, $55 million in outstanding debts. The vote came in: 55% for and 45% against the tax extension. That sounds pretty standard until you look at the numbers involved:

Out of about 71,000 registered voters, only about 33,000 showed up—well less than half. This number is higher than normal because the bond issue was tacked onto the ballot for the 2010 national mid-term elections. Thus, it was a general ballot which drew far more people than a special election. Of these, only about 31,500 voted on the school-bond tax. Of these 31,500, only about 17,500 voted for it, making up the 55%, with 14,000 against.

In other words, it was not 55% of "the people," but rather 55% of those few people who decided to vote specifically on the issue. In the end, the 17,500 pro-tax votes represented only about 25% of the registered voter base; and the margin of victory, 3,500 votes, made up less than 5% of registered voters. Thus, 5% of the voter base determined the imposition of a special tax on everyone else.

These are absolutely pitiful numbers, and yet they are nowhere near as pitiful as the turnout numbers when there are no *national* and/or *state* personalities on the ballot. This particular school bond tax vote was the fourth of its kind in fourteen years (1997, 2001, 2006, and 2010). It was the previous three that actually acquired all the bond debt, and thus these three were responsible for the outstanding millions at the heart of this latest legislation. Well, the previous three were all conducted via *special* elections, and as a result, not one saw a total voter turnout higher than 4,000 (the numbers were 3,905, 1,385, and 2,299 respectively). In other words, only a couple thousand people in favor of more debt and higher taxes—and in truth, only the few hundred who provided the margin of victory—were required for indebting and taxing the whole population. This means that only a tiny, tiny percentage determined the issue for everyone. And now there is no escape from it. If that's not tyranny—if that's not *ridiculous*—I don't know what is.

I have belabored these statistics to make the point that low voter turnout favors higher taxes and greater government debt. This is exacerbated when turnout is so low that only a few hundred votes can swing the outcome. In this case, it is mostly those who stand to benefit from the money—teachers, administrators, officials, contractors, etc.—who will be "in the know" and will work to keep "competition" (taxpayers) from opposing them in the vote. Thus the very people who call for the issuance of the bond, and who also control the public relations in regard to it, are the very ones who wish to keep voter turnout to a minimum.

And this is only their first trick. Another is more commonly known, yet also more commonly fallen for. It's the emotional appeal. If public relations become an issue, then you can pick your emotional appeal: if it's a tax for education, it's "for the kids" and "for a better tomorrow." If you oppose it, then you despise children and want us all to be uneducated, knuckle-dragging hillbillies with no hope for tomorrow. And since most people cannot imagine a world in which the government is not the single central benefactor in education, they actually believe this nonsense. If it's a tax for the police or fire, then you can be sure you will hear lots of appeal about "safety" and how brave and selfless every single policeman is, always there to "protect and serve." And if you oppose more of this, then you are promoting higher crime, kids hooked on drugs, women being raped in the streets, houses being left to burn to the ground with children and kittens inside, and illegal immigrants fleeing the scenes of accidents leaving little old ladies paralyzed for life.

This is not to say there are not some great policemen and firemen, but the romance novels written by propagandists here are endless—and people are in love with them.

Of course, it's funny, all those people who want bonds issued to pay for their children's education for a better tomorrow—they totally ignore the fact that their children will be the ones paying off those debts, along with the fat pensions of the public officials and teachers who called for those debts in the first place. Some "better tomorrow."

Then there is the theft of hope trick. It says, "We're going to have to pay for this somehow anyway, so you might as well vote for it." This is a false choice. In my local example, the deal was this: if the increased sales tax did not pass, then the county was going to use its authority to increase the school bond portion of property taxes anyway. Since, to most people, a 1% sales tax sounds less ominous than 3.6% higher property taxes, they jump at the deal. What remains unspoken is that there wouldn't have been any tax increased needed at all *if the money had not been borrowed and spent to begin with.*

Another trick deals with PR and public ignorance. Perhaps voters will turn out, so the big spenders will have to make their expenditure look like a good thing on the ballot. When the voter reads the issue (probably for the first time), he or she must be made to believe voting for it is a net good. By presenting the issue as the promotion of education in general, for example, the vote stands a greater chance of passing an apparently small tax than if the emphasis were placed on the millions of dollars in debt, the few it will actually help, the graft and waste involved, etc. Indeed, the amount of debt may not necessarily be legally required to appear on the ballot. Only some very brief and general description, like: "Provision 001: A vote to temporarily extend an existing 1% sales tax for bonds issued for Public Schools." Nothing is mentioned of even the alternative increase in property taxes or anything else. Thus, many voters are essentially uninformed, and functionally *mis*informed at the ballot box.

What needs to be done is an immediate spending freeze and drastic cuts in unnecessary local budgets in every local government in the nation. (The same is true for state and Federal government as well, but good luck on that. We must start locally.) This also means that all local public borrowing—all bond issues—should stop immediately as well, for it is the most insidious form of spending.

What can average individuals do to advance such a cause? The first is what I have already said—set up a monitoring website. As part of such a site, include a clear section regarding all public finance. Use requests for public information to your public officials for all the documents, facts, and figures you can get. Keep up with commission meetings and or other public officials' meetings. Most today are posted online. Learn and post any agenda item that will cost public money or imply increased taxes or debts. Make all of this information as simple and clear as possible—extract it from the obscurity of meeting minutes, detailed reports, etc. Just publish the clear and pertinent info for the public.

Second, all public bonds on all occasions are anathema, period. No more public debt, no more taxation on the backs of our futures and our children. It would be good to oppose these systematically at the polls, and inform your local representatives to do so as well. If people think some things are so important to fund, then let them organize and raise funds to do it privately. If it's worth doing, the money will not be hard to come by. Forcing everyone to pay for services only some use is a tyranny.

Third, if you profit from public contracts, especially based on bond issuances, then you should stop. If you have greatly enriched your business and/or yourself on such, then you should consider yourself like Zacchaeus (Luke 19:1–10), and you should pay restitution. Except, since it would be difficult to pay back every single taxpaying individual, I would recommend giving the money to a reputable public charity.

Fourth, start a local group—if one does not already exist—dedicated to spreading this information locally and increasing voter turnout. Make flyers for local businesses, the chamber of commerce, radio stations, etc. If you have a small non-profit foundation, you can take advantage of public service announcements on radio. This will help spread awareness and hopefully increase turnout. You can even use all of these outlets to inform the public of important details they will not get from the bond issuing authorities themselves, or the ballot, or anywhere else. If you have some wealth and are looking for a way to serve the public, setting up such a foundation would be a great idea (after donating to American Vision, of course!).

Fifth, there are other avenues to pursue. Investigate into your local public salaries and pension plans. These may very well be high, or even luxurious or exorbitant. Check it out. If you find something objectionable, then let the presses roll. Post it all clearly online. For the really adventurous, you could rent a public billboard or portable sign (check for legal places to put one first!) that largely and clearly exposes the waste. There are many ways to expose these things to the public. Be creative.

There is no doubt that the single most important measure for lowering taxes is to cut spending and oppose public bonds. The appeal to cut taxes must come simultaneously. It will do no good to leave revenues the same while cutting spending for a time. It would be no time at all before the government finds other ways to spend the revenue. We need simultaneous spending *and* tax cuts. Beat the bonds, break the taxes.

A loftier goal would be bond and tax referendum reform. It is absolutely ludicrous that a bare majority of even a tiny voter turnout is sufficient to indebt a whole population. There should be very high requirements: such as at least a two-thirds majority of all registered voters. Even this is not biblical for bonds, and is dubious for taxation, but it would at least ensure that the default answer on these issues is, "No." This would make it harder for big spenders to capitalize on voter complacency, ignorance, propaganda, or deception (all very likely). It would require great energy, organization, and personal expenditure on the part of anyone wishing to advance a new debt or tax. And even then, those who do not use the system should get tax exemptions.

This can, of course, only come through political change. It must include a movement to abolish all unbiblical forms of taxation, and minimalize what taxation may remain. Of course, before such a movement can begin, we need to see the rise of private alternatives—particularly in that main artery of local public expenditure, public education. That's why this project starts off with private education (and a call for tax exemptions for those who don't use the system). Then it goes to privatizing social insurances. There is no reason society could not also privatize police, fire, and EMT, or at least privatize the way they are funded. These few things would negate enormous chunks of public cost, and taxes could be slashed to match. In the meantime, there will be no viable and sustainable political pressure toward cutting spending and taxes if we do not first pull our kids from public schools, establish our own future funds and insurances, and take care of our own families, parents, etc. in these regards. These are the things we can do as average individuals; and we must do them in order to establish the moral high ground for future change. We can also immediately learn about and expose corruption, graft, and excess at the local level. There is nothing stopping us here, and this could have significant effects on slashing spending and taxes in the future. We must create both public will and public self-discipline. While we prepare for these things, we need to focus our efforts and our children's attentions on the details of local business, local politics, local issues, local culture, and local finance as much as the national.

6. Money

Money has become one of those things we rarely mentally separate from government. It seems printing money, coining coins, and regulating banks are simply things governments do, and most people cannot remember a time when this was not the case. Total government control of money is simply our common experience. But a whole generation is beginning to awaken to the fact that this state of affairs is not biblical, favors the few, and does not represent the best interests of American liberty. The ideal of freedom calls for a much different view of money and banking. In fact, by biblical standards of money, what we have today is an oligarchy, a scam, a tyranny, a sin, a crime.

Money in a Free Society

It helps to begin with definitions. What *is* money, after all? The answer is simple: money is the most marketable commodity in a given society at a certain time. This means money is the most universally accepted means of exchange in trade. If you have money, anyone who engages in business will be willing to trade their goods or services with you at any time in exchange for the accepted money. They will do this because they know that someone else will accept the same commodity later in exchange for other desirables. Money is therefore the product of human interaction. It arises naturally in a market as people make decisions to buy and sell.[1]

---

[1] Gary North, *Honest Money: The Biblical Blueprint for Money and Banking* (Tyler, TX: Institute for Christian Economics, 1986), 24.

In a free market, many things can act as money. American colonists used beaver furs and wampum as money in their trade with the Indians. In some parts of America, fish and corn worked as well. In Virginia, the most widely marketed commodity was tobacco. Into the eighteenth century, even taxes were still paid in pounds of tobacco. This was true also for government imposed fines. Warehouse receipts often circulated as currency, but these were backed by stores of tobacco.[2] When precious metals become available for this purpose, however, they tend to have a way of stealing the show.

Biblical View of Money

It is by no means necessary that metals be made into State-sanctioned coins, but this often occurs in practice. The conveniences of coinage—State-sanctioned or not—are portability and regularity. Each coin will, it is assumed, have a practical and consistent size and weight. This, of course, can be abused if the coining agent slightly decreases (cheats) the size, or debases the metal, and yet falsely maintains the same face value. This has been done thousands of times in history and continues today.[3] The Bible calls this stealing, and this applies whether it is done by private mints or agents of the government. The value of money does not originate from what is printed on the face of it. As we just saw, money arises naturally as a result of commerce. Its value is tied to its market-determined valuation as a commodity—and this can change over time. Its valuation is a function of *how much people want it*.

---

[2] See Murray N. Rothbard, *A History of Money and Banking in the United States: The Colonial Era to World War II* (Auburn, AL: The Ludwig von Mises Institute, 2002), 48.

[3] From 1909 until 1982, for example, American pennies were 95% copper. Around 1982, the copper value began to be worth more than the face value of the coin. The government switched to much cheaper zinc. In today's prices, a pre-1982 penny is actually worth 2.2 cents on the copper market. A post-1982 penny is worth about 0.5 cents on the zinc market.

The biblical standard for money is clear, and it is the same as the biblical standard for the exchange of any commodity: just and honest measurements. God says,

> You shall do no wrong in judgment, in measures of length or weight or quantity. You shall have just balances, just weights, a just ephah, and a just hin: I am the LORD your God, who brought you out of the land of Egypt. (Lev. 19:35–36)

This is repeated in more detail later:

> You shall not have in your bag two kinds of weights, a large and a small. You shall not have in your house two kinds of measures, a large and a small. A full and fair weight you shall have, a full and fair measure you shall have, that your days may be long in the land that the LORD your God is giving you. For all who do such things, all who act dishonestly, are an abomination to the LORD your God. (Deut. 25:13–16)

When anyone, including any agent of the civil government, manipulates the money supply, and thus devalues its purchasing power, he engages in diverse weights and measures. This is not just dishonest—according to God through Moses, it is an *abomination.*

Scripturally speaking, then, fiscal conservatism is just as important an issue as social conservatism. All those who make such a political issue over homosexuality—calling sodomy an "abomination" (which it is)—should be shouting a thousand times more that our money and banking system are an "abomination," because this biblical transgression is a much more pervasive evil and it affects everyone, everyday. The comparison in regard to frequency of offense is not even close. The Federal Reserve System is the abomination of abominations in our society, topped only by abortion. While the homosexual lobby is powerful in many places, the finance lobby is by far the largest of any, and it has influence in every office, party, and hall of government.

The biblical standard is just weights and measures. Ideally, this means a physical commodity as currency, such as gold or silver coins with a clear and honest (and verifiable) weight of metal content, or a paper receipt or certificate that is "backed" by a bank or other institution and freely redeemable for the stated amount of the physical commodity. The fact that banks do not keep 100% physical reserves ready to be redeemed for each paper receipt or certificate issued is simply fraudulent, though it is the standard practice today to keep only about 10% in reserve (which is not even gold or silver today anyway). Historically, banks have not been able to resist issuing more paper receipts than they have reserves to cover. This is called *fractional reserve banking*. It allows a bank to loan out and collect interest on more assets than it actually has.

Honest Money in History

Historically, the best example of honest money is by far the Byzantine Empire. With a consistent gold coin standard, prices remained stable for over 1,000 years. When America was at her best, things have operated closer to this standard. Despite episodes of paper inflation due to wars, the era of the international gold coin standard—from 1815 until 1914—was without measure the period of the most economic growth in America.

Perhaps the most widely-used coin in colonial times was the Spanish dollar. Despite British attempts to monopolize the coinage in the Empire, the American colonies continued to import the Spanish silver dollar—even smuggling them when they were outlawed.[4] Our word "dollar" today comes from this originally dependable silver coin. Today, of course, the dollar is completely unhinged from any physical standard of weight or measure.

---

[4] The Spanish dollar was cut into eight pieces, with each of the "pieces of eight" called a "bit." The label "two-bit" thus refers to the old quarter-dollar.

Banks and treasuries, as I said, have historically been unable to resist loaning out more than they have in reserve. This is true going back to the goldsmiths of the late middle ages. This was true also throughout much of U.S., including when we had a national or central bank, and especially in times of war.

There was at least one great exception in American history which illustrates how private currency issued by private banks backed completely by marketable assets (such as gold) can both thrive and help maintain a free market. Two Boston banks—the New England Bank of Boston, founded in 1814, and the Suffolk Bank, founded in 1818—were concerned over the excessive paper being issued by competing banks from farther out in the country. Since the country banks were more difficult to reach for redemption, they could more easily get away with issuing more paper, as fewer people showed up to redeem it. Many other city banks had refused to redeem their notes at all. Suffolk devised a system to buy up all the less valuable country bank notes, but would only redeem them if country banks agreed to keep gold deposits in Suffolk Bank. While country notes tended to trade at a discount in the city, Suffolk devised a "clearing house" that would enable them to be traded at par. Every other bank in the loop was thankful for this convenience and relief.

This system simultaneously forced the country banks to keep their paper issuances honest. Being forced to redeem in gold chafed them a bit, but the threat of being completely shunned by all the other banks in the circle was much worse. So they made their deposits of gold with Suffolk and closely monitored their paper. The system had the added benefit of lending new credibility to the country banks as long as they participated.

Suffolk's free market money and banking system prospered for forty years—from 1818 to 1858. In that year, a competitor arose with the same system—the Bank of Mutual Redemption—and a negative reaction from Suffolk cost it considerable market share. The real demise, however, was in 1861 and 1863, when Civil War measures stopped all redemption in gold and prohibited private issuance of paper.

In the end, "While it lasted . . . the Suffolk banking system showed that it is possible in a free-market system to have private banks competing to establish themselves as efficient, safe, and inexpensive clearinghouses limiting overissue of paper money."[5] Indeed, it is proof positive that a free market can regulate both money and banking: that it can curtail fraud, keep would-be cheaters accountable, provide viable private currency, protect wealth, and bring great profits to the most honest competitors.

So we can see that a free market in the creation and production of money, and a decentralized free market in banking, including a 100% reserve standard, are absolutely viable. It is the biblical standard, and it has been viable historically, most famously in the Byzantine Empire, but also right here in America in at least one regional example. So, free market money and banking are biblical and they work. There is no reason we could not restore this standard, although it would cause, probably, a short period of uncomfortable transition.

I have already said, however, that such freedom was compromised many times in American history. Truthfully, unbacked money and banking manipulations have been more often the norm than honest money.

The Loss of Monetary Freedom

We are all familiar with the present financial crisis which began in 2008. Most people have heard that this event is "unprecedented" except for the Great Depression of the 1930s. This is largely nonsense. Due to our limited historical experience and our short historical memories, we either do not know or have forgotten the many financial bubbles and bank bailouts caused mostly by dishonest banking and money all throughout American history. Today is just a variation on the same old

---

[5] Rothbard, *History of Money*, 122 (See pp. 115–122 for the whole story).

theme—played particularly loudly. Here are the true stories of how freedom in money and banking were lost in America.

Like the story of taxation and centralization in America, the history of money involves ratcheting tyranny. And like the story of taxation, an honest money and banking system has rarely existed in the United States. We could be picky about the point at which we start the criticism and the first acts to blame, but for all practical purposes it doesn't matter. The point is that, with few exceptions, most influential American banks 1) have never remained honest, 2) have never been forced to be honest, and 3) have actually been encouraged and promoted in their dishonesty by the civil government itself.

This has been especially true when the civil government has been a partner in the money and banking business. Instead of enforcing contracts—a primary responsibility of state governments—state and Federal governments have done just the opposite. They have created moral hazard by engaging in fractional reserve banking and inflating the paper and/ or digital money supply time and again. In times when private banks have inflated their bank notes against the amount of hard currency held in reserve, the state should have upheld any suit against the bank for theft by fraud. The bank should have been liable for any losses. Instead, more often than not, the scenario has been allowed to reach crisis status, and the crisis has been used to justify further fiat currency and the creation of central banks that create still more paper money. This is often coupled with the government-enforced prohibition on redeeming paper for hard currency. In other words, the government often refused to punish the fraudulent banking practice, refused to uphold the contract between the client and the bank, and instead enforced the exact opposite of the contract—that the people *cannot* redeem their bank or state-issued paper for gold or silver.

This has been true of private banks, state banks, and all nationally-chartered federal banks. Most modern discussions

of this topic evade this fact because they are politically motivated. Most people today read the modern Republican-Dem-
ocrat, conservative-liberal divide back into the nineteenth
century (with some justification), then choose sides, and then
try to paint the other side with as many warts as possible. Like
modern politics, the ones who emerge with the least mud on
their faces are supposed to be the "good guys." Problem: both
sides are covered in mud. Both sides have historically prosti-
tuted themselves to the fraudulent banking system. Colonial
banks did it; the Continental Congress did it. Hamilton did
it; Jefferson did it. Lincoln did it; the Confederate States did
it. Republican Progressives did it; Wilsonian Liberal Progressives did it. Republicans love the Fed; Democrats love the Fed.
Only a handful of politicians, historically, have opposed the
system in general: Andrew Jackson was one; he inspired a
whole party to oppose fractional reserve banking at one time.
Ron Paul is another today.

From very early, the national Congress tried to decree
wealth into existence out of nothing. When this failed, it tried
to impose legal tender laws—forcing people by law to accept
paper money according to its face value, despite its declining
worth. When this failed, the notes eventually sank into oblivion, and Congress eventually gave up. Speculators bought
the notes for fractions of a penny on the dollar. From just the
one very early example of the Continental paper dollar, the
Philadelphia merchant and astute observer Peletiah Webster
noted: "Perhaps this whole transaction affords the most strik-
ing proof conceivable, of the absurdity of all attempts *to fix the
value of money by a law, or any other methods of compulsion.*"[6]
Later, when Congress considered a resolution to forgo even
interest payments on their worthless paper, the great minister and statesman John Witherspoon stood and decried "the
last stab at public credit." A government, he iterated, without

---

[6] Pelatiah Webster, "Remarks on the Resolution of Council Of the 2^d of May,
1781, for raising the Exchange to 175 Continental dollars for 1 hard," *Political Essays
On the Nature and Operation of Money, Public Finances and Other Subjects*, 175n.

honest money and banking should not be trusted in any other matter either: "It will be in vain, in [the] future, to ask the public to believe any promise we shall make—even when the most clear and explicit grounds of confidence are produced."[7]

This early and very tragic lesson was immediately ignored, and has been ignored countless times over and again since. How was freedom in money and banking lost? Here's a partial list:

- It was lost with the Bank of North America in 1781.

- It was lost with the first Bank of the United States in 1791.

- It was lost with the second Bank of the United States in 1816.

- It was lost with Lincoln's National Bank system in 1861 and forward.

- It was lost with the Federal Reserve Bank in 1913. It was lost with countless government attempts to manipulate the value of money by decree: whether Continentals, Greenbacks, Federal Reserve Notes, or otherwise.

- It is lost every time a single bank or government agency inflates the money supply by fiat, and the government refuses to stop the fraud. It has been lost in modern times as the Dollar has lost 96 percent of its purchasing power since the Federal Reserve takeover in 1913. It takes almost $100 today to buy what $1 would buy in 1913.

- It was lost in every government-enforced refusal of banks to redeem their paper for gold or silver: 1814, 1837, 1861, 1933, 1971, an others.

- It was lost when Roosevelt confiscated the entire

---

[7] John Witherspoon, *On Money and Finance* (Powder Springs, GA: American Vision Press, 2010), 81.

nation's gold supply by executive order. He grabbed it for a government-mandated price of $20.67/oz., and then began selling it to foreign governments and banks nine months later for $35/oz. This executive tyranny was joined by Congressional action in 1934. Thus did the Federal government realize a return of 69 percent, by decree, on the gold it stole from the American people. (The Gold Reserve Act of 1934 also invalidated many contracts retroactively, thus illegally creating a virtual ex post facto law.)

• It was lost in 1971 when Nixon unhinged the dollar from the last remaining vestige of a gold exchange standard, refusing the redemption of international debts for gold coin. This act floated the dollar completely. The result has been the exponential skyrocketing of the national debt ever since (a graph of the national debt shows an exponential curve upward beginning roughly in the early 1970s).

Need we say more? Is this not enough to show how honest money and banking have been long lost and kept lost in American history?

For those who desire some more specifics, we can oblige. Space is not warranted here to tell the whole story, but here are some brief and partial historical highlights:[8]

America's Flight from Honest Money

Under the First Bank of the U.S. (1791–1811), designed by Hamilton, the number of paper-issuing banks jumped from three to eighteen. The paper currency supply was immedi-

---

[8] The following histories are based largely on Murray N. Rothbard, *A History of Money and Banking in the United States: The Colonial Era to World War II* (Auburn, AL: The Ludwig von Mises Institute, 2002), 45–147. See also Bray Hammond, *Banks and Politics in America: from the Revolution to the Civil War* (Princeton, NJ: Princeton University Press, 1967); Herman E. Kroos, ed., *Documentary History of Banking and Currency in the United States*, 4 vols. (New York: Chelsea House Publishers, 1983).

ately inflated. Wholesale prices rose 72 percent over the space of five years. The Jeffersonians, who ostensibly opposed the process, were even worse when they held the reins. Instead of abolishing the system (which would have been more consistent with their purported views of liberty), they subsequently ballooned the number of banks to 117. By the end of the first Bank's twenty-year charter, roughly four paper dollars were circulating for every dollar of metal in reserve. In other words, what was a dollar twenty years prior was now worth 25 cents.

While there was an interim between the first and second Banks of the U.S., the Federal and state governments were by no means inactive in manipulating the money supply. Indeed, this is where they made their greatest mistakes. First was the reaction of the easy-money addicts to the failure of an immediate re-charter. Second was the decision to enter and then finance the War of 1812.

When the charter of the first bank was up, Madison was president. He had opposed the first bank originally on more than one ground, not the least of which was his strict constructionist view of the Constitution. A very slight majority in Congress opposed the re-charter as well. While many today think the central bank's purpose was to control the inflationary wildness of state and local banks, the political support for re-charter at the time overturns this view: support from state banks, as well as the subsidized merchants, was overwhelming. Indeed, Hamilton's own Bank of New York applauded the institution specifically *for* its bail-out potential:

> [It was able] in case of any sudden pressure upon the merchants to step forward to their aid in a degree which the state institutions were unable to do.[9]

The bill for re-charter nevertheless failed. This did not deter the Federal government from encouraging more fiat

---

[9] Rothbard, *A History of Money*, 72.

paper. Congress simply turned to state banks and local banks. In doing so, the government perpetuated and exacerbated regional animosities. New England banks opposed a war with Britain, and were fairly conservative on inflation. But the government needed inflation to finance its war and to buy arms and supplies manufactured mostly in the North. So, the administration encouraged the proliferation of new government-friendly, fiat-friendly banks throughout the middle, southern, and western colonies. These banks inflated wildly in exchange for government debt. The government then took the loans and bought the manufactured goods in the North. Thus, in this interim period, 1811–1815, the number of banks jumped to 212. In addition to these, the government's wartime measures allowed for 35 unincorporated banks which were otherwise illegal in most states.

The inflation ratio during this period grew from 4:1 to 6:1 paper-to-specie. But this does not really capture the picture. It was really a Federal-government-driven regional war of newly created banks against New England banking integrity (what there was left of it). The regional results are disturbing: the inflation ratio in Massachusetts was less than 2:1. Rhode Island was around 2.4:1, and New Hampshire was at 2.7:1. Pennsylvania, however, had ballooned to over 19:1, and South Carolina and Virginia were well above 18:1 each. So the comparison shows how much the Federal government was using new banks as fronts to steal the wealth of its political opposition in the North.

This situation was completely unsustainable, of course. When the New England banks went calling upon the paper-issuing banks to redeem their currency, a massive shakeup was on the horizon. There was no way these massively counterfeiting banks could cover their debts while sustaining a fractional reserve ratio of 19:1. They clearly faced bankruptcy.

Not to fear: the government stepped in with a bank bailout. It was by no means the first, but it *was* massive. While there was, of course, no Federal Reserve to inject yet more fiat reserves, the bailout simply came in another form: the Federal and implicated state governments colluded and declared that banks in their states were no longer required to redeem in specie. It was that simple. When fraudulent behavior faced exposure, the government protected fraud and outlawed exposure—at the expense of the defrauded. It was almost exactly the same scenario as the big banks faced in 2008. The solution was mildly different, but the result was the same: protect and encourage fraud.

> In short, in one of the most flagrant violations of property rights in American history, the banks were permitted to waive their contractual obligations to pay in specie while they themselves could expand their loans and operations and force their own debtors to repay their loans as usual.[10]

As I said earlier, instead of enforcing contracts and ending the fraud, the government did just the opposite. And as a result, this moral hazard led to more of the same fraudulent behavior: in the following year, the number of paper-issuing banks jumped yet again, to 246, accompanied by further inflation. Again, during this period, wholesale prices jumped 35 percent. This was a government-mandated, easy-money time. It lasted until the change of administrations in 1817. Worse than the immediate perturbations was the precedent. Rothbard explains,

> It thus became clear to the banks that in a general crisis they would not be required to meet the ordinary obligations of contract law or of respect for property rights, so their inflationary expansion was permanently encouraged by this massive failure of government to fulfill its obligation to enforce contracts and defend the rights of property.[11]

---

[10] Rothbard, *History of Money*, 74.
[11] Ibid., 76.

If this is not fabulously prophetic of our more modern banking crisis, nothing is. The banks have been too big to fail since at least 1814, if not 1791. We hear today of an imminent collapse of the "entire financial system" and thus the need for multi-trillion dollar bailouts. But it has been the specially-protected fraud of bankers in this nation for over two hundred years.

We should reiterate that while central banking was the baby of big financiers and big-government Federalists like Hamilton, the allegedly freedom-loving Jeffersonians, including Madison, involved themselves to an even greater extent in inflationary theft. They did so through Federal debts, including war debt, and they allowed, indeed encouraged, the states to do so as well.

Indeed, the Democratic-Republicans in 1816 pushed as hard for a second bank as Hamilton had for a first. And whereas Madison had fought the first bank, he would nevertheless sign this new bill even in contradiction to his views of strict construction. Why? The state and private banks wanted to maintain their source of easy money. Senator William Jones (DE), despite being a Federalist, opposed the second bank. His understanding of its subversive purposes can stand as a valid criticism of all the national banks before and since. He saw that it was

> ostensibly for the purpose of correcting the diseased state of our paper currency by restraining and curtailing the overissue of bank paper, and yet it came prepared to inflict upon us the same evil, being itself nothing more than simply a paper-making machine.[12]

A paper-making machine it was indeed. Within the first two years of its existence, the bank ballooned its paper money supply to over a 9:1 ratio with specie, increasing the total national money supply by close to double. In the same period, the number of new banks rose to 338. In the great bubble-boom of this period, the exchange of paper stocks led to the creation of both

---

[12] Rothbard, *History of Money*, 85.

the New York Stock Exchange (NYSE), and the beginnings of large-scale investment banks (though the latter would not become a significant feature until the Civil War).

The Monroe administration noticed the banks were out of control, but it was too late. The Second Bank of the U.S. faced bankruptcy due to massive inflation and fraud. Frantically, its administrators began to contract their paper issues. The result was a huge contraction in credit and a pop of the investment bubble. The economy collapsed overnight in the so-called Panic of 1819. Prices plummeted, banks went bust, businesses went bankrupt, unemployment jumped, rural areas were reduced again to barter. Finally, honest money re-emerged, if only in a crude and partial way: whiskey once again acted as currency.

But the Second Bank of the U.S. survived the spell. In a line ominously echoed in the bailouts of today, one eyewitness noted, "the Bank was saved, and the people were ruined."[13] The Second Bank also learned nothing from the recession. Immediately after 1819, it began inflating again. In 1823, with the ratio of paper to specie at about 4:1, it ramped up the rate of increase. By 1832, the ratio was approaching 7:1. It is clear the central national bank was neither fiscally sound in itself, nor an improvement upon state and local banks.

Again, many historians and their readers today think that the purpose of the central bank was to rein in these wild local banks who were purportedly doing all of the inflating. The opposite is true. The central bank paid lip service to the hard money crowd in promising redemption in coin. This was the deal on paper, anyway (no pun intended, promise!). In reality, a backroom deal was made just prior to the bill's passage in 1816: it would create a $6 million injection of government paper to favored banks before it would require resumption of payment in specie. In this meeting, the stodgy New England banks were excluded. In addition to the huge subsidy, the banks pledged mutual support in case of emergency, a deal

---

[13] Quoted in Rothbard, *History of Money*, 90.

which everyone knew would lean in favor of the local banks. It was the assurance of a bailout given up front.

It is no wonder that the state and local banks favored the creation of another national bank. While this goes against the popular story, the facts support it. Indeed, part of Madison's justification for ignoring his own Constitutional scruples involved "the entire acquiescence of all the local authorities." Although not *entirely* true, in that not "all" acquiesced, this appeal to "local authorities" shows that a central national bank was no obstacle to them—they in fact profited from it just as they had without it. All through the period of the Second Bank of the United States (1816–1836), the state banks could profit. It is no surprise that when Bank president Nicholas Biddle ramped up his campaign for re-charter early in 1832, he complained how the Jackson administration had already poisoned the public with, as he saw it, anti-bank propaganda. This included "the imaginary injury done to the State Banks," and led Biddle to start a campaign for "proofs that the State Banks are in the main friendly to his institutions."[14] The historian's analysis shows that Biddle was correct: among the South and West, only Georgia had a state bank that opposed a national bank. In New England, support was understandably minimal, but the Middle States largely supported the measure.

Biddle's re-charter passed Congress, but met its demise at the desk of Andrew Jackson. Jackson opposed the Bank in principle as a looter of the people and feeder of a privileged few fraudsters. While the Bank would remain in theory to the end of its charter in 1836, Jackson vetoed the 1832 attempt. He then immediately began disemboweling the national bank by moving its assets to several state banks. These numbered 91 by the end of 1836. In that year, the Second Bank of the U.S. lost its charter and became an ordinary bank. Five years after losing its government-enforced monopoly privileges, it went bankrupt.

Meanwhile, Jackson had vetoed nearly every massive

---

[14] Quoted in Jan Alexander Wilburn, *Biddle's Bank: The Crucial Years* (New York: Columbia University Press, 1967), 32–33.

spending bill and sold off hoards of Federally-owned lands. Despite his deficiencies in other areas, he was the first and only president to pay off the national debt in its entirety, and the only president ever to be able to claim a true surplus in the treasury. This occurred in 1835. It has never happened again.

The Second Bust of the Bank of the United States again did not stop state and local banks from inflating paper, although they did maintain a consistent ratio of inflated paper for several years afterward. Nevertheless, an influx of silver specie into the country with this constant ratio meant that banks on average, 1833–1837, were inflating paper constantly as new specie came in. In that latter year, a disruption in international markets helped precipitate another credit contraction. The Panic of 1837 resulted. Again, however, had there been no inflation allowed to begin with, there could have been no subesquent malinvestment, bubble, and trouble to redeem. Credit contraction is simply not an issue in a world where inflation of credit is not practiced to begin with.

We have not even touched on many other issues of the nineteenth century: the Panic of 1857, The Civil War and Greenbacks, the Panics of 1873, the Recession of 1882–1885, the Panic of 1893. In all of these, official coercive attempts to uphold fraud extenuated social evils and pain.

In just three years of the Civil War, Congress created over $400 million in Greenback currency *ex nihilo*. Over the period of the war, the total money supply (including pre-existing fiat money and state bank notes) was pumped from $745.4 million to $1.77 billion—a huge 138% increase.[15]

We have only barely mentioned the behemoth culmination of all bank fraud—the Federal Reserve System, born in 1913. We have not discussed government attempts to fix the ratio of gold to silver, again by both sides—Hamilton in 1792,

---

[15] Not without flabbergasting irony, the original Greenback act (Legal Tender Act of 1862) specified stiff penalties for counterfeiting: up to $5,000 fine and 15 years hard labor. We can't have people running around just printing money willy-nilly, now, can we?

and Jackson in 1834. Plus many other failed exchange fixes: FDR in 1933 and 1934, Bretton Woods in 1944, Nixon in 1971 for example. We have also not put much emphasis on legal tender laws which are tantamount to armed robbery. The list is legion, because this demon is legion. And it has never been exorcised from American life.

The main point here is that the biblical (and common sense) principles of money and banking have not been followed in this country even from day one. We have not yet had a chance at a free market in money and banking. We have never seen honest money enforced on fraudulent, cheating banks and government treasuries. Not only have they not been followed or upheld by the government, but government has been the most active agent in abusing them and encouraging their abuse by others. Instead, perpetual fraud has been the rule, and government has instigated, encouraged, and protected it. We have no precedent for the pains of honest liquidation. We have way too much precedent for the public being stiffed and robbed by colluding governments (often voter-backed!) and bankers.

It is time this began to change. With a whole generation of people waking up to the fraud inherent in the international banking systems—the fraud that is the Federal Reserve System—and to the standard of truly sound money and accounting, there is great hope that things can indeed begin to change at all levels. The questions will be: What exactly needs to be one? What can we average people do? And are we willing to make the sacrifices necessary to do it?

Restoring Honest Money and Banking

What would it take to return society to biblical, honest money and banking? In all possible cases, the necessary ingredient will be a *commitment* to biblical ethics. Without a willingness to sacrifice up front and to stay disciplined throughout the process, no scenario will end in success. These conditions are the basic conditions whether the catalyzing event is a massive revival, a crisis or failure of the Federal government, a successful state or local alternative or even resistance movement, the legal advent of competing currencies, or some political miracle by which society commits to a gradual change of the system (the least likely scenario). Let us first discuss the larger goals, and then move on to steps an average person can take to prepare for a biblical system personally.

What is the overarching goal in regard to money and banking? In the big sweep of things, it should be to return to biblical standards of just weights and measures, and the enforcement of contracts. This means the enforcement of the eighth and ninth commandments within the sphere of money and banking (as within the rest of society). First, this means an end to fractional-reserve banking as well as all other forms of artificial monetary inflation.[16] Any bank or other institution that lends so much as a fraction of a percent more money than it has in hard assets in reserve should be liable to prosecution for fraud. Stated more practically, the moment a bank shows the slightest inability to redeem its checks or paper currency for gold or silver, then it should be considered in breach of contract.

Second, this means also that anyone would be able to withdraw up to the total of their deposits in the form of hard assets ("redeem" currency for gold or silver coin). They should be able to do this at any time (unless, of course, there is a contractually stipulated maturity period).

---

[16] The absolute end of all inflation is impossible. Even in a free money society where, for example, gold and silver act as money, mining companies constantly increase the metal supply and thus (it is assumed) the money supply. The difference is that the rate of increase is generally so small as to be statistically insignificant, and the mining industry is a product of legitimate business risk, investment, and labor in mining industry. Exceptions historically have been when tremendous discoveries have been made overnight and huge quantities entered the money supply in a brief period (such as the California gold rush of the 1840s–50s). Nevertheless, such events are sporadic, unpredictable, and few, and thus do not empower the predictive and predictable evils of bankers' whims.

Third, there should be no legal tender laws. No one should be forced to use or to accept any particular form of money. Forms of payment for debts, rents, and other contractual obligations should be agreed upon freely and stipulated in contracts up front as part of the contract. For standard business exchanges, the free market will determine what acts as money, and while a business owner should be free to decline payment even in these terms, he would be unwise to do so. These are the basics: only hard money or money backed 1-to-1 by hard assets in reserve, redemption of any bank paper for hard money upon notice, and the abolition of any civil compulsion to use a prescribed form of money (no legal tender laws).

Could such a society be reestablished? Yes, but not without lots of commitment and personal fortitude during the transition.[17] What would this look like? First, if we automatically switched to honest money and banking overnight, without wise planning, the economic system would collapse for most people and a period of chaos would ensue. People would starve, crime would explode, martial law would be imposed, and the public crisis would be used by scheming politicians to nix any future attempts at reform for generations to come. Societies are simply not designed for abrupt structural changes. Instead, we need to turn the boat slowly, and to work out the implications for many contracts, relationships, and related investments in the interim.

Ending Fractional Reserve Banking

Here are the steps to abolishing fractional reserve banking, each of which poses unique challenges: 1) Audit the Fed and the U.S. Treasury and determine the true inflation ratio of "paper" against hard assets; 2) for all existing institutions and legal agreements as far as possible, anticipate the ramifications and implications of deflating the money supply in

---

[17] North, *Honest Money*, 123–131.

correlation to the amount of the gold and silver that exists; 3) readjust all prices and financial figures according to the calculated ratio (this would create the deflation); and 4) move all Treasury- and Fed-owned silver and gold from government vaults into private circulation.

If we immediately required honest money and banking, then the money supply would probably contract massively overnight. I say "probably" because we may not know how much gold and silver actually exists at Ft. Knox or with the Federal Reserve—or indeed if there is any at all. So we have no definite idea what the initial monetary base would be, against which we would have to begin calculating the current measure of inflation. However, since the current monetary base is actually built largely upon government debt instruments (promises to tax the people in the future for repayment) in addition to the gold we assume exists, we know that a return to honest money would immediately contract the money supply to a great degree.

If so, this means prices would fall drastically across the board—on goods, services, and labor. Consumer prices would fall, but consequently so would wages by the same proportion. This would be a wash in many areas. For example, a grocer would be able to demand less money for his wares, but his overhead costs would all fall accordingly as well. In the simple view of standard business and exchange, nothing would change. These changes would be apparent to all. The shock that comes with such a drastic reduction, however, could be easily offset with a small amount of preparatory education.

What would *not* apparently fall in proportion would be any previous obligations, debts, mortgages, etc., which were written in dollars. So while incomes would fall drastically—say by 90%—people would still be stuck with $1,000 house payments monthly, car payments, etc. Under normal conditions, deflation hurts debtors. Of course, this would not be normal conditions. This is a problem that should be addressed with wisdom and a little forethought—before honest money could be fully enforced. It probably could be addressed by maintaining something like a "last call" dollar-to-gold ratio for the duration of those previous obligations which would be grandfathered in. This ratio would be made especially and only for such pre-existing contracts. At the time of the legislation ending all future use of the Fed paper, whatever gold was worth in dollars at the "last call" so to speak would become the fixed reference point by which a dollar-equivalent could be calculated into the future, and by which those pre-existing contracts would be fulfilled to their end. Thus those old mortgages, etc. could be paid off in the new money calculated by its equivalent to the old inflated money.

Then we have the problem of getting the gold and silver into the hands of the public. Supposing the gold actually exists, it would only take a simple act of Congress to force the Fed to redeem its gold to the U.S. Treasury. That's a small but necessary first step. A second would be the equitable distribution of those gold and silver reserves from the U.S. Treasury to every account holder in proportion to the previous dollar-values of their accounts.

Once all of the loose ends were tied up (and I have certainly left many loose ends out of this very brief discussion of practical consequences), then local communities, states, and even the nation (though I would prefer to leave the legislation as much as possible at the local level) could have a biblical system of honest money and banking in place. From here the issue would be maintenance of that system, meaning the enforcement of contracts and thus the swift and immediate punishment of any bank that tried to inflate upon its own reserves.

Practical Steps for the Individual

What can the average individual do toward such a goal? While at this point options are limited, there certainly are steps to take. The first is personally to purchase gold and silver while you can. This, of course, is an area not entirely free from investment dangers, scams, and confusion; for example, notice I did not say "invest" in gold and silver. Some people like to buy gold and silver for speculative purposes hoping the price will rise. They will then sell off the gold for a profit, so they expect. As part of preparation for a biblical system of money, I am not talking about this kind of transaction at all. After all, for what will you sell your gold at that future time? More inflated Federal Reserve dollars or digits? And what will you do with those dollars? For by that time, most likely, bread and milk prices, land prices, gas prices, and moon-pie prices will have risen by the same rate of inflation as gold prices, generally.

On top of this, sales of gold bullion are considered capital gains, and taxed at the highest capital gains rate—fifteen percent. Some people can beat this system, but they are generally the lucky few who are gifted at commodities speculation—not the vast majority of people. Nor is gold a good investment for barter during an impending crisis. In times of crisis, food and water will be far more valuable than gold (after all, you can't eat gold). I am speaking of none of this here.

Instead, I am recommending gold and silver simply as a very conservative, long-term valuable good that will be the natural choice for money and the monetary base in a biblical monetary system. For those awaiting the day for an honest monetary system, having at least 20% of your long-term savings in the form of gold and silver is nothing short of good preparation. In the meantime, it will be subject to the roller-coaster ride of any commodity.

So, step one, own some gold and silver. This is not difficult, but some tips will help. 1) Buy only bullion, not "numismatic" coins (these are antique and otherwise special "collectable" coins more suited to speculation than the reconstruction of society). 2) Try to buy from a dealer who sells only bullion coins; others will try to "upsell" or "bait-and-switch" you to the collectable coins with pressure sales tactics, and they are quite good at it. 3) Buy only coins with the lowest premium or commission: this should be around 2.5 to 3.5 percent max. Many people want to buy American coins ("Golden Eagles") because they are American, but these often sell for a much higher premium (6 to 9 percent or more). You are not concerned with nationalistic patriotism here: you want the gold content. South African Krugerrands, gold Mexican Pesos, or Austrian Coronas are just fine and will cost you less. 4) Keep your gold safe: do not advertise your purchase to friends or neighbors, don't show it off, keep it quiet; don't use a regular bank safe deposit box, but put it in a safe, hard-to-find place known only to you and your spouse (and perhaps one very closely trusted friend). Following these simple steps will save you possibly thousands of dollars with the dealer, and put you ahead of the game in preparation for an honest money society.

What else can be done? As with previous topics, you need to spread the word. Teach a Sunday school course in your church on honest money and banking.[18] Inform your local, state, and national representatives and officials of the lessons taught here in regard to honest money and banking.

It would also be great if we had the option to simply move our money to banks which themselves did not practice fractional reserve banking. Of course, this would not eliminate the same problem happening elsewhere above our heads, but it would eliminate one corner of it. The Federal Reserve system currently does not forbid banks from keeping one hundred percent reserves—it just doesn't require it, and all banks choose not to do it. It is certainly conceivable that some Christian banker somewhere could choose to keep one hundred percent reserves in his own bank and refuse to lend beyond that base. This could act as 1) a service to local Christians, 2) a testimony against the evil of fractional reserves, and 3) an example to other banks of how such a system could work. Such a bank, of course, may not

---

[18] You can follow Gary North's short book, *Honest Money: Biblical Principles of Money and Banking*—available as a free download from GaryNorth.com/ HonestMoney.pdf

be as profitable as banks that leverage their fractional reserve power, but then again profit is not the ultimate Christian virtue when it comes to money. Honesty is.

Again, however, such a bank would not restore biblical money in general, even for the customers of the bank, for at least two reasons: 1) banks are forbidden by the Federal Reserve system from keeping precious metals as their reserves. Any "one hundred percent reserve" bank would still only have, at best, vault cash as its base. Thus, 2) since the rest of the system would still be inflated and inflating the same currency that our example bank is forced to use, the devaluation of the whole money supply also devalues that of even the one hundred percent reserve bank. Such a bank can at best provide a "protest" example against a system in which all banks are forced to use inflated money.

There is something similar to one hundred percent reserve banking available in the online "gold bank accounts" provided by, for example, goldmoney.com and bullionvault.com. In these systems, you essentially purchase gold with dollars and the company maintains an account, valued in some form of "units" of gold, and the vault holds that actual amount of gold for you. The "value" of the gold will fluctuate over time with the market price. You can sell later and withdraw currency easily. The drawbacks are that there is nothing like a debit card or the convenience of modern checking accounts; and every conversion of gold units back into dollars is considered a sale and thus a taxable event. Thus, the account functions much like a gold-backed savings account. You would want to withdraw from it only for rare and major purchases, if at all.

You may also consider moving your money to a credit union instead of a bank. Granted, the change would not be greatly significant, but the move would eliminate at least one problematic aspect of banks. Many people don't know that a key factor in the 2008 financial crisis was something called the Community Reinvestment Act, expanded under Bill Clinton in 1995. I have written about this elsewhere.[19] In brief, this Act required all banks in the Federal Reserve System to make loans to people with poor or no credit. It was a recipe for disaster, and when the Fed-induced bubble finally popped, a myriad of risky loans turned into foreclosures. This act 1) filled many middle-class suburban areas with lower-income families with attendant crime and welfare rates, and 2) has left entire neighborhoods with rows of foreclosed, empty homes. In short, progressive manipulation of banking has left us with little to show for it but ghettos and ghost towns. But, here's the rub: credit unions by law are not required to participate in the Act. Thus, while they still may engage in fractional reserve banking, they are usually not participating in the direct government-led destruction of local communities. This much at least is laudable. Even here, however, you should research individual institutions, for some participate voluntarily in community improvement programs (which may or may not be desirable), and some are actually part of international organizations to which you may or may not wish to contribute.

There is the possibility also of alterative currencies. These are not "money" in the legal sense, but are legally legitimate. Several local systems have existed historically, and several smaller, localized versions exist still today. These are essentially paper-assisted barter systems. They tend to remain local because they require a network of businesses that agree to accept the currency. This could be a viable practice in the future if it became prevalent enough. For now, they are very limited in their utility.

In short, the best thing an average person can do for now is to buy some gold and silver, and to help spread awareness of the moral evil of fraudulent money and banking. By these efforts we are looking long term—hoping that education, preparation, the courage to face contraction, and the

---

[19] See Joel McDurmon, *God versus Socialism: A Biblical Critique of the New Social Gospel* (Powder Springs, GA: American Vision, Inc., 2009), 43.

willingness to sacrifice through it will pave the way for a better, more honest system in the future. As tough a challenge as this may seem, these things are all a moral imperative for society. Until we return to honest money, we are as a society trashing God's most fundamental laws—and God's longsuffering will not last forever.

7. Markets

The biblical prescription for markets and business is very simple: non-violence, enforcement of property rights, and enforcement of contracts. These principles are, of course, directly derived from three of the Ten Commandments: you shall not murder, you shall not steal, and you shall not bear false witness. Not only are they among the Ten, they all come from the second table of the law which is man's "kingly" duty—laws that primarily relate to man's relationship to man in society.[1] In brief, a biblical civil society is one in which people are *legally* free to engage in business and commerce in any way that does not violate their neighbor's person or property—life, liberty, or estate. Conversely, this means that individuals have a fundamental right to be free from coercion in these same areas. These are basics of God's law.

True Freedom in the Marketplace

The general right to freedom from coercion forbids State coercion as well.[2] Civil governments should not be in the business of erecting coercive markets: supporting some or all businesses through subsidies, taxation, protections, price controls, or any of the other various loopholes or exceptions that may exist. Civil government "bears the sword" because it

---

[1] This is distinguished from the first, or "priestly," table which delineates man's duty primarily to God. Thus Jesus said all of the law is summed up in the two greatest commandments: love the Lord you God with all your heart, etc. (priestly duty), and love your neighbor as yourself (civil, or kingly, duty) (Matt. 22:37–40).

[2] Excepting of course cases of punishment for crimes.

is "the servant of God, an avenger who carries out God's wrath on the wrongdoer" (Rom. 13:4). It is thus an agency of force to punish crime—"crime" being defined primarily as infractions of the three commandments mentioned already, as well as whatever other crimes are specifically revealed in Scripture as punishable offenses. Civil government should be involved only in this endeavor, and not in the promotion of favored businesses, corporations, the regulation of markets, etc. Individuals and businesses alike have a fundamental right to be free from the coercion of the State in all legitimate business and market matters.

The moment the State engages in manipulating the markets, it oversteps its boundaries. This moral evil almost always produces negative practical results as well; these can be seen as God's judgment on a society which departs from His law. But such results are not the *main* reason to keep markets free— this would be a merely pragmatic argument. The main reason is because God has created and commanded men to be free: to own property, to engage in production and exchange, to reap the fruits and rewards of these efforts, or, should it be the case, to bear the consequences personally when those efforts fail. Individual responsibility goes both ways: no one else has a legal right to the fruit of your labor, you have no legal right to anyone else's, and no one else has a legal obligation to subsidize your failures or shortcomings. Legally speaking, a "free market" is a biblical view of markets. Anything short of this is evil—even the slightest regulation.

This means, further, that no level of civil government should be able to tell you whom you can or can't hire, how you must compensate them, what benefits you must provide them, to whom you must provide goods or services, where you may or may not build or operate, or things of this nature. Nor should civil government be allowed to use public funds to enter into the markets—either directly through ownership and operation, or indirectly through planning and contracts.

This includes all construction, engineering, architecture, utilities, inspection services, legal services, financing services, and of course, education, as well as anything else. The moment the government enters the markets with public money, with regulation, the markets become distorted and can certainly no longer be called free. Instead, they must be admitted, at that point, to be to some degree *rigged* markets.

Taxation and the Market

We should back up a step at this point: in truth, the moment the government appropriates funds via taxation (by whatever name), the fundamental distortion has already been committed. This takes money from the economy in one area, to be used in another area as determined by the civil government. This has some negative effects: first, it reduces freedom at least in regard to the confiscated money, which would otherwise have been used freely by the individual or corporation. The individual now has no (or very little) say over how that money will be spent. Further, individuals also lose any interest they would otherwise have earned should they have chosen to invest that money. Also, the reduction of liberty has an attendant increase in coercion. Not only is a central agency now forcing you to spend money in ways you don't control and with which you may not agree, but the whole process can begin only when the government *takes* your money. This taking is a form of violence. Worse yet, this sets a social precedent for how any given agenda or project *may* in fact succeed: through the initial and sustained violence of government agents.

Second, coercive taxation breeds and feeds a class of opportunists who rely heavily on government grants and contracts for their market livelihood. On one level, it leads to the rise of businesses which otherwise would not have had as many market opportunities had not the government subsidized those opportunities with confiscated money. These government-underwritten businesses, which might have failed

on their own power, then thrive and grow while self-support-
ing businesses that may have prospered in a free market never
appear or are squeezed out. On another level, since most "government projects" are large-scale, only larger companies *even
within the same industry* will qualify to compete for the contracts. This subsidizes "big" business and withholds opportunities from the little guy to which he may otherwise have had
access. Thus, government contracts tend to prosper not only
certain businesses as opposed to others, but often certain *big*
businesses as opposed to smaller ones, even in the same field.

With the rise of such big parasites comes a great moral
hazard—the risk of a system of graft becoming self-perpetu-
ating. When such a company grows largely due to infusions of
tax money through government contracts, then the only way
it will often be able to sustain its operations is through similar contracts in the future. In short, once created, monsters
have big appetites. And more often than not, the monster will
not sit and wait, but will go hunt to find its own food. Big
government-contracted businesses then have an incentive to
promote projects, suggest projects, foster conditions in which
new public projects become "necessary" or "in the public
interest," and possibly even instigate crises—by which their
companies may grab new contracts to feed the beast.

Such moral hazard also breeds political problems. Large
companies often employ large numbers of people. Thus, *not*
providing more government contracts would mean potentially
laying off thousands of people. Now you have a graft problem
supported by a political obstacle. Thus, large voting blocks
grow dependent upon tax-funded projects, and become special interests which sway elections.

Murray Rothbard relates some of the main ways government market interventions have affected our society:

> Urban planning has controlled and regulated the cities.
> Zoning laws have ringed housing and land use with innu-
> merable restrictions. Property taxes have crippled urban

development and forced abandonment of houses. Building codes have restricted housing construction and made it more costly. Urban renewal has provided massive subsidies to real estate developers, forced the bulldozing of apartments and rental stores, lowered the supply of housing, and intensified racial discrimination. Extensive government loans have generated overbuilding in the suburbs. Rent controls have created apartment shortages and reduced the supply of residential housing.[3]

All of these represent destructions of liberty and property. And all of this starts with one initial act of violence—coercive taxation—on the part of the civil government. As they say, violence begets violence.

All of this is to say that government manipulation of markets is not only unbiblical in principle, but it also creates a ripple of adverse practical consequences as the principle of entitlement through violence becomes the norm for society.

Markets in America

How have free markets thrived historically in America? Much like we discussed concerning taxation and money, America has never had truly free markets, at least not across the board. Of course, since both taxation and money and banking lie at the heart of commerce, any lack of integrity in those areas will reflect in direct proportion to the lack of freedom in markets. But just as we saw with those areas, markets have at least been much freer in many ways than they are today.

In *The Enterprising Americans*,[4] perhaps the best single historical study of American business development and entrepreneurship, John Chamberlain explores American economic endeavors from colonial times up through World War II and

---

[3] Murray N. Rothbard, *For a New Liberty: The Libertarian Manifesto*, 2nd Ed. (Auburn, AL: Ludwig von Mises Institute, 2006), 93.

[4] John Chamberlain, *The Enterprising Americans: A Business History of the United States* (Tyler, TX: Institute for Christian Economics, [1961] 1991).

a little beyond. He wrote specifically to fill a void in American historiography at the time: to confront the old, and more often than not *false*, leftist caricature of American entrepreneurs and businessmen as "robber barons." Chamberlain rather more properly provides "a history which would treat business as a prime creative force" in society.[5]

As we have discussed earlier, most of early America was settled as land grants from the crown. The governors and trustees of these grants then surveyed the land and apportioned smaller grants of local lands for cultivation by settlers. Trustees would often use free land or temporary property tax exemptions to entice settlers to come. There were certainly also more ambitious types with visions of town planning, and leveraging port cities as centers of trade.[6] Merchants became more numerous as did other members of the middle class.

In early America, two famous examples will serve as good illustrations—though with a little bit of the "warts and all" we encountered earlier. The classic self-made boot-strapper was Benjamin Franklin. One of seventeen children born to a Puritan immigrant family, Franklin started with next to nothing and built himself into perhaps the most famous man in the western world before the Revolution. He started as an apprentice in his brother's printing business, suffered through several failed partnerships and personal tragedies, and ended up with his own printing business as well as scientific advancements, discoveries, and inventions (not to mention his vast political works). And yet what is commonly not stressed is that Franklin never missed an opportunity to leverage government power to tilt the markets in his favor. His business's first major achievement was to bring public shame to the existing "public printer" in Philadelphia and swipe away that company's lucrative post. He then entered the political arena for his own benefit: he published a

---

[5] Chamberlain, *Enterprising Americans*, xvii.

[6] See John W. Reps, *Town Planning in Frontier America* (Princeton, NJ: Princeton University Press, 1969).

tract on the hot issue of a new inflation of paper money in Penn-sylvania (1729). The tract was in favor of inflation and was key to getting the measure through the Assembly. Not ironically, the contract to print the new paper money was immediately given to Franklin's company. Franklin called it "a very profitable job and a great help to me."[7] Franklin and government power were rarely seen apart for the rest of his life.

On the other hand is the early life of our second example—the later arch-nationalist and nemesis from earlier chapters, Alexander Hamilton. As we mentioned before, he was an ille-gitimate child who was subsequently orphaned at age twelve. Whereas Franklin at least had sound if meager beginnings, the odds were totally stacked against Hamilton. Like Franklin, he educated himself by reading voraciously, and he was gifted with an enormous intellect. He was surely destined for great-ness in the merchant classes, but, as we saw, he grew bored of accounting. Having read the classics, he lusted for military and stately fame. He got the whole classic shebang—including an ending straight out of a Greek tragedy.

In the lives of both of these great figures, we see the abil-ity to start with nothing and work one's way to success—the classic American dream. In the case of each, ambition and lust for fame drove them to chase State power for themselves and their agendas. And yet, in regard to the original achievement of success in the marketplace, *neither man needed nor greatly profited from the intervention of the State.* This is especially true for Hamilton who could have used a State-run welfare system at one time, but instead profited greatly by the private charity of the merchants who took him in *voluntarily.*

Throughout American history, you will find essentially three attitudes towards the market. There are actually only two, but one side breaks into two more. You have noninter-

---

[7] See Murray N. Rothbard, *Conceived in Liberty, Volume 2, "Salutary Neglect": The American Colonies in the First Half of the 18th Century* (New Rochelle, NY: Arlington House Publishers, 1975), 65–66.

ventionists and two varieties of interventionists—left and right. Chamberlain captures the image of the early self-sufficient, non-interventionist types of American lore:

> The mystery—and miracle—of early America is that people went to places before there was any way to get there—and took care of their transportation and marketing needs afterward. They followed Boone's old trace to the Cumberland Gap and moved by Indian trails to the open "streets" trampled by the buffalo. They clawed their way over the Alleghenies, following the ridges above the tributaries of the Susquehanna and the Monongahela—and when they couldn't find a way of getting their corn or wheat to market because of its bulk, they distilled it into whiskey and shipped it back to civilization by pack horse. Pioneers settled in Marietta and Cincinnati (once called Columbia) on the Ohio River somehow—and once in the West, and presumably "cut off" from their old homes, they made seagoing ships that actually sailed all the way back to the Atlantic by way of the Ohio, the Mississippi, and the Gulf of Mexico. In less exalted fashion they used crude flatboats to get their produce to New Orleans, returning overland by the Natchez Trace, a devious wilderness road where they risked losing the profits of their husbandry to a new breed of land pirate that infested the gloomy woods and canebrakes.[8]

The other two groups we have already essentially discussed—their descendants became the Hamiltonians and the Jeffersonians. In promise, they each offer only relative improvements upon the other, and in practice, both resorted to centralization and government power to subsidize favored industries and impose tariffs, taxes, deficit spending, etc. Neither side, despite any lip service to liberty or free trade, stood on principle in the area of free markets.

---

[8] Chamberlain, *Enterprising Americans*, 63.

Nevertheless, two great successes for market freedom occurred in that founding era. The first came with the Constitution, and the other came with the rise of industry. First, the Constitution created the largest free-trade zone in the world. This is perhaps the most important advance in the western world next to the optimistic Christian worldview which made it possible. By unifying interstate commerce and eliminating potential trade wars and turf wars between states, the Constitution achieved this goal.

This was a consequence of the Constitution; however, we should note that it certainly would not have required the imposition of the whole Constitutional settlement to bring it to pass. In fact, we shall see how that whole fabric has actually abetted the gradual centralization of commerce that has occurred since. At most, a tweak of the Articles of Confederation—or a Congressionally approved treaty signed by any state that wished to participate (and few would have declined, all else being equal)—could have accomplished the same result.

In fact, an early attempt at solving some of these issues more locally could have been a successful model: the 1785 Mount Vernon Compact was an agreement reached between a few representatives of Maryland and Virginia during a meeting at George Washington's house. It was essentially a free trade agreement between the states to share the waters of the Chesapeake Bay and the Potomac and Pocomoke Rivers. It could not have been a legal *treaty*, of course, since the Articles forbade interstate treaties not approved by Congress, but the proposal and the agreement were certainly a model for success. Instead of pursuing this route, which would have remained uncoupled with greater political centralization, the gentlemen involved decided to have a bigger, better version of the Conference with all the states. This occurred the following year at Annapolis but was largely a failure due to low attendance from several states. A bigger, better Conference yet was pushed for by a small group of men, and achieved. This led to the Philadelphia Convention in 1787, but by now the nationalist coup was already well underway. Out of this came the Constitution and the system we have today.

The second major event was the industrial revolution. Vast increases in technology, manufacturing, transportation, and communications in a short period of time totally transformed production, lowered prices on consumer goods, and increased standards of living. Chamberlain provides a great example in one vignette:

> The year is 1803, and Terry, the teacher of a long line of Yankee clockmakers, is already making clocks in his Naugatuck Valley [CT] factory for which he has no storage space. With four clocks ready for sale Terry has to tear himself away from his mill, load the clocks into saddlebags, and take off over the hills toward "York State," walking beside his horse because the load is too heavy to permit a passenger. The clocks are offered at $25 each on the installment plan; when cash is entirely lacking they are "sold" for corn meal, beeswax, sailcloth, or woven cloth, commodities that can be bartered on the way home or passed on to workmen in lieu of cash wages. Four years later Terry has a bigger mill—and has adopted the full Eli Whitney technique of punching out standardized and interchangeable wheels and clock faces. He is now prepared to sell a clock for $5. . . .[9]

Thus in a mere four years did production techniques drop his product price by eighty percent. As soon as transportation caught up with the revolution—better roads, canals, the steam boat—sales would increase proportionally.

Of course, the process of developing these roads, canals, etc., as well as many other big ventures, was hardly left to free markets alone. In many, many cases, companies took loans and grants from the government or they secured monopolies (and thus profits) through government intervention. But even in

---

[9] Chamberlain, *Enterprising Americans*, 64.

an atmosphere of rigged markets, the free market was always close—ready to offer a viable alternative when monopolies stagnated. Chamberlain relates:

> Monopolies—oil was the most notorious of them—waxed fat only to recede into the pack, sometimes pursued by antitrust laws, as later arrivals came on the scene. Meanwhile new products and processes continually rose to compete with the old. Aluminum, even when there was only one company in the field, had to fight it out with wood at one extreme and steel at the other. Du Pont artificial fibers freed the textile business from dependence on cotton, silk, and wool. The railroads were controlled more effectively by competition from automobile and truck and airplane than they were by the ICC. From telephones to television, the electrical revolution leaped from dependence on wires to dependence on wave lengths in God's free ether. Came, too, the supermarkets and consumer credit, washing machines, home freezers, and the split-level ranchhouse which never looked upon a longhorn steer.[10]

With successes such as these, both left and right interventionists have always been able to speak in favor of free markets, but it's generally been a deception on their part. Free markets persist in many ways not *because of* either major party, but mainly *in spite of* their various interventions. We can say with confidence, however, that the free market has historically prevailed more here in America than anywhere else. This is what has made her great and wealthy, and this is what has established America's lasting reputation as a land of opportunity. The idea has been trampled many times, but it does shine through the cracks of the government superstructure that has so often overshadowed our greatest resource: the law of God—the belief in protecting private property, liberty, and life.

---

[10] Chamberlain, *Enterprising Americans*, xxii–xxiii.

We can also say with confidence that average Americans once understood this and sought to practice it—private property, enforcement of contracts—beginning with their own bare hands. And when allowed to remain free, free markets have indeed worked, and worked well. In fact, it took the efforts of many centralizers to railroad America into economic tyranny.

America's Not-So-Free Markets

Much like topics in previous chapters, to talk about "the loss of freedom" in regard to markets is not quite accurate. Although they have often been much freer than they are today, America has never had truly free markets. The causes for this are multiple—everything from ideology to graft, war and crisis, socialistic schemes and bank fraud, big business and big government. The list is really endless, but could be boiled down to covetousness and greed armed with the guns of government.

Mistakes abounded from day one. The first pilgrim colony attempted to enforce a communistic society. In months, the communal storehouse was almost exhausted. It did not take long for some to learn they could slack in working and yet receive the same amount of rationed victuals; meanwhile, those who did work hard to produce more did not receive compensation commensurate with their efforts—those who produced less consumed the extra fruits of those who worked more. Soon, everyone slacked and the storehouse was empty. Half of the settlers died in the first winter. The governors learned the hard way, though slowly; it took three years into the settlement when they finally took the advice of the farmers who were doing the work: land was divided into private plots. Greater prosperity soon followed. The story is well known. What is lesser known is that many elements of this quickly-privatized property economy remained under common ownership and government control. This improved only after 1675.[11]

---

[11] See Gary North, *Puritan Economic Experiments* (Tyler, TX: Institute for

The path toward great wealth in colonial America was often through State-sanctioned monopoly. In fact, many of the colonies were founded—as we have discussed—as land-grant charters from the English crown. These in themselves were meant to be monopolistic sources of wealth: ports were controlled, tariffs imposed, and merchants depended upon the crown to protect them from competitors in every way. This State-Big business alliance is called mercantilism and, in many ways, still exists today. It was criticized by Adam Smith, who published *The Wealth of Nations* the same year America declared independence.

Despite the ascendancy of Smith's views of freer economics, many early Americans favored the British model of mercantilism—not the least of which were Hamilton, Washington and the Federalist/Nationalist party. Indeed, as we saw earlier under the topic of states' rights, Washington, Hamilton, and Madison, among others, colluded to establish corporate welfare—essentially a form of mercantilism in which a few businesses get the special monopolistic favor and subsidy of government—as the rule in the new nationalized government. In the first-ever State of the Union address, Washington favored, as we noted, the establishment of a State-funded military-industrial complex during peacetime, but he also recommended State subsidies for manufacturing, Indian suppression, agriculture, commerce, transportation, postal services, science and education, as well as public finance. Here are his words:

> The advancement of agriculture, commerce, and manu-
> factures, by all proper means, will not, I trust, need rec-
> ommendation. But I cannot forbear intimating to you
> the expediency of giving effectual encouragement [that
> is, *money*], as well to the introduction of new and useful
> inventions from abroad, as to the exertions of skill and
> genius in producing them at home; and of facilitating
> the intercourse between the distant parts of our coun-

Christian Economics, 1988), 5–9.

try, by a due attention to the post office and post roads.

Nor am I less persuaded that you will agree with me in opinion, that there is nothing which can better deserve your patronage than the promotion of science and literature. Knowledge is, in every country, the surest basis of public happiness. In one in which the measures of Government receive their impression so immediately from the sense of the community, as in ours, it is proportionably essential. . . .

Whether this desirable object will be best promoted by affording aids to seminaries of learning already established; by the institution of a national university; or by any other expedients—will be well worthy of a place in the deliberations of the Legislature.

And Washington finished his speech with a populist nod to the "common good" which any modern liberal could love:

The welfare of our country is the great object to which our cares and efforts ought to be directed; and I shall derive great satisfaction from a co-operation with you, in the pleasing, though arduous task, of ensuring to our fellow-citizens the blessings which they have a right to expect from a free, efficient, and equal Government.

Thus, the precedent of America as a Welfare-Warfare State was solidified in her infancy—although the welfare at this point was mainly corporate welfare—early neo-mercantilism.

These beginnings were mild when compared to what would come, but they represent the very same principle in action. Federal subsidies gradually expanded to cover more special interest groups. After all, how very many things can be justified under the "great object" of the "welfare of our country." If a *little* funding for education is a good thing, then why not *a whole lot of it*? Why not compulsory government education? If a little funding for postal roads is a good thing, then why not for transportation in general? Especially since the promotion of "commerce" was already established in general, why not extend that principle to cover more convenient transportation of goods for those subsidized groups? Indeed, this is exactly what happened: the national government subsidized roads, bridges, canals, locks, dams, and eventually, the mother of all public-private schemes of the nineteenth century—railroads.

Both major parties embraced these schemes from early on. Jefferson's treasury secretary proposed a system of tax funded waterways, and nationalists like Henry Clay and John Quincy Adams favored a whole system of internal improvements including general transportation.[12] Early turnpike projects gained state charters, and in some cases state funding. The Eerie Canal was built based on state bonds floated under the persuasion of DeWitt Clinton.[13] Chamberlain declares candidly:

> The American people, though they had resented British mercantilism, were not averse to government help when it came to getting goods to market. . . . As in Britain, the pertinacity of businessmen seeking a profit contributed significantly to what modern economists choose to call the "public sector" of the economy.[14]

And again, this was often (almost always) justified by some appeal to the common good or the welfare of the nation. Well, as the saying goes, the road to hell is paved with good intentions. What the cliché neglects to mention is that the pavers are government employees, and that those "good" intentions are funded via hell's most egregious abuse—the public treasury.

The Destructive Power of the Commerce Clause

No area of American life displays this abuse more systematically than the progressive tyranny that has stemmed from the Commerce Clause of the U.S. Constitution (Article 1, Sec-

---

[12] Chamberlain, *Enterprising Americans*, 63–66.

[13] Ibid., 67–68.

[14] Ibid., 64–65.

tion 8, Clause 3). The Article empowers Congress "to regulate Commerce with foreign Nations, and among the several States, and with the Indian Tribes." The abuse has grown most particularly in regard to commerce "among the several States." Throughout American history, Congress has employed this Clause gradually to expand Federal control over every area of life. And, for the most part, the Courts have approved.

We have said quite a bit already about John Marshall's role in legislating Hamilton's (and the general Federalist) agenda from the bench and how this included centralized control over state power in courts, banking, taxation, and many other issues, including commerce. The Constitutional issue came to the fore in a 1995 Supreme Court case, *The United States v. Lopez*, which rehearsed a decent amount of the history in this regard, beginning, not surprisingly, with Marshall.

It was Marshall who vehemently upheld Congress's right to regulate Interstate Commerce. In 1824, he decided the landmark case, *Gibbons v. Ogden*, which confirmed that control of commerce was a primary motive of the centralizing instrument, the Constitution. Earlier, we reviewed Madison's comments in regard to New York and the real purposes of the Constitution: "which was among other things to take from that State the important power over its commerce." In *Gibbons v. Ogden*, we hear Marshall summarizing the same sentiment:

> Few things were better known, than the immediate causes which led to the adoption of the present constitution; and he [the plaintiff, on the nationalist side of the case] thought nothing clearer, than that the prevailing motive was to regulate commerce. . . .The great objects were commerce and revenue; and they were objects indissolubly connected.[15]

[15] 22 U.S. 1, 11 (1824); online at http://caselaw.lp.findlaw.com/scripts/getcase.pl?court=us&vol=22&invol=1 (acessed Sept. 25, 2012).

Again, "In the history of the times, it was accordingly found, that the great topic, urged on all occasions, as showing the necessity of a new and different government, was the state of trade and commerce."[16] Marshall reviews historical evidence backing this claim and concludes,

> We do not find, in the history of the formation and adoption of the constitution, that any man speaks of a general concurrent power, in the regulation of foreign and domestic trade, as still residing in the States. *The very object intended, more than any other, was to take away such power.*[17]

Quotations like this are reiterated throughout the decision. Marshall deemed it important to solidify national control in this area, and specifically to limit the role of individual states. For states to share in the power, Marshall concluded, "is insidious and dangerous." He warned of a slippery slope: "If it be admitted, no one can say where it will stop."

Of course, slippery slopes may run both ways. The same argument can be put against Marshall's centralized system: once Congress begins to regulate various aspects of commerce, no one can say where it will stop. It's one thing to strike down shipping monopolies one state grants to cargo ships travelling interstate waters (the subject in dispute in *Gibbons*). It's quite another thing to argue that the Federal government can intrude into local schools by defining "education" as "commerce," declaring potential crime in schools as a threat to the insurance industry (commerce), and then arguing that any threat to education is therefore a threat to the economy in general. Yet this is exactly what the government argued in 1995 in *U.S. v. Lopez*. Thankfully, the Supreme Court acknowledged, finally, that there has to be some limit on the Federal power; the gov-

---

[16] 22 U.S. 1, 11 (1824); online at http://caselaw.lp.findlaw.com/scripts/getcase. pl?court=us&vol=22&invol=1 (acessed Sept. 25, 2012).

[17] 22 U.S. 1, 13 (1824); online at http://caselaw.lp.findlaw.com/scripts/getcase. pl?court=us&vol=22&invol=1 (acessed Sept. 25, 2012). Emphasis added.

ernment had gone too far in regard to interstate commerce in this case, and the Court decided against the U.S.

Nevertheless, Marshall himself had expressed that this power is *unlimited*: "This power, like all others vested in Congress, is complete in itself, may be exercised to its utmost extent, and acknowledges no limitations, other than are prescribed in the constitution." The *Lopez* decision rehearses the long train of compromises, abuses, and usurpations which have piggy-backed onto the Constitutional power since Marshall's 1824 decision:

> For nearly a century thereafter, the Court's Commerce Clause decisions dealt but rarely with the extent of Congress' power, and almost entirely with the Commerce Clause as a limit on state legislation that discriminated against interstate commerce. . . .
>
> In 1887, Congress enacted the Interstate Commerce Act, and in 1890, Congress enacted the Sherman Antitrust Act, as amended. *These laws ushered in a new era of federal regulation under the commerce power.* When cases involving these laws first reached this Court, we imported from our negative Commerce Clause cases the approach that Congress could not regulate activities such as "production," "manufacturing," and "mining."[18]

In other words, even though this legislation increased tyranny, it still formally retained a view of limits upon Congress' power. But it was the first step toward serious compromise:

> Simultaneously, however, the Court held that, where the interstate and intrastate aspects of commerce were so mingled together that full regulation of interstate commerce required incidental regulation of intrastate commerce, the Commerce Clause authorized such regulation.[19]

---

[18] Emphasis added.

[19] 514 U.S. 549, 553–554 (1995), available online https://supreme.justia.com/cases/federal/us/514/549/case.html (accessed Sept. 25, 2012).

This arrangement lasted only until FDR's New Deal legislation moved to enforce labor and wage laws, and another new era was in view. The Courts at first struck these down:

> In *A. L. A. Schecter Poultry Corp. v. United States* (1935), the Court struck down regulations that fixed the hours and wages of individuals employed by an intrastate business because the activity being regulated related to interstate commerce only indirectly. . . . Activities that affected interstate commerce directly were within Congress' power; activities that affected interstate commerce indirectly were beyond Congress' reach. . . . The justification for this formal distinction was rooted in the fear that otherwise "there would be virtually no limit to the federal power and for all practical purposes we should have a completely centralized government."[20]

This decision was actually a death blow to FDR's New Deal legislation, for a moment. FDR and the progressive tyrants had no use for "limits to the federal power" in any way; this is when his great pressure on the Courts began. Sadly, the same Court that rejected the New Deal as unconstitutional in 1935 melted enough under pressure by 1937 to allow for radical reinterpretation:

> Two years later, in the watershed case of *NLRB v. Jones & Laughlin Steel Corp.* (1937), the Court upheld the National Labor Relations Act against a Commerce Clause challenge, and in the process, *departed from the distinction between "direct" and "indirect" effects on interstate commerce.* . . . The Court held that intrastate activities that "have such a close and substantial relation to interstate commerce that their control is essential or appropriate to protect that commerce from burdens and obstructions" are within Congress' power to regulate. . . .[21]

---

[20] 514 U.S. 549, 554–555 (1995)

[21] 514 U.S. 549, 555 (1995) Emphasis added.

The dikes were thus exploded, and so came the flood:

In *United States v. Darby* (1941), the Court upheld the Fair Labor Standards Act, stating:
"The power of Congress over interstate commerce is not confined to the regulation of commerce among the states. It extends to those activities intrastate which so affect interstate commerce or the exercise of the power of Congress over it as to make regulation of them appropriate means to the attainment of a legitimate end, the exercise of the granted power of Congress to regulate interstate commerce." . . .

See also *United States v. Wrightwood Dairy Co.* (1942) (the commerce power "extends to those intrastate activities which in a substantial way interfere with or obstruct the exercise of the granted power").

In *Wickard v. Filburn*, the Court upheld the application of amendments to the Agricultural Adjustment Act of 1938 to the production and consumption of home-grown wheat. The Wickard Court *explicitly rejected earlier distinctions* between direct and indirect effects on interstate commerce, stating:
"Even if appellee's activity be local and though it may not be regarded as commerce, it may still, whatever its nature, be reached by Congress if it exerts a substantial economic effect on interstate commerce, and this irrespective of whether such effect is what might at some earlier time have been defined as 'direct' or 'indirect.'" [In other words, the New Deal Court *completely* ignored judicial precedent.]

The Wickard Court emphasized that although Filburn's own contribution to the demand for wheat may have been trivial by itself, that was not "enough to remove him from the scope of federal regulation where, as here, his contribution, taken together with that of many others similarly situated, is far from trivial."

Jones & Laughlin Steel, Darby, and Wickard ushered in an era of Commerce Clause jurisprudence that *greatly expanded the previously defined authority of*

Congress under that Clause. In part, this was a recognition of the great changes that had occurred in the way
business was carried on in this country. Enterprises that
had once been local or at most regional in nature had
become national in scope. But *the doctrinal change also
reflected a view that earlier Commerce Clause cases artificially had constrained the authority of Congress to
regulate interstate commerce.*[22]

Thus the Commerce Clause has provided us the avenue to
tyranny—a highway to hell. Sure enough, Marshall's grant of
unlimited power clasically boasted good intentions: "The only
remedy has been applied which the case admits of; that of a
frank and candid co-operation for the general good."

As Gabriel Kolko's book *The Triumph of Conservatism*
(by "conservatism" he means big-business/big-government
partnership) makes clear, it was the Rockefellers, Carnegies,
Morgans, etc., who used Interstate Commerce regulation to
secure fat business contracts and monopolies at the expense
of taxpayers and small businesses, all in the name of trust-
busting, stabilization, and price controls. During this era:

> The federal government, rather than being a source
> of negative opposition, always represented a potential
> source of economic gain. The railroads, of course, had
> used the federal and local governments for subsidies
> and land grants. But various other industries appreci-
> ated the desirability of proper tariffs, direct subsidies in
> a few instances, government-owned natural resources,
> or monopolistic privileges possible in certain federal
> charters or regulations. . . .
>
> It was perfectly logical that industrialists who had
> spent years attempting to solve their economic prob-
> lems by centralization should have been willing to re-
> sort to political centralization as well.[23]

---

[22] 514 U.S. 549, 555–556 (1995). Emphasis added.

[23] Gabriel Kolko, *The Triumph of Conservatism: A Reinterpretation of Ameri-*

This is exactly what they did. Beginning with the creation of the Interstate Commerce Commission (ICC) in 1887 (as the *Lopez* case noted), the big-business magnates used government regulation to squeeze out smaller competitors.

Once the bureaucracies were in place, it made little difference who or what party took office. Thus, when the conservative Democrat Grover Cleveland took office, Andrew Carnegie's partner Henry Clay Frick glossed, "I am very sorry for President Harrison . . . but I cannot see that our interests are going to be affected one way or the other by the change in administration."[24]

Kolko notes the resilience of free enterprise despite increasing encroachments from the big-corporate-big finance-state alliance. After surveying the industries of iron and steel, oil, automobiles, agricultural machinery, telephones, copper, and meat packing up until 1890, he concludes that decentralized competition ruled the day despite efforts of major financiers to consolidate and monopolize the trades:

> The failure of the merger movement to attain control over the economic conditions in the various industries was brought about by the inability of the consolidated firms to attain sufficient technological advantages or economies of size over their smaller competitors—contrary to common belief and the promises of promoters.[25]

The big financiers—J. P. Morgan & Co., etc.—would not give up their quests for total domination simply because they could not win fairly in a free marketplace. They had no qualms at all about turning to government intervention and regulation. Thus, in the period immediately following the failed merger movement—the beginning of the twentieth century—we saw a rise in Progressive government domination. Indeed, "The dominant fact of American political life at the beginning

---

can History, 1900–1916 (New York: The Free Press of Glencoe, 1963), 59–60.

[24] Kolko, *Triumph of Conservatism*, 62.

[25] Ibid., 55.

of this century [20th] was that big business led the struggle for the federal regulation of the economy."[26] So we return to our earlier statement about covetousness and greed armed with the guns of government. Big business interests simply have used government coercion as a means of gaining a market advantage and forcing out smaller competitors.

And the big business was not shy about admitting their agenda clearly. For example, J. P. Morgan owned the agricultural machine company International Harvester. After Teddy Roosevelt established the Bureau of Corporations—designed allegedly to investigate and expose any monopolistic powers on the part of big corporations—IH came under suspicion and an investigation was ordered. The matter was a joke, for IH already had a back-room deal with the administration that an informal warning would give time to correct any "illegal" activity in the meantime. Indeed, IH's lawyer told the administration that the company welcomed exposure showing actual losses on the Company's behalf, "for then they would have just ground for raising American prices."[27] The Company was quite serious, and it raised prices with sanction from the Federal Bureau's reports "to prevent attacks from less friendly parties, and as a general shield."[28]

Noticeable also in this respect were the massive railroad companies. Not only had they used "federal and local governments for subsidies and land grants" from early on, but "railroads themselves had been the leading advocates of extended federal legislation after 1887."[29] Indeed, the railroads wanted to use Federal authority to guarantee their pooling agreements and thus free them from the disruptive pressures and temptations of the market."[30]

---

[26] Ibid., 57–58.

[27] Ibid., 119–120.

[28] Ibid., 120.

[29] Ibid., 59.

[30] Stephen Skowronek, *Building a New American State: The Expansion of Na-*

What has been said so far is a large part of the reason it is such a joke when modern leftists rail against free market principles as the historical cause of inequality, class warfare, and all our economic woes. There has been very little "free market" to begin with; this country hasn't had free markets very often at all, historically speaking. And the "capitalism" of the big bank-government collusion that we have today is hardly free-market capitalism. It's *rigged state capitalism*, which is to say it's socialistic to a large degree.

This arrangement extends into every industry and trade from finance to agriculture. Far from basic biblical protection of private property and enforcement of contracts, our governments have too often redistributed property in various ways (sometimes under the guise of free-market capitalism) and they have led the way in sidestepping contractual agreements. We have seen here only a smidgeon of how American governments have done so.

The solution is not what the leftists prescribe—it's not *more* government control and wealth redistribution. We've had enough of that already. Leftists just want to change the recipients of State welfare from the corporations to the masses. Nor is this to say big corporations are inherently evil in themselves—they are not corrupt of necessity. Proponents of the free market, however, want to establish true private property and abolish the State-enforced welfare scheme altogether—both for the masses and the favored businesses.

Putting "Free" Back Into Free Markets

If the road to hell is paved with good intentions, the road to freedom is rocky, uphill, and lined with thieves lying in wait. The path to restore freedom in markets and even to arrive at a

tional Administrative Capacities, 1877–1920 (Cambridge, UK: Cambridge University Press, 1982), 129.

totally free marketplace is the straight and narrow way indeed. Traveling it to its end will require personal integrity, fortitude, sacrifice, patience, and endurance. It will require these qualities in *society*—not just a few scattered individuals.

In simple terms, the road to free markets requires a personal and society-wide return to the principles that headed up this chapter: non-violence to a person's life or private property and enforcement of contracts. We must personally embrace these principles, and structure our lives, work, and businesses accordingly. More importantly, we have to *maintain* this discipline: we must absolutely refuse to depart from God's laws even when it is more profitable, more convenient, and more socially acceptable to do so. We won't have a moral leg to stand on until we practice fiscal integrity ourselves. We can't demand of society what we are unwilling to abide by ourselves. The model here is the Messiah, of whom David said in Psalm 15:

> O LORD, who shall sojourn in your tent?
>   Who shall dwell on your holy hill?
> He who walks blamelessly and does what is right
>   and speaks truth in his heart;
> who does not slander with his tongue
>   and does no evil to his neighbor,
>   nor takes up a reproach against his friend;
> in whose eyes a vile person is despised,
>   but who honors those who fear the LORD;
> who swears to his own hurt and does not change;
> who does not put out his money at interest
>   and does not take a bribe against the innocent.
> He who does these things shall never be moved.

This guy refuses to do anything dishonest, and this certainly applies to his business dealings. More importantly, he "swears to his own hurt and does not change." This does not necessarily mean he swears to his own hurt on purpose (even though Christ did go to the cross voluntarily), but when circumstances turn against him, he does not try to alter the promises or contracts he previously made simply to maintain profits or prevent losses. He bears the brunt of the deal and takes the sacrifice.

He will even go further. When he sees that society has departed from God's laws—that fraud and extortion have become socially accepted ways of life, that most people allow, depend on, or even thrive on coercive, rigged markets—he refuses to participate anyway. He will suffer the burdens of inconvenience, lower profits, decreased business, social stigma, and even persecution in order to remain faithful. Anyone who wants to return to freedom in the marketplace will have to embrace this level of sacrifice and commitment from the beginning.

This embrace will mean a clear application of the principle, "Don't take the cheese." Only now, it's not only to avoid the trap, it's also—perhaps *more* so—because it's immoral, unbiblical, unethical, and ungodly to take the cheese to begin with. This is not merely about personal and practical consequences, it's about *principle*. It's about faithfulness to God's law.

A large part of this effort will be mental and thus spiritual. People need to accept the mindset that the use of government force to gain a personal advantage is equivalent to theft. It is an unstated—ne'er to be stated—political maxim among conservatives: *Socialism is bad... except when it benefits me.* When the modern conservative says, "Socialism is bad," he really means, "The other guy's socialism is bad. Mine is good, right, laudable, and necessary." Until we leap this psychological hurdle, freedom is a distant goal.

Of course, getting people to do this by just stating it here is almost equivalent to asking, "Can't we all just get along?" Getting from where we are today to the point where the biblical mindset is both widely believed and widely practiced will require the same discipline and sacrifice for many people that we have already discussed in previous chapters. And these are key: *sacrifice* and *discipline.* Both will be necessary 1) to prepare a faithful remnant as a foundation and example into the future, 2) to facilitate the transition from where we are today to a free society, and 3) to *maintain* markets free of corruption, tyranny, and graft *after* a transition is effected.

Before I address the best way to make an impact, let's discuss a couple of ways this commitment could change your personal lifestyle. Embracing this commitment will probably mean changing where and how you shop and do business, what you buy to eat, wear, etc., what you drive, and where you live and what you live in (if such a change could be made practically at this point). You will no longer choose the best bargains, or make simply self-interested economic decisions. Self-interest is now replaced by sacrifice and discipline to God's law. If you don't believe in government-funded corporations, then why would you support them through your purchases if you have other options? Even if more private options cost you a little more, why not prefer the slightly more expensive, slightly less comfortable, or slightly less *prestigious* principle and integrity over minor personal gain?

The purist who wishes ideally to live completely without supporting companies that receive government subsidies will find this very difficult. Virtually everything in our economy today is in some way, at some level, to some degree, tainted by government interference. Of course, since the entire monetary system is rigged to begin with, as we have seen, then virtually no economic decision we make will be truly free of government manipulation and intervention. No bank we use is, or can be, truly honest at this point. The only way to avoid this is to swear off the use of Federal Reserve money altogether, and this would mean living by barter and self-sustaining agriculture—Amish style—and even then you could not totally escape the government's hand.[31] So, in many ways we are stuck in the unfair system of bank subsidy and privilege—and that leads to unfair investment and market subsidies as well.

---

[31] Study, for example, the difference between fee-simple ownership of property, and tax-free alloidal ownership which is almost non-existent and difficult to obtain.

One market that is seeing a resurgence of resistance is the food market. Many local people and towns, as we have already seen, are fighting to establish freedom and local sovereignty over food. The fact is, nearly every aspect of agribusiness today is massively subsidized. Between 1995 and 2010, the Feds have dumped more than $260 billion into agribusiness subsidies.[32] Subsidized (and overproduced) corn, wheat, and soybeans find their way into almost everything sold in grocery stores in the forms of corn syrup, enriched wheat flour, and soybean oil. Pick up any packaged or processed food and you will likely find at least one of these ingredients, if not all. It does save you a few dimes here and there, but comes at the cost of continual government intervention, and agricultural dependence on government handouts, not to mention the loss of nutrition in processed foods. Why not buy as much food as you can from local growers? Why not find a local milk producer who will sell to you directly? Why not buy as often as possible from local farmers' markets? Same with chicken, eggs, meat, and much more.

Same with sugary snacks, by the way (and I am no health-food Nazi!). American sugar is subsidized—by limiting the amount that can be imported. There are only a handful of American sugar producers, and they fight to maintain special protection from many foreign competitors. Since so sweeping a program provides so great an advantage to so few producers, the subsidy is actually staggering. Analyst James Bovard writes, "Since 1980, the sugar program has cost consumers and taxpayers the equivalent of more than $3 million for each American sugar grower." He concludes, "Some people win

---

[32] The Environmental Working Group (www.farm.ewg.org) has a fabulous website listing subsidy recipients by name and amount down to the level of your local ZIP code. If you wish to avoid subsidized companies, here's a tool. This is a great resource, and is funded through donations. Their major flaw comes in not opposing subsidy and regulation in principle, but only those they consider destructive to the environment. The group aims to continue subsidies, but merely shift them to other areas. This is not a free-market solution, although they offer a powerful free-market tool.

the lottery; other people grow sugar."[33] Since this market is so rigged, and sugar admittedly is a luxury item anyway, why not cut it from your diet as much as possible? This would eliminate your contribution to the subsidy of one sector. (Meanwhile, major candy companies have closed some operations in the U.S. and moved to Mexico where both the sugar and labor are cheaper. And since what they import to the U.S. is a finished manufactured good—not raw sugar—they dodge the sugar tariff problem.)

Another consumer issue is transportation. Here's the best formula for personal automobiles: buy used, pay cash, drive it until the wheels fall off. This helps minimize contributions to autoworkers unions whose collective bargaining rights leverage government power to increase worker benefits of all sorts. This is especially important for automobiles manufactured in states where collective bargaining rights hold sway and workers are forced to unionize. Due to their government-rigged market, auto workers make, on average, about $55/hour in wages and benefits.[34] That's a six-figure package *per worker* compared to the median *household* income in the U.S. of $45,000. United Auto Workers is so proud of its accomplishments that it produces a yearly updated website listing all the automobiles its unionized workers produce. I would suggest downloading this list, reviewing it, and making decisions on what to buy and what to avoid accordingly.

Purchasing used instead of new vehicles compounds the power of your decisions since you support only the local dealer—not necessarily the manufacturer. The previous buyer already paid the inflated price to the manufacturer. Of course, you will also support the financier unless you pay cash. But to make your used purchase have the greatest economic impact,

---

[33] "The Great Sugar Shaft," April 1998, http://www.fff.org/freedom/0498d.asp (accessed November 10, 2011).

[34] See "Auto Worker Salaries," See "Auto Worker Salaries," http://www.fact-check.org/2008/12/auto-worker-salaries/.

drive it forever. This keeps one more customer (you) from further supporting a union-rigged market.

This type of thinking can be taken to any extent you wish, and into every facet of every market you desire. I have only included a couple examples here—food and personal transportation—to demonstrate *how* to think in this regard. How can you apply the same principle—avoiding companies that leverage government coercion for their profits—in every other area of your life? I leave that up to you.

You could also support organizations which fight for the free-market principles you believe in. There are public interest law firms that specialize in all manner of property rights, free market rights, gun rights, and many others.[35] Firms like these are usually non-profit and can be supported via tax-deductible donations. There are certainly many more. You should search for one regionally, or one which you prefer; research it carefully; talk to staff and leaders if possible to determine a sense of their values and goals. And then, if you wish, support their cause.

But the best way you can personally impact society in regard to free markets is to start a business. Legitimate, honest businesses generate wealth, provide services to communities, and create jobs. Sure, this will not in itself decrease the number of taxes, subsidies, and regulations in society—if anything, you will discover various taxes you never knew existed. But this in turn will give you further incentive to fight for a free society. Greater Christian, ethical entrepreneurship is the key to spreading the interests of freedom in society.

Business and entrepreneurship will require education for some people. It should be an educational priority especially for

---

[35] There is, for example, a National Right to Work Legal Defense Foundation based in Springfield, VA (http://www.nrtw.org/). They exist for the purpose of "defending America's workers from the abuses of forced unionization." There is the Pacific Legal Foundation in Sacramento which "fights for limited government, property rights, individual rights and a balanced approach to environmental protection" (http://www.pacificlegal.org/). The Southeastern Legal Foundation in Marietta, GA is another (http://www.southeasternlegal.org/).

your children as well. Without proper guidance, children are indoctrinated to socialistic principles from early ages. A study done years ago by John Hunter revealed no significant difference in economic worldviews between Christian and secular colleges. Thus, despite having the Ten Commandments allegedly at their base, Christians have no advantage in learning and embracing free markets. This is true not just in college but at an early age. The Nehemiah Institute has conducted extensive tests that show significant departures from biblical thinking can begin as early as fifth and sixth grade. This organization offers educational resources on biblical economics and government. There is also the similarly named but independent Nehemiah Project, which offers many training courses, books, and resources on biblical principles for entrepreneurship and business.

As Christians, we must attend to more than just the economic, political, or legal aspects of free enterprise. Christian business is as much an endeavor of *stewardship* as it is anything else. If we are to perpetuate a free society, we must value more than just the bottom line. Indeed, in many cases, people and values should come before profits. This does not mean that we need government interventions for wage and price controls, etc.—far from it. But it does mean that God's moral laws call us to treat workers with dignity and respect, pay them well, as well as reduce waste in executive expenses, etc. Sure, it should be perfectly *legal* to do otherwise, but it's still poor practice in God's eyes. Business owners, officers, and executives that embrace such license—exploiting employees for gain, etc.—should recognize increases in government regulation and socialistic tyranny as God's judgment against a society where such things abound. This is not by any means to defend government-labor relations or the vast body of regulations as "godly" in the way some liberal progressive "Christians" do. Rather, just as God used pagan Babylon to enslave a disobedient nation of Israel, so He today will use tyranny to punish careless, heartless business practices in society.

Some great companies have already set precedents in this regard. The Guinness brewing company spread God's kingdom-charity through the care it showed for its workers. It has historically paid its workers much higher wages than average (thereby recruiting and retaining the best and brightest talent, while helping others who might otherwise have been left poor). But this was not all. Journalist Stephen Mansfield relates the following Guinness company benefits from a 1928 company report (at the height of international corporate greed right before the Great Depression):

- All employees with their wives and children enjoyed the services of an on-site clinic staffed by full-time doctors night and day; these doctors also made house calls.

- Medical services included company-dedicated dentists, pharmacists, nurses, home sanitation consultants, and a masseuse.

- Retirees received pensions, in some cases even when they never contributed to the fund. Pensions extended to widows.

- Most funeral expenses for company families and family members were paid by the company.

- The company had its own bank, and provided mortgages for company families.

- The company spurred living standards with domestic skill competitions. It gave cash awards for sewing, cooking, decorating, gardening, and hat making. The same was true for crafts, trades, and sports of all kinds.

- The company provided concerts and lectures for moral and intellectual improvement, especially for housewives.

- Guinness paid for employees' education: they could advance in technical school, trades, side-businesses, or more advanced education. The company paid all and provided a library and lounges for study.

- The company provided paid vacations including train fares and spending cash.[36]

Many of the workers enjoying these benefits had just fought a decade earlier in World War I, but they did not fear losing their benefits: Guinness guaranteed their jobs would be available for them when they returned.[37]

Yet these workers were *entitled* to none of these things (and the government was involved in demanding and/or requiring none in this case). No business owes anything to its workers except a fair-market compensation (and thus whatever the parties agree upon, Luke 20:1–16). All of these special benefits were private, voluntary subsidies—*Christian charity distributed through regular business.*[38] Christian businessmen should emulate this example with their employees, in some cases above and beyond the minimum government mandate.

Other great examples to review are the efforts at leadership and employee relations successfully revived and reformed by Christian business leaders such as Wayne Alderson. He developed the "Value of the Person" program to rescue labor management at a struggling Pittron Steel company. It was Christian-based and highly successful. So much so that a young R.C. Sproul, Sr., wrote a book about the episode called, *Stronger Than Steel.* Other great conservative success stories include Lemuel R. Boulware's awesome but unfortunately-titled book, *The Truth About Boulwarism*, and the wonderful private charity and leadership of William Volker, described in *Mr. Anonymous* by Herbert C. Cornuelle. All of these deserve

---

[36] Stephen Mansfield, *The Search for God and Guinness: A Biography of the Beer that Changed the World* (Nashville, TN: Thomas Nelson, 2009), xix–xxii.

[37] Ibid., xxviii.

[38] I have excerpted these comments on Guinness from my book, *What Would Jesus Drink?: A Spirit-Filled Study* (White Hall, VA: Tolle Lege Press, 2011), 121–123.

greater exploration which I plan to provide in supplemental articles and videos.

If you really want to expand the principle of freedom, you should aim not only at the reduction of taxes and regulations, but also at the privatization of roads, bridges, ports, parks, libraries, museums, education, and every other government subsidized or owned area of life. Of course, this is a very large goal which is beyond the capacity of some people even to imagine as feasible, let alone embrace as a practical goal. While there are workable and viable long-term plans for such goals, the general public is no more ready for them than it is for the great revival necessary to make them happen.

These more radical goals aside, the steps I have outlined here are very practical, simple, and honestly do not require that much lifestyle sacrifice. If we are serious about freedom and desire to have a return to free markets, then we should be able to start making minor adjustments to our lifestyles to begin with, and then working toward educating ourselves and others, including our representatives, on free market principles and reduction of government interference in markets— local, state, and national. Beginning of course with the education and lifestyle changes described in the first two chapters of this book, these later measures fall right in place for the person committed to long-term sacrifice and discipline for the cause of liberty.

8. Courts

As with taxation, there is no specially-revealed biblical form of government or courts. The standard biblical passages dealing with these issues (e.g., Exod. 18; Rom. 13) describe aspects of providence and common grace. Unlike civil taxation, however, God certainly does establish and ordain civil rulers *in general*—and does so for the specific function of punishing crime (Gen. 9:5–6; Rom. 13:1–4). But He does not give us a prescription for the form of that rule. These details are left to His providence.

Courts of Law in a Free Society

The lack of a detailed prescription for courts does not mean, however, that just any form of government or jurisprudence can be considered godly in the sense of the ideal of liberty. In many cases—in most cases—the providentially-ordained system is a tyranny and is thus an indicator of God's judgment on that land. God's providence is not willy-nilly: He acts according to His law and sanctions in society. Thus a society's government will be a manifestation of that society's faithfulness to God. This means, ultimately, that *freedom* and *faithfulness* are inextricably linked. We will return to this idea in a moment.

The Bible tells us, for example, that bigger government is an indication of more pervasive wickedness in society: "When a land transgresses, it has many rulers, but with a man of understanding and knowledge, its stability will long continue"

(Prov. 28:2). The corollary is, of course, that in a land where knowledge and understanding of God's will lead to self-government on the part of the people (righteousness), there will be little need for civil government. Thus, in a free society, we should expect "few rulers."

Biblical Principles of Government Structure

While not specially revealing the ideal system of government, God does give us theological principles to guide ourdecisions of form and method of selection. Without writing a treatise on Christian government here, we'll highlight the more important and relevant of these principles: *representation, election, qualification,* and *decentralization.*

First, representation is primarily a *theological* principle which has ramifications in all covenantal settings, including civil government. Adam represented all of humanity in the fall; Christ represents all believers in His work of redemption (Rom. 5:12–21). Each is a covenant head. Believers are in turn Christ's representatives on earth. Following the covenant headship of Christ, "we are *ambassadors* of Christ, as though God were making an appeal *through us*" (2 Cor. 5:20; cp. Eph. 6:20). The idea that we are in some sense God's redeemed representatives in this world reaffirms and renews the fact that we are created in God's image. In a Christian civilization, we expect to see this principle at work in our civil covenant. Civil rulers are to be representative servant-leaders of the people, and thus biblical government is *representative* government.

Biblical government is also *elective.* Unless there is some specially revealed leader legitimized by public divine activity (Moses, Samuel, Jesus), the leaders—including civil leaders—are ideally to be *elected,* not imposed on the people from above by appointment or right of inheritance. We see this principle illustrated in the New Testament in regard to church government—specifically the office of deacon:

> And the twelve summoned the full number of the dis-
> ciples and said, "It is not right that we should give up
> preaching the word of God to serve tables. Therefore,
> brothers, *pick out from among you* seven men of good
> repute, full of the Spirit and of wisdom, whom we will
> appoint to this duty" (Acts 6:2–3).

These "servers" (deacons), the Apostles instructed, were to be chosen from among the people and by the people. Then, once so elected, the apostles confirmed them in their offices.

These two aspects of election and appointment work together, however, and the basis for appointment is *qualification.* The apostles did not choose the representatives, the people did. But the apostles would not confirm just anyone—they have to meet certain standards. Thus we see Paul later putting these qualifications in written form to Timothy and Titus— leaders of local congregations responsible for electing and appointing their own elders and deacons (see 1 Tim. 3:1–13; Titus 1:5–9). Thus, there is a biblical principle that potential leaders must be godly and sound individuals, having already proven their leadership abilities in their homes and among their peers, *before* even being considered for office.

The final principle here is *decentralization.* I will highlight this momentarily.

These principles all pertain to official leadership in general—obviously ecclesiastical leadership, for which they are directly prescribed, but there is no reason they should not also apply to civil leadership as well. And thus, there is no reason they should not be the ideal for biblical *courts* also.

Two primary passages in Scripture address the nature of a biblical judiciary system. One describes a practical, decentralized system of civil courts throughout society; the other prescribes private courts as the ideal for Christians. The classic model for a biblical system of civil courts comes in Jethro's advice to Moses (Exod. 18:13–26). While Moses was the sole civil judge for the three million or so Israelites, the court system was clogged and everyone suffered, including Moses. Jethro advised delegation of judiciary powers through a greatly decentralized model:

> Moreover, look for able men from all the people, men who fear God, who are trustworthy and hate a bribe, and place such men over the people as chiefs of thousands, of hundreds, of fifties, and of tens. And let them judge the people at all times. Every great matter they shall bring to you, but any small matter they shall decide themselves. So it will be easier for you, and they will bear the burden with you (Exod. 18:21–22).

All of the previously discussed elements of biblical government are either explicitly or implicitly described here. Each new judge took over the duties of a smaller constituency; was taken from among the people; had to meet certain qualifications of godliness, honesty, and incorruptibility; and the system greatly decentralized the work which was bottlenecked at Moses. Most small matters were settled at the very local level, and only great issues made their way to Moses.

It is also likely that these new judges were elected. Although they are said to have been chosen by Moses, this is most likely speaking by proxy—as Moses was the leader of the whole people and thus gets "credit" so to speak. But think of the task before him. There were 600,000 *men* in Israel (Exod. 12:47). Just using this number of men alone, a program of chiefs for "thousands, of hundreds, of fifties, and of tens" would require 78,600 appointments. There is no way Moses could have appointed this many judges by himself, especially since he would have had to analyze each one's character, reputation, and integrity individually. Even if he chose only the top rung and then had each of them choose the lesser authorities, he still would have had to examine 600 men individually. At a rate of even ten examinations a day, this would take two months. It seems more likely to me that there had to have been some kind of election process involved, at least at the lower levels. Chiefs of tens would require 60,000 appointees. Just as the apostles had the people choose their own servants, so there was probably a mass announcement for small groups to choose a representative judge from among them.

Whatever the exact mode of selection, the upshot was a drastically decentralized court system which still left in place a system of appeals for more momentous or difficult cases. Again, this is a system based on the advice of Jethro and not specially revealed by God Himself; nevertheless, the principles involved are affirmed elsewhere in Scripture. Thus we can safely affirm that a biblical court system can indeed be a state court system, but should definitely feature elected and representative judges, biblically qualified judges, and a greatly decentralized system of local courts with appeals.

The Christian Ideal: Private Courts

But state courts are neither the only, nor even the most desirable, system given in Scripture. The second significant passage in regard to courts shows us a better way—private courts. And whereas the state court system exemplified by Moses is based on the pragmatic advice of a man along with piecemeal biblical principles, the private court system we shall see is directly revealed as the Christian ideal by the apostle Paul. Thus, this should be accepted and embraced by Christians as the most biblical method for resolving judicial disputes. Paul applies the Christian principle of private courts in 1 Corinthians 6:

> When one of you has a grievance against another, does he dare go to law before the unrighteous instead of the saints? Or do you not know that the saints will judge the world? And if the world is to be judged by you, are you incompetent to try trivial cases? Do you not know that we are to judge angels? How much more, then, matters pertaining to this life! So if you have such cases, why do you lay them before those who have no standing in the church? I say this to your shame. Can it be that there is no one among

you wise enough to settle a dispute between the brothers,
but brother goes to law against brother, and that before
unbelievers? To have lawsuits at all with one another is already a defeat for you. Why not rather suffer wrong? Why
not rather be defrauded? But you yourselves wrong and
defraud—even your own brothers! (1 Cor. 6:1–8)

What this shows is first, all believers are judges. We are
called to be judges first and foremost of ourselves. All of
Christian life is about making and living by decisions that
are faithful to our Lord—and this requires faithful *judgment.*
Since civil government is instituted only to punish crime, then
courts will need to exist only to the extent that people fail in
their efforts to judge themselves faithfully.

But, it is assumed that since we are still sinners even as
Christians, and we live in the midst of a fallen world, that conflicts of judgment will abound both personally and interper-
sonally. Thus, courts will be necessary to decide such conflicts.
Paul's admonition here is to exalt the Christian virtues of forgiveness, love, and self-sacrifice and thus limit the number of
conflicts that 1) go to suit at all, 2) go to suit between believers,
and 3) get heard before state courts. All these should be held
to an absolute minimum.

For cases that do arise, private courts are usually the best
alternative. This means church courts, arbitration panels, medi-
ation boards, and industry and professional courts. A society
neglecting these outlets and the attitude of self-government will
easily be paralyzed by endless litigation, massive bureaucracies,
and countless administrative laws.[1] Toward this aim, all contracts between Christians should include some form of private
dispute settlement clause—Christian arbitration being a common one. Christians should seek to resolve all possible contract
disputes privately, between Christian brethren, and eliminate
state courts in all but the most extreme cases.

---

[1] Gary North, *Moses and Pharaoh: Dominion Religion Versus Power Religion*
(Tyler, TX: Institute for Christian Economics, 1985), 284.

Private courts may sound like a utopian dream to many people today, simply because—as has been the case with so many of our topics—we have rarely been exposed even to the idea, let alone the practice, in our generations. But the truth is, private courts not only sound good in theory, they have existed widely in western Christian history, and they worked quite well.

Arbitration grew popular after the Civil War in the U.S. Judicial panels handled corporate and labor disputes and were widely accepted, despite the fact that they were completely *voluntary* and *not legally binding* up until 1925. It was only when some corporations determined to streamline the process in 1920 that New York enacted a state takeover of arbitration, backing all arbitration suits with the force of the state.[2] So, the abuses of a few got answered by the loss of even the option of purely private courts. The U.S. government followed five years later by nationalizing the same principle. This has been revised several times since to give us the modern Federal Arbitration Act which overrides all arbitration cases and state laws pertaining to arbitration. But keep in mind, this was not the case before 1925, and it came about only because of the political clout of large corporations for whose benefit the civil government took over the process.

The idea of private industry or private merchant courts has deep historical roots in the Middle Ages when private courts often made state enforcement unnecessary. From the Middle Ages until the 1920s, merchants relied on private courts, and, if necessary, boycott and ostracism. Author William Wooldridge explains,

> Merchants made their courts work simply by agreeing to abide by the results. The merchant who broke the understanding would not be sent to jail, to be sure, but neither would he long continue to be a merchant, for the compliance exacted by his fellows, and their power over his goods, proved if anything more effective than

---

[2] Murray N. Rothbard, *For a New Liberty: The Libertarian Manifesto* (New York: Collier Books, 1978), 223–224.

physical coercion. Take John of Homing, who made his living marketing wholesale quantities of fish. When John sold a lot of herring on the representation that it conformed to a three-barrel sample, but which, his fellow merchants found, was actually mixed with "stickle-backs and putrid herring," he made good the deficiency on pain of economic ostracism.[3]

In other words, this was an honor system on steroids: break the code of honor, and you lose your livelihood. Once it was made known that a business ignored the decision of an arbitration panel, no one would do further business with it.

And while it may be natural to think things were just so different in the Middle Ages than today, it was not so long ago that an industrialist like Owen D. Young, president and chairman of GE, spent a good portion of his time advocating for private arbitration, writing several essays on the subject. He advised the U.S. Chamber of Commerce "to support and develop the moral sanction upon which arbitration outside the law must depend."[4] Indeed, where the law is not in force, *moral sanction* is the necessary and very effective key. Young "concluded that the moral censure of other businessmen was a far more effective sanction than legal enforcement."[5] This was 1915. Today, with internet, various databases, and other powerful communications, *nationwide* ostracism would be even more powerful. It could be public and worldwide within seconds of an arbitration panel's decision.[6]

So we have seen then that a biblical view of the judiciary involves several principles, the most challenging ones being that judicial decisions be *radically decentralized* and *priva-*

---

[3] Quoted in Rothbard, *New Liberty*, 224.

[4] Quoted in Josephine Young Case and Everett Needham Case, *Owen D. Young and American Enterprise: a biography* (Boston, MA: David R. Godine, Publisher, Inc., 1982), 245.

[5] Rothbard, *New Liberty*, 224.

[6] Ibid.

tized as far as possible. We have also discussed how the United States was once a bit closer to these principles, considering a few examples of the effectiveness of private courts. These examples are just a small taste of the vast literature on both the theory and practice of private courts, arbitration, etc. We do know that our society at least does have decent options in many cases, especially in private contracts and church courts. We also know that we once had options in this regard to an even greater degree than we do today. In the next section, we will discuss how our judicial systems have been hijacked and abused from very early on, and how this has ultimately resulted in the vast judicial tyranny we have today.[7]

Judicial Tyranny in America

How American freedom was lost *in* and *through* the judiciary should already be apparent from our discussions in previous chapters. We have seen how the John Marshall court ener-gized and applied the centralizing effects of the Constitution and the power of the "Federalist" *coup* in the areas of localism, states' rights, commerce, money and banking, taxation, and more. The precedent set by Marshall's activism was embraced by later justices who picked it up and ran in the areas of edu-cation, welfare, and again, much more. Legislation by the bench has been an American tradition—tyrannical as it may be—since the beginning.

Partisan Politics and the Supreme Court

If you remember correctly, the establishment of a single national Supreme Court was one of the major issues objected

---

[7] We have also not yet addressed the most important issue, by the way, and that is the basis upon which courts must operate. Far more important than form, method, or procedure is the *law* itself. Without some ultimate legal system, the very idea of a court must give way to not mere anarchy, but social chaos and lawlessness.

to by the Anti-Federalists. Candidus warned that the court would "occasion innumerable controversies." "A Friend to the Rights of the People" said the Supreme Court may prove "a source of mischief and ruin to thousands" by which "the course of public justice may be much obstructed, the poor oppressed, and many undone."[8] "An Old Whig" called the Court's Constitutional appellate power "destructive to the principles of liberty," and yet this power could not be extinguished even by legislation.[9] Brutus, as we noted earlier, warned clearly, "If . . . the legislature pass any laws, inconsistent in the senses the judges put upon the constitution, they will declare it void; and therefore in this respect their power is superior to that of the legislature." He saw the great danger of unelected and unaccountable judges to the future peace of the country:

> when this power is lodged in the hands of men independent of the people, and of their representatives, and who are not, constitutionally, accountable for their opinions, no way is left to controul them but *with a high hand and an outstretched arm.*[10]

For reasons such as this, The Federal Farmer believed "we are in more danger of sowing the seeds of arbitrary government in this department than in any other." He saw the established state courts as largely adequate and warned against expansion:

> Judicial power is of such a nature, that when we have ascertained and fixed its limits, with all the caution and precision we can, it will yet be formidable, somewhat arbitrary and despotic—that is, after all our cares, we must leave a vast deal to the discretion and interpretation—to the wisdom, integrity, and politics of the judges.[11]

---

[8] Storing, *Complete Anti-Federalist*, 4:241.

[9] Ibid., 3:47.

[10] Ibid., 2:442.

[11] Ibid., 2:315.

The "politics of the judges" indeed became a major factor. The American judiciary was *politically* compromised
from very early on as most Court appointees held Nationalist sympathies. We have mentioned how Marshall spent his
career legislating Hamilton's state papers from the bench. It
was much more widespread than just Marshall—his brand of
judicial activism trickled down to all inferior courts as well.

The District Court was crawling with partisanship. In
1793, a Federalist civil servant "commented that the federal
judiciary had 'assumed a party complexion.'" That same year,
William Ellery wrote to Alexander Hamilton saying of the
federal judges, "They have become a band of political preachers." Another critic in 1797 said, "It has . . . become a regular
practice of the federal judges to make political discourses to
the grand jurors throughout the United States."[12] These men
were politically committed before they ever got to the bench.
Indeed, out of twenty-eight district court judges during the
Nationalist-dominated 1790s, twenty-one had been politically
active in support of the Federalist cause; of these, fourteen
were either delegates to the Constitutional Convention or to
state ratifying conventions.[13] Only three ever even questioned
nationalization, and these came to favor it afterward. Throughout their careers these judges remained active in party politics
and were often described in, or even labeled themselves by,
such terms. Nathaniel Chipman of Vermont, for example, was
one of the State's "major political strategists," and an "effective
and unscrupulous practitioner of magnate politics."[14]

Federal judges during this era openly participated in party
meetings and election campaigns. Some did not shy from private intimidation. Judge James Duane—a former delegate to
the Constitutional Convention and member of the Hamiltonian cabal of New York—owned large tracts of rental prop-

---

[12] Carl E. Prince, *The Federalists and the Origin of the U.S. Civil Service* (New
York: New York University Press, 1977), 242.

[13] Ibid., 242–243.

[14] Ibid., 244.

erty in upstate New York. He is described as a "powerful land-lord" who would "exert undue pressures on tenants at election time."[15] Duane eventually took his partisan eagerness too far when he seized French ships in violation of existing treaties. When confronted by fellow Federalist and Secretary of State Edmund Randolph for his offense, the New York cabal cited a Jeffersonian conspiracy of "partizans of the French Sans Culottes [revolutionaries]." The propaganda effort failed and Duane was eventually forced to resign.[16]

And of course, being the main part of their job, their judi-cial decisions reflected their biases. In one case, District Judge David Sewell of Maine used his bench to bully a jury into a guilty verdict against his political rivals. Certain defendants had been charged with violating the wildly unpopular Jay Treaty. "Sewell instructed the jury to find him guilty. In his charge to the jurors, he pointed out that both the defendant and his defense attorney were political opponents of the gov-ernment and Constitution."[17]

After John Adams' Alien and Sedition Acts of 1798, Fed-eralist political activism grew even more overt and pervasive. Despite the despotic nature of the Acts which allowed Adams to deport people who merely criticized him or the government in print—a blatant infraction of the First Amendment—a full half of the sitting district court judges *eagerly* enforced the new laws.[18] In various politically-motivated cases during this time, political rivals in court were specifically targeted as examples, ridiculed and mocked, denied copies of court documents per-taining to their hearings, had juries stacked against them (a practice encouraged and promoted by judges), were refused time to prepare an adequate defense, and even rushed to trial without their lawyers present.[19] The historian concludes:

[15] Prince, *The Federalists*, 246.

[16] Ibid., 248–249.

[17] Ibid., 249.

[18] Ibid., 250.

[19] Ibid., 251–252.

What happened in the district and circuit courts in the 1790s cannot simply be written off as the bias of a few partisan judges involved in a handful of isolated cases. . . . Political activism helped loosen political emotions and corrupt the objectivity of otherwise distinguished, highly qualified jurists in every part of the nation. Thus, it may be said, if an independent federal judiciary did emerge as a basic building block of American liberties, it was a lodgment that took place only *after* the generation of the Founding Fathers.

It is clear . . . that both the first United States district and circuit courts were among the most thoroughly politicized federal judicial institutions in American history.[20]

The Establishment of Broad Construction

Among those most annoyed by judicial partisanship in this era was the most outstanding spokesman of the rival party, Thomas Jefferson. He was involved directly in the landmark case Marshall alley-ooped to himself, *Marbury v. Madison* (1803). As Secretary of State under Adams, and in the waning days of that administration, Marshall signed and sealed several appointments of "midnight judges" to further pack the judicial system with Federalist activists. But upon the change of administration, Jefferson took office and forbade the Secretary, Madison, from delivering the letters. But Marshall had orchestrated the whole thing. One of the appointees, William Marbury, filed suit to obtain his office anyway. The case went to the Supreme Court and Marshall decided it. Thus, while Secretary of State, he tossed the case in the air, then moved over to the Justice position and slam-dunked it.

And in its decision, he made a very clever move: he used the judicial function of the Court itself to declare that the Court itself had no jurisdiction to decide the case! In the process of this decision, he declared the Judicial Act of 1789—

---

[20] Prince, 252.

which had given the Supreme Court power to hear such cases as this—was actually unconstitutional. Thus Marshall used the trivial case of Mr. Marbury as a Trojan horse to trump legislation with judicial dictum. The activity has since been called the doctrine of "judicial review."

Jefferson was quite perturbed by Marshall's activism. Late in his life, in a letter to Justice William Johnson (whom he had appointed in 1804), Jefferson opined:

> This practice of Judge Marshall, of travelling out of his case to prescribe what the law would be in a moot case not before the court, is very irregular and very censurable. I recollect another instance, and the more particularly, perhaps, because it in some measure bore on myself. Among the midnight appointments of Mr. Adams, were commissions to some federal justices of the peace for Alexandria. These were signed and sealed by him, but not delivered. I found them on the table of the department of State, on my entrance into office, and I forbade their delivery. Marbury, named in one of them, applied to the Supreme Court for a mandamus to the Secretary of State, [Mr. Madison] to deliver the commission intended for him. The Court determined at once, that being an original process, they had no cognizance of it; and therefore the question before them was ended. But the Chief Justice went on to lay down what the law would be, had they jurisdiction of the case, to-wit: that they should command the delivery. The object was clearly to instruct any other court having the jurisdiction, what they should do if Marbury should apply to them. Besides the impropriety of this gratuitous interference, could anything exceed the perversion of law? . . . Yet this case of Marbury and Madison is continually cited by bench and bar, as if it were settled law, without any animadversion on its being merely an *obiter* dissertation of the Chief Justice.[21]

---

[21] Jefferson to Judge Johnson, June 12, 1823, *The Works of Thomas Jefferson*, ed. Paul Leicester Ford (New York and London: G. P. Putnam's Sons, 1905), 12:256–

That letter, written in 1823, is a long lament of how the nationalist/Federalist party had already corrupted so much of what America had promised to be. This included the tyrannical power of her court system, for which even the Bill of Rights was no match:

> The States supposed that by their tenth amendment, they had secured themselves against constructive powers. They were not lessoned yet by Cohen's case, nor aware of the slipperiness of the eels of the law. I ask for no straining of words against the General Government, nor yet against the States. I believe the States can best govern our home concerns, and the General Government our foreign ones. I wish, therefore, to see maintained that wholesome distribution of powers established by the constitution for the limitation of both; and never to see all offices transferred to Washington, where, further withdrawn from the eyes of the people, they may more secretly be bought and sold as at market.[22]

These "constructive powers"—and the "slipperiness of the eels of the law"—Jefferson by this late age knew all too well. In his 1791 argument with Hamilton over the establishment of a national bank, Jefferson fought these powers with his "strict construction" view of the Constitution. He was joined by Madison against Hamilton, who argued that Congress had the power to do anything necessary as a means to its ends—and this included incorporating a national bank even though such an animal was nowhere mentioned as a Congressional power in the Constitution. Hamilton (and Marshall) would argue such a means to an end was an *implied* power.

In this debate, though Madison sided with Jefferson on the constitutionality of the bank bill, his own writings came back to bite him. For he himself had written of the very "necessary

---

257n.

[22] Ibid., 12:258–259n.

and proper" clause in the *Federalist Papers* No. 44: "No axiom
is more clearly established in law, or in reason, than that wherever the end is required, the means are authorized; wherever
a general power to do a thing is given, every particular power
necessary for doing it is included." It was nothing less than
this "original intent" of the Constitution which Hamilton and
his party wished to leverage. For the necessary end of solidify-
ing public credit, a national bank should be authorized. When
Madison's own words were recalled on the floor on Congress,
the debate was essentially over. The two sides in the personal
written admonitions of Jefferson and Hamilton reached their
final battleground upon Washington's desk. The president
sided with his Treasury Secretary and the Bank was born.

Thus prevailed the doctrine of "broad construction" and
"implied powers" of the Constitution—a doctrine by which
the rule of law becomes a wax nose wrung in the hands of
activist judges. It was this same doctrine Marshall upheld,
applied, and elucidated in *McCulloch v. Maryland* (1819)
(another bank case!):

> The subject is the execution of those great powers on
> which the welfare of a nation essentially depends. It
> must have been the intention of those who gave these
> powers, to insure, so far as human prudence could in-
> sure, their beneficial execution. This could not be done,
> by confiding the choice of means to such narrow limits
> as not to leave it in the power of congress to adopt any
> which might be appropriate, and which were conducive
> to the end. This provision is made in a constitution, in-
> tended to endure for ages to come, and consequently, *to
> be adapted to the various crises of human affairs.*[23]

This, of course, places a tremendous premium on the
opinions and decisions of the leadership—particularly the

[23] 17 U.S. 316, 415; online at http://caselaw.lp.findlaw.com/scripts/getcase.
pl?court=us&vol=17&invol=316 (accessed Sept. 25, 20120).

judges and those in positions to influence legislation, as was Hamilton. In short, a broad construction view of the Constitution immediately breeds elitism and cronyism. The historian Prince notes the elitism of the judicial activists of the era:

> The Federalist judges believed that talented, superior men like themselves, by virtue of their inherent stature, could stretch and dilute their judicial mandate with impunity in the best interests of the nation and its people as they saw those interests.[24]

This is the exact same elite impulse by which every other politician, government official, senator, president, and judge has decided *they too* have the ability to reinterpret and bend the law as they see fit—from Hamilton and Marshall to the leftists judicial activists of more recent decades. Indeed, it could be said that the "living constitution" view of partisans like Oliver Wendell Holmes Jr., Louis Brandeis, Woodrow Wilson, Earl Warren, and the radicals of today is the direct logical outworking of the so-called "broad construction" view of Marshall and Hamilton (and Washington). Indeed, Marshall's landmark decision in *McCulloch* provides one of the key evidences that modern liberal proponents of a living constitution use in their favor.

There is a fundamental problem with such elitism, however. What happens when elected—and especially *unelected*—leaders depart from traditional values and foundations of law? In such a case, you have not only judicial tyranny, but judicial destruction of society. And when such degeneration of legislative, and especially *judicial*, values is simultaneously entrusted with the power of broad construction and implied powers, you have a recipe for the decay of the whole civilization.

For this reason, the Anti-Federalists warned of placing undue trust in great leaders. As we have seen, Candidus foresaw a time when illustrious elites would not be available:

---

[24] Prince, *The Federalists*, 252.

"Though this country is now blessed with a Washington, Franklin, Hancock and Adams. . . posterity may have reason to rue the day when their political welfare depends on the decision of men who may fill the places of these worthies." Another, "An Old Whig" announced the same warning: "We ought not to repose all our liberty and all our happiness in the virtue of our future leaders. . . . Idolatry is the parent of errors in politics as well as religion;—and an implicit confidence in our rulers now, will be abused as much as implicit confidence in priests ever was in the days of superstition." For this reason, he concluded, "If we perish in America, we shall have no better comfort than the same mortifying reflection, that we have been the cause of our own destruction."[25]

True to the warnings, strange leaders did arise, new values did present themselves. Constitutional lawyer Herb Titus explains how, in 1887, Oliver Wendell Holmes Jr. "overthrew a 600-year old tradition with a single paragraph."[26] The paragraph was from Holmes' attack on *The Common Law*:

> The life of law has not been logic: it has been experience. The felt necessities of the time, the prevalent moral and political theories, intuitions of public policy ... even the prejudices which judges share with their fellow-men,... [primarily] determine the rules by which men governed. The law embodies the story of a nation's development through many centuries.... In order to know what it is, we must know what it has been, and what it tends to become.[27]

Holmes' disciple, Louis Brandeis, replaced all former Supreme Court precedent with Holmes' view in a 1938 decision, *Eerie Railroad Co. v. Tompkins*. In that case Brandeis proclaimed it a "fallacy" to assume there is any "transcenden-

---

[25] Storing, *Complete Anti-Federalist*, 3:47–48.

[26] Herb Titus, *The Common Law* (Chapel Hill, NC: Professional Press, 1998), 5.

[27] Quoted Titus, *Common Law*, 5. Emphasis Titus's.

tal body of law" by which Federal or state courts could judge common cases. Instead, only the laws of state legislatures or opinions of state Supreme Courts should stand as binding. In other words, only the laws of men and state institutions are valid—there is no such thing as a transcendent (godly) law.[28] Out of these same humanist-driven Court precedents has come Supreme Court protected abortion, easy-divorce, and homosexual marriage, just to name a few.[29]

And thus, the very means used for making an allegedly strong, dependable nation under Marshall and Hamilton became the means for making an unstoppably progressive, liberal nation—a massive Welfare State built on a Warfare State—under Wilson, FDR, LBJ, etc.

Perhaps one of the most egregious offenses came with the so-called Reconstruction Amendments, particularly the Fourteenth. While certainly aiming at some admirable goals, this Amendment essentially became the means for extending central government powers into every crevice of American life—under the guise of the "due process" clause. This includes *Roe v. Wade*, as we discussed earlier. The Amendment basically reversed the original intent of the Bill of Rights—which was to protect state freedoms from encroachments, or legislation, by the National government. Now, the Supreme Court uses the Fourteenth Amendment as a means of interpreting and enforcing *upon the states, lower governments, and citizens* a whole array of laws allegedly *implied* in the Bill of Rights or Constitution. Thus what was intended as a control upon the central government has become the central government's means to control the people.

This judicial tyranny is so much the case that Raoul Berger could write of *Government by Judiciary* in 1977:

> The Fourteenth Amendment is the case study par excellence of what Justice Harlan described as the Su-

---

[28] Ibid., 6.
[29] Ibid., 6–7.

preme Court's "exercise of the amending power," its continuing revising of the Constitution under the guise of interpretation.[30]

There is so much more we could say in this regard that we could write an entire book just on the subject of judicial tyranny in America. Indeed, whole books have been written.[31] What we have written so far should be enough to conclude that the biblical ideal of courts described above has been absolutely treaded upon and obliterated by political partisanship from the earliest minutes of this Constitutional Republic. And the precedents of elitism and broad construction established by Hamilton and the Marshall Court became the tools of judicial activism which demolished the moral and spiritual foundations of our legal heritage. And these are just the political considerations; we have not even really touched upon corporate influences (except for the banks) which joined the political powers in perverting our Court systems.

The decline and degradation are thus clear. The question of course is: What can we do to reestablish freedom in our Courts?

Creating a Free Judiciary

What can be done to return society to a biblical judicial system? In this section we will cover two main avenues to recovering a free society: the establishment of voluntary and private courts, and jury nullification.

---

[30] Raoul Berger, *Government by Judiciary: The Transformation of the Fourteenth Amendment* (Cambridge, MA: Harvard University Press, 1977), 1.

[31] See Carroll D. Kilgore, *Judicial Tyranny: An Inquiry into the Integrity of the Judiciary published at the beginning of the Third Century of American Independence* (Nashville, TN: Thomas Nelson, 1977); See also Raoul Berger, *Government by Judiciary*.

Private Christian Courts

In light of what has been said so far in reference to biblical courts, the most important thing we can do today is to attempt at all costs, as far as possible, as often as possible, to settle interpersonal disputes *privately*. What does this look like in practice? We will also discuss the commitment to Christian virtue necessary to make this work.

For Christians, private settlement means first, forgiveness whenever possible. Secondarily, it means private *Christian* courts. This was Paul's main argument to the Corinthians, as we reviewed before. Christians need to recover this doctrine and put it into action. In general, Christians should:

1. Appeal only to *Christian* "courts."

2. Allow only *Christian* judges or arbitrators to resolve disputes between Christians.

3. Allow only biblical law as the standard of judgment in such cases.

4. Provide only such remedies or restitution as biblical law allows.

5. Provide some measure for finality of the decision.

Christ Alone

Let's consider each of these five aspects. The first point is an application of the idea of sovereignty. Christians have one ultimate King and Judge, the Triune God. It is He who presides, ultimately, over all of life. Only courts that honor Him ultimately have validity. The universe is His courtroom, and no one has removed the Ten Commandments from this courtroom, nor will they. The point is intimately tied with the other four, but especially with point three—that of law. Law in every society is ultimately religious in origin, and the source of law in any given society is that society's God.[32] Christians, as members of God's holy society, the temple of God on earth (1 Pet. 2:5–10), must recognize the ultimate validity of God's law alone, and thus God-honoring courts. Courts judging according to some other legal standard are courts of some other god—no matter how much any constituent part or party of any case may say "so help me God." This has major implications. Christians must generally consider modern state courts to be mostly ungodly. However they may have been originally founded, they have long since abandoned, as we have seen, any formal recognition of Christian law and have instead embraced Holmes's humanistic standard of evolutionary, relativistic law. Granted, some traces of Christian judicial heritage may remain, but traces only indicate past history, they do not legitimize the courts as still acceptably "Christian" today. We will address secular courts more in a moment. For now, it is expedient merely to acknowledge their apostasy and avoid them as much as possible.

Paul's admonishment to the Corinthians here seems to have had some precedent in Jewish rabbinical law. *The Mishnah*—an early collection of ancient rabbinical deliberations which forms the basis for the later *Talmud*—contains a strikingly similar opinion: "A bill of divorce given under compulsion is valid if ordered by an Israelitish court, but if by a gentile court it is invalid."[33] The Jewish legal scholar George Horowitz refers to the phrase, "tribunals of idolators." He quotes the *Talmud*, which is commentary upon the earlier statement of the *Mishnah*:

> If it is impossible to adjust amicably, and the parties must go to law, they should resort to a *bet-din* ["house of judgment"] of Israel. It is forbidden to litigate before judges or tribunals of idolators even when their law is similar to Jewish law, and even when both par-

---

[32] See R. J. Rushdoony, *The Institutes of Biblical Law* (The Craig Press, 1973), 4ff.

[33] Herbert Danby, *The Mishnah* (New York: Oxford University Press, 1933), 320. See *Gittin*, 9.8.

ties agreed to submit their case before them and, even if they bound themselves thereto by kinyan [a binding agreement] or by instrument in writing. Such agreements are null and void.[34]

In other words, these Jews considered non-Jewish courts to be courts of idolatry. Since these courts do not submit to biblical law, they must have submitted to a false god. It is important to see that Paul was applying a very similar mindset when instructing Christians in 1 Corinthians 6. As Christians, we dare not turn to pagan courts—that would be idolatry—but rather should despise them as inferior Christian courts ruled by Christian law.

God's law, God's court must be made preeminent by Christians, who then must expand godliness outwardly into the state courts where it is lacking. Rushdoony explains,

When a state or its laws are godly, its courts are legitimate and can be used. The state then, despite its sins and shortcomings, is an aspect of the Kingdom of God. Present civil law is in the process of becoming radically humanistic, but its framework is still to a large degree Biblical. It is the duty of Christians, not to withdraw from civil law (i.e., the law of the state), but to make it Biblical.[35]

Representing Christ

Closely related to the issue of sovereignty is the second aspect, representation of authority. Every court has representatives of its sovereignty—earthly incarnations of its authority—its judges. God's court is no different—in fact, it is the original model for this. Ideally, all civil judges' oaths of office would include swearing allegiance to Jesus Christ and His Word— they would be *His* representatives—but this simply is not the case today. In a decentralized world, of course, we would have

---

[34] Quoted in George Horowitz, *The Spirit of Jewish Law* ((New York: Central Book Company, 1963), 650.

[35] R. J. Rushdoony, *Law and Society: Volume 2 of the Institutes of Biblical Law* (Vallecito, CA: Ross House Books, 1982), 344.

a much better chance of having at least local judges willing and ready to take such an oath, but we are not there yet. In the meantime, every judge represents the law of his court, and thus the source of that law. An idolatrous court is an idolatrous jurisdiction and should not be accepted as ultimate for the Christian. Rushdoony again explains,

> A judge or court whose premise is other than the law of God is an untrustworthy administrator of justice. Justice is not impossible with such a man, but it is not to be expected.[36]

The moment a judge begins representing a law other than the law of God, that judge is representing a false law, and his court has assumed the position of a false god.

> If church or state, or any other agency, function as the creator of law, i.e., *issuing laws without a transcendental basis*, then they have made themselves into gods. Their *right* to command is then gone.[37]

In light of this, Christians should seek only *Christians* as arbiters of their disputes. Indeed, they should preferably seek Christians who have an understanding of Whom they represent *as* judges and the Word according to which they are to judge. We want to submit only to judges who in turn submit to God and His Word. This is not to say, of course, that all Christian elders, arbitrators, and "judges" of all kinds, as opposed to all pagan judges, will always be perfectly just in their sentences. But justice, honesty, and impartiality are to be expected from godly leaders, whereas such cannot be expected from a judge who refuses to submit to the rule and law of God Almighty. Christians should therefore seek out willing and able Christians to arbitrate and settle disputes among them.

---

[36] Rushdoony, *Law and Society*, 345.

[37] Rushdoony, *Institutes*, 620.

The Standard of Christ

We have already said enough about the third aspect—law. It takes center stage throughout the process and infuses each of the other aspects. The standard throughout is God and His sovereignty, God and His Word. Every court must submit to God's Law, else the Christian cannot accept it as ultimately authoritative. This raises questions which I will address in a minute. More importantly, every *Christian* and every *church* must accept God's law as the standard of every area of life, of structuring family life and business life, and of "judging the world" (1 Cor. 6:2–3). Unless the individuals and their respective leaders within the church accept the godly standard, we can hardly expect it to ever to be adopted as a source of conflict resolution by civil courts; and more importantly, we can hardly expect the blessing of the Final Judge who gave us that Law to begin with. Without embracing God's Law, Christians today are—despite whatever growing numbers and massive churches we may display—absolutely *lawless* in the eyes of our God.

Biblical Remedies

The fourth aspect, *sanctions*, is tied to the Law as well. Christian courts must seek remedies and resolutions to problems that apply God's sanctions revealed in His law, and no further. For example, the Bible provides clear guidelines for restitution of property in several types of cases: different degrees of theft, embezzlement, negligence, workers' responsibilities, and more (Exod. 22:1–17). Christian "judges" should study these cases carefully to determine the biblical guidelines that apply, and then declare accordingly. Decisions that go beyond these boundaries—even if determined by secular "authoritative" courts, should not be accepted by the Christian. Biblical sanctions will provide godly justice, and at the same time prevent frivolous cases, malicious cases, and cases of greed, envy, or human whim.

Consider, for example, the famous "hot coffee lawsuit" from a biblical-law view. In this case, a woman sued McDonald's after she spilled her coffee and suffered third-degree burns on 6% of her body. Since the restaurant served its coffee far beyond the temperature of any other (near boiling-point in fact!), the liability issue was strongly against the restaurant. Meanwhile, the woman originally asked only for her medical expenses to be covered—about $20,000. But the case escalated, and the jury eventually awarded her $200,000 in compensation, *plus* a whopping $2.7 million in *punitive* damages. Now, biblical law does call for both restitution and *at least* 100% punitive damages, awarded to a victim of theft (Exod. 22:4), of which this was a sort. It even calls for four- or five-fold restitution in cases involving valuable property which produces returns or has required costly investment. But not even the most extreme of cases prescribes a ten-fold restitution *plus* a 135-fold punitive award. And ironically, this determination was not driven by greed, but by the jury's whim, based on the defense attorney's statement that McDonald's should be punished one or two days' coffee revenues. Indeed, this was not a frivolous case—as many have supposed—but a frivolous *application* of *sanctions* to the remedy. The judge did succeed in lowering the penalties, and further appeals by the defense actually resulted in the woman getting less than she could have settled for in the original case. That much was due to greed, no doubt. But the jury's decision was unbiblical, and thus unjust in itself. Christian courts and tribunals which are allowed to adjudicate only according to *biblical* law would avoid such ridiculous decisions.

Finality and Perpetuity of Decisions

Finally, we have perhaps the most difficult aspect of private Christian courts—indeed, of *all* systems of private arbitration, etc.—finality. Every court decision is likely going to be uncomfortable to one party. This means that there will always be an incentive to appeal to a higher court or greater power. Indeed, unless there is a final "buck stops here" voice of judicial authority, appeals in a free market of private courts would be endless.

Even the completely anti-State anarchist Murray Rothbard, in his very helpful system of libertarian thought, conceded that there must be some accepted final arbiter: "Obviously, in *any* society legal proceedings cannot continue indefinitely; there must be *some* cutoff point."[38] While he criticizes the idea of a state Supreme Court as an "arbitrary" cutoff point, he nevertheless recognizes the necessity of a legally-mandated limit to appeals among private courts:

> In the Libertarian society, there would also have to be an agreed-upon cutoff point, and since there are only two parties to any crime or dispute—the plaintiff and the defendant—it seems more sensible for the legal code to declare that *a decision arrived at by any two courts* shall be binding.[39]

Obviously, even this standard cannot be upheld without some ultimate point of coercion. What if, despite the legal code, the defendant still refuses to submit to the judgment, or yet another court agrees to hear the case even if the other party remains *in abstentia*? In such cases, it would be up to society at large to enforce the prior decisions, and this may or may not be very easy. There still remains the possibility that a decision has no practical finality. And who will determine whether the prior *two courts'* concurring decisions were arrived at justly? Wouldn't that require yet another third-party examination of law, facts, and *procedure*? Thus we introduce yet another type of appeal—but won't *this* appeal also be subject to dispute? It seems that there must be some "arbitrary" aspect to arrive at finality and continuity of decision in any humanly-enforced judicial system.

In either Christian courts, or Rothbard's "Libertarian society"—we could simply say a "free society"—the key factor that will give continuity to legitimate court decisions is public virtue

---

[38] Rothbard, *New Liberty*, 227.

[39] Ibid.

based in personal devotion to God's law. Rothbard is correct to say that "there will have to be a legal code," it must be "generally accepted," and the standard of limited appeals must arise from that legal code.[40] But if a legal code does not derive from a truly authoritative source, then even a "generally accepted" legal code can only arrive at something like finality *pragmatically*, not in principle. True binding authority over man can derive only from a Source higher than man, meaning a Law higher than man's. This law must be God's law, and this standard must be upheld by courts, especially private Christian courts.

Rothbard is absolutely correct on the practical side: people and the courts must generally agree on the authority of that particular legal code and the courts' adherence to it. Without people who agree ahead of time to place limits on their appeals for more litigation—which in a free society are really attempts at self-justification against the prior decisions of a plurality of your closest and often self-chosen peers—then the very principles of justice are undermined in our hearts to begin with, and such a society cannot expect to be free. The absence of such virtue is the main ingredient which keeps tyrannical States in operation. As long as people are unable to agree voluntarily to limit appeals to self-justification, and as long as enough of the rest of society refuses to impute continuity to the legitimacy of those limits, then some form of coercive State solution will arise and persist to enforce the arbitrary limits determined by the interested and ruling parties. Of course, this is true in many areas of civil life, not just the legitimacy of court decisions.

The Necessity of Civic Virtue

The issue of civic virtue touches the heart of the spiritual and psychological nature of society, and this is clearly true in reference to the judiciary in any society. Criminal and civil cases multiply only when people cannot or *will not* govern them-

---

[40] Rothbard, *New Liberty*, 227.

selves—a point made many times already—but also where people desire to exact as much revenge or remuneration as possible for acts against them. Paul makes this point in reference to the Corinthians. Some of them were bringing frivolous or even fraudulent cases against their brethren, just to profit at their expense. Thus Paul condemned them: "You yourselves wrong and defraud—even your own brothers!" (1 Cor. 6:8). Rushdoony comments that "just as they give more worth to pagan courts than they deserve so they give more worth to their own contentions than they deserve."[41] This is basic to fallen human nature—the source of all fraud in human society. The point, however, discovers the vital link between human vice and the persistence of pagan courts: deviant hearts wish to avoid godly courts. Instead, they seek out ungodly avenues of authority in order to profit from their vices.

Further, such fraud can exist in degrees: a case need not be completely illegitimate to be considered fraudulent. It may rather be a legitimate injury *magnified* beyond its true warrant. In fact, this is probably a more likely scenario, for it allows vice and plunder to proceed under at least *some* cover of law. This, again, is a product of the fallen human heart. It is sometimes by conscious design—aimed at enriching oneself or destroying another purposefully. It is sometimes unconscious. Either way, one should take the advice offered in the essay "On Private Revenge, III," written by a young John Adams:

> Let me conclude, by advising all men to look into their own hearts, which they will find to be deceitful above all things and desperately wicked [Jer. 17:9]. Let them consider how extremely addicted they are to magnify and exaggerate the injuries that are offered to themselves, and to diminish and extenuate the wrongs that they offer to others. They ought, therefore, to be too modest and diffident of their own judgment, when their own passions and prejudices and interests are concerned, to desire to judge

---

[41] Rushdoony, *Law and Society*, 345.

for themselves in their own causes, and to take their own
satisfactions for wrongs and injuries of any kind.[42]

Paul's remedy for these situations is spiritual: it is self-sacrifice. He writes, "To have lawsuits at all with one another is
already a defeat for you. Why not rather suffer wrong? Why not
rather be defrauded?" (1 Cor. 6:7). This would eliminate pur-
posely fraudulent cases between brethren, it would eliminate
frivolous cases, and it would go a long way toward eliminating *most* cases. Those cases that would survive this reduction—
and *should* survive—are those in which the issue under dispute
would significantly weaken the well-being of the victim. But the
path to this state of affairs is one of self-government—controlling the passions, jealousies, and other emotional vices which
drive us to magnify our "injuries" beyond warrant. Indeed, the
true Christian spirit will go further than self-government. I will
progress to self-sacrifice—reining in even the desire to justify
one's injuries in many or most cases.

There was a time when our legal scholars acknowledged
this basic fundamental of common law. Again, Adams writes,

> The divine Author of our religion has taught us that trivial
> provocations are to be overlooked. . . . Little injuries and
> insults ought to be borne patiently for the present, rather
> than run the risk of violent consequences by retaliation.
>   Now, the common law seems to me to be founded
> on the same great principle of philosophy and religion.[43]

A necessary step, then, in recovering a free judiciary system
is for people to adopt this Christian mindset. We must increase
individual, personal government—beginning at the spiritual
level—before we can expect society in general to reflect a less
litigious, coercive spirit which leverages government courts
and force as a means of self-justification. The basic summary

---

[42] John Adams, in *The Revolutionary Writings of John Adams*, ed. C. Bradley
Thompson (Indianapolis, IN: Liberty Fund, 2000), 17.

[43] Adams, *Revolutionary Writings*, 12–13.

is this: "*If men will not obey God, they will not obey men.*" And when disobedience is the common standard, "they will then require the gallows and the gun as the necessary instruments of order."[44] Unless we learn more often to crucify that flesh, we will not progress beyond such institutionalized force, and we must despair of seeing a free society.

But crucifying that flesh has practical manifestations and applications. The spiritual must manifest in the material—as we pray His will be done "on earth as it is in heaven." Christian arbitration or Christian private courts—or a free society in general—would further address the problem of continuity by encouraging relevant clauses in *contractual* agreements. If parties engaging in business had clear arbitration clauses in their contracts up front, then any arbitration decision that followed would become a legally enforceable instrument under contract law. If a contract specifies that, should any conflicts arise, these parties agree to settle by means of arbitration, and that the decision of the arbitration panel will be accepted by both parties as final, then that aspect of the contract becomes a legally-enforceable decision under contract law in civil courts. This would make any recourse to state courts at least predictable if not pointless. Of course, such a situation would be extreme; Christians should be content to accept the contractual means of conflict resolution without needing recourse to State enforcement. The point being made here, however, is about finality. Christians solve the endless appeals problem simply by contractually agreeing to stop at the decision of a pre-determined panel of arbitrators or elders.

So here are five principles of Christian courts which individuals and churches need to learn and implement. Considering that Christians (of some confession or other) make up about seventy-five percent of the U.S. population, if every dispute between "Christian" and "Christian" were settled this way,

---

[44] See Rushdoony, *Institutes*, 620.

privately, it would have several great effects in society. It would make a huge impact on the clogged court system. It would set a powerful precedent of Christian law, virtue, peace, and brotherly love for the rest of society. It could also have an educational effect upon a greater number of Christians in at least two ways: 1) it would require us to seek answers to more of life's practical considerations from God's Word, and thus would force us back to the texts of Scripture more frequently than is currently normal for most Christians, and 2) it would teach Christians in general to learn and rely on the Christian doctrine of self-government. Just apprehending these two lessons would go a long way toward improving society and increasing freedom.

Christians Under Pagan Judicial Tyranny

Earlier we mentioned the problem of secular courts which judge according to a law other than God's law, and thus set themselves up as rival gods. We noted with Rushdoony how justice is not impossible with such a court, but it should not be expected. In the American system which still has vestiges of its Christian legal heritage, we might expect proper justice more often than in some other societies, but the possibility still arises—and in fact arises more increasingly as society departs from biblical truth—that the rival gods will uphold and enforce satanic laws and sanctions. It may be that courts call for Christians to engage in acts that are sinful. It may even be that courts threaten punishments upon such Christians in these cases, or that courts provide remedies to others who wish to coerce Christians in these regards. What should the Christian do in these cases?

There is a progression of resistance for Christians to follow. First, we must resist peacefully using the instruments of the law, such as peaceful protest and legal appeals. Second, where the issues are merely local or state issues, we can leave the jurisdiction and move to another which better reflects our values. This option is, of course, greatly magnified under this project's proposal of "county rights," where the highest civil authority enforcement for such matters would exist only at the local level. In the absence of such a decentralized ideal, it may be best in some cases to leave a state, or even leave the country. Third, when protest and activism are ineffective, and emigration is not practical or preferable, then the Christian must make a judgment as to the severity of the offense to determine whether civil order or Christian conscience should have priority. It may be the case that "while the powers have no right to command apart from God's Word, sometimes the duty to obey remains as the moral course, and the pragmatic course," and thus we must obey as unto God, for the sake of order, not for the sake of the particular human decision. Fourth, where a particular law is egregious enough, however—for example, in reference to abortion or sexual deviancy—Christians absolutely must engage in civil disobedience. But this must be done in "conscious obedience to God rather than man," and preferably in concert with public proclamation by some recognized Christian authority.[45]

Civil disobedience in egregious cases—necessary cases—is a long accepted and ancient Christian right and practice which modern Christians need to recover. This is especially true in the United States where we retain many vestiges of a formerly Christian society: the delusion created by these vestiges means that we tolerate the rotten guts of socialism and humanism in virtually every corner of government and society merely because there remains a paper veneer of Christian heritage over top of it. The greatest advances, however, of Christianity in society throughout history have come when Christians have confronted the rottenness. Toward this motivation, the words of Francis Schaeffer are worth quoting at length:

> Throughout the whole history of the Christian Church (and again I wish people knew their history; in *A Christian Manifesto* I stress what happened in the Reforma-

---

[45] For these four "routes" of resistance, see Rushdoony, *Institutes of Biblical Law*, 620. The direct quotations here are all from the same reference.

tion in reference to all this), at a certain point, it is not only the privilege but it is the duty of the Christian to disobey the government. Now that's what the founding fathers did when they founded this country. That's what the early Church did. That's what Peter said. You heard it from the Scripture: "Should we obey man?... rather than God?" That's what the early Christians did.

Occasionally—no, often—people say to me, "But the early Church didn't practice civil disobedience." Didn't they? You don't know your history again. When those Christians that we all talk about so much allowed themselves to be thrown into the arena, when they did that, from their view it was a religious thing. They would not worship anything except the living God. But you must recognize from the side of the Roman state, there was nothing religious about it at all—it was purely civil. The Roman Empire had disintegrated until the only unity it had was its worship of Caesar. You could be an atheist; you could worship the Zoroastrian religion.... You could do anything. They didn't care. It was a civil matter, and when those Christians stood up there and refused to worship Caesar, from the side of the state, they were *rebels*. They were in civil disobedience and they were thrown to the beasts. They were involved in civil disobedience, as much as your brothers and sisters in the Soviet Union are [in 1982]. When the Soviet Union says that, by law, they cannot tell their children, even in their home, about Jesus Christ, they must disobey and they get sent off to the mental ward or to Siberia. . . .

The early Christians, every one of the reformers (and again, as I'll say in *A Christian Manifesto*, I go through country after country and show that there was not a single place with the possible exception of England, where the Reformation was successful, where there wasn't civil disobedience and disobedience to the state), the people of the Reformation, the founding fathers of this country, faced and acted in the realization that if there is no place for disobeying the government, that government has been put in the place of the living

God. In such a case, the government has been made a false god. If there is no place for disobeying a human government, that government has been made God.[46]

It is simply time that Christians informed themselves on these matters, exalted the proper God to His throne in both their hearts and their society, and get prepared to decide and act accordingly. The early Christians did it, the Reformers did it, and American Christians did it. There is no reason God's people today should not be equally prepared.

Jury Nullification

Another currently available avenue through which we can restore the principles of liberty is through jury nullification. This practice, once widely accepted among Christians and early American jurists and lawyers, has been largely forgotten until very recently. Thanks to the increasing interest in liberty, civic involvement, and the advance of individual rights, we are seeing a resurgence of this principle.

The principle itself is quite simple: juries have the perfectly legal right to determine *both* the facts and the *law* in cases over which they sit in judgment. This concept sounds radical to most modern ears, but it's absolutely true. In cases where the application of a currently law would actually cause an unjust outcome, or where the applicable law itself is unpopular or simply a bad law, the jury can remedy the situation—even if the defendant is technically guilty of breaking the law—by refusing to find that defendant guilty, by declaring the person innocent. Juries have this right *even if the judge instructs them otherwise in any way.*

Several of the founding fathers understood the fundamental importance of jury nullification. Even a Fox News report

---

[46] Francis Schaeffer, "A Christian Manifesto," from a lecture given at Coral Ridge Presbyterian Church in 1982; http://www.peopleforlife.org/francis.html (accessed November 25, 2011).

on the subject quoted John Adams to this effect: "It is not only [the juror's] right, but his duty . . . to find the verdict according to his own best understanding, judgment, and conscience, though in direct opposition to the direction of the court." [47] Likewise, the first Chief Justice of the U.S. Supreme Court, John Jay, "you have nevertheless a right to take upon yourselves to judge of both, and to determine the law as well as the fact in controversy. . . . Both objects are lawfully, within your power of decision."[48] Unsurprisingly, Jefferson joined these Federalists in this view. He explained why we should support jury nullification: because "to consider judges as the ultimate arbiters of all constitutional questions," he wrote, is "a very dangerous doctrine indeed, and one which would place us under the despotism of an oligarchy."[49]

This power was preserved as basic to preventing government abuse of power. During the ratification debates, this power was upheld as the fundamental check against potential abuse under the Constitution. During the debates in Massachusetts, Theophilus Parsons—a supporter of the Constitution and later state Supreme Court Chief Justice—proclaimed:

> The people themselves have it in their power effectually to resist usurpation, without being driven to an appeal to arms. An act of usurpation is not obligatory; it is not law; and any man may be justified in his resistance. Let him be considered as a criminal by the general government, yet only his own fellow-citizens can convict him; they are his jury, and if they pronounce him innocent, not all the powers of Congress can hurt him; and inno-

---

[47] Quoted in "Justice Often Served By Jury Nullification," August 1, 2005, *FoxNews.com*; http://www.foxnews.com/story/0,2933,163877,00.html (accessed November 24, 2011).

[48] *Georgia v. Brailford*, 3 U.S. 1 (1794); http://openjurist.org/3/us/1 (accessed November 25, 2011).

[49] Jefferson to William Charles Jarvis, *The Works of Thomas Jefferson*, 12 vol., ed. Paul Leicester Ford (New York and London: G. P. Putnam's Sons and The Kinckerbocker Press, 1905), 12:162..

cent they certainty will pronounce him, if the supposed law he resisted was an act of usurpation.[50]

The framers recognized the importance of this issue from the hard lessons of previous generations. William Penn, founder of Pennsylvania, was a defendant in a 1670 case in England in which he was tried for unlawful assembly. He had violated the so-called "Conventicle Act" of 1664 which forbade religious assemblies of more than five persons for non-establishment protestants. This act was part of the Elizabethan acts of Unity which aimed to centralize the English Church and suppress all Puritans and other Protestants. Penn was one of these. When drawn into court, he pleaded not guilty. The jury upheld his innocence—not because he had not broken the law, but because they esteemed the particular law unjust. The bench was furious, and threatened the jurors with imprisonment and deprivation. It finally settled upon fining each member and imprisoning them until it was paid. A higher court, however, later released them. The episode was very famous; it was fundamental to our framer's understanding of how courts would become tyrannical and uncontrollable unless we preserved the right of jury nullification.[51]

Unfortunately, today it is a practice of most judges to remain silent about this aspect of the law and instead specifically *mislead* juries only to consider the *facts* in the case and not the *law*. An 1895 Supreme Court decision even ruled that this practice is Constitutional—judges are not required to explain to juries their right of jury nullification. But this by no means makes the right itself any less important. (It just means that judges are elit-

---

[50] In Jonathan Elliot, ed., *The Debates in the Several State Conventions, on the Adoption of the Federal Constitution*, 4 vols. (Washington, 1836), 2:94. Partially quoted also in Thomas Woods, Jr., *Rollback: Repealing Big Government Before the Coming Fiscal Collapse* (Washington, D.C.: Regnery, 2011), 179.

[51] See the whole court transcript, "The Trial of William Penn and William Mead, at the Old Bailey, for a Tumultuous Assembly: 22 Charles II. A. D. 1670," at http://www.constitution.org/trials/penn/penn-mead.htm (accessed November 24, 2011).

ist, not wanting average people to have a say in the righteousness of any given law, that they are pressured by large beneficiaries, or that they for some other reason lean toward the side of
the prosecution in all cases. Whatever the cause, it's unethical
and counterproductive to liberty in most cases.) Despite the
judges' shifty silence, the Supreme Court itself has upheld the
right more than once in American history:

> In 1952, for example, the Court found that "juries are
> not bound by what seems inescapable logic to judges."
> And in 1972, that "The pages of history shine on in-
> stances of the jury's exercise of its prerogative to disre-
> gard instructions of the judge."[52]

The application of the right has a deep and meaningful American heritage as well. Juries exercised it against the
Alien and Sedition Acts of Adams and against the Fugitive
Slave Laws in the 1850s. It was used against growing corporate power during the height of the progressive era, used frequently against alcohol control laws during Prohibition, and
even in a few cases for Vietnam War protestors.[53]

Keeping right with the theme with our project, the Fox
News report says,

> A common question I get from people disturbed by
> these kinds of cases is, "What can we do?" Well, here's
> one thing the average citizen can do: Serve when you're
> called to jury duty, and while there, refuse to enforce
> unjust laws. If a defendant is guilty of harming someone
> else, certainly, throw the book at him. But if he's guilty
> of violating a bad law, or if you feel the law has been
> unjustly applied to him, by all means, come back with
> "not guilty," no matter what the judge, the prosecutor, or
> the evidence says.

---

[52] "Justice Often Served By Jury Nullification," *FoxNews.com*

[53] See "A History of Jury Nullification," by the International Society for Individual Liberties; http://www.isil.org/resources/lit/history-jury-null.html (access
November 25, 2011).

For those wishing to have as immediate an impact as possible in this regard, they should embrace jury duty when called, and actively work to spread knowledge of the right among their families, communities, churches, and in public wherever possible. Likewise, interested parties should read and learn as much as possible about the subject. There is at least one organization devoted to this issue—the Fully Informed Jury Association (fija.org). They provide resources for education, including a DVD lecture series for churches.

There is yet another avenue by which the people have some control over the judiciary, albeit indirectly. This is Congress' Constitutional power to regulate the Supreme Court's jurisdiction over any of its legislation. Believe it or not, the Constitution gives Congress this power. Article 3, Section 2 states,

> In all Cases affecting Ambassadors, other public Ministers and Consuls, and those in which a State shall be Party, the supreme Court shall have original Jurisdiction. In all the other Cases before mentioned, the supreme Court shall have appellate Jurisdiction, both as to Law and Fact, *with such Exceptions, and under such Regulations as the Congress shall make.*

In many cases, then, Congress can declare "Exceptions" and "Regulations" upon the jurisdiction of the Court, and indeed it has done so in the past. This power has certain limitations and drawbacks, of course, but is very real, should be taken seriously, and our Senators and Congressman should be well-informed of it.

Conclusion

The average person concerned about judicial tyranny has practical things to do even in this seemingly incontestable area. We can promote private courts or private arbitration: When applicable, we can settle our own disputes there and pledge to remain content with the results. This is especially true for Christians who should have had such courts established for themselves long since. Further, Christians should do as much as they can individually to limit litigation in society—this often means self-sacrifice for minor infractions, debts, etc. Finally, jury nullification is a powerful tool to halt tyranny in individual cases—and if enough cases strike down the same law, it will set a precedent for changing that law. Interested Christians should research, learn about, and then inform their elders of all of these principles and practices. Granted, these steps will not transform the entire judiciary system overnight. But then again, as we have stressed from the beginning, we are planning and working for our children and grandchildren.

9. Defense

It is now time to focus on some vitally important topics in American life today: the military, war, and defense. Why do I say these topics are so vitally important? Because biblically and historically speaking, no tyranny can rule without military force, and when a central government has access to a standing army, then not even long traditions, faith, or well-entrenched legal systems can constrain a tyrant's whim. Many nations throughout history have risen and fallen by the fateful recompense of military lusts, and America is no exception to these forces.

Yet many Christians uncritically praise every advance of American ship and jet, hailing every missile strike with strains of "God Bless America." These same Christians have probably never read how openly and clearly the Bible forbids a nation to have a large standing army. They have probably never read the Bible's rules for raising armies and waging war. Considering the hundreds of billions of dollars of debt our wars lay upon us each year, not to mention hundreds of thousands of casualities in just the past decade, *it is time for Christians to address this issue.*

When a nation's identity grows too dependent upon military power, that power soon grows intertwined with every other branch of government and civic life: the economy, education, welfare, political power, special interests, taxation, money and banking, manufacturing and trade, courts, and of course the other Executive power functions. In turn, each of these becomes moulded and shaped, and, in some cases, grows dependent upon that large, *active*, standing army. Thus, the lust for a standing army transforms the entire character of a nation from liberty to centralized nanny-state, as we shall further see in the second part of this topic.

While the biblical teaching on war and the military presents a nearly radical picture to the modern mind, the Bible is the only proper place to find foundations for "national defense in a free society." Indeed, the biblical direction is so contrary to what we have known and come to accept as normal, that were it not God's Own Word, many Americans would refuse even to tolerate hearing it for a second. But hear it we must, because change we must.

Preventing a Warfare State

The biblical picture is found primarily in two passages of Deuteronomy: the laws for kings (Deut. 17) and the laws for warfare (Deut. 22). First, let us simply read the laws for kings, stated in Deuteronomy 17:14–20:

> When you come to the land that the LORD your God is giving you, and you possess it and dwell in it and then say, "I will set a king over me, like all the nations that are around me," you may indeed set a king over you whom the LORD your God will choose. One from among your brothers you shall set as king over you. You may not put a foreigner over you, who is not your brother. Only he must not acquire many horses for himself or cause the people to return to Egypt in order to acquire many horses, since the LORD has said to you, "You shall never return that way again." And he shall not acquire many wives for himself, lest his heart turn away, nor shall he acquire for himself excessive silver and gold. And when he sits on the throne of his kingdom, he shall write for himself in a book a copy of this law, approved by the Levitical priests. And it shall be with him, and he shall read in it all the days of his life, that he may learn to fear the LORD his God by keeping all the words of this law and these statutes, and doing them, that his heart may not be lifted up above his brothers, and that he may not

turn aside from the commandment, either to the right hand or to the left, so that he may continue long in his kingdom, he and his children, in Israel.

While not all of these criteria explicitly refer to the military, they are still proper to review here. First, the law stipulates that rulers should be "From among your brothers . . . not a foreigner." In other words, to use a catch phrase commonly heard today, the ruler must be a "natural born citizen." The U.S. Constitution exhibits this biblical idea, which was a response in part to the fact that King George III was not a native Brit, but of the German House of Hanover. Moreover, he had an alliance with continental banking interests, and when Parliament wished to further tax the American colonies, he remained indifferent to the Colonists he was sworn to defend. The U.S. Constitution returned to the pre-1066 Anglo-Danish standard of "kith and kin." The word "King" is related to the English "kin" which has an ethnic reference. "Kith and kin" means "same country and family." Without this quality in a leader, there cannot be any true loyalty to the people. And while this sounds like a side matter, it is not: a ruler who identifies with the people almost as a family will fight to defend them and their liberties. A ruler without that loyalty, however, will more likely be less interested in defense. It's the difference which Jesus taught between the shepherd and the hireling:

> The good shepherd lays down his life for the sheep. He who is a hired hand and not a shepherd, who does not own the sheep, sees the wolf coming and leaves the sheep and flees, and the wolf snatches them and scatters them. He flees because he is a hired hand and cares nothing for the sheep (John 10:11–13).

Notice how the issue manifests itself especially in times of *defense* and *protection*, when the hireling's own life or goods may be at risk.

The King's self-interests can pervert society in other ways as well, and the law therefore forbids him from acquiring three categories of things: horses, wives, and wealth. While it may not be apparent to the modern reader immediately, these three things all relate to foreign policy, the military, and war. First, horses. In those days, horses were an *offensive* weapon with great range and quick-strike ability; they were thus a means of military conquest. To acquire many horses was to have a standing cavalry ready for an expansive empire. God did not save His people to be a large War State. Horses were the favorite tool of War States. There were other means sufficient for defense.

This also means in principle that God's people, with their King, were not allowed to have a standing army. This does not mean they could not have a well-trained, well-prepared, and well-ordered militia system, as we shall see; it means no *permanent* standing army. A standing army is a perpetual temptation for a king to impose his will by force *somewhere*, if not abroad in imperial conquest, then in tyranny upon the people at home—or both. This is the very reason God punished David for taking a census, which was the first step in raising an army (2 Sam. 24).[1] For this sin of militarism, God plagued Israel.

The law against multiplying horses had a second part: forbidding the King from causing "the people to return to Egypt in order to acquire many horses, since the LORD has said to you, 'You shall never return that way again.'" This is, on its surface, a law against foreign arms exchanges, but it is much more. Two things stand out. First, the king is not to "cause" the people to do this. The Hebrew verb "return" is specifically in the *causative* form: the King shall not cause them to return—that is, he shall not *force* them to return to Egypt. This is not a literal blanket prohibition against visiting or even migrating to Egypt. Jesus did so with his parents by divine prompting

---

[1] Compare Numbers 1:1–3 where numbering the people was in reference to those able to go forth to war. The book of Numbers is the account of God's holy army in its first days in the holy land.

(Matt. 2:13ff). Rather, this is speaking of the King forcing people into service, presumably as mercenaries or perhaps plain
slaves for Egypt in exchange for horses. This is made clearer
when we study the second aspect, God's command that the
people "shall never return that way again."

By "that way," God is not talking about the literal road to
Egypt—again, Jesus' flight to Egypt makes this interpretation untenable. By "that way" God is speaking of the slavery
involved in the people being forced into State servitude. How
is this clear? Ironically, from something that is *un*clear: the
verse clearly says that God *told* the Israelites this command:
"since the LORD has said to you, 'You shall never return that
way again.'" Yet this command appears nowhere in the story
of God's people up to that point—indeed, it appears nowhere
else in Scripture. We have no record of any prohibition of a
return to Egypt like this, let alone a literal return. While it is
possible God told them this beforehand and that revelation
was not recorded, it makes much more sense if understood in
reference to the slavery of Egypt. For in reference to slavery to
a god-State like Egypt, God *did* give His people a general prohibition. It was given to all of them clearly and loudly:

> And God spoke all these words: "I am the LORD your God,
> who brought you out of Egypt, out of the land of slavery.
> "You shall have no other gods before me" (Exod. 20:1–3).

This is the preamble to the Ten Commandments and the
First Commandment. Here, God makes it clear that His relationship to them as their God was one of deliverance from
slavery to a total State. Egypt here is equated with slavery, and
God brought them out of it. He subsequently *commanded*
them to have no other God but Him—the God of liberation
and deliverance. In other words, the people were not to return
to the way of Egypt—in the judicial sense of the word.

This understanding is further reinforced by the sanctions
of Deuteronomy 27 and 28, where God detailed the bless-

ings Israel would enjoy if she remained faithful, as well as the curses the nation would suffer should she disobey. The very last sentence of the list of curses makes the point:

> The LORD will bring you back in ships to Egypt, a jour-
> ney that I promised that you should never make again;
> and there you shall offer yourselves for sale to your en-
> emies as male and female slaves, but there will be no
> buyer (Deut. 28:68).

Should Israel disobey, they would be returned to the slav-ery of Egypt—not necessarily literal Egypt (for when the nation did disobey, it was carried captive into Assyria and into Baby-lon) but certainly a physical bondage, even if self-imposed.

So the law against horses is, in its fullness, a law against offensive armies, standing armies, imperialism, and *conscrip-tion*—all based in God's condemnation of slavery and of salva-tion by conquest, by man. All of these things are manifestations of humanism and idolatry: man trusting man, man exalting man, man serving man, man being forced to serve man.

Second, the King was not allowed to have many wives. In today's culture—where we have the strange mixture of a gen-eral repugnance of polygamy in conjunction with easy divorce and growing acceptance of homosexuality among politicians and leaders—it may be difficult to comprehend why a King should be prohibited many wives. But the reason is quite simple. In the ancient days—and really right up until modern times—Kings would use marriages to seal political alliances. Thus, polygamy was often intertwined with foreign policy.

Again we have an allegiance issue, just as with the require-ment that the King come from among the people. If he is married to many foreign women, his heart is susceptible to compromise in favor of her people and against his. The same is true of multiple marriages (or women) even of his own people—there is in that case an increased competition for his heart, will, and capacities which detracts further from his ability to do his job as King. We see these problems develop in Solomon's womanizing (1 Kings 11:1–4), and his "heart was not wholly true."

Third, the King was not allowed to have much money—that is, "excessive silver and gold." This is a prohibition against a large public treasury, and certainly against a virtually infinite public treasury like the Federal Reserve. Again, this is about loyalty: a King with independent wealth can have a divided heart as he has no need for trust or dependence upon the people. The issue, however, is more importantly about *power*. A large treasury has the power to make large portions of the public dependent upon the government. It can also be used to buy those war toys and standing armies and to wage wars. In fact, there is a powerful connection between money, power, and war. As Cicero said, "The sinews of war are infinite money."[2] God's people were not to be a people of conquest; their King should not have the tools of conquest, including excess funds (and certainly not a central bank with fiat powers!).

The final verse of this passage tells us that the King is to make himself a personal copy of God's law, and have his copy approved by the priesthood (for accuracy at least). He must read in that law daily, and, most importantly, obey it. In all of these things, we see a King who is not a self-motivated, power-hungry leader, but rather a man first and foremost submitted to God's Word. And that Word continues on to tell us exactly why that King should do so: so that he remains in the fear of God, with humility and equal station with his constituents, to preserve justice according to God's law, and to maintain peace and prosperity in the land for the long term.

The goal here is a State or civil society that is small; restricted by God's law; not equipped for offensive conquest, with no standing army and thus not tempted to wars of imperialism, expansion, colonialism, or nation building; not hav-

---

[2] Quoted in John Brewer, *The Sinews of Power: War, Money, and the English State*, 1688–1783 (Cambridge, MA: Harvard University Press, 1988), v.

ing a large treasury and thus not capable of acting as a Welfare State or a Warfare State. It will have a public and constant emphasis on the ruler not having his heart lifted up above the people—thus, no elitism, and no sense of government being the highest leaders of every facet of life, for *they are not messiahs or saviors* of the people. They are there for one purpose alone—civil justice according to God's Law.

Raising an Army

The second relevant passage covers both the laws for raising a militia and for waging warfare, all found in Deuteronomy 20:5–20. The first part of this covers the raising of a militia:

> When you go out to war against your enemies, and see horses and chariots and an army larger than your own, you shall not be afraid of them, for the LORD your God is with you, who brought you up out of the land of Egypt. And when you draw near to the battle, the priest shall come forward and speak to the people and shall say to them, "Hear, O Israel, today you are drawing near for battle against your enemies: let not your heart faint. Do not fear or panic or be in dread of them, for the LORD your God is he who goes with you to fight for you against your enemies, to give you the victory." Then the officers shall speak to the people, saying, "Is there any man who has built a new house and has not dedicated it? Let him go back to his house, lest he die in the battle and another man dedicate it. And is there any man who has planted a vineyard and has not enjoyed its fruit? Let him go back to his house, lest he die in the battle and another man enjoy its fruit. And is there any man who has betrothed a wife and has not taken her? Let him go back to his house, lest he die in the battle and another man take her." And the officers shall speak further to the people, and say, "Is there any man who is fearful and fainthearted? Let him go back to his house, lest he make the heart of his fellows melt like his own." And when the

officers have finished speaking to the people, then commanders shall be appointed at the head of the people.

There are several principles involved here. First, the militia
is raised in a defensive situation. The Israelites are first confronted with the armies of their enemies before they begin
this process. The principle here is that a militia is raised for
the cause of repelling invaders.

Second, an army is religious in nature, for war is religious
in nature: it is God's judgment on earth, as we shall see later.
So the first to speak to the assembled people (not yet an army)
is a priest. The army is to be motivated by God's sanction and
find their primary courage in His favorable presence. Now,
the people would already know for a fact that God does not
approve of offensive wars, so had they been assembled for
such, this motivational prayer would have been an act of public
hypocrisy. And the people—not the government or the priesthood, nor any other top-down authority—have the final right
to decide this. This prayer is a final reminder to the assembled
men that, ultimately, God decides the outcomes of battles, and
they should consider the call before them in such light.

Third, based on this fact of God's sovereignty in the affairs
of men, and building on God's prohibition of offensive wars,
God leaves the final decision of joining the fight *up to the
individuals themselves*. This is apparent in the militia-raising
process that follows. The militia was purely voluntary: anyone
who had any unfinished business (whether property, business,
or family) was given multiple clear notices, and allowed to
leave. Able-bodied males over 20 years old were called, and
by implication were *expected* to fight in any just cause. But the
exit door was broadly open for a wide scope of reasons. The
civil rulers were not allowed to make exceptions for anyone,
but were required by God generally to let those who chose to
abstain freely leave.

And if the latitude had not been given widely enough
already—land, vineyards, wives—the Law mandated that any-

one who was simply *fearful* could freely leave the militia: "Is there any man who is fearful and fainthearted? *Let him go. . . .*"

These "freely leaving" measures provided several benefits to the whole scenario: In case the militia had been organized for offensive or dubious purposes—most soldiers would leave, and the campaign would likely fall apart. When given a choice, people will not fight in these conditions. Yet in the case of a legitimate cause, the Law provided every possible out for the fearful, the distracted, worrisome, or otherwise distracted soldiers to be removed from the scene. This protected both those who left—who would not have fought wholeheartedly if at all—and also the willing soldiers who would not want to have to fight beside, or rely on, those with divided loyalty or lack of courage. If the cause is just, the end result is the most willing, able, and focused army possible (Uriah's unwillingness to leave his brethren in battle even at the behest of King David is evidence of this spirit; see 2 Samuel 11:11). At this point, the militia was raised. (Consequently also, if the cause were unjust and clearly so, there would be great difficulty on the part of the bloodthirsty, tyrannical government to raise much of a militia at all. A general lack of willingness would drive all those able bodied males readily to accept the various "outs" and leave little more than a meager force standing to serve the corrupt leaders.)

Finally, after all objectors and abstainers left, then, and only then, were commanders *appointed*. Note that the military leaders had to be appointed: for as there was no standing army, there would be no lifetime, career military men. There would, of course, probably always be veterans around, skilled in battle and administration from past wars, but these were to return to the private sector when the battle was over. Should another just cause arise, they would probably—though not necessarily—be appointed as commanders again.[3]

---

[3] In such a free society, there would probably also exist private institutions providing combat training and skills during peacetime, thus keeping military skills and knowledge in the land sharp during peacetime, yet unavailable as a

What is clear here is that God's society makes no provision for a standing army and none for military conscription or a draft. Indeed, a military conscription was simply another type of State slavery from which God had delivered Israel, and which He forbade their kings to practice, as we saw above. And when Israel finally rejected God in choosing for themselves a king like other nations, military conscription was one of the curses which God said that tyrant would bring upon them (1 Sam. 8:11–12). Instead, God protected peace, freedom, and, by giving His people every chance to leave a potential militia, He left the final judgment of any particular war's justness to the individual—not the government. This is decentralization at its finest.

Contrast this with the modern American mentality in regard to the military and war. Not only have we had a draft in more than one instance, we have a tradition of ridiculing objectors, calling them cowards, traitors, and "un-American," and in some cases even passing laws against detracting from a war effort or discouraging enlistment. From just what we have seen so far, this attitude can only be judged as ungodly— and God is no pansy when it comes to issues of war and judgment in the earth. He nevertheless has a higher standard for conscience and freedom. We have more often than not gotten His standard exactly backwards: whereas He gives men every opportunity to abstain from a battle and invites those who would leave to do so, we often force everyone to fight (upon threat of civil penalties) and ridicule those who object. This is to place nationalism over godliness, and thus to make an idol of one's nation or armed forces.

The Laws of Waging War

The second part of this passage (Deut. 20:10–20) covers the laws of war. Intertwined in this passage are several aspects that pertain only to Israel's special situation in the land, yet

---

political resource.

since we also learn here the general principles of waging warfare, we must focus on these.

Before we can understand these rules of warfare, we have to understand their theological foundation in the laws concerning judgment of false witnesses. These appear in the previous chapter of Deuteronomy.

> A single witness shall not suffice against a person for any crime or for any wrong in connection with any offense that he has committed. Only on the evidence of two witnesses or of three witnesses shall a charge be established. If a malicious witness arises to accuse a person of wrongdoing, then both parties to the dispute shall appear before the LORD, before the priests and the judges who are in office in those days. The judges shall inquire diligently, and if the witness is a false witness and has accused his brother falsely, then you shall do to him as he had meant to do to his brother. So you shall purge the evil from your midst. And the rest shall hear and fear, and shall never again commit any such evil among you. Your eye shall not pity. It shall be life for life, eye for eye, tooth for tooth, hand for hand, foot for foot (Deut. 19:15–21).

While not apparent at first, this passage has a profound connection to the rules of warfare. War is God's judgment upon whole societies and nations, and it involves the ultimate sanction of God's judgment in earth—the death penalty. For there to be a sanction of armed defense (especially to the point of killing the aggressor) lawfully applied, there must first have been an aggression that justifies it. Out of this principle comes the theory of "just war." Thus any nation that acts with deadly force is by implication saying to its target, "You have committed an offense which justifies God's judgment of the death penalty."

At this point, the laws against false witness provide a check. Just as with individuals who bring false accusations, any nation aggressing against another *without* just cause is making that implied accusation *falsely*. An unwarranted aggression is a false declaration of God's judgment, which means also that those in charge of the decision to aggress have set themselves up as false prophets or even false gods. But God's laws against false witness in regard to the death penalty state that the bearers of such false accusations themselves should receive the penalty in question—in this case, death or subjugation.

This is, in part, the theological justification for waging war against an aggressor nation. But unlike cases involving individuals, national disputes have no higher court other than God Himself to decide the evidence in the case and then punish a false witness. National leaders must deliberate among themselves and then, if the attack is unjustified, choose to enact the sanctions against the aggressors themselves. In the end, God will determine which cause was just—and this may very well be reflected in the results on the battlefield.

Even at the point of defensive attack, however, the Bible calls leaders to offer terms of peace. They must allow for the admission of guilt on the part of the false-witness aggressor, and then allow the possibility of restitution and peaceful subjugation as opposed to bloodshed. This is a measure to advance peace over warfare. Thus we get to the passage on the laws of waging war:

> When you draw near to a city to fight against it, offer terms of peace to it. And if it responds to you peaceably and it opens to you, then all the people who are found in it shall do forced labor for you and shall serve you. But if it makes no peace with you, but makes war against you, then you shall besiege it. . . .
>
> When you besiege a city for a long time, making war against it in order to take it, you shall not destroy its trees by wielding an axe against them. You may eat from them, but you shall not cut them down. Are the trees in the field human, that they should be besieged by you? Only the trees that you know are not trees for food you

may destroy and cut down, that you may build siegeworks against the city that makes war with you, until it
falls (Deut. 20:10–20).

Be clear here: the "terms of peace" proposal is in no way
to let the aggressor nation off the hook. They are instead to
be forced into restitution and servitude. This does not require
occupation necessarily, certainly not at the level of local task-
masters—that is not the point. The point will be civil atonement for the aggression, and the punishment must fit the
crime. This is establishing a principle of war reparations to be
paid by an entire generation of the aggressing nation. This is
no light penalty, but it is just and is to be preferred above the
waging of war for the preservation of social peace and life.

Nevertheless, if the aggressor refuses the terms—which
would be to persist in declaring the validity of its false judgment—then war and bloodshed are justified, and should
indeed be carried out as a matter of cosmic justice. But note,
by looking at the big picture here, war and bloodshed are
acceptable only in defense, and only as a last resort.

The laws pertaining to trees here sound obscure and perhaps obsolete, but just the opposite is true: they have both
fundamental theological significance and modern practical
relevance. The theological significance lies in the significance
fruit-bearing trees have for life (stemming all the way back to
the Garden). Biblical economist Gary North addresses this
issue with powerful insight:

> This law of warfare reminded man that fruit-bearing
> trees sustain man's life. For this reason, they must not
> be used to impose man's death. . . .
>
> This law makes it clear that holy warfare is not just a
> means of inflicting death and destruction. It is a means
> of extending life. Holy warfare is not destruction for de-
> struction's sake. It is destruction for God's sake. There

is an element of disinheritance in war, but it is always to be offset by an element of inheritance.[4]

The passage goes on to say that the Israelites could cut down non-fruit-bearing trees to make siegeworks—implements for battle in the days of walled cities. But these days ended with the invention of gunpowder and its application in the West in the fifteenth century. Nevertheless, the fruit trees must remain alive. The Israelites could eat the fruit, but must preserve the fruit-bearers.[5]

Both aspects of this law have modern applications. The destruction of-non fruit trees is still allowed, and has benefits in some conditions of war. Defoliants in jungle warfare are certainly allowable where necessary.[6] Nevertheless, fruit trees are not to be cut to make war implements, certainly, but the theological principle of "that which sustains man's life" has much broader modern applications than the narrow instances in which fruit trees could somehow serve as modern weaponry. The principle means also that *crops* must be preserved during times of war, as well as water sources and systems, livestock, beehives, and other sources of food and health. The doctrines of total warfare and the "scorched earth" policy run completely counter to God's law here. Deaths of innocent civilians, "collateral damage," and destruction of private property in general should be condemned. Medical centers and pharmaceutical plants should remain protected. So should most factories and businesses—for these centers of economic production pertain directly to the sustenance of life for many people. Those factories directly involved in any war efforts, however, thereby include themselves in the hostilities, and therefore give up the protections afforded civilian life.

---

[4] Gary North, *Inheritance and Dominion: An Economic Commentary on Deuteronomy*, 4 vols. (Harrisonburg, VA: Dominion Education Ministries, Inc., 2003), 759.

[5] Gary North discusses several implications of this law in Israel's context.

[6] See North, *Inheritance and Dominion*, 769.

Biblical Ideals in America

So we have seen the basic biblical ideals for the state in regard to the military, the raising of a militia, and the waging of war. The reader will realize that we are a long way from these ideals today. But that has not always been the case in American history. We were once closer to the biblical doctrines.

In fact, in early colonial times, we were much closer. British citizens, especially those involved in business, disparaged war, and wanted a separation of party politics and commerce. For the hundred years from 1660 to 1760, the eminent historian Charles Andrews tells us,

> Most, though by no means all, of the mercantilists—merchants, tradesmen, and manufacturers as well as pamphleteers—hated war and the diplomacy that led to war, as interfering with the prosperity of the nation, and they resented the influence of party politics in determining any governmental programme that affected trade.[7]

Those that defected from this view, Andrews adds, were a group who wanted war with Spain as a license to raid Spanish plate fleets for gold bullion. These were essentially would-be pirates who did not succeed in their desires.[8]

Daniel Defoe, the famous author of *Robinson Crusoe*, wrote in favor of free commerce in 1713:

> What has trade to do with your political quarrels, and what business have party men with the commerce of the nation? Trade is neither Whig nor Tory, Church or Dissenter, High Church or Low Church. If parties come to govern our trade, all our commerce will be at an end.[9]

---

[7] Charles M. Andrews, *The Colonial Period of American History: England's Commercial and Colonial Policy,* Volume 4 (New Haven and London: Yale University Press, 2011), 321–322.

[8] Ibid., 321n1.

[9] Quoted in Ibid., 322.

Another pamphleteer, under the name "Thomas Merchant, Esq.," wrote of "Peace and Trade, War and Taxes or the Irreparable Damage of New Trade in Case of War."[10] This desire to separate political power and commerce helps preserve the biblical injunction to deprive the king of a large treasury, which applies to Parliaments as well. As soon as parties realize they can keep themselves in power by promising handouts or advantages to special interests, then corruption takes over and incentives for war mount. Thus, they should not be allowed any recourse that affects trade pro or con. The biblical mindset was prevalent, even if primarily originating on the British side, in colonial America.

The same was true in regard to voluntarism in the militia. The 1641 Massachusetts Body of Liberties was the first legal code established in the Colonies and was written by a Puritan minister. It outlawed military conscription:

> 7. No man shall be compelled to go out of the limits of this plantation upon any offensive wars which this Commonwealth or any of our friends or confederates shall voluntarily undertake. . . .

This continued for forty-five years until it was disregarded by Charles II and again by James II. Nevertheless, colonists were not regularly compelled to fight for Britain, even in their own colonies. In cases where local militia aided British "regulars," they were referred to as a secondary class, "provincials." Yet these "provincial" militias were enough of a threat that the first thing the British tried to do at the outset of the American Revolution was disarm them. Indeed, it was Britain's planned raid on their respective armories that led to the battles of Lexington and Concord.

During the American Revolution, recruitment still had a voluntary element. In one example, the famous Lutheran minister and friend of George Washington, John Muhlenberg,

---

[10] Ibid., 322n1.

gave a rousing sermon on the "time for war." At the end, he disrobed to reveal his own full military regalia and encouraged men to enlist. He signed up three hundred on the spot. This was the common view up to the time: American military was by recruitment of a militia in response to a just cause. Thus, a military historian reminds us, "Standing armies are a relatively recent institution in the history of warfare."[11]

Many of the American Framers, having learned of and observed the militaristic imperialism of Europe, lauded individual arms and opposed standing armies on principle. Thus, in *Federalist* 46, Madison lauded

> the advantage of being armed, which the Americans possess over the people of all other countries. . . . Notwithstanding the military establishments in the several kingdoms of Europe, which are carried as far as the public resources will bear, the governments are afraid to trust the people with arms.[12]

During the Constitutional ratification convention in Virginia, George Mason recalled how Britain aimed "to disarm the people—that was the best and most effective way to enslave them." This statement came on suspicion of the standing army which was proposed in the Constitution; he feared it would replace or overpower the state militias. The nationalists' response, which was supposed to alleviate this fear, could only do so by presupposing that state militias and private gun ownership would remain the status quo and would be enough to deter a takeover by the national army.

---

[11] Mark Mayo Boatner III, "Militia in the American Revolution," *Encyclopedia of the American Revolution* (New York: David McKay Company, 1966), 705.

[12] Quoted in Lawrence D. Pratt, "Tools of Biblical Resistance," in *Tactics of Christian Resistance*, ed. by Gary North (Tyler, TX: Geneva Divinity School Press, 1983), 441–442. This quotation, and others below, are found in *The Right to Keep and Bear Arms: Report of the Subcommittee on the Constitution of the Committee on the Judiciary in the United States Senate*, Ninety-Seventh Congress, Second Session (Washington: U.S. Government Printing Office, 1982), unpaginated.

Noah Webster argued:

> Before a standing army can rule, the people must be disarmed as they are in almost every kingdom in Europe. The supreme power in America cannot enforce unjust laws by the sword, because the whole body of the people are armed, and constitute a force superior to any band of regular troops that can be, on any pretense, raised in the United States.[13]

The British politician and reformer, James Burgh, whose work was very popular in the colonies (and influenced Jefferson), wrote in his *Political Disquisitions* (1774),

> Those, who have the command of the arms in a country, says Aristotle, are masters of the state, and have it in their power to make what revolutions they please. . . . there is no end to observations on the difference between the measures likely to be pursued by a minister backed by a standing army, and those of a court awed by the fear of an armed people. . . . No kingdom can be secured otherwise than by arming the people. The possession of arms is the distinction between a freeman and a slave. . . .

Even Alexander Hamilton, besieged by Anti-Federalist complaints about a standing army under the proposed Constitution, proposed in *Federalist* 29 a militia training program and individual possession of arms:

> If circumstances should at any time oblige the [national] government to form an army of any magnitude, that army can never be formidable to the liberties of the people while there is a large body of citizens, little, if at all, inferior to them in discipline and the use of arms, who stand ready to defend their own rights and those of their fellow-citizens. This appears to me the only substitute that can be devised for a standing army, and the best possible security against it, if it should exist.

---

[13] Quoted in Pratt, *Tactics of Christian Resistance*, 441.

Unfortunately, as I explore further in *Restoring America*, Hamilton neither truly believed this nor intended to practice it once he and his nationalists got their way. The Anti-Federalists remained closer to the older colonial view and greatly feared a standing army. We have already heard Mason in Virginia. Brutus in New York also held this view and would also not fall for the nationalist/Federalist response. He warned that the standing army was already planned by many of the nationalists and would become inevitable should the Constitution pass:

> The idea that there is no danger of the establishment of a standing army, under the new constitution, is without foundation.
>
> It is a well known fact, that a number of those who had an agency in producing this system, and many of those who it is probable will have a principal share in the administration of the government under it, if it is adopted, are avowedly in favor of standing armies. It is language common among them, "That no people can be kept in order, unless the government have an army to awe them into obedience; it is necessary to support the dignity of the government, to have a military establishment." And there will not be wanting a variety of plausible reasons to justify the raising of one, drawn from the danger we are in from the Indians on our frontier, or from the European provinces in our neighborhood. If to this we add, that an army will afford a decent support, and agreeable employment to the young men of many families, who are too indolent to follow occupations that will require care and industry, and too poor to live without doing any business, we can have little doubt, but that we will have a large standing army, as soon as the government can find money to pay them, and perhaps sooner.[14]

---

[14] Quoted in *The Complete Anti-Federalist*, ed. Herbert J. Storing (Chicago and London: University of Chicago Press, 1981), 2:410–411; minor grammatical edits added for readability.

"Centinel" (probably Judge George Bryan or his son, Samuel, of Philadelphia) feared the broad military power given to Congress. Speaking of Article 1, Section 8 of the proposed Constitution, he wrote,

> This section will subject the citizens of these States to the most arbitrary military discipline, even death may be inflicted upon the disobedient; in the character of a [national] militia, you may be dragged from your families and homes to any part of the continent, and for any length of time, at the discretion of a future Congress: and as a militia, you may be made the unwilling instruments of oppression, under the direction of government; there is no exemption upon account of conscientious scruples of bearing arms; no equivalent to be received in lieu of personal services. The militia of Pennsylvania may be marched to Georgia or New Hampshire, however incompatible with their interests or consciences;—in short, they may be made as mere machines as Prussian soldiers.[15]

The State of Pennsylvania—being populated largely by Quakers and other conscientious objectors to war—saw the same concerns addressed in a report of the Minority's "Dissent" to its Convention. Along with several other changes to the proposed constitution, the Minority proposed that "as standing armies in the time of peace are dangerous to liberty, they ought not be kept up."[16] The "Dissent" also warned that a standing army may be used to enforce the collection of taxes, and to enforce any laws it creates from which even the majority of people dissent.[17] This would be "inconsistent with every idea of liberty." The report warned, "For the same force that may be employed to compel obedience to good laws, might and probably would be used to wrest from the people their

---

[15] Ibid., 2:160–161.

[16] Ibid., 3:151.

[17] Ibid., 3:162, 163–164.

constitutional liberties."[18] The Minority certainly did not trust the Convention:

> The framers of this constitution appear to have been aware of this great deficiency; to have been sensible that no dependence could be placed on the people for their support: but on the contrary, that the government must be executed by force. They have therefore made a provision for this purpose in a permanent STANDING ARMY, and a MILITIA that may be subjected to as strict discipline and government.[19]

Luther Martin, who had been a delegate, addressed the Maryland Assembly in regard to the proceedings of the Constitutional Convention: "It was further observed, that when a government *wishes* to deprive their citizens of freedom, and reduce them to slavery, it *generally makes use of a standing army* for that purpose, and *leaves the militia in a situation as contemptible as possible, lest they might oppose its arbitrary designs.*"[20] Nevertheless, he continues to reveal, this concern and many like it were steamrolled by a single majority vote on the floor.

"John DeWitt" of Boston saw the Constitutional grant of power for a standing national army as the beginning of the subversion of state militias, and all defenses of that power were but a cover for the greater plan of centralization. But it started as an apparently *small* grant of power, for "They are aware of the necessity of catching Samson asleep to trim him of his locks." He added,

> It is asserted by the most respectable writers on Government, that a well regulated militia, composed of the yeomanry of the country, have ever been considered the bulwark of a free people; and, says the celebrated Mr. Hume, "without it, it is folly to think any free govern-

---

[18] Ibid., 3:163–164.

[19] In Storing, *Complete Anti-Federalist*, 3:164.

[20] Ibid., 2:59.

ment will have stability and security. . . ." It is universally agreed, that a militia and a standing body of troops never flourished on the same soil. Tyrants have uniformly depended upon the latter at the expense of the former. . . . No, my fellow-citizens, this plainly shews they do not mean to depend upon the citizens of the States alone to enforce their powers, wherefore it is their policy to neglect them, and lean upon something more substantial and summary.[21]

The principle that the militia should be decentralized, local, and composed of "yeomanry of the country" parallels the biblical ideal that rulers should be from among their own people. If they are not, they have less interest in the land and the people they are supposed to defend. "The Federal Farmer" recognized this problem, and thus warned "that all regulations tending to render this general militia useless and defenceless, by establishing select corps of militia, or distinct bodies of military men [both instances of a central army], *not having permanent interests and attachments in the community* [are] to be avoided."[22] In a much earlier essay, the same writer expressed—as did many of the writers on both sides—that the Constitution would lead eventually to a civil war. The Federal Farmer argued this could happen in two ways, and a national, central army would be the key factor in one of them. He wrote,

No position can be truer than this, that in this country either neglected laws or a military execution of them, must lead to a revolution, and to the destruction of freedom. Neglected laws must first lead to anarchy and confusion; and a military execution of laws is only a shorter way to the same point—despotic government.[23]

---

[21] Ibid., 4:36–37.

[22] Ibid., 2:341; emphasis added.

[23] Ibid., 2:234.

We could follow with yet further quotations showing a general fear and suspicion of standing armies and centralized armies in the United States, or the Colonies, before the Constitution. Indeed, the Declaration of Independence itself states that one of the colonists' grievances against George III was that "he has kept among us, in times of peace, Standing Armies without the Consent of our legislatures." This was one of the very reasons America declared independence to begin with!

Nevertheless, despite the few dozen grievances listed, the colonists followed the biblical principle of making war a last resort, making numerous appeals for peaceful redress to both the King and the British people:

> In every stage of these Oppressions We have Petitioned for Redress in the most humble terms: Our repeated Petitions have been answered only by repeated injury. . . .
>
> Nor have We been wanting in attentions to our Brittish brethren. We have warned them from time to time of attempts by their legislature to extend an unwarrantable jurisdiction over us. We have reminded them of the circumstances of our emigration and settlement here. We have appealed to their native justice and magnanimity, and we have conjured them by the ties of our common kindred to disavow these usurpations, which, would inevitably interrupt our connections and correspondence. They too have been deaf to the voice of justice and of consanguinity. We must, therefore, acquiesce in the necessity, which denounces our Separation, and hold them, as we hold the rest of mankind, Enemies in War, in Peace Friends.

This principle and the discipline to apply it exhibit strongly the Reformed Christian heritage—so much of which the early Puritans brought with them to this land. John Calvin himself had urged the use of war only as a last resort:

> [If Kings] must arm themselves against the enemy, that is, the armed robber, let them not lightly seek occasion

to do so; indeed, let them not accept the occasion when offered, unless they are driven to it by extreme necessity. For . . . surely everything else ought to be tried before recourse is had to arms.[24]

Calvin's colleague Pierre Viret was even more tenacious on the subject. He called war a "sickness" and said "there is nothing which Christians should be more wary to employ nor which is less suited to their profession."[25] Distinguished Professor Robert D. Linder notes how Viret "denounced those who made their living manufacturing military equipment and munitions," for it was pursued in view of profit via the shedding of blood.[26] The resulting military-industrial complex, he argued in so many words, then had an interest in creating and sustaining more and more wars: it magnified the differences between peoples so that "hateful, ambitious, greedy people who hoped to profit from the war" increased their chances of starting one. Viret considered the wars of religion as largely products of such avaricious greed.[27] While he believed in a doctrine of just war, he also thought it should be used only as an absolute last resort, for even just wars have unwelcome consequences.

These beliefs are, of course, merely extensions of the previously quoted laws of kings and laws of warfare taken from Scripture. There were to be no standing armies and no large treasury from which the king could draw to fund a war. Every measure was to be taken to avoid war when necessary.

These theological principles held by the early American colonies helped them retain much of this spirit of peace and reasonableness. While the colonies certainly did not develop a fully biblical view of the military and war, they were far closer to one than America is today. But those principles were com-

---

[24] Calvin, *Institutes of the Christian Religion*, 4.20.12 (Battles' translation).

[25] Quoted in Robert D. Linder, "Pierre Viret: A Christian View of War," *Faith for All of Life*, March/April 2011: 9–10.

[26] Ibid., 10.

[27] Ibid.

promised as early as the Constitution, making even some of the grievances of the Declaration—just eleven years prior—appear hypocritical to many of our ancestors. In the years that followed—the Civil War, and the subsequent Progressive Era of empire for starters—those early principles were more and more abused. In the next section, we will more closely examine how these ideals of freedom were further compromised and eventually lost.

How Freedom Was Lost

The destruction of the early Puritan-American views of the military, and of biblical, voluntary militias, etc., began in this country with the first skirmish of the first world war—not World War I, mind you, but what was perhaps the first truly world war. Here's the story:

The Real First World War

In the 1750s, the French began to solidify and fortify their claims along the rivers of what is today western Pennsylvania. The Ohio Company of Virginia, a massive land speculation group subsidized by government land grants in the area, viewd the French as competition and pressured the acting governor of Virginia, Robert Dinwiddie (conveniently a shareholder in the Company), to confront the French *encroachments*. Dinwiddie could not fund a large enough force to be a real threat, so he bought time with an emissary to advise the French to "desist."[28]

The emissary he chose was a lanky, 21-year-old army officer, early heir of a decent estate, connected to the Ohio Company, who out of a lust for military fame (just as we saw earlier with Hamilton and others) jumped at the chance to go. With the sea-

---

[28] Fred Anderson, *Crucible of War: The Seven Years' War and the Fate of Empire in British North America, 1754–1766* (New York: Vintage Books, 2000), 41.

soned Iroquois leader Tanaghrisson as a tracker and guide, the young man led a tiny troop westward into the woods. Unskilled in French or diplomacy, and untested in battle, he was unaware of what he would soon set in motion.

The British ventured too close to a French encampment of scouts. Upon being discovered, the British officer commanded his company to fire on the French. The French scouts, out-numbered, asked for quarter; their wounded leader, Joseph de Jumonville, presented his diplomatic letter; the British officer accepted, walked a few paces, and began reading. Then to every-one's shock, Tanaghrisson approached the wounded Jumon-ville and said, "You are not yet dead, my father"; he hacked the Frenchman's skull several times with his hatchet, and liter-ally washed his hands in the brain matter.[29] It was an Iroquois blood-atonement ceremony. Tanaghrisson had been holding a personal vendetta against the French, and he used Dinwiddie's troop to put him in position to make the sacrifice.

The kill would have far-reaching consequences. Upon hearing of their defeat, the French prepared a larger detach-ment headed by Jumonville's half-brother who was eager for revenge. A month later, they cornered the British troops in a makeshift fort at Great Meadow. Everything went wrong for the British, and they were soon forced to surrender.

At eight-o-clock that night, a call rang out for the nego-tiation that no one knew would change the course of history. The French offered generous terms if the British would aban-don Ohio territory for the space of a year. The British emis-sary's friend and translator returned that night with a copy of the terms, and the two struggled to read the rain-soaked document, written in French, by candlelight. For some reason, apparently, they did not realize that the document described the death of Jumonville a month earlier as not merely a kill, but an "assassination." By signing that document, as he did

[29] Ibid., 52–59.

a few minutes before midnight on July 3, 1754, that 21-year-old *George Washington* officially declared the British crown responsible for an act of war against France. The next morning—a not-so-happy Fourth of July—the beaten British began their journey back to Virginia with the news.

It was the beginning of the Seven Years' War—the "French and Indian War"—which would spread throughout the world, sucking in Prussia, Austria, parts of the left-over Holy Roman Empire, Sweden, Russia, the Netherlands, Spain, India, the Caribbean, the Philippines, and more. It was truly the first *world war*, and it was truly sparked by Washington's ambling into the frontier seeking glory as a military agent for the British public-private partnership, the Ohio Company. That war would lead to the compilation of such massive debt on the part of the British that the crown began looking throughout its Empire for new sources of revenue. When it was realized in the 1760s that the American colonies were the least taxed by far, a wave of tariffs and other measures were instituted. These led to revolts like the Boston Tea Party, and eventually the Declaration of Independence, the American Revolution, and thus, of course, America's own war debts, and then the problems with Hamilton and the central banks, etc. In short: no Jumonville, no War, no debt, no centralized government in America.

Now that may sound like a stretch to many readers. And indeed, we must not be so reductionistic as to cite Jumonville's death as *the* cause of the American Revolution, and certainly not all of our tyrannical woes today; but were it not for the lust for war-fame—a kid itching for a fight in order to make a name for himself—things would have been much different, and very likely much more peaceful. Even the definitive historian on the subject thinks so: "Without the Seven Years' War, American independence would surely have been long delayed, and achieved (if at all) *without a war* of national liberation."[30] Indeed, it was not only America:

---

[30] Anderson, *Crucible of War*, xviii.

It would be difficult to imagine the French Revolution occurring as it did, when it did—or, for that matter, the Wars of Napoléon, Latin America's first independence movements, the transcontinental juggernaut that Americans call "westward expansion," and the hegemony of English-derived institutions and the English language north of the Rio Grande.[31]

All of this can be laid, at least in part, on the use of military force to gain advantage in speculative markets—to enrich a big corporation and its interested shareholders in high government positions. And young Washington strode right into the midst of this practice, with his brothers Lawrence and Augustine on the corporate side, and he on the military.

Carryover to the Constitution

It was this same Washington who would later team with Hamilton in the call for a strong national military-industrial complex, as we have seen, built on the back of brand-new Constitutional powers for a *standing army*. But there was still a significant faction, a majority in fact, that expected traditional freedoms. As we have seen, the battle over the Constitution produced numerous responses on this issue. The epitome of that opposition was inscribed by Benjamin Workman, a math professor in Philadelphia, writing under the name "Philadelphiensis":

> My fellow citizens, the present time will probably form a new epoch in the annals of America: . . . We are now publicly summoned to determine whether we and our children are to be *freemen* or *slaves;* whether liberty, which we have so recently purchased with the blood of thousands of our fellow countrymen, is to terminate in blessing or curse.
> In regard to religious liberty, the cruelty of the new government will probably be felt sooner in Pennsylva-

---

[31] Ibid.

nia than in any other state in the union. The number of religious denominations in this state, who are principled against *fighting* or *bearing arms*, will be greatly distressed indeed. In the new constitution there is no declaration in their favor; but on the contrary, the Congress and President are to have an absolute power over the *standing army, navy,* and *militia;* and the President, or rather *Emperor*, is to be the commander in chief. Now, I think, that it will appear plain that no exemption whatever from militia duty shall be allowed to any set of men, however conscientiously scrupulous they may be against *bearing arms*. Indeed from the nature of the qualifications of the president, we may justly infer, that such an idea is altogether preposterous: He is by profession a *military man*, and possibly an old soldier: Now such a man, from his natural temper, necessarily despises those who have a conscientious aversion to a military profession, which is probably the very thing in which he principally piques himself.[32]

So many state delegates so greatly feared the military powers surrendered in the Constitution that the appeasement measures for the Anti-Federalists—the Bill of Rights!—specifically addressed the issue. Not many people realize that the Second Amendment—so revered by conservatives—had roots in the repeated warnings against the dangers of a standing army. The Congressional discussions of this amendment reveal that the original intent of the right to bear arms was as a potential defense against our own Federal government. It was meant specifically to alleviate the historical threat which the Constitution had just enshrined as a Federal power.

While the final form of that Amendment may not be explicit enough for us to see it, the Congressional debate makes it clear. Elbridge Gerry of Massachusetts introduced it:

---

[32] In Storing, *Complete Anti-Federalist*, 3:107.

This declaration of rights, I take it, is intended to secure the people against the mal-administration of the
Government; if we could suppose that, in all cases, the
rights of the people would be attended to, the occasion
for guards of this kind would be removed. . . .

What, sir, is the use of a militia? It is to prevent the
establishment of a standing army, the bane of liberty.
. . . Whenever Governments mean to invade the rights
of people, they always attempt to destroy the militia, in
order to raise an army on their ruins. This was actually done by Great Britain at the commencement of the
late revolution. They used every means in their power
to prevent the establishment of an effective militia to
the eastward.[33]

Later in the discussion, Mr. Gerry moved to change the
language so that a standing army could not even be considered as "a secondary" security to the militias. Aedanus Burke
of South Carolina preferred to be more explicit. He proposed
an Amendment which added,

A standing army of regular troops in time of peace
is dangerous to public liberty, and such shall not be
raised or kept up in time of peace but from necessity,
and for the security of the people, nor then without
the consent of two-thirds of the members present of
both Houses; and in all cases the military shall be sub-
ordinate to civil authority.[34]

Thus it is clear that the Second Amendment was intimately
related to the standing army powers delegated to the central
government by the Constitution itself.

This view was maintained for several years afterward. St.
George Tucker, a prominent professor of law at the College

---

[33] *Annals of Congress*, 1:749–50; quoted in Philip B. Kurland and Ralph Lerner,
eds., *The Founders' Constitution*, 5 vols. (Chicago and London: University of Chicago Press, 1987), 5:210.

[34] Quoted in Ibid., 5:211.

of William and Mary, and later a Federal District Court Judge, assumed the same connection between the individual's right to bear arms and the threat of a standing army. In his 1803 edition of *Blackstone's Commentaries*, he called our Second Amendment the "true palladium of liberty," for,

> Wherever standing armies are kept up, and the right of people to keep and bear arms is, under any colour or pretext whatsoever, prohibited, liberty, if not already annihilated, is on the brink of destruction.[35]

A Tale of Two Rebellions

In regard to original intent, a mere Amendment would not be enough to withstand the military powers its larger brother, the Constitution itself, gave to the new central government. This problem is best illustrated with a tale of two rebellions—one taking place prior to, and the other after, the Constitutional settlement. In the first, the lack of central military powers ultimately left the decision to form a militia up to the people of the state. In the second, the national government used its coercive power to raise an army of 13,000 to squash a revolt.

The first is the oft-maligned Shays' rebellion. Granted, there were revolutionary undertones within parts of the Shays' movement, and likely more than undertones among a few of the rebels; but the rebellion has largely been understood only according to the propaganda of its enemies. That is, until fairly recently: Leonard Richards' work *Shays's Rebellion: The American Revolution's Final Battle.*[36]

The story commonly runs that western Massachusetts farmers were heavily indebted to eastern banks. When time came to collect those debts and the farmers could not pay, they revolted in a quasi-class-war against private property. George

---

[35] St. George Tucker commenting on *Blackstone's Commentaries*, quoted in Kurland and Lerner, eds., *The Founders' Constitution*, 5:212.

[36] Op. cit., (Philadelphia: University of Pennsylvania Press, 2002).

Washington's friend, former general Henry Knox, warned him at the time of a proto-communistic uprising:

> They feel at once their own property compared with the opulent, and their own force, and they are determined to make use of the latter in order to remedy the former. Their creed is that the property of the United States has been protected from the confiscations of Britain by the joint exertions of all, and therefore ought to be the common property of all. . . .[37]

This is how the story was told to George Washington, and how it has been told pretty much ever since. But Knox was primarily motivated by a desire for a stronger union, and he knew he had to get Washington on board for any such venture. Thus, he stretched as far as he could, and what he didn't say is as important as what he did. Here's the rest of the story (in a nutshell):

Like other states, Massachusetts had helped fund the American Revolution with that wretched excuse for money, colonial scrip. It was so overinflated after the war that it was sold on the speculators' market for fractions of a penny on the dollar. This money virtually died—but it was only mostly dead. Many of those western farmers, and especially former soldiers who were paid almost exclusively with the paper, suffered through the inflation and couldn't get rid of the worthless money fast enough. But a cabal of Boston speculators and other investors sat holding the paper just hoping it would recover—in the case of the speculators, for a handsome profit, and in the case of the more conservative establishment bankers, to save themselves from massive losses.

The cabal then made its move. No doubt better connected in the State Assembly than the frontier farmers, the investors

---

[37] Henry Knox to George Washington, October 23, 1786, Gilder Lehrman Collection Documents, http://www.pbs.org/georgewashington/collection/pre-pres_1786oct23.html, (accessed Dec. 9, 2011); quoted in Gary North, "John Hancock's Big Toe and the Constitution," http://www.lewrockwell.com/north/north247.html (accessed Dec. 9, 2011).

got a *law* passed that the worthless scrip would be redeemable at *face value* and worse yet, all interest retroactively paid in silver. It was a rigged market if ever one was. But it didn't stop there. To pay off these now massively, artificially, over-valued investments, the Assembly raised taxes, the vast majority of which would fall on the common people including the western farmers. It was nothing short of a bailout for the failed Boston investors; worse yet, it double-punished the farmers who first were forced to use the money in its devalued state, and now forced to pay it off at face value to the very people who forced them to suffer through its demise.

It was even worse yet. The taxes got passed only because the Senate rammed in a self-interested governor. The former governor John Hancock sympathized with the soldiers especially and had refused to enforce collection of taxes for some time. He was very popular. But an illness forced him from running again in 1785. The new governor—himself a holder of over £3,000 in the debased notes, ready to make a killing on the enforcement of the new taxes—immediately began enforcement not only of the taxes, but of all past taxes as well. This was more than many of the country people were able to pay or willing to tolerate. It is understandable, therefore, why a revolt broke out: a *tax revolt*, not a proto-communist movement.

But more to the point is the reaction to the organized revolts led by former Revolutionary War captain Daniel Shays, after whom the "rebellion" was named. When the governor tried to raise a militia from the state's ranks, it failed miserably. The state petitioned Congress; it's sympathizers in Congress even lied saying they needed help with an Indian war. Congress pledged 1,320 troops, but Massachusetts had to raise half. Congress could convince only one hundred of its soldiers to go. Back in Boston there was decent response, but the western counties largely ignored the governor. Out of over six hundred war veterans, only twenty-three showed up. Gary North relates,

Baron von Steuben, who had served under Washington, identified the problem in an article signed "Belisarius." Massachusetts had 92,000 militiamen on its rolls. Why did the state need military support from Congress? He provided the correct answer: the government was not representative of the opinions of the people.[38]

A group of Boston merchants then paid former Generals Benjamin Lincoln and William Shepherd to get involved and they were able eventually to raise a combined 4,000 men, mainly from the cities Boston and Springfield. Shepherd beat Shays to the Springfield armory and illegally—that is, against orders and without the required Congressional approval—raided the armory and awaited the approaching Shays' forces. When they approached, Shepherd fired "warning shots" that killed four men and wounded twenty. This began the decline of the resistance which was over within a month.

Whatever may be said of either side in these skirmishes, the central fact to take away is how difficult it was to raise an army for a corrupt cause prior to the Constitution. Granted, the corrupt forces still eventually won out, but even this was a function of powerful centralized controls: first the imposition of colonial fiat paper, then the bailout laws for the banks and speculators, and the centralizing of the whole state's legal system largely under the power of the Bostonians. Even here, out of 92,000 enrolled militiamen, only a tiny fraction was willing to support the cause.

And the corruption did not stop with the Bostonian bailout and its mercenary militia, it continued in Knox's leveraging of the crisis to convince Washington into the Constitutional Convention. Knox wrote,

> What is to give us security against the violence of lawless men? Our government must be braced, changed, or altered to secure our lives and property. . . .

---

[38] North, "John Hancock's Big Toe."

The men of property and the men of station and
principle there are determined to endeavor to establish
and protect them in their lawful pursuits; and, what
will be efficient in all cases of internal commotions or
foreign invasions, they mean that liberty shall form the
basis,—liberty resulting from an equal and firm administration of law.

They wish for a *general government of unity*, as they
see that the *local legislatures must naturally and necessarily tend to the general government.*[39]

Urged on by others as well—not to mention by his own
predilections for stronger central government—Washington
bit. You know the rest of the story: we got that "government of
general unity," along with its new military powers, including a
standing army and central control over state militias.

In light of this new government, we now move to the second rebellion in this tale of two: the Whiskey Rebellion of 1792.
The situation was very much similar to Shays': the government
(national now as opposed to state) had now centralized all the
war debts from the Revolution, and Hamilton was seeking new
sources of revenue to pay them off. He studied how he could best
raise taxes while angering the fewest people. His answer was
what we today would call a "sin tax"—a tax on all distilled spirits. Madison agreed surprisingly quickly, and the two rammed
the bill through Congress. But not everyone accepted it as wise.
Senator William McClay of Pennsylvania, (not to be confused
with the later Congressman of the same name from the same
state) wrote a startlingly accurate prophecy in his journal: "War
and bloodshed are the most likely consequence of this."[40]

Within a few months of the bill taking effect, reports of widespread revolt were reaching Washington. Instead of rescinding

---

[39] Henry Knox to George Washington, October 23, 1786, Gilder Lehrman
Collection Documents. Quoted in North, "Hancock's Big Toe."

[40] Quoted in Ron Chernow, *Alexander Hamilton* (New York: Penguin Books,
2004), 343.

or even reconsidering the tyrannical tax, the administration planned stiff coercion. Hamilton—eager as always to impose his will by force—immediately called for a swift and harsh military solution. Washington welcomed whatever was necessary to suppress the revolts, as long, he said, as the solution was Constitutional. Before all-out military suppression could take place, however, the administration needed at least two things: it needed to appear to the public as having attempted a peaceful solution, and it needed to expand its militia-raising powers so that it could *draft* soldiers by compulsion.

The draft powers came with the two Militia Acts of 1792. Whereas the Constitution had already centralized military powers, it generally left the power to *call up* the militia within the powers of Congress, and then it was only a call, not compulsion. The first Militia Act of 1792 remedied the first problem, delegating power to the President to call up the militia to repel invasions, etc. This was ostensibly in response to Indian Wars in the Northwest Territory, but the statute included language directly applicable to the tax revolts of late: the President could call up the militia "whenever the laws of the United States shall be opposed or the execution thereof obstructed, in any state, by combinations too powerful to be suppressed by the ordinary course of judicial proceedings." The second Militia Act ensured that such a call would be answered; by decree, it conscripted every able-bodied male between 18 and 45 years of age (Congressmen and Senators, however, were conveniently excepted) into their respective state militias, ready to be called up, and provided some unifying structure throughout. (And with great irony, this conscription—which as we have seen before is a form of slavery—applied to "each and every *free* able-bodied white male citizen.")

Within months, Hamilton began drafting a proclamation condemning the revolts in western Pennsylvania which Washington eventually delivered on September 15, 1792. Ignoring the obvious imposition of the tax itself, the letter praised "the moderation which has been heretofore shewn on the part of the government," and promised every "necessary step" would be taken and "all lawful ways and means will be strictly put in execution" to enforce collection of the taxes. Hamilton was already ready for the military option, but the time was not quite ripe for it.

Hamilton eventually ramped up a campaign of propaganda and outright deception to move the nation toward his goal. During this window, from 1792 to 1794, Hamilton engaged in a general attack on his political opposition by claiming they were agents of the French Revolution, atheism, and anarchy—all of which accusations were false. With the multiple efforts at secession and refusal to pay the tax, and now the Militia Acts in place, Hamilton sensed a perfect "opportunity for successful assertion of federal dominance."[41] His campaign deceptively portrayed the rebellion as uniquely located in a few western Pennsylvania counties—though he knew otherwise that opposition was widespread. He pulled out the conspiracy theory card, claiming these revolts were the work of a few local elites and "malcontent persons" aiming "to confirm, inflame, and systematize the spirit of opposition."[42]

Washington concurred with Hamilton's sentiments. He feared the rebellion was fomented by French revolutionary-style activism in political clubs that arose in the wake of a visit to the U.S. by French Ambassador Charles Genêt. The conspiratorial paranoia is evident in Washington's letters: the clubs were designed "primarily to sow the seeds of jealousy and distrust among the people of the government" and spread "nefarious doctrines with a view to poison and discontent the minds of the people."[43]

---

[41] Thomas P. Slaughter, *The Whiskey Rebellion: Frontier Epilogue to the American Revolution* (New York: Oxford University Press, 1986), 192.

[42] Quoted in Ibid., 193.

[43] Quoted in Ibid., 194.

Both pretended that the whole political fabric of America hung on suppressing this allegedly small, local rebellion. Washington feared "anarchy and confusion." Hamilton went over the top, writing, "It appears to me that the very existence of government demands this course."[44] In this same letter to Washington, on August 2, 1794, Hamilton provided a very specific plan of action for raising the militia of several states: that is, the raising of at least 12,000 troops to shock and awe the rebels. Newspapers picked up the French conspiracy motif and the exaggeration, decrying "total subversion of government" due to "sans culottes of Pittsburgh."[45] And yet despite the alleged threat to the whole foundation and existence of government itself, Hamilton revealed the real issue at the root of the administration's firmness: "The immediate question is whether the government of the United States shall ever raise revenue by any internal tax." Determined to solidify and uphold this central power, Hamilton was willing to exercise another—the military—and shed American blood.

But the military means to the end couldn't be on the surface of the program lest the administration risk alienating the public. This is not to say they respected the will of the people, for Hamilton would write Washington later saying he had "long since learned to hold popular opinion of no value" while pursuing his own unpopular agendas.[46] Instead, they saw public opinion as an obstacle to be maneuvered around and manipulated. Thus, they began preparing for war as much as possible, and yet going through the motions required for a peaceful solution with the mind that these motions would fail. Hamilton went so far as purposefully to

---

[44] For Washington see Slaughter, 193; for Hamilton see "Hamilton to Washington," August 2, 1794, in *The Works of Alexander Hamilton*, 12 vols., ed. Henry Cabot Lodge (New York and London: G. P. Putnam's Sons and The Knickerbocker Press, 1904), 6:356.

[45] Slaughter, *Whiskey Rebellion*, 194–195.

[46] Quoted in Ibid., 123.

undermine peace negotiations with a series of letters under the pseudonym "Tully"—again propagandizing the public with the conspiracy plot.[47] Around the same time, he was having General Henry Lee begin the draft and prepare the troops with the command to keep it secret and to postdate all written orders to September 1, to make it look as if the administration had not been planning attack all along. The whole effort was a public façade:

> For "particular reasons" of a political nature, no one was to know that the decision to raise an army had been made before August 25. The peace negotiations were a sham, but a necessary political maneuver to forestall criticism of the administration's policy. It must *appear* that the President had made every effort to settle the dispute without resort to arms, even though he privately longed to teach the western Pennsylvanians a stern lesson.[48]

That lesson would come upon these western Pennsylvanians, but whereas Hamilton had earlier pretended the revolt was localized there, he now prepared a show of force calculated to include opposition joined by several other surrounding states and counties. From this he concluded the need for at least 12,000 soldiers. And he was out for more than the suppression of the rebellion. He wanted to make public examples of some of the rebels, as he would later write to Washington, November 11, 1794: "Tomorrow the measures for apprehending persons and seizing stills will be carried into effect. I hope there will be found characters fit for examples, and who can be made so."[49] With the power of the Militia Acts behind them, an inter-state militia of 13,000 was raised, and personally led by Washington and Hamilton on horseback to quash the "rebellion."

---

[47] Ibid., 198.

[48] Slaughter, *Whiskey Rebellion*, 198–199.

[49] Lodge, *Works of Alexander Hamilton*, 6:457.

These two rebellions, however, illustrate the power of the centralized militia and thus the ability for the central government to impose its will on its subjects. Before the Constitution, the people of Massachusetts could choose whether or not to support the Governor's call to raise a militia, and most did not. People were left free to decide if the cause were just—a much more biblical design. All of this changed with the advent of the Constitution. Now, the standing army power was enshrined and the Hamiltonian machine was dedicated to making it even more powerful. And every "free" able-bodied man was forced into the slavery of conscription—whether they agreed with the justness of the cause or not. And many people did disagree, and Washington knew it: he was fearful that even the Militia Acts would not be powerful enough to force the raising of the militia.[50] These fears were, of course, allayed, and thankfully, there was very little bloodshed as the overwhelming forces melted any organized opposition. But this was never the point: the point was to have the military power to enforce the will of the central government despite the possible unpopularity of its decrees—*the very thing the prescient Anti-Federalists had warned against.*

Thus, while some twenty men were arrested in the raid, and several indicted in Philadelphia, only two were ever convicted in court, and George Washington eventually pardoned them. After all that public façade and exercise of overwhelming force, why finally pardon the only convicts out of a movement which he and Hamilton both had described publicly, repeatedly, as "treason"?[51] Because the point was never really to uphold justice: it was rather to impose the will of the central government. It was to crush all possibility of political control beyond the taxing and

---

[50] Slaughter, *Whiskey Rebellion*, 196.

[51] See Washington's "Proclamation," August 7, 1794, in *The Works of Alexander Hamilton*, 6:391, 393; and "Proclamation" September 25, 1794, *Works*, 6:443; cf. Hamilton to Washington, August 2, 1794, *Works*, 6:355; Hamilton's "Tully III," August 28, 1794, *Works*, 6:420; "Tully IV," Sept. 2, 1794, *Works*, 6:425.

warring dictates of Washington, D.C. In this, the response to the Whiskey Rebellion was successful, and it was built on the back of the Constitution. In these regards, the United States departed further from the biblical standard of a free society—specifically in the creation, expansion, and use of its military power.

This change was a small but effective beginning. It was also a precedent for much more to come. Yes, the Constitution created this power, and it was used overwhelmingly to crush political dissent to Hamilton's tax scheme. But at least the national forces remained somewhat small. Prior to the Civil War, the entire active peacetime militias stood at a total of only 16,000 troops. And at least during this time, those forces were not used *beyond* Constitutionally-achieved powers. But the next step in the growing loss of freedom in this area would do just that.

Lessons of These First Conflicts and Beyond

Just stop momentarily and consider what freedom had been destroyed militarily just to this point. We have not even included the Civil War. Beginning with Washington's appearance on the scene of American history, we have seen virtually every one of the biblical principles of war completely trampled. We have seen 1) wars started unnecessarily for corporate influence and profit, 2) wars waged by governments on their own people in order to impose taxes and prevent secession, 3) taxes imposed by military force in order to pay off previous war debts held by central banks, 4) the creation of a standing army, 5) military conscription of every able-bodied male, 6) the suspension of trial by jury, 7) the unconstitutional opposition of a Supreme Court order by the President backed by his standing army. At this point, it is helpful to recall the words of the political advocate of peace, James Burgh, whom we quoted earlier:

> There is no end to observations on the difference between the measures likely to be pursued by a minister backed by a standing *army*, and those of a court awed

by the fear of an *armed people*. . . . No kingdom can be secured otherwise than by arming the people.

Indeed, there is no end to the differences. In fact, there *has been* no end to the differences, as America continued down the path of more greatly centralizing its armed forces. Without getting fully into the Civil War, its very early days saw Lincoln oppose a Supreme Court order by using the military to withstand a U.S. Marshal from serving a writ of habeas corpus. Thus we could add to the list above 6) the suspension of trial by jury, 7) the unconstitutional opposition of a Supreme Court order by the President backed by his standing army. But this was just the beginning.

Freedom was lost when the war hawks—led by General Sherman—applied their "scorched earth" policy throughout the South: burned crops, destroyed livestock, destroyed property of all sorts, including innocent businesses, towns, churches, and infrastructure.

Freedom was lost as Sherman fought to maintain a standing army after the war and applied his total war policy to Indian "pacification." That campaign ended after many trails of tears and most Native Americans were herded onto reservations out west. Sherman also advocated using the standing army to suppress labor revolts, and promoted a campaign designed to consolidate the state militias eventually into a single national system ruled by a military bureaucracy.

Freedom was lost when a coup led by private American corporatists in Hawaii was being suppressed by natives, and the well-connected conspirators summoned a group of Marines to squash the counterrevolution. Cleveland opposed the actions, but McKinley ascended to the presidency and annexed Hawaii, thereby eliminating the tariffs for his cronies.

Freedom was lost under the McKinley & Co. administration as we were led unnecessarily into the Spanish-American War. The result was full-blown empire as the treaty with Spain gave us the Philippines and the government embraced those islands with a fresh war. The U.S. wiped out entire villages, erected concentration camps, and shot detainees found outside after an early curfew. The U.S. had condemned these same policies, using them as a pretext for war with Spain in Cuba. But in the Philippines the, U.S. had systematized this brutality and turned it into a sport. In all, between 200,000 and a million Filipinos were killed.

Freedom was lost as the militia consolidation effort advanced slowly but surely, and was gained under the pressure of Secretary of State Elihu Root and the Dick Act of 1903, revised and strengthened in 1908 and again in 1916. This was the final metamorphosis of the American military into a full standing army almost completely at the behest of an imperialistic Federal government. The act was a drastic move away from biblical freedom and toward the humanistic Warfare-Welfare State.

The military's own historical account laments the fact that prior to the Act, local militias were simply too voluntary: a compulsory standing army was needed. State guardsmen "were under no legal obligation to volunteer, and a significant number refused either because of fears over how their unit would be treated by the Regular Army or from concern over hardships that volunteering would impose on their families."[52] In other words, before the Dick Act—as it was called after the Congressman—the state militias were closer to a biblical model. Moving away from this empire-hindering system was, in the words of one military historian, "the most important national legislation in militia history."[53]

Freedom was lost further under the Wilson War State during World War I, through the whole period leading up to FDR's New Deal and on into World War II. This period shows the final merger of the Warfare and Welfare States in all their

---

[52] William M. Donnelly, "The Root Reforms and the National Guard," http://www.history.army.mil/documents/1901/Root-NG.htm (accessed Dec. 21, 2011).

[53] Ibid.

glory, and the powers ceded to government during the time have not only been retained, they have been increased and compounded. We will consider the transformation of the Executive power via the use of emergency powers in the next chapter. For now, we must note the evil twins:

The Warfare-Welfare State

Perennially, war has been the greatest centralizing mechanism to achieve the Total State. This was noted in recent times by the famed military historian, Martin van Creveld:

> Had it not been for the need to wage war, then almost certainly the centralization of power in the hands of the great monarchs would have been much harder to bring about. Had it not been for the need to wage war, then the development of bureaucracy, taxation, even welfare services such as education, health, etc. would probably have been much slower. As the record shows, in one way or another all of them were bound up with the desire to make people more willing to fight on behalf of their respective states.
>
> To focus on the field of economics alone, the Bank of England as the first institution of its kind originated in the wars which Britain fought against Louis XIV. Early in the nineteenth century the first modern income taxes were likewise the product of war, as were both legal tender and its most important specimen, the greenback. Later, to cite but three examples, neither some of the early attempts to provide social security, nor the abandonment of the gold standard in 1914, nor the Bolshevik Revolution (representing the attempt to institute total state control over an economy) would have come about in the form they did, had it not been for the need of the state to mobilize its resources and wage war against its neighbors.[54]

---

[54] Martin van Creveld, *The Rise and Decline of the State* (Cambridge, UK: Cambridge University Press, 1999), 336.

These are bold assertions, but the facts bear them out. Van Creveld's last few examples refer to the early Twentieth Century, the era leading up to World War I. Consider the changes in America under Woodrow Wilson during this war.

The Overman Act of 1918 gave President Wilson expansive powers over every aspect of American life during the war. His centralizing efforts decked the government with countless new bureaus: the War Labor Policies Board, Shipping, Food Administration, the War Industries Board (WIB), and many more, all with absolute power over their sphere.

The WIB was one of the most egregious as it established a genuine military-industrial complex that would disband, in name at least, only after the War. It created national moral hazard that led to the nationalization of unions, mines, railroads, and other industries.[55] This created a monopolistic system that many businesses and groups did not want to give up once the war was over. They began to use their influence to pass new laws to restore their positions. As a result, despite the fact that Wilson disbanded the WIB immediately after the War, there was "no returning to prewar conditions."[56] Wilson's move was merely a political shift for the complex which resulted in Congress being in charge instead of the Executive. This meant that now, all the special interests of Congress were involved in trying to control and get a share of the military-industrial booty. The structure created by the emergency control was still in place, it just had new masters.

If national moral hazard were not enough, the Wilson War State also created it internationally. America became the conscious model for Germany itself (which copied Wilson in a final attempt to reorganize and win the war), Lenin's "War Communism," and Mussolini's early version of Fascism. All were modeled on Wilson's accomplishment, and all have

---

[55] *Moral hazard* is a tendency to continue risky behaviors based on the artificial absence of punitive consequences.

[56] Skowronek, *Building a New American State*, 242.

had devastating effects for decades thereafter and helped bring about World War II.

The effect of the combined Welfare and Warfare State—the Total State—is effectively to replace freedom with central planning across the board. After WWI in the U.S., there was a steady effort on the part of leftists and social Darwinists of all stripes to leverage the lingering centralized structures of the War State. The War had created a ripe opportunity for more elitist control. A slogan which first appeared in the 1920s was popularized by George Soule, then editor of *New Republic* magazine, in his 1932 book, *The Planned Society*: "We planned in war, why not in peace?" It was cry for central planning at the national level, and the outright replacement of local community and local sovereignty with national community.

To do this requires the government to replace local community—genuine community—with the appearance of a "community" at the national level. FDR did this explicitly in his first inaugural address, March 4, 1933, in which he mixes the language of a military mission with that of a national community:

> If I read the temper of our people correctly, we now realize as we have never realized before our interdependence on each other; that we can not merely take but we must give as well; that if we are to go forward, we must move as a trained and loyal army willing to sacrifice for the good of a common discipline, because without such discipline no progress is made, no leadership becomes effective. We are, I know, ready and willing to submit our lives and property to such discipline, because it makes possible a leadership which aims at a larger good. This I propose to offer, pledging that the larger purposes will bind upon us all as a sacred obligation with a unity of duty hitherto evoked only in time of armed strife.

This replaces local community with national community, personal morals with national ethics, religious language with political coercion, peacetime with wartime. But it was right about one thing: it would "bind upon us all" an obligation to the State previously experienced only under the threat and stress of war. Not only was the old freedom gone, but even what relaxation occurred in the War State after the War was now reestablished and extended. Wilson's temporary War State became FDR's Welfare State, and every expansion of it since. Every political battle fought since has been fought in light of that new reality, and only in terms of the Welfare State. Since the New Deal era, the question is never Welfare State or no Welfare State, but what kind of a Welfare State and how big?

For all of his talk of willingness and sacrifice among the people, FDR couldn't have cared less about their willingness. He planned to solve the nation's problems through central planning and sheer control if he believed it necessary:

> I shall ask the Congress for the one remaining instrument to meet the crisis—broad Executive power to wage a war against the emergency, as great as the power that would be given to me if we were in fact invaded by a foreign foe. For the trust reposed in me I will return the courage and the devotion that befit the time. I can do no less.
>
> We face the arduous days that lie before us in the warm courage of the national unity; with the clear consciousness of seeking old and precious moral values; with the clean satisfaction that comes from the stern performance of duty by old and young alike. We aim at the assurance of a rounded and permanent national life.

From day one, the Warfare and Welfare States have been evil twins, constantly feeding and empowering the other; and war itself is the vampire which sucks the free blood out of their prey. War is waste, war is plunder, war is loot, war is destruction of wealth, morals, fidelity, and social bonds. Government-run welfare is all of those things, too. The two things are one and the same, fueled by the same lusts, toward the same ends, by the same spirit.

War is Hell

After his Indian-slaughtering days were all but over, General Sherman spent his final military days touring and lecturing students. During one speech, he gave the line that has since been paraphrased as, "War is hell." There is little indication at all that Sherman was a religious man, and in fact he seems to have been critical of religion for most of his life. The "war is hell" sentiment for Sherman was more about scorched earth strategy than religious teaching. But he had no idea how religious it indeed was.

God's covenantal promises to His people concluded with a list of blessings that would come upon them if they obeyed, but also a list of curses they would suffer for rebelling against Him. The curses for national disobedience are found in Deuteronomy 28:15 and following. Verses 15–19 and 25–33 are particularly relevant:

> But if you will not obey the voice of the Lord your God or be careful to do all his commandments and his statutes that I command you today, then all these curses shall come upon you and overtake you. Cursed shall you be in the city, and cursed shall you be in the field. Cursed shall be your basket and your kneading bowl. Cursed shall be the fruit of your womb and the fruit of your ground, the increase of your herds and the young of your flock. Cursed shall you be when you come in, and cursed shall you be when you go out. . . .
>
> The Lord will cause you to be defeated before your enemies. You shall go out one way against them and flee seven ways before them. And you shall be a horror to all the kingdoms of the earth. And your dead body shall be food for all birds of the air and for the beasts of the earth, and there shall be no one to frighten them away. The Lord will strike you with the boils of Egypt, and with tumors and scabs and itch, of which you cannot be healed. The Lord will strike you with madness and blindness and

confusion of mind, and you shall grope at noonday, as the blind grope in darkness, and you shall not prosper in your ways. And you shall be only oppressed and robbed continually, and there shall be no one to help you. You shall betroth a wife, but another man shall ravish her. You shall build a house, but you shall not dwell in it. You shall plant a vineyard, but you shall not enjoy its fruit. Your ox shall be slaughtered before your eyes, but you shall not eat any of it. Your donkey shall be seized before your face, but shall not be restored to you. Your sheep shall be given to your enemies, but there shall be no one to help you. Your sons and your daughters shall be given to another people, while your eyes look on and fail with longing for them all day long, but you shall be helpless. A nation that you have not known shall eat up the fruit of your ground and of all your labors, and you shall be only oppressed and crushed continually.

While there is obviously not a one-to-one correlation in every respect—mainly due to the fact that we don't live in walled cities or have siege warfare situations—the main aspects of this judgment in history are the same. They are the destructive effects of war:

- Destruction of life
- Destruction of property
- Spread of disease
- Destruction of the family
- Economic hardship, scarcity
- Political tyranny and oppression
- Triumph of rabid selfishness
- Low birth rates
- Enormous debt that remains for generations
- No reprieve from heaven (ratchet effect)

There is another saying among military men, again a paraphrase: "The army is not an insurance company. The purpose of the army is to kill people and blow up stuff."

The pagan ruler Sun Tzu, author of the classic *The Art of War*, wrote the famous dictum, "All warfare is based on deception." Governments, you see, must continually lie to prosecute war: deceive the enemy for advantage, yes; but also lie to its own people about the need for war in the first place. They will lie about the cost of the war, the bloodiness of the war, the long-term plans for war, and the extent of war, and then they will add the promise, "Things will return to normal once the war's over." It's all, or nearly all, a continuous lie covering the face of the earth.

Sun Tzu continued on about the economic effects of war: "Where the army is, prices are high; when prices rise the wealth of the people is exhausted. When wealth is exhausted the peasantry will be afflicted with urgent exactions [taxes, provisions for the army]." The State must continue its wars, no matter the cost, the debt, the burden—and it will be a burden.

There you have it in a nutshell, from the most famous theoreticians of war in history, as well as biblical law: war is destruction, death, lies, and theft. There's a convenient summary of all this in Scripture: "The thief comes only to steal and kill and destroy" (John 10:10).

If you don't believe war is hell, then you don't understand the Bible... or war. If you still want American imperialism and its wars after this, then you must think hell is the cure for the world's problems. You must think America is hell, and hell is salvation.

But Jesus finished that verse by saying this: "I came that they may have life and have it abundantly."

How to Get Freedom Back

How can we restore the freedoms we once had, long ago, in the areas of war and the military? It starts with changing our personal views from the celebration of aggression, destruction, death, and *hell*, to the celebration of freedom and life—and not just life, but as Jesus put it, life "abundantly." It proceeds to personal commitments, actions, spreading the word, and then a larger agenda. Let's discuss these steps.

First, we need a radical change of mind. I hope the foregoing lessons on the biblical principles and the innumerable infractions of them in American history will help begin that change. It will be quite easy for some: the Bible says it; that settles it. Many such people may have never even read the relevant passages or considered their modern applications, but immediately upon understanding them, faithful Christians will simply embrace Scriptural truth. For others, however, different types of impediments will hinder this mental and spiritual process. For some, loyalty to a particular imperial political tradition—whether "strong Hamiltonian Federalism," or Unionism, or Republican Progressivism, Expansionism, or Wilsonian, Leftist Progressivism—will create a barrier to embracing freedom in the military. People accustomed to spreading their values by the use of force, theft, destruction, and murder will find it difficult to adjust to a peaceful mission.

Christian Missions Secularized

The concept of *missions* is a real spiritual issue at the heart of the modern war problem: what form shall missions take? *All* of the coercive measures mentioned above are simply secularized versions of the Christian great commission. Whether under the guise of spreading civilization, education, protecting citizens from themselves, serving the expansion of transportation and commerce, purging the land of dangerous savages, saving the Union, modernizing the world, making the world safe for democracy, or fighting "treachery" or "terror"—in all cases, the use of government force to spread peace is a false version of the Christian mission. And in many cases, these "solutions" were devised by people operating explicitly out of traditions that had secularized the Christian message—Unitarians, humanists, social Darwinists, etc.

The classic expression of such secularization was the American abolitionist and terrorist John Brown, who put into action the belief of some Unitarian activists that it is acceptable to employ violence to bring about social change. Sure enough, Brown's intellectual and financial backing came from a group of six Unitarian clergymen called the "Secret Six."[57] But this was only one radical expression. The principle of threatening or forcing people into righteous behavior is the same whether it's John Brown murdering political rivals, Woodrow Wilson waging a war to make the world safe for democracy and to institute a League of Nations, or Horace Mann prescribing a compulsory State education mandate upon threat of fines or kidnapping. Each constitutes a mission to improve society, but each case replaces the Spirit-persuasion of the Gospel mission and the protections of liberty found in God's law with the "persuasion" of intimidation and physical coercion. The basis of the Great Commission—the influence of the Gospel, the move of the Spirit, the change of hearts, and discipleship—is completely blown out of the picture and replaced by the barrel of a gun.

This, of course, is the mode of secularistic and atheistic regimes historically. Most people have heard Mao Zedong's famous saying, "Political power grows out of the barrel of a gun." Most have not heard the thoughts which followed:

> Having guns, we can control Party organizations. . . . We can also create cadres, create schools, create culture, create mass movements. . . . All things grow out of the barrel of a gun. . . . Whoever wants to seize and retain state power must have a strong army. Some people ridicule us as advocates of the "omnipotence of war." Yes, we are advocates of the omnipotence of revolutionary war; that is good, not bad, it is Marxist. . . . Only with guns can the whole world be transformed.[58]

---

[57] See Otto Scott, *The Secret Six: John Brown and the Abolitionist Movement* (New York: New York Times Books, 1979).

[58] "Problems of War and Strategy," *Selected Works of Mao Tse-Tung* [Zedong],

Just as Wilson and his contemporaries, like H. G. Wells, believed they were fighting the "war to end all wars," Mao concluded, "We are advocates of the abolition of war, we do not want war; but war can only be abolished through war, and in order to get rid of the gun it is necessary to take up the gun."

Likewise, Friedrich Engels was quite blunt in his essay "On Authority":

> A revolution is certainly the most authoritarian thing there is; it is the act whereby one part of the population imposes its will upon the other part by means of rifles, bayonets and cannon—authoritarian means, if such there be at all; and if the victorious party does not want to have fought in vain, it must maintain this rule by means of the terror which its arms inspire.[59]

But we must not make the mistake of thinking this principle applies to only radical leftists, revolutionaries, and communists; again, these are merely the *explicit* and *extreme* expressions of the principle of social change by violence—the logical conclusion of it, if you will. But the exact same principle underlies every attempt by man to transform man and society—even to advance the "common good"—through *coercive* means: compulsory state schooling, "sin" taxes, welfare schemes, drug wars, substance control laws, wealth redistribution, corporate welfare, public-private partnerships, government contracts, and thousands more. It's the same principle applied in many ways, and it has been applied in these ways from very early on in our history.

If American Christians, especially fundamentalists and evangelicals, are serious about the Bible and biblical freedom, they have got to end their love affair with America's standing

---

Volume II (Peking [Beijing]: Foreign Language Press, 1967), 224–225.

[59] Friedrich Engels, "On Authority," *Basic Writings on Politics and Philosophy: Karl Marx and Friedrich Engels*, ed. by Lewis S. Feuer (Garden City, NY: Anchor Books, 1959), 485.

army. It is unbiblical; it is outrageously, unbiblically expensive; and it is invasive, destructive, and deadly, most often not in pure defense. We have to stop the mentality that pronounces—as a popular country singer put it—"we'll put a boot in your ***, it's the American way." We have to stop applauding everything the military does as if it were automatically the gleam of national greatness, quit praising all soldiers all the time as sacrosanct individuals, and quit forbidding any criticism of the military as if it were the holy of holies. It is simple: for many people, the use of force—deadly force—and the military that embodies that power are idols. And like David taking a census of the people for battle against God's will, we too often trust more in our nation's military capacities than in God. This has got to end if we are ever to see freedom in our country once again.

Bible Prophecy

While for some the mental hurdle will be political loyalties, others cling to military might because of their view of Israel and the end times. I am not going to go into a full discussion of eschatology and foreign policy here except to say that this view is false. It takes a very special, recent, and convoluted view of Bible prophecy to derive the position that Christians today should specially favor the modern nation called "Israel" with foreign aid and military support, and help her against her Islamic neighbors. This view is most often supported by referring to the promise to Abraham, "I will bless those who bless you, and him who dishonors you I will curse" (Gen. 12:3). The most definitive work expressing this view is also the clearest: "Politically speaking, this statement is God's foreign policy to the Gentiles in their relationship with the Jewish people."[60]

This view is easily debunked (though not thoroughly debunked, which would take too much space here) by sim-

---

[60] Arnold G. Fruchtenbaum, *Israelology: The Missing Link in Systematic Theology* (Tustin, CA: Ariel Ministries, 1994), 838.

ply considering the biblical context: this promise was given to Abraham *before* he had *any* children. If we are to take just this verse at this point in Scripture—as so often is done—as the basis of blessing nations in relation to "Abraham," then we must apply it equally to *all* of Abraham's children. This includes Ishmael, the father of the Arab nations. This would mean of course that we should give just as much foreign and military aid to all of modern Israel's Arab neighbors! But this is absurd from a biblical viewpoint, as the definitive author above would agree. On what basis is it absurd? It is so because *later Scripture qualifies and narrows the definition of Abraham's seed.* Agreed.

But herein lies the rub: the means of qualifying who actually inherits the promise becomes the very means of *dis*qualifying modern-day Israel as well. The argument is that later Scripture qualifies the promise as not to Ishmael, but to Isaac, and then not to Esau, but to Jacob, who is later renamed "Israel." True enough. But this sets a precedent of narrowing that does not—as the proponents of this view would like you to believe—*stop* with Jacob. Paul himself uses this very method of argument in Romans 9 to prove that *Israel* also shall be redefined in light of Christ, "For not all who are descended from Israel belong to Israel" (9:6). He concludes,

> What shall we say, then? That Gentiles who did not pursue righteousness have attained it, that is, a righteousness that is by faith; but that Israel who pursued a law that would lead to righteousness did not succeed in reaching that law. Why? Because they did not pursue it by faith, but as if it were based on works. They have stumbled over the stumbling stone, as it is written, "Behold, I am laying in Zion a stone of stumbling, and a rock of offense; and whoever believes in him will not be put to shame." (Rom. 9:30–33)

In other words, the kingdom of God, the kingdom of the seed of Abraham, is made up of the faithful, not the physical Jews per se. It is based on faith and not on bloodlines. Indeed, in the apostolic era, *most* Jews did not make it into the kingdom, and yet the resulting entity would still be called "Israel"— that is, the *new* Israel, the Church. Now it is clear why Jesus could tell the Jewish leadership of the day that they were not the seed of Abraham nor even children of God, but "You are of your father the devil" (John 8:44). For this very reason, He would put them on the cursed end of "God's foreign policy." Quoting the same prophecy of the stumbling stone as Paul did (Rom. 9:32–33; cf. Isa. 8:14–15; 1 Pet. 2:8), Jesus said to the Jews of His day,

> Therefore I tell you, the kingdom of God will be taken away from you and given to a people producing its fruits. And the one who falls on this stone will be broken to pieces; and when it falls on anyone, it will crush him. (Matt. 21:43–44)

American Christians have simply got to get past the view that there is something special about the ethno-political entity established in the land of Israel in 1948. This is a huge mental hurdle for many Christians, but it is also an enormous theological delusion that leads so many to continue promoting an unbiblical view of war and the military, especially in regard to having a strong threatening presence in the Middle East.

A Pro-Life Issue

Christians must also realize that the biblical perspective on the military and war correlates to pro-life issues. It doesn't make much sense to cry out against abortion while at the same time demanding our sons and daughters—and other people's children—be sent into unnecessary wars at the risk of their lives. This does not discount fighting in just wars when necessary, for these are wars to protect life against aggression. But the war-missions mentality is almost always contrary to this principle. The sad fact is, too many Christians who decry the government-protected slaughter of children in the womb are way too tolerant of government-mandated slaughter of kids at nineteen or twenty, not to mention the slaughter of thousands of civilian bystanders. A consistent pro-life view will avoid this terrible oversight.

Unnecessary war, along with abortion, is a modern form of human sacrifice, akin to the *Moloch* worship forbidden in Scripture.[61] As I write in *God versus Socialism*,

> it should be obvious that if any war is waged unjustly, and troops are killed in that battle for an ungodly cause, then the *perpetrators of that war have offered human blood as an agent of social change*, rather than relying on godly principles. This is human sacrifice pure and simple. Christians should not be afraid to oppose war, to oppose it vigorously, and to oppose hasty wars especially.[62]

In fact, Christians ought to be leading the opposition to such wars by overwhelming numbers and with deafening cries.

Practical Steps

What practical steps can individuals take toward the goal? Simple. *Don't join the current standing armed forces.* Don't join unless there is an invasion of our land or a biblical defensive cause which you deem worthy of fighting for. Thankfully, the one redeeming quality of our massive standing army is that enlistment is currently voluntary, at least at the point of joining. Once you join, of course, it becomes a binding contract, and that is important to remember. Once you report to basic training for the first time, you are obligated to be enlisted for

---

[61] (See Lev. 18:21; 20:1–5; Deut. 12:29–32; 18:9–10; 2 Kings 16:3; 21:6; 17:17; Jer. 7:31–32).

[62] Joel McDurmon, *God versus Socialism: A Biblical Critique of the New Social Gospel* (Powder Springs, GA: American Vision Press, 2009), 24.

eight years, probably half of which will be active duty, and it is difficult to get out.

While there is no current obligation to join, the vestiges of the old draft system remain in place just in case. Every male 18 to 25 years old must register with the "Selective Service System" so that the government has him on a list in case it needs to reinstate the draft. In its own words, the SSS exists to "provide our Nation with . . . the most prompt, efficient, and equitable draft possible, if the country should need it."[63] Failure to register (your duty by law) remains punishable as a felony including up to five years in prison and up to a quarter-million dollar fine.[64] In short, you cannot legally avoid military conscription in this country if the government demands that you fight, and in the meantime, the government continues like David to number its people for war. But at least for now, actual enlistment is voluntary. (And by the way, recruiters have been known to lie about benefits and much else to get young men to enlist.)

If you do decide to join a military force in the event of a just cause, you should consider your local state guards first, rather than immediately joining the National army. State defense forces are separate from the National Guard units that often bear the names of their states—these latter were completely nationalized in 2007 so that Governors no longer have any control over them. Nevertheless, many states have their own defense forces which serve various purposes. Extreme caution is needed here, however. Only some of these forces are armed; *some even go so far as to prohibit carrying weapons while in uniform!* This ironic twist on a "defense force" should ward off anyone who thinks, according to the Second Amendment, that the right to bear arms shall not be infringed. The regulations and goals differ from state to state, so research your own state and make informed decisions.

---

[63] www.sss.gov/what.htm (accessed January 3, 2012).

[64] www.sss.gov/FSinternet.htm (accessed January 3, 2012).

Further, don't support political candidates who have militaristic or imperial agendas. Don't support those who provoke unnecessary wars, call for huge defense spending, and military interventionism. This greatly narrows the field of viable candidates today, but it is the necessary view if biblical freedom is ever to prevail in this land again. Political choices arise to meet overwhelming demand. If we don't change our demands along with our attitudes, our political choices won't change; and if our political choices don't change, the tyranny will continue.

The first chief justice of the Supreme Court, John Jay, is often quoted by Christians in regard to the U.S. being a Christian nation and the need for statesmen to be Christians. He is famously cited: "It is the duty as well as the privilege and interest of our Christian nation to select and prefer Christians for their rulers." This is all good and true, but rarely is this quotation given in its context. Jay was not speaking merely in general, but in the particular context of foreign policy, peace, and *war*. Here's the context of his letter:

> It appears to me that the gospel not only recognizes the whole moral law, and extends and perfects our knowledge of it, but also enjoins on all mankind the observance of it. . . .
>
> It certainly is very desirable that a pacific disposition should prevail among all nations. The most effectual way of producing it is by extending the prevalence and influence of the gospel. *Real* Christians will abstain from violating the rights of others, and therefore will not provoke war.
>
> Almost all nations have peace or war at the will and pleasure of rulers whom they do not elect, and who are not always wise or virtuous. Providence has given to our people the choice of their rulers, and it is the duty as well as the privilege and interest of our Christian nation to select and prefer Christians for their rulers.[65]

---

[65] John Jay to John Murray, October 12, 1816, *The Correspondence and Public*

We cannot, of course, fully endorse Jay's politics, for he was squarely on the side of the Nationalists and the Constitution which got us into this military mess; but at least at this one point he had the doctrine correct. And ironically for its "pacific" tone, the letter was a reply to the issue of *pacifism*, which Jay adequately rebutted. In other words, even while promoting a doctrine of justifiable war, Jay nevertheless upholds the principles of individual rights, international peace, non-aggression, that missions should be based on the spread of the gospel, and that Christians should choose candidates who do not desire to provoke further wars. Christians should commit to these aspects of political theory.

This commitment must extend beyond our view of government: it should also apply to the entire military-industrial complex to a large degree. If you own a business, don't contract with the military unless you are absolutely sure the military is not using the technology, products, or services you provide for the purposes of unjust wars. Perhaps there is room here in some instances for pleas of ignorance, but certainly if you know for a fact that you are supplying unnecessary aggression, then there is moral culpability for the bloodshed and destruction on your part. It's a difficult decision, of course, when livelihood and lifestyles are at stake, but you at least have to ask the question of yourself. You should be more than willing to do so if you're a Christian. For consumers, try as much as possible to avoid patronizing companies that contribute to such wars.

Consider just for a moment the vast industry that has grown up around military aggression. If a company exists which manufactures, for example, guided missiles, that company makes profits only when it contracts with the government to sell those missiles. But what happens if the military stockpile reaches its capacity of missiles? No more orders come in. The company has no income, no future. Several people—maybe hundreds or thousands—who work for that company will face job loss and hardship. These are people with families, children in school, mortgages, and bills. Unless that company gets more orders for its bombs, it does not move forward and these people stand to lose everything. But unless the military actually *uses* its missiles, it does not need to order any new ones. Thus the company has a vital—perhaps desperate—economic incentive for the military to indeed fire missiles, and fire them continually, in order to maintain cash flow and the employment and lifestyles of its employees. This can mean only one thing: there are many economic incentives and motives driving America to go to war. And those profiting from the military-industrial complex are a significant example.

Now, consider that there are literally hundreds of such companies across this country. The Department of Defense writes new contracts daily, publishing only those larger than five million dollars. In 2010 alone, the Department contracted out over 300 billion dollars worth of contracts to private businesses. This means literally thousands—perhaps hundreds of thousands—of people are dependent upon revenue from the military.

The same moral culpability argument applies equally to those massive construction firms that share in rebuilding contracts after war has wreaked its havoc and a new city and State must be built from the rubble. If the war was unjust to begin with, being paid by the perpetrator to clean it up—while slightly more redeeming than aiding the destruction itself—is still wrong.

No doubt, it's important to have a strong defense system in place, but this can be accomplished effectively through biblical means without resorting to a standing army, drafts, or wars of aggression. If this were not the case, God would not have written His law the way He did. Our challenge today is 1) to look beyond the massively powerful army with which we are enamored and see it for the unbiblical system that it is, 2) have the conviction and courage to call it unbiblical even while it's unpopular to do so, 3) begin to make personal commitments that align with biblical values, and 4) begin to call and work for greater political change. With this, we must simultaneously develop a decentralized system for recruiting and training voluntary, biblical militias for genuine defense. We should do so beginning at the local level.

Churches could greatly strengthen both the convictions and efforts of individuals in this regard by simply teaching and preaching on the relevant passages and their implications as discussed in the first part of this chapter. Then, they should lead their people vehemently in prayer against all our enemies, including the ones in our own nation who would involve us in unnecessary wars. "Pray for peace." While to some it may sound like lame advice taken from the old hippie Jesus movement, it is actually a necessary and effective part of the advance of God's kingdom and the protection of freedom in the military. I recommend the following prayers, adapted from the *Book of Common Prayer* of the Reformed Episcopal Church:

For Our Country

Almighty God, Who has given us this good land for our heritage, let us always be mindful of Your favor. Bless us with industry, prosperity, learning, and purity of life. Save us from discord and violence, and from pride and arrogance. Preserve us from public calamities, pestilence, and famine; from war, conspiracy, and rebellion; and especially from national sins and corruption. Defend our liberties, and give wisdom to those in authority so justice and peace may prevail. Make us strong and great in the fear of God, and in the love of righteousness, so that with Your blessing we may be a blessing to all people. In prosperity fill our hearts with thankfulness, and in trouble do not let our trust in You fail. We ask all of this in the name of Jesus Christ our Lord.

For the Armed Forces of Our Country

Almighty God, the refuge and fortress of Your people, we ask that You bless and protect all those who serve in the defense of our country, upon land, and on the water, and in the air. Ever spare them from being ordered into a war of aggression or oppression. Use them, if need be, as Your instruments, in the defense of our life and liberty. But restrain the greed and wrath of man that wars may cease in all the earth. Deepen in the hearts of our defenders the spirit of peace; and, for His sake, may they ever love and serve the Prince of Peace, our Lord and Savior Jesus Christ. Amen.

For the Coming of Christ's Kingdom and Universal Peace

Almighty Father, we pray that You would hasten the coming upon earth of the kingdom of Your Son, our Lord and Savior Jesus Christ, and draw the whole world of mankind into willing obedience to His blessed reign. Overcome all His enemies, and bring low every power that is exalted against Him. Cast out all the evil things which cause wars and strife among us, and let Your Spirit rule the hearts of men in righteousness and love. Repair the desolations of former days; rejoice the wilderness with beauty; and make glad the city with Your law. Establish every work that is founded on truth and equity, and fulfill all the good hopes and desires of Your people. Manifest Your will in the brotherhood of man, and bring in universal peace; through the victory of Your Son, Jesus Christ our Lord. Amen.

10. Executive

At the Federal level, the functions of the executive branch pertain to both domestic and foreign policy. I have already explained how I think government in general should be greatly decentralized stateside with a focus on county rights first, then states' rights, then a very limited federal instrument—in other words, true federalism. For this reason, we need not really discuss how we were once free in these regards, for we have already largely described it in so many ways. We have also already covered most of the fall into tyranny in this regard—particularly with welfare, taxation, and the military—so we will reserve comments in this regard to the two most dangerous stateside issues: the abuses of executive orders and administrative law.

Domestic and foreign policy are separate areas, but hardly have separable consequences. In this regard, we will discuss the loss of freedom in regard to the President's enumerated power to sign treaties—a power which is checked only partially by the legislative branch. Because of this power, Americans have always have been, and remain, vulnerable to tyranny by foreign entanglements.

Lord Acton is credited with the famous saying, "Power corrupts, and absolute power corrupts absolutely." A corollary to this is to say the closer you get to absolute power, the more potential there is for you to be tempted with corruption. Solutions to the various problems of society appear more within reach when viewed through the scope of a comprehensively armed and funded coercive apparatus. Thus, the larger and more centralized the Executive institution becomes, the more tempting it becomes to bypass clumsy Congress and a lumbering Judiciary and instead administer as extensively as possible via Executive decree alone. And as soon as the Executive tastes the efficiency of government by decree, like sharks with blood, it goes crazy for more.

Freedom and the Executive Branch

For these reasons, along with their colonial experiences of abuse, Americans were especially wary of a strong executive power too much like a monarch. In fact, among those many grievances we have highlighted in the Declaration of Independence, all are charges against King George III—the Executive—who had trampled the colonies' rights in all other areas of legislation and courts. He had abused his executive power with the colonies and was denying the rights of representation and due process promised them as citizens under English common law. The precursor to the Declaration of Independence, the Declaration of Rights of 1774, complained of being governed by "unconstitutional powers." This in particular was in reference to Parliament, but the point was that Britain and her colonies were supposed to be governed by *laws*. And the laws should apply equally to the rulers as to the people. Laws stand over the government, not the government over laws. It is this principle which is thrust aside the moment the Executive power is defined too broadly or given too much power.

Such a powerful central Executive was one of the many points of controversy during the Constitutional debates. Opponents feared the president would be no different, essentially, than the monarch from whose tyranny they had just fought to free themselves. America already had some history of dealing with corrupt and autocratic state governors—like Dinwiddie in Virginia—and these were often bad enough. Now, the Constitution threatened to create just such an office at the national level.

At the Constitutional Convention in Philadelphia, Edmund Randolph (Governor of Virginia and later Secretary of State for a year and a half under Washington) argued that executive power should not be vested in one man but rather at least three. He—along with many others—criticized a unity in the executive as too close to a monarchy. Responding to those whom he thought desired to mimic the British government, he called the presidency "the foetus of monarchy."[1]

This was a major theme throughout the Anti-Federalist writings during the ratification era. "An Old Whig" expressed the feelings of those who feared the great centralization of power to be vested in a single Executive agent:

> In the first place the office of President of the United States appears to me to be clothed with such powers as are dangerous. To be the fountain of all honors in the United States, commander in chief of the army, navy and militia, with the power of making treaties and of granting pardons, and to be vested with an authority to put a negative upon all laws, unless two thirds of both houses shall persist in enacting it, and put their names down upon calling the yeas and nays for that purpose, is in reality to be a KING as much *a King as the King of Great Britain.*

Such power, Old Whig continued, would be a great temptation to corruption—even to the point of seizing indefinite power and refusing to relinquish it. All that would stand in the way of such corruption is the want of unprecedented character:

> It will cost a man many struggles to resign such eminent powers, and ere long, we shall find, some one who will be very unwilling to part with them. . . . So far is it from its being improbable that the man who shall hereafter be in a situation to make the attempt to perpetu-

---

[1] Quoted in *The Founders' Constitution*, ed. by Philip B. Kurland and Ralph Lerner, 5 vols. (Chicago and London: The University of Chicago Press, 1987), 3:491.

ate his own power, should want the virtues of General Washington; that it is perhaps a chance of one hundred millions to one that the next age will not furnish an example of so disinterested a use of great power.[2]

As we have seen, not even Washington was so "disinterested" as the Old Whig here assumes. And while no such refusal to leave the office has yet occurred, it is safe to say that the abuse of the great power for self-interest and party-interest is abundantly enough documented as to make the Old Whig's prediction too accurate.

One of the chief proponents of the one-man Executive view was James Wilson of Pennsylvania, a prominent and influential lawyer who later served as one of the original Supreme Court Justices. His arguments hold some merit as far as they would have been applicable; he thought a single-person Executive would force transparency and accountability:

> The executive power is better to be trusted when it has no screen. Sir, we have a responsibility in the person of our President; he cannot act improperly, and hide either his negligence or inattention; he cannot roll upon any other person the weight of his criminality; no appointment can take place without his nomination; and he is responsible for every nomination he makes.[3]

This might have been great had the Executive ever truly been designed and run with literally only one person. But some of Washington's earliest presidential deeds were to create cabinet positions with delegated responsibility. These provided the very "screens" of which Wilson warned (yet Wilson, a strong nationalist, never decried them after the fact). Hamilton was a notable screen for whose agenda, as we have seen, Washington was often largely a front. And this was within one year of Wilson's persuasions. Today, the Executive branch has

---

[2] Storing, *Complete Anti-Federalist*, 3:37–38.

[3] Quoted in Kurland and Lerner, *Founders' Constitution*, 3:501.

dozens of levels of bureaucracy, cabinet positions, etc., and literally millions of employees—all of whom can and do provide screens for irresponsibility, corruption, waste, etc., throughout their many different levels.

Executive "Care"

Another Anti-Federalist warned about what has turned out to be a real danger of the president: his actual job description for executing the law. This appears in Article 2, Section 3 of the Constitution and is left extremely broad (not an uncommon feature in our Constitution): "He shall stake Care that the Laws be faithfully executed." In a letter to Captain Peter Osgood of Massachusetts, William Symmes described the problem:

> Can we exactly say how far a faithful execution of the laws may extend? or what may be called or comprehended in a faithful execution? If the President be guilty of a misdemeanor, will he not take care to have this excuse? And should it turn against him, may he not plead a mistake! or is he bound to understand the laws, or their operation? Should a Federal law happen to be as generally expressed as the President's authority; must he not interpret the Act! For in many cases he must execute the laws independent of any judicial decision. And should the legislature direct the mode of executing the laws, or any particular law, is he obliged to comply, if he does not think it will amount to a faithful execution?[4]

In other words, the Constitution defines the President's power so broadly that he can essentially create new laws by interpreting undefined areas of existing law according to his own agenda, interpreting how to implement existing laws, or he can perhaps even ignore specific laws of Congress if he thinks they infringe upon the broad interpretations he comes up with. In this way, the President has great latitude under the guise of his "care" to faithfully execute the laws.

---

[4] Quoted in Ibid., 4:126; cf. Storing, *Complete Anti-Federalist*, 4:60.

Compare this recipe for confusion and tyranny with the biblical function of the executive power. Here the famous Romans 13 passage is very helpful in its simplicity. Concerning the magistrate:

> He is God's servant for your good. But if you do wrong, be afraid, for he does not bear the sword in vain. For he is the servant of God, an avenger who carries out God's wrath on the wrongdoer (Rom. 13:4).

The executive power's function is simply to punish those who disobey the law. His job is not to make the laws, nor to interpret the laws, nor to judge cases at law, but rather to apply punishments and enforce the laws. And note two things: first, the making of laws must be already established before enforcement can be executed legitimately. There must never be a time in which the Executive feels free to create laws for itself and then enforce those laws; if such a new law needs to be created, it must go through the legislative process. In the meantime, the sword must not be used to enforce such a dubious law. Second, in a society governed by laws, the punishments themselves must be prescribed by law. The use of the "sword" itself must be predictable. Only that which the Bible says is punishable should be punished, and that which is punished should be punished only according to the principles laid down in Scripture.

Both of these reasons taken together derive from the principle that the executive power is itself subject to the law—both in *what* it enforces and in *how* it enforces it. The executive at every level of government is "a man under authority," and must be made to behave accordingly. This is why the laws for kings which we reviewed earlier (Deut. 17) state that the King must make himself a copy of the Law and read in it daily. He must know exactly what he is empowered to do, what he is not empowered to do, and what he is explicitly forbidden to do. The law itself, in other words, should restrict the Executive's "care that the laws be faithfully executed."

In the biblical system, the supreme Executive is obvious: He is God. The "powers that be" in whatever executive systems we enlist on earth must all rule in God's service, according to God's laws, according to God's facts, and must punish only according to God's revealed standards of punishment and restitution. In fact, God must be the head of all our branches of government, "For the Lord is our judge; the Lord is our lawgiver; the Lord is our king; he will save us" (Isa. 33:22). The biblical Executive is a ministry accountable to God, not a demigod which has the people accountable to it.

As we shall see, today's Executive of the United States is a long way from this simple biblical model.

How Freedom was Lost

American freedom was lost *in* and *through* the Executive branch under three main headings: 1) treaty powers, 2) the abuse of executive orders, and 3) government by national emergency. The first two of these have been greatly leveraged by the abuse of the third, as we shall see.

Tyranny by Treaty

A Constitutionally valid, signed international treaty can have the same force domestically as the U.S. Constitution or statute law. This issue, however, has not been settled legally and if a controversial enough treaty were passed it would undoubtedly create a Constitutional crisis. Meanwhile, the ease of passing a treaty is efficient for government's sake, but leaves the liberty of the people vulnerable. Article 2, Section 2 of the Constitution gives the President "Power, by and with the Advice and Consent of the Senate, to make Treaties, provided two thirds of the Senators present concur."

The President has a full monopoly on the actual negotiation of treaty details. According to Supreme Court Justice

Sutherland in *United States v. Curtiss-Wright Export Corp.*
(1936), "He alone negotiates. Into the field of negotiation,
the Senate cannot intrude; and Congress itself is powerless
to invade it."[5]

The requirement of a two-thirds vote of the Senators present refers only to a *quorum* of the Senate, as per Supreme
Court decision. A quorum requires only 51 Senators officially,
but the Senate's own website indicates that an even smaller
number could constitute a quorum if only a voice vote is
taken: "the Senate presumes that a quorum is present unless
the contrary is shown" by a roll call vote or quorum call."[6] This
means that a treaty can become the law of the land with as few
as 34 Senators voting in agreement.

Taken together, these legal requirements indicate that an
activist President could sign a radical treaty and have it pass
the Senate quickly if the conditions were right. He would need
the support of only a loyal minority dedicated to the agenda.

This potential Executive abuse was debated very little during the Convention. When it *was* debated, the main tension
arose over the need for "secrecy" in treaty-making versus the
need to reserve legislating power to the Congress only. James
Wilson suggested that since treaties will operate like laws,
"they ought to have the sanction of laws also."[7] Roger Sherman
questioned "whether the power could be safely trusted to the
Senate," which at the time was designed to be a voice of states'
power only, not the people at large.

Opposition did arise. Delegate George Mason, expressed
himself in some personal notes to his draft copy of the Constitution; these later became a pamphlet circulated during the

[5] Quoted in the Congressional Research Service's *Annotated Constitution,*
http://www.law.cornell.edu/anncon/html/art2frag14_user.html#art2_hd65 (accessed January 11, 2012).

[6] http://www.senate.gov/reference/glossary_term/quorum.htm (accessed January 11, 2012.

[7] Kurland and Lerner, *Founders' Constitution,* 4:36.

ratification period. He bemoaned the exclusion of the people and Congress from the treaty-making power, and he stressed the need for "distinctions" in treaties:

> By declaring all treaties supreme laws of the land, the Executive and the Senate have, in many cases, an exclusive power of legislation; which might have been avoided by proper distinctions with respect to treaties, and requiring the assent of the House of Representatives, where it could be done with safety.[8]

James Iredell, a leading nationalist in North Carolina and later U.S. Supreme Court Justice, responded to Mason in print. His rebuttal emphasized the secrecy needed for treaties and questioned the safety of trusting Congress. The new system, he assured, would be better because it would have the additional check of "a President with high personal character."[9] In other words, "Just trust us, we're good people."

Mason's point of making distinctions in treaties was echoed by others. The Federal Farmer elucidated on the distinctions between treaties of alliance, peace, and commerce, the latter of which does not require secrecy like others. Such treaties of commerce "almost always involve in them legislative powers, interfere with the laws and internal police of the country, and operate immediately on persons and property."[10] Yet he thought that the Constitutional power of the legislature to regulate commerce with foreign nations was enough to give it "proper control over the president and senate in settling commercial treaties."[11]

An interesting exchange took place between James Madison and Patrick Henry during the ratification debates in Virginia. Henry decried the treaty powers as excessive and dangerous:

---

[8] Ibid., 4:38; See also Max Farrand, ed., *The Records of the Federal Convention of 1787*, 3 vol. (New Haven, CT: Yale University Press, 1911), 2:639.

[9] Quoted in Kurland and Lerner, *Founders' Constitution*, 4:41.

[10] Ibid., 4:41; cf. Storing, *Complete Anti-Federalist*, 2:293.

[11] Ibid.

[C]onsider the condition this country would be in if two thirds of a quorum should be empowered to make a treaty: they might relinquish and alienate territorial rights, and our most valuable commercial advantages. In short, if any thing should be left us, it would be because the President and senators were pleased to admit it. The power of making treaties, by this Constitution, ill-guarded as it is, extends farther than it has in any country in the world. Treaties are to have more force here than in any part of Christendom; for I defy any gentleman to show anything so extensive in any strong, energetic government in Europe. Treaties rest on the laws and usages of nations. To say that they are municipal is, to me, a doctrine totally novel. To make them paramount to the Constitution and laws of the states, is unprecedented.[12]

Madison countered by arguing that the proposed Constitution was not unprecedented among world powers in this regard, for the King of Britain himself had similar power. Henry rebutted that the English system was actually more limited than the proposed American Constitution in regard to treaties—we should be so lucky as only to have such a king. As it stood,

The constitutions of these states may be most flagrantly violated without remedy. . . . I say again that, if you consent to this power, you depend on the justice and equity of those in power. We may be told that we shall find ample refuge in the law of nations. When you yourselves have your necks so low that the President may dispose of your rights as he pleases, the law of nations cannot be applied to relieve you. Sure I am, if treaties are made infringing our liberties, it will be too late to say that our constitutional rights are violated. . . . A treaty may be

---

[12] Quoted in Kurland and Lerner, *Founders' Constitution*, 4:49;cf. Jonathan Elliot, ed., *The Debates in the Several State Conventions on the Adoption of the Federal Constitution*, 5 vol. (Philadelphia: J. B. Lippincott Company, 1907), 3:500.

made giving away your rights, and inflicting unusual punishments on its violators.[13]

The main federal salvo against such an abuse would be the hope that the Senate would not be able to ratify the treaty. Otherwise, the whole of Congress could later essentially repeal a treaty by passing new legislation to override the unwanted effects; but the Supreme Court has warned that this could constitute an infraction of international law and would thus be possible grounds for war:

> Its infraction becomes the subject of international negotiations and reclamations, so far as the injured party chooses to seek redress, which may in the end be enforced by actual war. It is obvious that with all this the judicial courts have nothing to do and can give no redress.[14]

The number of treaties to which Americans have been bound through this Executive power are legion. They are so many that no comprehensive publication of the texts of all current binding Treaties has ever been attempted. The State Department does publish a volume merely listing all the Treaties and international agreements in force as of 2011. Merely *listing* them all by name and date, organized by country, fills a volume of 484 pages.[15] Of course, not all of these are necessarily invasive, intrusive, or otherwise necessarily bad. But the sheer volume of binding agreements in which we have little if any voice should be alarming in itself. The sheer volume greatly increases the risk, if nothing else, that abuses and

---

[13] Quoted in Kurland and Lerner, *Founders' Constitution*, 4:50; cf. Jonathan Elliot, ed., *The Debates in the Several State Conventions on the Adoption of the Federal Constitution*, 3:503.

[14] Quoted in the Congressional Research Service's *Annotated Constitution*, http://www.law.cornell.edu/anncon/html/art2frag16_user.html#art2_hd71 (accessed January 11, 2012).

[15] *Treaties in Force: A List of Treaties and Other International Agreements of the United States in Force on January 1, 2011*, http://www.state.gov/s/l/treaty/tif/index.htm (accessed January 11, 2012).

intrusions *will* occur, and indeed they have been attempted. Here are a few recent examples:

Gun Control Laws

First, consider the United Nations plan of global disarmament— a goal which would impose strict gun-control measures upon its members, including the rightfully gun-loving U.S. There are at least two public efforts aimed at essentially circumventing the U.S. Second Amendment: a treaty to regulate small arms trade between nations, and the more comprehensive *International Small Arms Control Standards* (*ISACS*) project. The first seems more innocuous, though we are unsure what exactly it will contain. The UN assures us it is merely to help fight terrorism and suppress rogue states, but several conservative critics believe even that mild-sounding objective could have far-reaching implications for gun registration and licensing, even leading to outright international gun control laws.

But the UN seems focused mainly on the finalization of *ISACS*—a detailed outline for international small arms policy and implementation. *ISACS* is a product of the United Nations Coordinating Action on Small Arms (CASA). The latest draft of this document calls not only for regulation of international trade, but for "National controls over the access of civilians to small arms and light weapons," "National controls over the manufacture of" small arms and light weapons, and eventually "Collection, "Stockpile management," and "Destruction" of weapons and ammo.[16] It is clear that the agenda here aims far beyond restricting the availability of AK-47s to terrorists. Indeed, the "Programme of Action" on the UN's "Implementation Support System" website exhibits all of these goals in considerable detail and explicitly states that such new laws and regulations shall apply "within the State's jurisdiction."[17]

---

[16] "Project on International Small Arms Control Standards, Phase 2" May 4, 2010; http://www.un-casa-isacs.org/isacs/Documents_files/ISACS%20Phase%20 2%20Project.pdf (accessed January 12, 2012).

[17] "Programme of Action to Prevent, Combat and Eradicate the Illicit Trade in

The Obama administration, particularly Secretary of State Hillary Clinton, already signaled in 2009 that they were ready to begin negotiations with the UN on such a treaty.[18] If they succeed, they will have essentially accomplished what the Anti-Federalists and Patrick Henry warned of: the use of treaty powers to trash U.S. liberties. Indeed, this will have occurred in the worst form: the practical annulment of a clear Constitutional Amendment. This would certainly created a Constitutional crisis which the Supreme Court would likely—though not definitely—strike down. Fifty Senators have already signed a letter to Hillary Clinton saying they will not vote for any treaty which infringes on civilian arms; but remember, it takes only thirty-four if conditions are right. So those opposed must actively resist and stay vigilant lest we be taken unaware.

Global Governance in Your Town

The second example of the danger of treaty powers is the much more ambitious but ceaseless attempt for international governance. This appears in such forms as the UN's Convention on Biological Diversity and its sister development, Agenda 21, which could be imposed in the U.S. via a treaty. While you may not have heard of either of these specific United Nations programs, and probably have not heard of any *serious* attempts to impose international governance on the U.S. in general (at least not without talk of "tinfoil hats"), such attempts sadly have been very real. One would have succeeded were it not

---

Small Arms and Light Weapons in All Its Aspects," http://www.poa-iss.org/PoA/poahtml.aspx (accessed January 12, 2012).

[18] Colum Lynch, "US Puts Condition on Joining Talks on Conventional Arms Trade," *Washington Post*, Oct. 16, 2009; http://www.washingtonpost.com/wp-dyn/content/article/2009/10/15/AR2009101503659.html; also Maxim Lott, "Proposed U.N. Treaty to Regulate Global Firearms Trade Raising Concerns with U.S. Gun Makers," August 5, 2011; http://www.foxnews.com/world/2011/08/05/proposed-un-treaty-to-regulate-global-firearms-trade-raising-concerns-for-us/; and Larry Bell, "U.N. Agreement Should Have All Gun Owners Up In Arms," June 7, 2011; http://www.forbes.com/sites/larrybell/2011/06/07/u-n-agreement-should-have-all-gun-owners-up-in-arms/ (all accessed January 12, 2012).

for the last-minute efforts of four investigators who provided crucial, uncirculated information to a handful of Senators.

In 1992, a United Nations "Earth Summit" was held in Rio de Janeiro. Out of this conference came a book-length document titled *Agenda 21* popularizing the slogan "sustainable development." Basically, every time you hear the world "unsustainable" used in public it's a by-product of this agenda. According to the online version of the document, *Agenda 21* "is a *comprehensive plan of action to be taken globally, nationally and locally* by organizations of the United Nations System, Governments, and Major Groups in every area in which human impacts on the environment."[19] What follows is nearly 300 pages of two-column fine print providing guidelines for a global Treaty controlling every area of life—everything from all science, business, and industry down to the very air we breathe and water we drink—and calling for international revenue sources (taxes) and mechanisms to pay for it. The preliminary estimate was roughly $600 billion annually just in *developing* countries, which effectively means a transfer of that proportion of wealth from developed nations to third world partners.[20] It was all couched in terms of saving the environment, and thus providing laws to promote "sustainable" living.

The liberal establishment in the U.S. drooled over the plan. Only months after the Rio Summit, Bill Clinton was sworn into office. Democrats already controlled the Senate, but they still had to walk circumspectly to some degree. Clinton spent precious political capital early pushing a universal health-care plan (which would ultimately fail), NAFTA, and the Brady Bill, as well as weathering the Whitewater affair. Clinton signed the Biodiversity Treaty in June of 1993. Over the next few months, Al Gore and a coalition of environmental groups planned a strategy for ramming the Treaty through Congress. When it

---

[19] http://www.un.org/esa/dsd/agenda21/index.shtml (accessed January 11, 2012).

[20] *Agenda 21*, 251.

finally reached Congress in November, the State Department requested it be put on the "fast track." The Treaty was reviewed in the Senate Foreign Relations Committee until June of 1994 when the Committee approved it for vote. Grassroots efforts were then only beginning to mount opposition to the plan of which most Senators were largely oblivious. Quickly, Majority leader George Mitchell (D-ME) announced on August 3 that the Treaty vote was set for August 8. Grassroots went into overdrive leveraging a well-connected system of fax machines to get Senators' attention. The effort paid off, landing a letter from 35 Republicans on Mitchell's desk. He rescinded the hasty vote for the moment. This last-minute effort created room for more widespread awareness to solidify opposition as Congress recessed between August 26 and September 12.

On September 29, Mitchell announced the vote would be rescheduled for 4 p.m. the following day. Already alerted to the radical United Nations agenda behind the Treaty, opposing Senators showed up with large maps of land confiscations, property rights infringements, agricultural controls, and the overall radical environmental agenda displayed for all to see—details which were not supposed to be revealed until *after* the nations agreed to the treaty in general.[21] Senator Kay Bailey Hutchison (R-TX) led in condemning the foolishness of signing a treaty before its details were known in full. On the floor of the Senate she said,

> Under the treaty, a conference of parties will meet after the treaty is in force to negotiate the details of the treaty. We need to know how the Senate, in fulfilling its constitutional responsibilities to concur in treaties, can review the provisions of a treaty that will not be written until the meeting of the conference of parties.

---

[21] For the full narrative from which the above is taken, see "How the Convention on Biodiversity was Defeated," http://sovereignty.net/p/land/biotreatystop.htm (accessed January 11, 2012).

She revealed the plot:

> I am especially concerned about the effect of the treaty on
> private property rights in my State and throughout Amer-
> ica. Private property is constitutionally protected, yet one
> of the draft protocols to this treaty proposes "an increase
> in the area and connectivity of habitat." It envisions buffer
> zones and corridors connecting habitat areas where hu-
> man use will be severely limited. Are we going to agree to
> a treaty that will require the U.S. Government to condemn
> property for wildlife highways? Are we planning to pay for
> this property? One group, the Maine Conservation Rights
> Institute, has prepared maps of what this would mean. I
> do not know if they are accurate yet, but that is my point.
> Neither do the proponents of this treaty. . . .
>
> This bio-diversity treaty could preempt the deci-
> sions of local, State, and Federal lawmakers for use of
> our natural resources. The details that are left for ne-
> gotiation could subject every wetlands permit, building
> permit, waste disposal permit, and incidental taking
> permit to international review.
>
> We would be subjecting property owners to inter-
> national review, which would be yet another step in the
> already egregious bureaucratic processes, just to have
> the very basic permits necessary for the use of their
> own private property.[22]

Along with several others, Senator Wallop (R-WY) immediately agreed:

> I ask you, can the United States Senate, in good faith,
> give its consent to this treaty without having had an op-
> portunity to scrutinize the completed convention? The
> best advice we can give President Clinton right now is
> to wait until the Convention on Biological Diversity has
> been completed before asking for our consent.

---

[22] Congressional Record Volume 140, Number 140 (Friday, September 30, 1994), http://www.gpo.gov/fdsys/pkg/CREC-1994-09-30/html/CREC-1994-09-30-pt1-PgS22.htm (accessed January 11, 2012.)

The last-minute outcry from these Senators created enough awareness and opposition to table the consideration of the Treaty indefinitely. To this day it has never been voted on.

Now ask yourself what would have happened if this small group of concerned grassroots citizens had not sniffed out a genuine conspiracy, been able to alert their fax lists, and been able to convince a few key Senators of the facts. Consider, because of the nature of the Treaty powers of the President and limited Senate, how narrowly we avoided having an international socialist tyranny completely alter the landscape of America.

But the tabled status of the Treaty in the U.S. meant it was also not definitively squelched; it could be resurrected anytime. In fact, where the Convention on Biodiversity's own website lists the Parties to the Treaty (193 to date), the United States is still listed as a signatory waiting to ratify before becoming a full Party.[23] They're still waiting on us. They're patient. (The only others refusing assent are the Vatican and the tiny mountain enclave of Andorra.) In the meantime, the UN masquerades the plan under different names and renewed efforts. The Agenda 21 website confidently states,

> The full implementation of Agenda 21, the Programme for Further Implementation of Agenda 21 and the Commitments to the Rio principles, were strongly reaffirmed at the World Summit on Sustainable Development (WSSD) held in Johannesburg, South Africa from 26 August to 4 September 2002.[24]

A toothier document appeared from the UN affiliate the International Union for the Conservation of Nature (IUCN). First published in 1995, the third edition of the "Draft International Covenant on Environment and Development" arrived in 2004. It aims "to achieve environmental conservation and sustainable development by establishing integrated rights

---

[23] http://www.cbd.int/convention/parties/list/ (accessed January 11, 2012).

[24] http://www.un.org/esa/dsd/agenda21/ (accessed September 18, 2012).

and obligations."[25] This is the groundwork, further detailed, for imposing an international legal authority that transcends American sovereignty.

Executive Orders

Like the patient internationalists, American leftists like former President Bill Clinton were undeterred in their long-term goals by the defeat of the U.N. treaty in the Senate. Clinton demonstrated another outlet by which the Executive can wield its power to advance agendas even when opposed by the people and their Legislature: the executive order.

Though Clinton could not effect the adoption of international law via treaty, he could still help the UN goal of influencing American governments. He wasted no time on this. A full year before the Treaty made it to the floor of the Senate, Clinton signed Executive Order No. 12852 establishing the "President's Council on Sustainable Development." This Council was to advise the President on all matters of "sustainable development" and "develop and recommend to the President a national sustainable development action strategy that will foster economic vitality."[26] In 1997, Clinton revised the Council's Charter. Whereas the original aimed merely at developing strategy, the new Charter included advising on policy, disseminating educational material, and assessing progress—no doubt the very strategy it had previously devised. The Council was not only to advise on policy, but "to encourage and demonstrate *implementation* of sustainable development in real world settings" and "report on successes and recommend strategies to *replicate* those successful projects *throughout the United States.*"[27] The

---

[25] http://www.i-c-e-l.org/english/EPLP31EN_rev2.pdf (see p. 2), (accessed January 11, 2012).

[26] http://www.archives.gov/federal-register/executive-orders/pdf/12852.pdf (accessed January 11, 2012).

[27] Revised Charter, April 25, 1997; http://clinton2.nara.gov/PCSD/Charter/index.html (accessed January 11, 2012); emphasis added.

new policy bulldog was created, funded, and maintained without any input from Congress or the voice of the people.

The Council's influence was intended to be comprehensive in scope, including local governments. After all, *Agenda 21* said greatest resistance comes at that level, and thus "the participation and cooperation of local authorities will be a determining factor in fulfilling its objectives."[28] Thus the new Council's job was to encompass "national *and local* sustainable development plans." The revised Charter specified the following as one of several official activities for the Council:

> The Council should create and participate in projects that help forge partnerships among representatives of federal and state agencies, urban centers, suburban areas, and rural communities with the goal of solving, in a comprehensive way, local and regional sustainable development issues."[29]

What you're seeing here is the leftist, one-world government, top-down control version of the very project you're studying in my book. But instead of *restoring* America one county at a time, they are *destroying* America one county at a time. Instead of cutting the size of government and returning local government to local responsibility, they are increasing government, imposing yet another higher level of it (global), and coercing (or seducing) local governments to make their local citizens responsible to global agencies.

One of the grassroots activists who fought this at the time (and still does) could lament its progress already in November of 1994:

> This vision of local governance leaves city councils, county commissions, soil conservation districts, regional water authorities, and state legislatures com-

---

[28] *Agenda 21*, 233.

[29] Revised Charter, April 25, 1997; http://clinton2.nara.gov/PCSD/Charter/index.html (accessed January 11, 2012).

pletely out of the environmental, land use, sustainable development picture. Never happen? Don't be too sure. It is already happening.

Literally thousands of private and municipal land use decisions have been blocked by federal regulations. Land use, and therefore resource use, is no longer within the authority of local, or even state governments. Local planning commissions and local county commissions may go through the motions, but their deliberations are likely to center more on compliance with federal regulations than on what's best for the community. When decisions are reached at the local level, they are still subject to approval or reversal by the federal government.

Local and state governments are further intimidated by the now common practice of withholding federal highway funds, or education funds, or medicare funds, or other funds—until the local government falls into line with the federal demand.

The explosion of unfunded federal mandates in recent years has further weakened the effectiveness of state and local government. By demanding that local and state governments implement federal laws and regulations, the federal government has effectively usurped local government's authority and ability to pursue its community objectives. As the unfunded mandate trend continues, local and state governments are reduced to little more than administrative units of the federal government.

The transition to bioregional communal, if not tribal, governance, is not going to happen by declaration. Treaty proponents already fear a backlash, and they are much too smart to deliberately precipitate a rebellion. The goal is long-range and fully integrated into a comprehensive program designed to achieve the desired result. Maurice Strong has said the international framework must be in place by 2012. The biodiversity documents anticipate a transition period of 20 to 50 years.[30]

[30] Henry Lamb, "The Convention on Biological Diversity: Cornerstone to the New World Order," http://freedom.org/reports/srbio.htm (accessed January 11,

In 1999, Clinton signed Executive Order 13112, advancing an innocuous-sounding plan for combating "invasive species."[31] It was a back-door ploy to advance the sustainable development agenda throughout American government. This seemingly obscure issue of invasive species for some reason required the institution of a national "Invasive Species Council." And while you might think such a Council would involve scientists and biological experts—perhaps it did—it included and demanded compliance from the Secretary of State, the Secretary of the Treasury, the Secretary of Defense, the Secretary of the Interior, the Secretary of Agriculture, the Secretary of Commerce, the Secretary of Transportation, and the Administrator of the Environmental Protection Agency—some of the biggest and most comprehensive bureaucracies of the Federal government.

Why? Ostensibly for targeting "invasive species" within their respective jurisdictions; but in reality, it was part of the Agenda 21 plan to increase Federal control over every corner of American life. Sure enough, entire UN colloquies have been written on the use of "invasive species" as a means of advancing international law and Agenda 21 specifically.[32] The trick was to find one obscure environmental issue for which the Executive could corral so many important Federal agencies to focus on one agenda.

More recently, Barack Obama has implemented the same tactic only on a broader scale with Executive Order 13575, "Establishment of the White House Rural Council." Again it touted good intentions: "enhance the Federal Government's efforts to address the needs of rural America . . . to better coordinate Federal programs and maximize the impact of Federal investment to promote economic prosperity and

---

2012).

[31] http://frwebgate.access.gpo.gov/cgi-bin/getdoc.cgi?dbname=1999_register&docid=fr08fe99-168.pdf (accessed January 11, 2012).

[32] See Odd Terje Sandlund, Peter Johan Shei, and Aslaug Viken, eds., *Invasive Species and Biodiversity Management* (Dordrecht, Netherlands: Kluwer Academic Publishers, 1999).

quality of life in our rural communities." But again, there was a vast consolidation of agenda throughout Federal agencies, this time including a much larger list: the Departments of the Treasury, Defense, Justice, Interior, Commerce, Labor, Health and Human Services, Housing and Urban Development, Transportation, Energy, Education, Veterans Affairs, Homeland Security, EPA, FCC, Office of Management and Budget, Office of Science and Technology Policy, Office of National Drug Control Policy, Council of Economic Advisers, Domestic Policy Council, National Economic Council, Small Business Administration, Council on Environmental Quality, White House Office of Public Engagement and Intergovernmental Affairs, White House Office of Cabinet Affairs—and just in case any had been left out, "other executive branch departments, agencies, and offices as the President or the Secretary of Agriculture may, from time to time, designate."[33]

The new Council's scope of mission is just as broad. It shall

> coordinate and increase the effectiveness of Federal engagement with rural stakeholders, including agricultural organizations, small businesses, education and training institutions, health-care providers, telecommunications services providers, research and land grant institutions, law enforcement, state, local, and tribal governments, and nongovernmental organizations regarding the needs of rural America.

In other words, the Executive branch via its own fiat now aims to have direct influence over all these areas of private life, business, law, and police at the local level. This was accomplished without legislation, without Congressional approval or scrutiny, purely by the whim of the Executive himself.

These abuses of power illustrate the problem William Symmes mentioned long ago and which we already noted:

---

[33] http://www.gpo.gov/fdsys/pkg/FR-2011-06-14/pdf/2011-14919.pdf (accessed January 11, 2012).

without clear definitions of the power and laws which the president must take "care" to be executed, he is broadly at liberty to define his own according to his agenda, or another's.

Keep in mind we have only touched on a tiny few executive orders here. There have been many. The total number is unknown because the government didn't start counting them until 1907, numbering retroactively from 1862. Still, the consecutively-numbered orders stand currently at No. 13,596—the last one signed December 19, 2011 by Barack Obama. FDR was the king of the Executive Order, signing 3,728 of them. Only one other modern president is even over 500. But just consider the fact that presidents have signed 13,596 different interpretations or applications of their power that are not explicitly stated in the Constitution. There have been 38 presidents in office since 1862. This means that a mere 38 men have been allowed to circumvent the Constitutional legislative process 13,596 times— an average of 357.8 abuses per president.

Of course, not all orders are actual abuses. Many are exercises of powers already ceded to the President, and some are simply frivolous. Some of these orders have been more important than others. In 1952, one of Eisenhower's orders would have seized control of all steel mills in the country. The Supreme Court found this disturbing enough to review it and shoot it down. But in recent times, this type of check on presidential power is a rare exception to the rule—it has occurred only twice.

In 1999, Bill Clinton essentially waged the war in Kosovo entirely by Executive Orders and without Congressional declaration of war. In Order No. 13088, Clinton declared the civil war in Kosovo a "an unusual and extraordinary threat to the national security and foreign policy of the United States" and thus a "national emergency."[34] Leveraging previous Acts of Congress which were allegedly designed to prevent open-

---

[34] June 9, 1998, http://frwebgate.access.gpo.gov/cgi-bin/getdoc.cgi?dbname=1998_register&docid=fr12jn98-162.pdf (accessed January 13, 2012).

ended abuses of emergency powers, Clinton empowered himself to seize assets, block property, and prohibit trade with then-Yugoslavia. When military action was inevitable to fulfill the agenda, Clinton shot first and asked questions later. Actually, he never *asked* at all: he shot first and then made requisite demands later. Between March 24 and April 7, 1999, Clinton simply informed Congress multiple times that he was sending troops to the region to support the NATO effort. On April 13, he signed order No. 13119 declaring Yugoslavia and its airspace a "combat zone" by referencing an obscure section of IRS tax code.[35] More importantly, the order retro-dated the commencement of "combatant activities" to March 24, 1999, the date NATO bombings had begun and a full three weeks prior to the order. On April 27, Clinton signed E.O. 13120, ordering reserve forces to active duty.[36]

Congress's apparent objections were highly suspect while Clinton effectively steamrolled them. On April 28, the House shot down a declaration of war overwhelmingly, and then appeared to oppose war even further when it passed a bill forbidding the use of ground troops. There is a certain amount of deceptive PR detectable in these moves: the bill which passed suspiciously neglected to forbid the use of troops *in general* (only expressly mentioning "ground" troops) or aircraft, etc. Then, not even a month later, the House passed a supplemental appropriations Act giving implicit assent to the war by approving billions of dollars to pay for it.[37]

---

[35] http://frwebgate.access.gpo.gov/cgi-bin/getdoc.cgi?dbname=1999_register&docid=fr16ap99-163.pdf (accessed January 13, 2012). The particular section in view is now 26 U.C.S. 112 and essentially provides a tax break for soldiers serving in undeclared wars, including serving in "combat zones." The section defines "combat zone" as "any area which the President of the United States by Executive Order designates, for purposes of this section or corresponding provisions of prior income tax laws, as an area in which Armed Forces of the United States are or have (after June 24, 1950) engaged in combat" (27 U.S.C. 112(c)(2)).

[36] See Cliff Kincaid, "How Clinton Waged War Through Executive Order," http://www.usasurvival.org/kosovowar.html (accessed January 13, 2012).

[37] Abraham D. Sofaer, "The War Powers Resolution and Kosovo," *Loyola of Los*

Even after the NATO air campaign was officially over (June 11–12, 1999), Clinton continued to tout the "national emergency" his E.O. declared. In fact, in the final days of his presidency, Clinton moved to "lift" and "modify" some of the measures taken against Yugoslavia, and yet still referred officially to "the continuing threat" and "national emergency" decreed previously.[38] The order remained in effect until George W. Bush finally revoked it in 2003 with E.O. 13219. Yet Bush's E.O. itself referred to yet another national emergency described in yet another E.O. from two years earlier which this new one replaced and amended, and thus *continued*. Bush also declared a national emergency on September 14, 2001, just after the 9/11 attacks, for obvious reasons.

This is just the tip of the iceberg. It turns out that wars and national emergencies are the real powers behind Executive tyranny, and they have been used widely since at least the Civil War to allow the President to circumvent Congress.

Emergency and War Powers

We observed earlier in the chapter on war how the Warfare State and Welfare State have a symbiotic relationship. In modern American history, the "tie that binds" these unholy partners until death do them part has been "emergency powers." Ostensibly an extreme measure for war-time only, modern presidents have increasingly relied on declarations of emergency in order to exercise vast powers domestically and during peacetime.

You probably don't realize it, but you have lived probably the entirety of your life under national emergency. You almost certainly have if you were born after 1933. In that year, President Roosevelt transformed the United States into

---

Angeles Law Review 34/1 (Nov. 2000): 75; http://llr.lls.edu/volumes/v34-issue1/sofaer.pdf (accessed January 13, 2012).

[38] E. O. 13192, January 17, 2001; http://frwebgate.access.gpo.gov/cgi-bin/getdoc.cgi?dbname=2001_register&docid=fr23ja01-141.pdf (accessed January 13, 2012).

a peacetime Executive tyranny. We have mentioned FDR's first inaugural address on a couple of occasions, noting how the president applied the language of warfare to a peacetime problem. It was no mere metaphor, as he clearly said he wanted "broad Executive power to wage a war against the emergency." The solution would come by "treating the task as we would treat the emergency of a war." He used the word "emergency" four times in that address to describe the American dilemma. It was no coincidence. He gave that speech on March 4, 1933. Five days later, he declared a national emergency which gave the Executive near total control over American life—again, in peacetime.

In 1973, Congress took temporary interest in the subject of emergency powers, long enough at least to discover their history in a Senate study, and to pass an Act purporting to limit those powers. The Act, as we shall see, has done nothing but formally codify and regularize them. That 1973 study begins by saying,

> Since March 9, 1933, the United States has been in a state of declared national emergency. In fact, there are now in effect four presidential proclaimed states of national emergency: In addition to the national emergency declared by President Roosevelt in 1933, there are also the national emergency proclaimed by President Truman on December 16, 1950, during the Korean conflict, and the states of national emergency declared by President Nixon on March 23, 1970, and August 15, 1971.[39]

"Four separate national emergencies" sounds crazy, but believe it or not, those were the good ol' days. Today it is difficult to get an accurate account of all the outstanding national emergencies. The latest revised edition (2007) of a Congressional Research Service report on "National Emergency Powers"

---

[39] *Emergency Power Statutes: Provisions of Federal Law Now in Effect Delegating to the Executive Extraordinary Authority in Time of National Emergency,* quoted in Eugene Schroder and David E. Schechter, *War, Central Planning and Corporations: The Corporate State* (Cleburne, TX: Buffalo Creek Press, 1997), 11.

lists *fourty-two* declared national emergencies just between 1976 and August, 2007.[40] Only twenty-two of these have been rescinded, leaving twenty in effect. We know Obama added several others on top of those.

The powers given to the Executive under these declarations are broad and numerous:

> Under the powers delegated by these statutes, the President may: seize property; organize and control the means of production; seize commodities; assign military forces abroad; institute martial law; seize and control all transportation and communications; regulate the operation of private enterprise; restrict travel; and, in a plethora of particular ways, control the lives of all American citizens.[41]

> There are various stand-by laws that convey special emergency powers once the President formally declares a national emergency activating them. In 1973, a Senate special committee studying emergency powers published a compilation identifying some 470 provisions of federal law delegating to the executive extraordinary authority in time of national emergency. The vast majority of them are of the standby kind—dormant until activated by the President.[42]

That 1973 report led eventually to the National Emergencies Act, signed into law in 1976. A companion bill, called the International Emergency Economic Powers Act, came the following year. These Acts placed some light checks upon the Executive power but did little more than codify the practice of Executive rule via national emergency into statute law. Thus it

---

[40] Harold C. Relyea, "National Emergency Powers," *Congressional Research Report*, August 30, 2007, No. 98–505; http://www.fas.org/sgp/crs/natsec/98-505.pdf (accessed January 16, 2012).

[41] *Emergency Power Statutes*; quoted in Schroder and Schechter, *War, Central Planning and Corporations*, 11.

[42] Relyea, "National Emergency Powers."

received legal sanction. The end result has been a vast *increase* in the practice rather than a Congressional limitation on it. The 1973 report (and a follow-up in 1974) exposed a huge list of dangerous Executive powers, but the Acts that issued from these reports were preposterously feeble. One is tempted to say they were mere smokescreens.

We do know that the achievement of these vast powers on behalf of the Presidency involved considerable work "behind-closed-doors." This came on the part of government officials and non-governmental collaborators, namely the Rockefeller-funded Spellman Fund. One of the main legal obstacles impeding FDR in 1933 was the states' rights doctrine that still remained residually in the southern and western states. Any open move on behalf of the President would have caused widespread opposition among the people, which could have stalled the nationalistic agenda. So the elites moved stealthily.

Remember that inaugural address on March 4, 1933. Well the immediate day after, a coordinated effort began to get every state governor essentially to effect a state-level emergency power grab in preparation for handing that power directly to FDR. A telegram was received by Kansas Governor Alfred M. Landon stating:

> We respectfully submit to your consideration that the dire need of the hour calls for national unity in support of our president, a unity even more complete and unselfish than that necessary in war. . . . Prompt and decisive action of a national scope in several directions is necessary to prevent economic collapse throughout the land. The ordinary operations of government that prevail and are suitable in time of prosperity with normal conditions may be too slow to meet adequately this emergency and avoid the danger of this economic avalanche carrying all before it. . . . We, a Coalition Committee of different groups and political and religious

faiths, respectfully request that you join the other Governors of our country in the issuance of a Proclamation on Wednesday, March 8, 1933, in support of the President of the United States.[43]

The message was signed by a variety of leaders with national profiles: Richard E. Byrd (a celebrity Naval Officer and explorer), Mrs. Calvin Coolidge, Nicholas Murray Butler (president of Columbia University and chair of the Carnegie Endowment for International Peace), H. G. Harriman (president of the U.S. Chamber of Commerce), Rev. Harry Emerson Fosdick, Walter Lippman, plus labor and farm leaders, as well as hold-outs from the Wilson War State. A national governor's meeting was called in Washington, D.C. Those who could not attend got the telegram. Landon responded willingly. Merely a few days later, a new telegram announced "Complete success of program of simultaneous proclamations by all governors of states. . . . Plans being made ready for reading your proclamation in every church in your state."[44]

Indeed, it was successful. Following the proclamations, legislation was rammed through state legislatures. In Colorado, the governor made such a proclamation on August 2, 1933. Two weeks later, the legislature gave the governor all the power he asked for. These new laws so closely paralleled the Governor's requests and the President's designs that given the brief turnaround time, it is likely they were given pre-approved templates from which to work.[45]

But the power grab was unprecedented and not without opposition, however futile. The Colorado Supreme Court

---

[43] Quoted in Schroder and Schechter, *War, Central Planning and Corporations*, 29. See Franklin D. Roosevelt: "Letter Urging Support of the President," March 6, 1933. Online by Gerhard Peters and John T. Woolley, *The American Presidency Project*. http://www.presidency.ucsb.edu/ws/?pid=14639 (accessed September 18, 2012).

[44] Quoted in Schroder and Schechter, *War, Central Planning and Corporations*, 30.

[45] Ibid., 27–28.

decided to review the measures, and declared that they were profoundly unconstitutional (though its views were apparently not legally decisive):

> We venture the assertion that no man, able to read and understand ordinary English, however otherwise educated or uneducated, wise or foolish, would question for a moment that this bill was a plain violation of the [state] constitutional prohibition [against contracting state debts for other than defense]. . . .
>
> If the people's "Thou shalt not" can be brushed aside by the simple *ipso dixit* of the public servants thus bound, the mandate is impotent. Such a construction, once adopted, breaks the barrier, and future legislatures, protected by precedent, might pile up mountains of debt on future generations, resulting in inevitable imporverishment or ruthless repudiation.[46]

It did not matter. The state governors persuaded the state legislatures and the President got his "broad Executive power to wage a war against the emergency." Almost immediately, the President's "National Planning Board" began issuing circulars to the states. The fifth of these letters, on December 11, 1933, called for the creation of state planning boards. These would oversee the implementation of Federal guidelines for public works, land use planning, zoning, use of rural lands, transportation, agriculture, housing, population redistribution (yes, that's the government telling you that you have to leave your property and move were they tell you, Trail of Tears style), conservation, water resources, recreation, fiscal programming, and more. The circular stated, "A full fledged state planning project will eventually include all of these items, and others as well."[47]

A later letter from Kansas Governor Landon to the Chancellor of the University of Kansas reveals it was not all purely

---

[46] Quoted in Schroder and Schechter, *War, Central Planning and Corporations*, 26–27.

[47] Ibid., 32.

political. As we have seen so many times in this study, particularly with education, banking, tariffs, money, and war,
there were corporate and religious-ideological forces at work
as well. Landon says in his letter, "We are of course dependent on the National Resources Board and the Spelman Fund
for the continuance of effective work."[48] The Spelman Fund
was a Rockefeller Oil endowment directed by Beardsley
Ruml, who, along with Elihu Root, is among the most influential men you've never heard of. He was a psychologist of
the behaviorist school, a leader at the University of Chicago,
and a Macy's executive. After serving as a director of the Federal Reserve Bank of NY, he became the Ben Bernanke of his
day and chaired it. In 1942, he invented income tax withholding so that average people would not feel the pain of writing
a single, large, year-end check to the government. Taxing in
small increments creates less resistance and allows the government 1) to take more in the long run, and 2) to bank and
to earn interest on what they collect in the meantime. These
were some of the ideological forces pushing for consolidation
of executive power in this era.

   Meanwhile, the history of the Progressive era, as we saw,
was one of empire and corporate growth, and Rockefeller was
one of the kings, if not *the* king. After a coal mine strike in
Colorado (involving workers from one of Rockefeller's mines)
led to a massacre of miners courtesy of the National Guard
(Sherman would be proud), Rockefeller took the national lead
in calling for increased employee benefits, protections, wage
protections, and representation. The so-called "Colorado
Plan" became something of a blueprint for centrally planned
"Industrial Relations" as Rockefeller funded programs in several major universities throughout the nation.[49] The following

---

[48] Ibid., 33.

[49] See Rockefeller's own description of the Colorado Plan in "John D. Rockefeller,
Jr., on Labor and Capital," *New York Times*, January 6, 1916; on the funding of programs, see Schroder and Schechter, *War, Central Planning and Corporations*, 42.

section from Schroder and Schechter is worth its length for its incisive summary:

> Princeton, Yale, Harvard, and Columbia were heavily funded by John D. Rockefeller, Jr., but the political science department at the University of Chicago, under the leadership of Charles E. Merriam and Beardsley Ruml, became the headquarters for the new "science" of industrial relations. Whether the increased cost of providing for laborers' "human weaknesses" would be offset by increased profits turns out to be immaterial. If government could provide these benefits, at no cost to the corporations, any increased productivity would be a windfall profit to the corporate owners. It was this goal that the Rockefeller interests pursued through their foundations, university funding, and government collaborations, and that they ultimately achieved in 1933. The only problem to be overcome was the peacetime constitutional limitations on government to create money and "tax and spend" at will. President Roosevelt, the Congress, and the states solved this problem on March 9, 1933, by declaring that a state of national emergency existed, thereby eliminating prior constitutional restraints. . . .[50]

The first hundred days of the Roosevelt administration were by and large no more than an implementation of the Rockefeller "Colorado Plan" by the national government in cooperation with the state and local governments, with purported Constitutional authority under a state of declared national emergency that previously had been assumed to apply only in wartime.

Indeed, one Rockefeller-funded adviser of FDR briefed him nearly a year before his presidency, stating for a fact that corporations we already in control: "65% of American industry is owned and operated by about six hundred corporations."

---

[50] Schroder and Schechter, *War, Central Planning and Corporations*, 42–43.

He would go on to praise this as an opportunity to advance toward Soviet-style socialism:

> At the present rate of the trend, the American and Russian systems will look very much alike within a comparatively short period—say twenty years. . . . [For] there is no great difference between having all industry run by a committee of Commissars and by a small group of Directors.

Thus FDR was advised to make it part of his campaign that the Corporate-State should set up "monopolies at will" and "should include power to require uniform prices; to control security issues; and to control further consolidation."[51]

On the same day he declared the national emergency, the Emergency Banking Act gave FDR total control of national finance. He declared a bank holiday and forbade redemption of paper for gold. A month later he confiscated the nation's gold coins from all private individuals at the set price of $20.67/oz. A year later he declared the price to be $35/oz. which effectively inflated the money supply by 70 percent (or decreased the nation's debt burden by that amount, depending on how you look at it). Out of this same emergency atmosphere came the Emergency National Industry Recovery Act which exempted corporations from anti-trust and anti-monopoly laws, a central National Resources Board, the Home Owners' Loan Act, the Emergency Relief Act, the Social Security Act, and the Emergency Agricultural Adjustment Act which placed national controls on farms, prices, etc.

A similar spirit has prevailed ever since. What President Clinton did in Kosovo via executive orders and declared national emergencies was already long-since the norm for advancing central planning and political agendas. Presidents today regularly use emergency powers in both war and peace to expedite agendas under the guise of "governing effectively," "national security," and many other justifications.

---

[51] Ibid., 46.

Conclusion

While there is certainly no limit to the tyranny of an Executive who has both the ambition and opportunity, there is enough here to show how a once freer America has been subdued. This has come primarily through three key Executive powers: the Treaty-making power in this country, the abuse of executive orders, and the ascendency of government-by-emergency. We have seen how the latter of these has been the main catalyst for executive tyranny, especially in more recent times, and also as it unleashes a greater potential for the abuse of executive orders.

The greatest irony of all here is probably that, of all tyrannies and abuses, Americans are most complacent with this one. Consider for a moment how broadly these Executive excesses have been indulged by both Republican and Democrat administrations in recent times. In both cases, partisans praise the abuses of their party and condemn those of their opponents. The message is clear: "We will tolerate Executive tyranny as long as our guy gets to stick it to the other guys." Understandably, the two major political parties in this nation have become merely two expressions of big government Executive tyranny. The one says give us protections for social welfare programs, the other says give us protections for corporate banks and big business. In short, there seems to be no escape from this game of big spending and massive debts: it only seems to be a matter of who gets to profit on the front end.

But there is an alternative worldview. While change in the executive functions of our governments—especially at the Federal level—is definitely a long way off, barring some major collapse and catastrophe, there are still some goals for which to aim.

Restoring Freedom from Executive Tyranny

In light of all these Executive excesses, what can be done to restore the freedom Americans once had? Even better, how can we return to a society even more free than before—something more akin to biblical controls on Executive tyranny? The answer is two-faceted: first, things average people can do now, and second, larger goals for the future.

As far as things average people can do now, we must first remember our priorities. Go back to the first topic of this project and work your way through. Pull your kids from public schools; plan and fight for your family autonomy in old age, insurance, etc.; focus on localism, local politics, local control, and start exposing and fighting the massive wastes, corruption, and debts that exist in the thousands of halls of local governments; start focusing on state-level solutions to problems like abortion, exercise Tenth Amendment rights, nullification, etc. Just these first four topics, if put to practice by groups in every county across this nation would go a long way toward softening the scaly underbelly of Leviathan, leaving the monster vulnerable to the forces of freedom. But these topics must come first because hearts and minds must change through education, and local individuals must set the example. The serious, the faithful, and the courageous must make the necessary sacrifices first. As volume nine of the *Biblical Blueprints* series encourages,

> I am not calling for wholesale revisions of the Constitution today. These changes must be implemented only after a full-scale revival and the clear-cut political triumph of Christians as self-conscious Christian voters. Attempting to amend the Constitution before you have the votes is suicidal; this would play into the hands of the humanist left wing. Just as internationalism prior to international revival is extremely dangerous, so is attempting any Constitutional amendment nationally before national revival. This would be a top-down political transformation, something quite foreign to Christian

social theory. It puts the cart before the horse. The religious transformation must precede the political transformation; the political transformation must precede
the Constitutional transformation.

We must therefore content ourselves for the present with small steps.[52]

There are many Christians today who cannot see this, or
who deny it. If society is left to their influence, Statists will
dominate, there will be no revival of faith and freedom, and
society will decline under God's judgment, or even possibly
face a catastrophic collapse. It will not matter who the president, congressmen, or judges are if they do not first have a
biblical worldview and a biblical doctrine of power. Changing
our priorities and acting accordingly is the first step in creating a generation of properly-focused leaders and citizens.

Secondly, Christians must change their view of the scope of
missions. It was a false de-Christianized view of missions that
led us into the tyranny we have today—both in regard to messianic warfare and messianic central planning. You can't have
messianic social progress unless the Messiah is in absolute control—legally, judicially, and executively. This means that instead
of seeking change through coercion—whether the central planning state or the warfare/nation-building state—we must have
a more concerted effort of evangelism and proper, full biblical-
worldview, biblical-society discipleship. A colleague of mine
pioneered this field in international missions, particularly in
Bulgaria, with a simple translation ministry, translating the pro-
Christian society writings of R. J. Rushdoony, Gary North, Greg
Bahnsen, and others. People are beginning to replicate this
effort in places like Brazil, Puerto Rico, Chile, Italy, and more.
Bojidar is also currently writing a book on missions done the
biblical way, to be published hopefully this year. But we must
not make the mistake of thinking "missions" means interna-

---

[52] Gary North, *Healer of the Nations: Biblical Principles for International Relations* (Ft. Worth, TX: Dominion Press, 1987), 301.

tional missions alone. As one missionary once told me, "Don't fly over one mission field to get to another one." As far as learning how biblical freedom applies to every area of government and life, America is nearly as needy a mission field as anywhere else. Indeed, many places are less problematic because they haven't already grown up with the façade of a Christian heritage deceiving them into false assurance and pride.

Educational matters aside, what can individuals *do* to combat Executive tyranny (like treaty powers, executive orders, and abuses of emergency powers)? What you can do is get involved in local politics and become an influence *against* things like Agenda 21. You can form an unofficial local group dedicated to exposing and raising awareness of such intrusions into local government and life. Alert your local sheriff, council members, and the local public to these programs along with the examples of those who are already fighting encroaching tyranny in their own counties.[53] Through efforts like these we can withstand intrusions at local and even state levels in a highly visible way. This sends a message of popular support for organized resistance to tyranny. The more small groups there are doing this across the country, the more visible and pervasive that message will be.

Larger Goals

The *larger* social and political needs are more easily stated but harder to achieve. These include revamping the Constitutional treaty-making process, curtailing the power of the Executive departments, as well as the presidential use of emergency powers and executive orders. The policy suggestions I provide here are largely based on the recommendations given in Gary North's *Healer of the Nations*:

---

[53] For example, there is http://www.countysheriffproject.org/, http://supportruralamerica.ning.com, http://www.siskiyoucountywaterusers.com/, http://www.defendruralamerica.com/DRA/Home.html, http://pienpolitics.com/, http://24hourpatriots.com/, http://www.constitutionalsheriffs.com/, as well as the pioneering efforts of Sheriff Richard Mack at http://sheriffmack.com/.

First, we absolutely need a Constitutional amendment that places greater checks on the President's treaty-making powers. No treaty should be ratified without full two-thirds majorities (not just of a quorum) in *both* houses of Congress. We should at least consider making distinctions between treaties of commerce and treaties of peace or alliance as the Federal Farmer suggested. And since treaties of commerce have much more effect on internal laws, they should be held to the same standard of passage as all domestic legislation. Any treaty that has such effects should be treated so.

We need transparency and accountability in the State department. That huge book listing all of the treaties we mentioned? Those treaties should be compiled in one place online, indexed in every way possible, searchable, and in full text. There should be a complete study done as to which ones are still in force and how they currently affect U.S. Code.

Second, we need to get out of the United Nations. The United States should never send a dime to the UN. It is a messianic organization designed to redistribute wealth throughout the world, centralize global public policy, advance a pagan nature-religion, and work toward implementing global government at local levels through comprehensive programs like Agenda 21 and others. UN staff members are required to take an oath of allegiance to the UN. The office of the Secretariat's own website says,

> As international civil servants, staff members and the Secretary-General answer to the United Nations alone for their activities, and take an oath not to seek or receive instructions from any Government or outside authority. Under the Charter, each Member State undertakes to respect the exclusively international character of the responsibilities of the Secretary-General and the staff and to refrain from seeking to influence them improperly in the discharge of their duties.[54]

---

[54] (accessed January 17, 2012); cf. North, *Healer of the Nations*, 295–296.

Any American taking such a job—and thus such an oath— should automatically be required to revoke their U.S. citizenship or face charges of treason. This harsh-sounding reaction gets to the heart of what the UN is about: it is a would-be global government designed to transcend national sovereignty. Only Jesus Christ has any claim to legitimate global sovereignty.

Third, we need to cut the size and reduce the number of Executive departments. The State Department currently has a budget of $27.4 billion annually and a staff of 49,900 employees. George Washington ran it with six. This is just one department of several. The IRS alone employs over 100,000. In an age in which government spending has become virtually the biggest threat to future liberty, the size of these bureaucracies is simply Executive insanity.

Fourth, the president should veto any appropriations bill that does not balance the budget, and frankly, in light of the ballooning national debt, he should veto any spending bill that does not follow a plan to create a surplus and begin eliminating huge chunks of the national debt. Such reductions would likely take care of the war and nation-building problem as well. And while he's at it, he should veto absolutely any bill that construes the Constitution to increase the powers of the Federal government. Period. The veto is an awesome power rarely used for the public good.

Fifth, the president should rescind all 13,600+ Executive Orders. Granted, he would have to use an executive order to do so, but this one would at least have the virtue of being *negative*: cancelling government powers rather than creating more of them. Congress should then enact a bill treating all future executive orders like any other law: not actionable unless passed by both chambers of Congress and *then* signed by the President.

Sixth, we need an Act which *genuinely* and forcefully binds the Executive in regard to national emergencies and emergency powers. The Acts passed in 1976 and 1977 under the guise of reining-in the abuse of emergency powers have done nothing but codify the abuse by statute while placing only mild checks upon them. The result has been a drastic increase in the number of declared emergencies and the attending Executive powers normally reserved only for war. These feeble Acts must either be drastically revised or repealed and replaced with legislation that requires full congressional approval of declared emergencies, again via recorded roll call votes.

The main goals of these actions are twofold: first to check the power of the Presidency and bring that power back as close to the people as possible. In each of these proposals, Congress becomes responsible for the legislation, or other governmental actions which have the force of legislation. Congress stands responsible for spending, war, tyranny, emergency, invasive measures, etc., and they are on record as to who voted for what. In the case of bills which the President vetoes, it's even better. This means a supermajority of Congress would be required to pass it. If Congress still issues a declaration of war—meaning more debt, infractions of civil liberties, etc.—then the President's veto *forces Congress to own it.* Any unpopular bill passed by a supermajority at that point will put a lot of Congressmen out of work.

The second major goal is to remove the massive infrastructure of tyranny that has grown up since the New Deal in 1933. If we could get past Wilsonian and Civil War precedents, that would be even better. But a pre-1933 level of Federal intrusion in our lives would at least free us from most of the emergency powers abuses, bloated Federal bureaucracies, peace-time central planning, and abuses of executive orders. Even here, however, we need structural changes in order to hinder any attempts to resume such powers again in the future.

Conclusion

Again, these larger structural changes can come about and have lasting effects only if a massive change of hearts and minds occurs first. There are waves of this change happening right now, so there is hope. But we have a long way to go. The most important steps to take now are local: begin individual and organized opposition to local spending, local debts, and intrusions into local sovereignty. A hundred counties eventually telling the EPA and the FDA, "No" will lay an impressive foundation for genuine social change toward liberty, and will send a strong message to the bureaucrats and central planners who wish to make marionettes of us all. A thousand counties would be better. A thousand counties backed by state governments would be even better yet.

Epilogue

Roughly speaking, I reasearched and wrote this book over the space of nine months. It was a labor of love. Most of the main ideas I already knew and held firmly, but I did learn some new things along the way. What I learned strengthened my already-held views as well as my distaste for centralized government solutions. Sharing this development, I think, can help you remain encouraged through what will certainly be an uphill journey, as all self-sacrificial decisions tend to be, even when they're rewarding in the end.

Most importantly, my understanding of just how much freedom in America has been eroded—by factors often stemming directly from and relying upon the Constitution itself, and often in the name of conservatism or the Republican tradition—has been greatly intensified from what I originally believed. This was so often the case that I had to check myself several times against becoming a cynic—and I assure you I am not one!—in regard to the value of the whole political process and the possibility of regaining our freedom. Nevertheless, being honest about the scope of the losses and the depth of the entrenchment of statist and socialistic principles (in both major parties and beyond) forced me to develop biblical outlooks and solutions even more refined than I would have been able to conceive previously.

This has come in two main aspects. First, in seeing the true nature of the outgrowth of many things from the Constitution—and the consistency in all political parties in either abusing it with impunity or using it for the purposes of tyranny with impunity—I have felt ever more free and justified in criticizing it. It's not that I never criticized the U. S. Constitution in the past, but that I have realized more than ever how central a role it has played in, well, centralization, and all of the attendant evils that come along with that. As truth often does, even when we are at first hesitant to acknowledge it due to whatever fear, prejudice, or hangup, a tremendous burden was lifted from me. Something counterintuitive results: where it is human nature to shrink somewhat when faced with the prospect of preaching what will certainly be perceived as an unpopular message (even to the point of being ridiculed), I have nevertheless felt freer before God than ever before to simply stand up and say the truth. In a sense, truth, no matter how unpopular, is *liberating* when embraced.

Second, with this new awakening and new boldness also comes a greater love and dependence upon the pure Word of God. It's only when you see the true nature of the problem that you can formulate a proper solution to it. And even though we have held the Word of God firmly in our hands all this time, we have often failed to put forth a fully biblical platform for all of life specifically because we have been applying it piecemeal to a faulty view of the problems. If, after all, we think that the public school system, or the monetary system, or the military only needs a fix here and there rather than being entirely unbiblical from the root up, then we will consistently fail to propose a truly biblical goal for society. In short, we have too often allowed our society to influence our reading of the Bible, rather than letting the Bible determine our reading and structuring of society.

As I completed this phase of this project, I realized that I had grown even more bold and more determined to put forth only biblical answers, no matter how unpopular, and no matter what the cost. And the more I pursue this, the more I find out, *I love doing so.*

And it's not just me. Whereas I fully expected to be shot down and ridiculed at every turn, I have more often than not been surprised by positive feedback from many, often unexpected, angles. While speaking candidly to a few hundred conservatives about the need to stop supporting the military automatically in everything it does merely because it's the military, etc., I was shocked to see nods of agreement across the entire room punctuated with a few quiet amens. Over this nine months I have been contacted by people of all ages and stations in life: businessmen, lawyers, presidents of chambers of commerce, county commissioners, party delegates, political activists, and many average Janes and Joes who desire to see America free once again. Like me, and I hope like you, these people are ready and willing to make serious sacrifices in their lives in order to restore a free America to the glory of God.

Some of these are among the younger "liberty movement" crowd, but many are fifty and older. Among this latter group there are people who were at one time politically active, but grew disillusioned with the failures of the Religious Right and similar groups to make any real change or progress, or even hold the Republican Party to its repeated but failed promises. Having dropped out long ago, the political climate since 2010 and the rise of the TEA party and liberty movements has encouraged them to see new hope and get involved once again. These wisened, hardened Christian liberty patriots are not fooled by the same old Party nonsense, they come out seeking something deeper and more substantial. In many cases, they have found my project and contacted me.

Among the younger crowd are many Christians who have learned much from the quickly rising "libertarian" (small "l") and "Ron Paul" movements, but desire something more firmly founded upon the Bible in order to understand and apply specifically Christian liberty—the only true liberty. These have not only embraced this project, but have often been led on the road of the same experience as me in the process: awakening to the true roots and depth of the centralized tyranny in our nation, accompanied by both a boldness to say it plainly and a reinvigorated devotion to God's Word as the only true blueprint for solutions to society's problems. Indeed, one of the editors for the video version of the project—herself already a devout Christian and conservative—told me upon completion of her work that her life had been radically changed by it, and that for the good.

It is my sincere hope that the bold and uncompromising approach of this project, its radical honesty, along with the encouraging fact that countless individuals across the spectrum out there are waiting to get involved in such substantial changes to the glory of God, will help mitigate the hesitance that may hinder the "average" Christian from making a start. There are people around you, already in your county, who are willing to get involved if only someone stands up first as a beacon for other eager locals to focus upon and gather around. I want to encourage you to be that person, or if someone has already begun in your area, to join them and help draw others. You will find out quickly that God rewards your boldness in faithfulness to Him. God rewards those who state, in a very plain and simple way, the basic but tough truth before others. You will find out that there are more people than you think willing to listen and to discuss these issues candidly at a very practical level.

We are digging the first trenches and pouring the first footings of the foundation here. It takes people with a vision of the larger structure even to begin in that effort. But we must begin. For the sake of your children and grandchildren, for the sake of liberty, and for the glory of God, grasp that vision. Put your hand to the shovel, the plow, the block, and begin.

APPENDIX

Repeal the Seventeenth Amendment

The Seventeenth Amendment was an important assault on states' rights. The product of a time when Populism and Progressivism were sweeping large sections of America, it jammed a wedge of pure democracy into the Constitution where it was never designed to belong. This upset the Constitutional checks-and-balances system, weakened state rights and power, and magnified the power of special interests in Washington.

In the original bicameral design of the Constitution, the Legislature was divided between a House and a Senate. Members of the House represent the people of the United States; these representatives are therefore elected in each state by popular vote. The Senate today is the same—also directly elected by the people—but this was not originally the case. The Senate was originally designed not to represent the people, but to represent the *states*, and thus protect states' rights and powers from Federal encroachment. Thus, Senators were elected by the legislatures in each state. With this arrangement, each state had popular representation according to population in one house, and equal representation for the state itself in the other.

The change came, as I said, during the era of the rise of populism and progressivism—both of which movements placed heavy emphasis on democracy at the expense of republicanism (the idea, not the party). The change did not come about due to sober reflection upon American political science, tradition, the Constitution, or other state papers; there was little philosophical analysis; the change came about due to pure party politics building up until it could seize the right moment in Congress. It was enabled, however, sadly, by corruption which was exploited toward that political goal.

It is not without irony that the centers of populism—the Midwest and Northwest mainly—were also the centers fighting most for Senate election reforms. These same states during this era saw direct-democracy reforms passed into their Constitutions in the form of initiative and referendum powers, backed mainly by farm and labor unions. Along with these efforts, most of these states were also allowing election of their Senators by some form of referendum or popular input. They were, in effect, already practicing direct popular election of Senators.

But it was not enough for these ideologues—as it rarely is for any leftists or Statists—to rest content with their own States (the way state issues ought to be treated). They hungered to force direct election of Senators upon every other state in the union as well. And aided by the very procedures outlined in the original tool of centralization—the Constitution—they eventually achieved their goal. While the popularly elected House continually proposed an Amendment for the measure, the Senate—understandably—rejected it just as often. This occurred until 1911. By this time, the Senate was dominated by Senators from states where direct election was being practiced. Thus, Senatorial resistance to the issue was broken down, and the Amendment bill finally passed the Senate.

After the bill subsequently passed the House, a massive media campaign was begun to expose state legislatures as tools of corporate special interests. Aided by special exposés and accusations of bribery, etc., progressives were able to portray the Constitutional system as having become corrupt and in need of immediate change. Implicated, the state legislatures were powerless to withstand. By 1913, thirty-six of the fourtyeight states ratified. One—Utah—explicitly rejected it, and nine simply refused to back a lost cause resistance once the amendment was ratified by the requisite three-fourths. The nine holdouts were the states that have historically respected the need for states' rights: Mississippi, Alabama, Georgia, Florida, Virginia, Kentucky, Maryland, South Carolina, and of course, Rhode Island.

No doubt, the state legislatures and thus the Senators had indeed become corrupted by massive corporate influences, lobbies, and special interests. But consider two things: first, the farm and labor unions that pushed for popular democracy were no different! They themselves were essentially incorporated collectives formed for the sole purpose of advocating the special interests of farmers and laborers. So the special interest and lobbying problem wasn't truly solved by this means, it was merely shifted from domination by one special interest to another.

Second, not only was the power shifted from one special interest to another, but the degree, focus, and scope of power of that special interest shifted as well. Now, instead of dealing with state-wide lobbies, and interests and corporations within their respective states, Senators are now subject to the corrupting power and influence of *national* lobbies and special interests. Now, instead of dealing merely with the local rich and powerful, Senators can be compromised by influences from outside their own states. This means, the people of a particular state may be subjected to the power and influence of a powerful corporation or organization—or especially a national union—from outside their state. So from this perspective, the special interest problem is not only unsolved, it is actually exacerbated and even more entrenched than before.

Thus, the very reason for proposing the Seventeenth Amendment in the first place has become one of the leading reasons for it to be repealed.

This was noticed by Senator Zell Millier, a conservative Democrat who retired from the Senate in 2004. Upon his retirement—perhaps the only occasion for which he could speak so openly—he criticized the Senate for having become "one big, bad, ongoing joke held hostage by special interests."[1] His subsequent remarks were illuminating and interesting:

One man inquiring into the prospect of a Senate race observed the body with disgust, and concluded the Senate to be composed of, Miller says:

> A bunch of pompous, old—and I won't use his word here, I would say "folks"—listening to people read statements they didn't even write and probably don't believe.

Meanwhile, the laws of this country are subject to special interests like environmentalists and judicial activists. Indeed, "Most of the laws of the land, at least the most important and lasting ones, are made not by elected representatives of the people but by unelected, unaccountable legislators in black robes who churn out volumes of case law and hold their jobs for life." To this we could easily add: unelected lobbyists and bureaucrats writing volumes of regulations and administrative law.

Miller criticized the turn toward democracy at the expense of a republic:

> No matter who you send to Washington, for the most part smart and decent people, it is not going to change much because the individuals are not so much at fault as the rotten and decaying foundation of what is no longer a Republic. It is the system that stinks, and it is only going to get worse because that perfect balance our brilliant Founding Fathers put in place in 1787 no longer exists. . . .
>
> You see, the reformers of the early 1900s killed it dead and cremated the body when they allowed for the

---

[1] Congressional Record, April 28, 2004 (S4503). Following quotes from same source.

direct election of U.S. Senators. Up until then, Senators were chosen by State legislatures, as James Madison and Alexander Hamilton had so carefully crafted. Direct elections of Senators, as great and as good as that sounds, allowed Washington's special interests to call the shots, whether it is filling judicial vacancies, passing laws, or issuing regulations. The state governments aided in their own collective suicide by going along with that popular fad at the time.

Note how the problem is not just special interests in general—for you'll never eliminate those—but "Washington's special interests." The stage has indeed shifted to bigger, more powerful, *national* special interests, as I said.

Now more democratized in nature, the Congress no longer works to protect states' rights. As a result, we have unfunded Federal mandates placed upon the states in which the Federal government essentially tells states what to do and makes them pay for it—to the tune of $33 Billion a year at the time Miller was speaking (2005). Miller asks, "Can you imagine those dreadful unfunded mandates being put on the states . . . if Senators were still chosen by and responsible to the state legislatures?"

Of course not. But the same special interests that weaken the power of the states also keep the Senators themselves personally interested in maintaining direct election. Where do you think their campaign funding comes from? Miller answers:

> Make no mistake about it. It is the special interest groups and their fundraising power that elect Senators and then hold them in bondage forever. In the past five election cycles, Senators have raised over $1.5 billion for their election contests, not counting all the soft money spent on their behalf in other ways. Few would believe it, but the daily business of the Senate in fact is scheduled around fundraising. . . .

As a result, we have a tyranny of special interests and unions empowered and entrenched at the national level instead of merely at the state level. The states themselves, rather than being represented properly, essentially act as one more lobby for Senators' attention, except the states can't buy them off:

> The election of Senators by the state legislatures was the lynchpin that guaranteed the interests of the states would be protected. Today state governments have to stand in line because they are just another one of the many special interests that try to get Senators to listen to them, and they are at an extreme disadvantage because they have no PAC [Political Action Committee].

Miller concludes that the Seventeenth Amendment "destroyed federalism forever," and it "was a victory for special-interest tyranny and a blow to the power of state governments that would cripple them forever."

Concluding his speech, Mr. Miller introduced a bill to repeal the Seventeenth Amendment, which was like asking each one of his fellow Senators to bite the hands that fed them. The proposed bill never made it out of committee.

Then, in a brave display of fighting national special interests, Miller became a board member of one of the largest lobbies in Washington, the NRA.

Are things really this hopeless?

I disagree with Miller's conclusion. True federalism and the power of state governments have not been destroyed "forever." With the groundswell of interest in self-government and limited government arising with the Tea Parties and similar groups, a lot has changed even in the few years since Miller's 2004 speech. A much bigger and more eager audience than ever before is embracing the message: decentralization and restrictions on higher levels of government. Recovering states' rights is an important piece of that puzzle. Restoring proper representation of state interests in Washington—and thus the repeal of the Seventeenth Amendment—is an important step in recovering that piece. Simple education about that Amendment and its history is awakening many people to the importance of repealing it.

No, it will not eliminate special interests (this is perhaps impossible). But it will decentralize them. This is surely something worth pursuing. And while it certainly is not sufficient toward the overall effort to decentralize power and government, it certainly is necessary. It is certainly worth contacting and educating your state and national representatives about.

Scripture Index

Genesis

9:5–6 245
12:3 339

Exodus

12:47 248
18 245
18:13–26 247
18:21–22 248
20:1–3 289
20:15 157
22:1–17 269
22:4 270
30:11–16 155

Leviticus

19:11, 13 157
19:35–36 185
20:30–33 156

Numbers

1:1–3 288n

Deuteronomy

6:4–7 13
14:22–29 156
17 286, 354
17:14–20 286–287
19:14 157
19:15–21 296
20:5–20 292–293
20:10–20 295,
        297–298
22 286

25:13–16 185
27:17 157
27–28 289
28:15 333
28:15–19 333
28:25–33 333–334
28:68 289

1 Samuel

8:11–12 295
8:15–17 156

2 Samuel

11:11 294
24 288

1 Kings

11:1–4 291

Psalms

15 235

Proverbs

22:28 157
23:10 157
28:2 246

Isaiah

8:14–15 341
33:22 355

Jeremiah

17:9

Matthew

2:13 289
21:43–44 341
22:37–40 211

Luke

20:1–16 243

John

8:44 341
10:11–13 287

Acts

6:2–3 247

Romans

5:12–21 246
9:6 340
9:30–33 340
9:32–33 341
13 245
13:1–4 245
13:4 212, 354
13:7 159

1 Corinthians

6 267
6:1–8 249–250
6:2–3 269
6:7 274
6:8 273

2 Corinthians

5:20 246

Ephesians

6:1–4 13
6:20 246

1 Timothy

3:1–13 247

Titus

1:5–9 247

1 Peter

2:8 341
2:13–17 159

Subject Index

A

abortion 341–342
  ending at state level 148–150
Abraham 339–341
Acton, Lord 349
Adair, Douglas
  "Fame and the Founding Fathers" 125
  religion of Alexander Hamilton 134
Adams, Charles Francis Jr. 28–29
Adams, John 273
  on jury nullification 280
Adams, John Quincy 115, 225
Adams, Samuel
  as "Candidus" 90
Agenda 21 361–369, 385–386
  via Executive Order 367
aggression 297, 346
agricultural subsidies 238
Alderson, Wayne 243
Alien and Sedition Acts 282
alliances 290
America - attitudes toward war 295, 300
American dream 217
Americanism 26–27
American Revolution 301, 312
American Sociological Association 52
Amish 33, 66, 237
Andrews, Charles 300
Anonymous, Mr.
  Herbert C. Cornuelle 243

Anti-Federalists 76–77, 83–93, 112–113, 117–122, 254, 261, 304, 314, 325, 361
  summary of arguments from 85–86
Articles of Confederation 113, 114, 130, 219
Art of War, The 335–336
asylum 29–30, 48–49
ATF
  product of taxation 172
Attorney General 97
Augustine, Aurelius 74

B

Babylon 121
balanced budget 387
banking
  Bank of Mutual Redemption 187
  fractional reserve banking 186
  New England Bank of Boston 187
  Second Bank of the U.S. 197
  Suffolk Bank 187
Bank of Mutual Redemption 187
bearing arms 302, 303, 314
Biblical Blueprints 383
Biddle, Nicholas 198
Bill of Rights 314
Bismarck, Otto von 49–53
bonds 178–180, 225, 332
Book of Common Prayer 347–348
Boston Latin School 15

Boston Tea Party 163, 312
Boulware, Lemuel C.
  Truth About Boulwarism, The
    243
Bovard, James 238
Brandeis, Louis 261
Bretton Woods 200
Brown, John 20
  and The Secret Six 337
Brutus 254, 304
  "necessary and proper" 88
  Supreme Court 89
  taxation 86–88
Bureau of Public Assistance 55
Burgh, James 303
  Political Disquisitions 303
Burr, Aaron 133
Byzantine Empire 186

C

"Caesar" 126–131, 278
Calvin, John 308–309
"Candidus" 92–93, 254, 261
  Supreme Court 90
Carnegie, Andrew 232
"Cato"
  letters of 127, 128, 129, 130
  on the Philadelphia Convention
    129
Chalcedon, Council of 75
Chamberlain, John
  Enterprising Americans 215
Chamber of Commerce 109, 377
  United States 252
Charles II (king) 301
cheese ix, 4–6, 32, 56–58, 94–97,
    101, 109, 138, 167, 236
Chipman, Nathaniel 255
Christendom 130
civic religion 26–27
civic virtue 272–275

civil disobedience 277
  Francis Schaeffer on 277–279
civil law 80–81, 267
Civil War 56, 82, 92, 117, 121–
    122, 136, 170, 172, 187,
    192, 197, 199, 251, 310,
    326–327, 373, 388
  Greenback inflation 199
Clay, Henry 225
Cleveland, Grover 232
Clinton, Bill
  war on Kosovo, by Executive
    Order 371–372
Clinton, DeWitt 225
Clinton, George 127
Clinton, Hillary
  gun control by treaty 361
Cohens v. Virginia 91
collateral damage 299
Colorado Plan 379
commerce 300
Common Law, The 262
Communist Manifesto 49
Community Reinvestment Act
    208
Comptroller General 57
Confederacy
  taxation 171
Congress (U.S.) 305
conscientious objection 295–296
conscription 139, 290, 295,
    301–302, 321, 325, 343, 346
Constitution 5, 6, 33, 42, 43, 76,
    77, 83–99, 107, 112–128,
    134–141, 146, 149–151,
    161, 166, 219–220, 253,
    256, 260–263, 280–283,
    287, 302–326, 345, 350–
    359, 371, 383, 391–396
  Commerce clause 225
  debate over intrepretation 259
  free trade and 219

implied powers 259
Income Tax Amendment 171
interstate commerce 219
"living constitution" 261
Second Amendment 360
Seventeenth Amendment 154,
     395–400
Sixteenth Amendment 171
Constitutional Convention
     319–320
Continental dollar 190
contracts 6, 39, 46–47, 72–74,
     81, 100, 105, 174, 189–196,
     202–204, 222, 236, 250,
     275, 338, 345–346
  during deflation 204
  government/public 179, 214
    defense contracts 346
    and employment 214
Conventicle Act of 1664
  William Penn and 281
Convention on Biological Diver-
     sity 361
Coordinating Action on Small
     Arms
  UN gun control 360
corporations 27, 93, 139, 212,
     233–234, 237, 251, 380–
     381, 397
county 72
  definition 72
County Commissioners 105
County Rights viii, xi, 5, 71, 122
courts 6, 73, 74, 85, 89, 154, 226,
     245, 249, 251, 253, 254, 257,
     263, 264, 265, 266, 269, 270,
     271, 272, 273, 274, 275, 276,
     281, 283, 284, 285, 350, 359
  biblical principles for 245–253
  biblical remedies 269
  biblical, restoring 265–278
  early judicial activism 255

endless appeals 270
  John Marshall's 253
  necessity of 250
  pagan 267, 273
  private Christian 249–252,
     265–270
    contractual agreements 275
    self-sacrifice and 274
  private courts
    forms of 250
    in history 251
covenant 44–45, 75, 78–79, 246
credit union 208
Cremin, Lawrence 13–16
crime
  definition of 212
criminal law 80
curriculum 17, 35, 37, 38

D

David, King of Israel 294
Davie, William R.
  argument for revenue sharing
     138
death penalty 296
deception 335
Declaration of Independence 76,
     88, 107, 112, 115, 117, 140,
     148, 161, 308, 310, 312, 350
  Mecklenburg County, NC 108
Declaration of Rights of 1774 350
defense contracts 345–346
Defoe, Daniel 300
Democratic-Republicans 112
denominations 17–18
Department of Defense 346
  defense contracts 346
Department of Justice 97
  DNA Initiative 97
DeWitt, John
  on Constitution and army 306

Dick Act of 1903 328
Dinwiddie, Robert 310, 350
DNA Initiative 97
dollar
  Spanish 186
Duane, James 255

E

Education viii, x, 4, 9–40, 44, 45,
    47, 48, 54, 56, 61, 97, 100,
    101, 131, 140, 144, 178, 181,
    240, 243, 244, 253, 283, 285,
    329, 336, 337, 368, 370, 383,
    401
  bond financing and 177
Eerie Canal 225
Eerie Railroad Co. v. Tompkins
    (1938) 262
Egypt 288–289
Election 246
Electoral College 94–95
Ellery, William 255
Emergency Banking Act 381
emergency powers 373–381
emotional appeal 177
Engels, Friedrich 49, 338–339
enlistment 342
Enterprising Americans, The 215
entrepreneurship 215, 240, 241
Environmental Working Group
    238
excise taxes 172
executive branch 137, 349, 370
  biblical view of 354
  compared to monarchy 350
  emergency powers 373–381
  job description 353
  national emergency 373–382
Executive Order 366–372
  FDR and 371

President's Council on Sustain-
    able Development 366
president should rescind 387
war by (Kosovo) 371–372
White House Rural Council 369

F

Fabian socialism 55
Fabius 128
Falk, Isidore 54
farm subsidies 96
FBI 97
"Federal Farmer" 84, 92, 116, 123,
    254, 307, 386
  consolidated government 84
  Supreme Court 89–90
  treaties 357
Federal government
  subsidies from 96–97
federalism 75, 76, 153, 349, 400
  and taxation 153
Federalist 83, 84, 85, 86, 87, 88,
    89, 90, 92, 93, 112, 113, 114,
    115, 116, 117, 118, 123, 124,
    127, 129, 130, 131, 138, 196,
    223, 226, 253, 254, 255, 256,
    257, 259, 260, 261, 262, 302,
    303, 304, 306, 314, 351, 352,
    353, 357
Federalist Papers 302–304
Federal Reserve 5, 33, 82, 98, 139,
    185, 191, 195, 200–208,
    237, 291–292, 379
feudalism 72
fifth commandment 13, 47
food
  free market in 238
forced servitude 289–290
Fosdick, Rev. Harry Emerson 377
Fourteenth Amendment 92, 150,
    263, 264

Fox News
  report on jury nullification 279
fractional reserve banking 186,
  201
Franklin, Benjamin 15
  business career 216
  Poor Richard's Almanack 43
free market 15–16, 16–17, 39–40,
  46–47, 184–185, 187–188,
  188–189, 200–201, 202–
  203, 212–213, 221–222,
  240–241, 244–245
free markets
  government interference 213
  in American history 215–221
free school lunch 109
French and Indian War 165
French Revolution 132, 133, 313,
  322
Frick, Henry Clay 232
Fugitive Slave Laws 282
Fully Informed Jury Association
  283

G

Gales, Joseph 91, 92, 141
Genêt, Charles 322
George II
  George Washington as 136
George III 75, 148, 162, 165, 350
Gerry, Elbridge 314
Gettysburg 117
Gibbons v. Ogden 91, 141, 226
global governance
  via treaty 361
gold
  tips for buying 206
Gore, Al
  and Agenda 21 362
Great Commission 336–337
Great Depression 41, 188, 242

Great Society 82
Greenbacks 199
Guinness 242
gun-control
  via treaty 360

H

Hamilton, Alexander 83, 89,
  123–142, 170, 196, 200,
  217, 226, 255, 260–263,
  303, 304, 310, 312, 313, 320,
  321, 321–326, 352, 399
  Bank of New York 193
  Julius Caesar, love of 126
  childhood war lust 124
  Constitutional interpretation
    259
  Constitution "frail and worthless
    fabric" 137
  early life and success 217
  expansion of Treasury powers
    137
  fame, lust for 125
  First Bank of the U.S. 192
  mercantilism and 223
  Newburgh Conspiracy 124
  religion 131–133
  Secretary of Treasury 136
Hancock, John 318
Hayek, F. A. 102, 103
  The Road to Serfdom 103
health care 45
health insurance 42, 49, 53, 54, 56
Henry, Patrick 77, 113, 361
  on treaty powers 357
Hitler, Adolf 50
Hoey, Jane 55
Holmes, Oliver Wendell, Jr. 261,
  266
  The Common Law 262
home schooling 2, 34–38

Hopkins, Harry 53
Horowitz, George 266
hospitals
  charitable 45
Hutchison, Kay Bailey
  exposes Agenda 21 363

I

immigration 19–20, 26–27, 31–32
Immigration 26–27
imperialism 290
income tax 171
  of 1861 171
Income Tax Amendment 82
industrialization 27–28
industrial revolution 19–20, 27–28, 220–221
inflation 6, 62, 161, 186, 194–205, 317
  as bank fraud 201
  Benjamin Franklin and 217
  in Pennsylvania 217
International Small Arms Control Standards
  and gun control 360
International Union for the Conservation of Nature 365
Interposition 147
interstate commerce
  United States v. Lopez 226
Interstate Commerce Commission 232
Iredell, James
  on treaty powers of executive 357
IRS 165, 172, 372, 387
Israel 339–341

J

Jackson, Andrew 190, 198

James II (king) 301
Jay, John 344–345
  on jury nullification 280
Jeffersonians 90, 112, 256
Jefferson, Thomas 43, 77, 126, 147, 257–258
  on jury nullification 280
Jethro
  advice to Moses 247
John Birch Society 80
Johnson, Lyndon B. 21, 82, 172, 263
Johnson, William 258
Josiah 121
J. P. Morgan & Co. 232
judicial review 258
jury nullification 279–282
just cause 294, 302, 309
just war 296, 309, 345

K

Kentucky Resolutions (1798) 147
kings 286, 290–291
Knox, Henry 317–319
Kolko, Gabriel 231
  The Triumph of Conservatism, 231

L

laissez-faire 52
Landon, Alfred M. 376
League of Nations 337
Lee, Richard Henry 84, 116, 123
legal tender 202
Lerner, Max 123
lesser magistrate 148
Lincoln, Abraham 117, 149, 191, 319, 327
Linder, Robert D. 309
literacy
  in the colonies 15–16

local food 107
localism viii, 1, 71, 76–82, 253,
    383
  public finance
    all bonds anathema! 179
    tricks 175–178
Louisiana Purchase 83

M

Madison, James 91–92, 136, 141,
    302–303, 320, 399
  on treaty powers 357
Magna Carta 73, 74
mankind
  perfection of 19
Mann, Horace 20, 24, 29, 48, 337
Mansfield, Stephen 242
Marbury v. Madison 90, 257
marriage vow 44–46
Marshall, John 90, 122–123, 226,
    253
Martin, Luther
  on standing army 306
Marx, Karl 49, 338
Mason, George 302
  on treaty powers of executive
    356
Massachusetts 20, 24, 77, 194,
    280, 301, 314–319, 325, 353
  State Board of Education 24
Massachusetts Body of Liberties
    301–302
McCulloch v. Maryland 90, 260
  basis for liberal view of Consti-
    tution 261
McDonald, Forrest 125, 135
McDonald's
  hot coffee lawsuit 269
McKinley, William
  annexation of Hawaii 327
  Spanish-American War 327

Mecklenburg County 108
Medicare 41, 56, 57, 66, 67, 160,
    172
Mein Kampf 51, 54
Mennonites 66
messianic State 21
military-industrial complex 5,
    140, 223, 309, 313, 330,
    345–346
militia 288, 293–294, 300–302,
    306–307, 315, 325
  biblical principles for 292–294
  laws of war 295
  voluntary 293
Militia Acts 321–323
  of 1792 139, 321
Millier, Zell 398
missions 17, 336–339, 342, 345,
    384–385
Mitchell, George 363
money viii, 6
  biblical view of 185
  Bretton Woods 200
  Continental dollar 190
  definition of 183
  fiscal conservatism 185
  free markets and 184
  gold and silver as now 205
  government and fraud in 189
  Greenbacks 199
  in American history 186–187
  retirement/savings 56–68
  Sunday school lesson on 206
  whiskey as 197
monopolies 221
Monroe, James 197
moral hazard 330
  and public contracts 214
Morgan, J. P. 232, 233
Morison, Samuel Eliot 14, 15
Morris, Robert 139

Mount Vernon Compact (1785) 219
Muhlenberg, John
  recruitment during American Revolution 301

N

national defense 286
National Emergencies Act 1976 375
national emergency 373–382
"National Emergency Powers" report 374
National Guard 343
nationalism 295
National Planning Board 378
National Right to Work Legal Defense Foundation 240
natural born citizen 287–288
Nazi 50, 51, 238
Neutrality 10, 11, 12
Newburgh Conspiracy 124
New Deal 51, 82, 141, 229, 230, 328, 332, 388
  George Washington's 134
New England Bank of Boston 187
New York Stock Exchange 197
Nicaea, Council of 75
Nisbet, Robert A. 82
non-combatants 299
Nullification 147
  and Tenth Amendment issues 145

O

oath 44, 45, 46, 80, 386, 387
  courts and representation 268
Office of Justice Programs 97
"Old Whig"
  on the executive branch 351

warning against trust in political leaders 262
Osgood, Peter 353
ostracism 252
  as economic penalty 252
Overman Act 330

P

Pacific Legal Foundation 240
pacifism 345
Panic of 1837 199
Panic of 1857 199
Panic of 1893 199
Panics of 1873 199
Parents 11, 44, 47
parochial schools 26
Parsons, Theophilus
  on jury nullification 280
Patriot Act 83, 92
patriotism 339–340
Paul, Ron 190
peace 297–298, 347
Penn, William
  on jury nullification 281
pensions 100, 108, 178, 180, 242
Personal finance
  401k 62
"Philadelphiensis"
  on standing army 313
  on standing army and religious liberty 313
Philippines
  American brutality in 328
pilgrims 222
Pinckney, Charles Cotesworth 114
"Plebeian" 86, 91
  summary of Anti-Federalist arguments 85
  Supreme Court 89
politics 301

polygamy 290
Poor Richard's Almanack 43
Populism 395
Post Office 82
President's Council on Sustainable
    Development 366
prison 28–29, 48–49, 343–344
private insurance 46, 48, 65
Prohibition 282
  jury nullification during 282
propaganda 102, 180, 198, 256,
    316, 322
property tax 30, 38–39, 79,
    157–161, 216
  modern feudalism 158
prophecy 339
Puritans 308

Q

Quakers 305–306

R

rabbinical law
  on courts 266
railroads 29, 221, 225, 231, 233,
    330
Randolph, Edmund 351
ratchet effect 55, 173, 189, 334
Reconstruction 92, 122, 263
rehabilitation 29–30
reinsurance 46
religion and war 293
reparations 298
representation 85–86, 89, 94–95,
    98, 104, 166, 171, 174, 246,
    252, 267, 350, 379, 395, 400
resistance
  Christian 276
restitution 297–298
Revenue Act of 1913 171
Robin Hood 80

Rockefeller Foundation 53
Roe v. Wade 145, 148, 149, 263
Roosevelt, Franklin 51, 53, 57, 82,
    92, 122, 172, 200, 229, 263,
    328, 331–333, 371, 374,
    376, 380–381
  confiscation of gold 381
  Emergency Banking Act 381
  national emergency and consoli-
    dation of power 376
  National Planning Board 378
Roosevelt, Theodore 53, 233
Root, Elihu 328
Rothbard, Murray 214, 271
rule of law 74, 260
rules of war 295–296
  in the Bible 286–287
Ruml, Beardsley 379
Rushdoony, R. J. 95, 266–268,
    273–277, 384
Russell, James Earl 24

S

sales tax 158
Samaritan Ministries 66
school board 175
scorched earth 299, 333
Second Amendment 314–316,
    343
Second Bank of the U.S. 197
Secret Six 337
Section 8 109
Sedgwick, Maine
  food laws 107
Selective Service System 343
sermons on war 302
Seventeenth Amendment 154,
    395–400
Seven Years' War 310–313
Shays, Daniel 318
Shays' rebellion 316–319

Shearon, Marjorie 49, 54
sheriff 2, 5, 80–81, 385
Sherman, Roger 356
Sherman, William Tecumseh 228,
    333, 379
  Indian pacification 327
  scorched earth 327
  "war is hell" 333
shire 72
Shirer, William 50
single mom 36
Sixteenth Amendment 171
Smith, Adam 223
  The Wealth of Nations 223
Smith, William L.
  letter from Hamilton 132
social Darwinism 49
socialism 20, 22, 32, 49–51,
    55–56, 94, 103, 236, 277,
    381
Social Security 4, 41–69, 160, 172,
    381
Soule, George 331
Southeastern Legal Foundation
    240
Spanish-American War 327
special-interest groups 93, 95
Spellman Fund 376
Spencer, Herbert 52
Sproul, R.C., Sr. 243
  Stronger Than Steel 243
Stamp Act (1765) 163
standing army 285, 288, 290–294,
    302–309, 313–314, 325–
    326, 338, 342, 346
state (military) guards 343
states' rights viii, 5, 71, 77, 90, 92,
    111–152, 253, 349, 376,
    395–400
Stevens, Thaddeus 23
Stronger Than Steel 243

subsidies 96, 139, 211, 215, 223–
    224, 231–233, 237–240
  agricultural 238
  Environmental Working Group
    238
  sugar 238
  voluntary 243
Suffolk Bank 187
sugar
  subsidized 238
Sumner, William Graham 52
Sun Tzu 335–336
Supreme Court 33, 54, 81, 89–90,
    104, 122, 148–151, 171,
    226–227, 254–263, 271,
    280–283, 326–327, 344,
    352, 355–361
  early justices all nationalist
    253–256
  judicial review 258
  of Colorado 377
  opposes Eisenhower 371
swing vote, 95
Switzerland 103
Symmes, William 353, 370

T

Talmud 266
Tariff
  Morrill (1861) 171
  of 1789 135, 167
  of 1789, 1790, and 1792 171
  of 1824 171
taxation v, 4, 5, 12, 18–21, 29,
    36–38, 48–49, 57, 64–69,
    77–80, 85–86, 100, 106,
    112, 134, 138–139, 153–
    166, 172–175, 180–181,
    226, 253, 285, 318, 329, 338,
    349
  and markets 213–214

and public-private partnerships
   213
biblical prinicples for limited
   159
bond financing and 174
etymology 165
excise taxes 172
"head tax" in Exodus not civil
   155
in American colonies 161
income tax 157
no biblical form for civil gov
   155–159
parallel to slavery 156
principles for curtailing 160–
   161
property tax unbiblical 158
"public" services and 154
sales tax 158
Tea Act (1773) 166
and Boston Tea Party 163
teachers unions 175
Ten Commandments 72, 80, 211,
   241, 265, 289
Tenth Amendment 90, 91,
   144–148, 152, 383
Jefferson on 259
Tenth Amendment Center
   144–145
terrorism 20, 21, 360
Thirteenth Amendment 42
tithe 155
Titus, Herb 148, 262
tobacco 161, 162, 168, 172, 184
as tax revenue 162
Tocqueville, Alexis de 78
total warfare 299
Townshend Acts (1767) 163, 166
treason
UN oath as 387
treaties 355–365

Constitutional amendment
   needed 386
global governance 361
Senate's roll in 356
trees
warfare and 298–299
Triumph of Conservatism, The
   231
Truth About Boulwarism, The 243
Tucker, St. George 315

U

unions 100–101, 114–115, 126,
   240, 314, 317, 397
Unitarianism 19–21, 24–29, 48,
   337
United Auto Workers 239
United Nations 360–363, 386
Convention on Biological Diver-
   sity 361
need for U.S. to pull out of 386
*United States v. Curtiss-Wright
   Export Corp.* 356
United States v. Lopez 226–228
urban planning 214

V

van Creveld, Martin 329–330
Vietnam 82, 282
Viret, Pierre 309
Virginia Resolution (1798) 141
Volker, William
Mr. Anonymous 243
volunteer military 293

W

Walker, David 57, 58
Walpole, Robert
Alexander Hamilton as 136
war
and central planning 331

as hell 333–335
as pro-life issue 341–342
biblical rules for 295–297
false witness and 296
scorched earth 299
total warfare 299
Ward, Lester Frank 49, 51
Dynamic Sociology 49
Warfare-Welfare State
van Creveld on 329
War Industries Board 330
War Labor Policies Board 330
War of 1812 171
Warren, Earle 261
War State 56, 121, 288, 328–332, 377
George Washington and 139
Washington, George 2, 32, 81–83, 89–93, 100–101, 110, 115, 123–142, 164, 173, 224, 259–262, 281, 301–302, 312–313, 317–326, 351–352, 361, 377, 387, 395
"American Fabius" 128
call for corporate welfarism 139
mercantilism and 223
Mount Vernon Compact 219
State of the Union address 139, 223
Wealth of Nations, The 223
weaponry 288, 337, 345
Webb, Sydney 55
Webster, Noah 303
definitions of "Nation" and "State" 119
Webster, Peletiah 190
Welfare State 4, 43–49, 57, 263, 292, 328–332, 373
Wertenbaker, Thomas Jefferson 78
whiskey
as currency 197

Whiskey Rebellion 89, 139, 170, 320–326
Wilson, James 352, 356
Wilson, Woodrow 53, 171, 261, 330–332, 337–338
Witherspoon, John 190
Wooldridge, William
on medieval merchant courts 251
Works Progress Administration 53
World War I 53, 243, 310, 328, 330
World War II 102, 184, 192, 215, 328, 331

Y

Yates, Robert 86, 91
Young, Owen D. 252
YouTube x, 33, 106

Z

Zedong, Mao 337
zoning laws 214